A Transnational History of Forced Migrants in Europe

A Transnational History of Forced Migrants in Europe

Unwilling Nomads in the Age of Two World Wars

Edited by
Bastiaan Willems and Michał Adam Palacz

BLOOMSBURY ACADEMIC
LONDON • NEW YORK • OXFORD • NEW DELHI • SYDNEY

BLOOMSBURY ACADEMIC
Bloomsbury Publishing Plc
50 Bedford Square, London, WC1B 3DP, UK
1385 Broadway, New York, NY 10018, USA
29 Earlsfort Terrace, Dublin 2, Ireland

BLOOMSBURY, BLOOMSBURY ACADEMIC and the Diana logo are trademarks of
Bloomsbury Publishing Plc

First published in Great Britain 2022
Paperback edition first published 2024

Copyright © Bastiaan Willems and Michał Adam Palacz, 2022

Bastiaan Willems and Michał Adam Palacz have asserted their right under the Copyright, Designs and Patents Act, 1988, to be identified as Editor of this work.

Cover image: Heiligenstaedt, c. 1919, printed by Flüchtlingsfursorge des Bundes der deutschen Grenzmarken-Schützverbände.
From the private collection of Bastiaan Willems.

All rights reserved. No part of this publication may be reproduced or transmitted in any form or by any means, electronic or mechanical, including photocopying, recording, or any information storage or retrieval system, without prior permission in writing from the publishers.

Bloomsbury Publishing Plc does not have any control over, or responsibility for, any third-party websites referred to or in this book. All internet addresses given in this book were correct at the time of going to press. The author and publisher regret any inconvenience caused if addresses have changed or sites have ceased to exist, but can accept no responsibility for any such changes.

Every effort has been made to trace copyright holders and to obtain their permissions for the use of copyright material. The publisher apologizes for any errors or omissions and would be grateful if notified of any corrections that should be incorporated in future reprints or editions of this book.

A catalogue record for this book is available from the British Library.

A catalog record for this book is available from the Library of Congress.

ISBN: HB: 978-1-3502-8107-3
PB: 978-1-3502-8108-0
ePDF: 978-1-3502-8109-7
eBook: 978-1-3502-8110-3

Typeset by Deanta Global Publishing Services, Chennai, India

To find out more about our authors and books visit www.bloomsbury.com and sign up for our newsletters.

Contents

List of illustrations — vii
List of contributors — viii
Foreword — xii
Acknowledgements — xv

Introduction. Unwilling nomads: A four-dimensional model of diaspora *Bastiaan Willems and Michał Adam Palacz* — 1

Part I Internees and evacuees during the First World War

1. Population movement, evacuation and internment in Habsburg Galicia during the First World War: Considering the four-dimensional model of diaspora *Serhiy Choliy* — 13
2. Humiliated and insulted: The multiple categories of Austro-Hungarian civilian internees, 1914–17 *Egor Lykov* — 29
3. Between suffering and displacement: The case of the Istrian Evakuirci *Diego Han* — 43

Part II Political emigrants in the interwar era

4. Salvaging the 'unredeemed' in Italy: The Kingdom of Yugoslavia and the Julian March émigrés *Miha Zobec* — 59
5. Ukrainian emigration in the Weimar Republic and its role in German foreign policy *Veronika Weisheimer* — 75
6. Protecting the national identity of Russian emigrants and their children in interwar Eastern Europe *Aleksandra Mikulenok* — 89

Part III People on the move in fascist Europe

7. Stefi Kiesler: A librarian as 'Intellectual Refugee Service' *Jill Meißner-Wolfbeisser* — 105
8. The catalysts of 1938: European child evacuations as humanitarian innovation *Chelsea Sambells* — 119
9. 'And Without a Hat!': Refugee women in the transit country Portugal after 1933 *Katrin Sippel* — 136

10 Many journeys of exile: Spanish Republican refugees in France, 1939–46 *David A. Messenger* — 152

11 Reclaimed for the *Volk*: Forced migration and assimilation in the wartime Third Reich *Bradley J. Nichols* — 165

Part IV Refugees and displaced persons and the Second World War

12 The surviving remnant: Subjectification and self-organization in the Jewish DP camp Bergen-Belsen, 1945–8 *Lennart Onken* — 183

13 Resettling, repatriating and 'rehabilitating' Polish displaced persons in British-occupied Germany, 1945–51 *Samantha K. Knapton* — 199

14 Ethnopolitical humanitarianism: The post-war resettlement of 2,446 Danube Swabians to Brazil *Cristian Cercel* — 215

15 Anti-communists, communists and migrants in France, 1917–53 *Aaron Clift* — 231

Conclusion. Polish refugees and East Prussian expellees: Applying the four-dimensional model *Bastiaan Willems and Michał Adam Palacz* — 245

Concluding remarks *Pertti Ahonen* — 261

Further reading — 269
Index — 270

Illustrations

Figures

5.1	Pavlo Skoropadskyi with his officers and members of the Ukrainian government, Kyiv, spring 1918	76
8.1	A convoy of Belgian children arrives in Switzerland, 1942	129
9.1	Picture in the Portuguese newspaper *Mundo Grafico* showing the legs of women sitting on an esplanada, 1943	146
11.1	A Polish family selected for re-Germanization, *c.* 1941	169

Maps

1.1	Austro-Hungarian Empire, 1910	12
4.1	Kingdom of Yugoslavia, 1930	58
14.1	Settlement of Danube Swabians in south-eastern Europe, 1930	214

Contributors

Pertti Ahonen is professor of history at the University of Jyväskylä in Finland. He received his PhD in modern European history from Yale University in 1999 and previously taught at the University of Sheffield (1999–2005) and the University of Edinburgh (2005–14). He specializes in contemporary European history, with a particular thematic emphasis on forced migrations and a primary geographical focus on Central Europe. His main publications include *After the Expulsion: West Germany and Eastern Europe, 1945-1990* (2003) and *Death at the Berlin Wall* (2011).

Cristian Cercel is a research associate in the Institute for Social Movements at the Ruhr University Bochum (Germany). His research interests focus on memory studies, nationalism and ethnicity, minority politics and German identities outside the German nation state. His book *Romania and the Quest for European Identity: Philo-Germanism without Germans* was published in 2019.

Serhiy Choliy is an associate professor of history at the Igor Sikorsky Kyiv Polytechnic Institute. During the past decade, he has investigated the processes of military manning in Europe with an emphasis on Austria-Hungary. His second research interest is the interrelation of the processes of technological development and population relocation. His most recent publications are: Communities in Fukushima and Chernobyl – Enabling and Inhibiting Factors for Recovery in Nuclear Disaster Areas' and 'Military Desertion as a Counter-Modernization Response in Austro-Hungarian Society, 1868–1914' (both 2020).

Aaron Clift is a lecturer in modern history at Jesus College, University of Oxford, UK. His research interests include anti-communism, the Cold War, ideology, interest group politics, international migration, European integration and, broadly, the political and social history of modern France and Europe. His doctoral dissertation *Anticommunism in French Politics and Society, 1945-1953* is forthcoming.

Diego Han is a researcher at the Centre for Historical Research in Rovinj, Croatia. His research interests focus primarily on Istrian contemporary history and the history of fascism and nationalism. He has published various articles on local and regional interwar history and is currently a PhD candidate at the University of Zagreb (Croatia).

Samantha K. Knapton is an Assistant Professor in History at the University of Nottingham. Her research interests focus on twentieth-century central and East-Central Europe, displacement and international humanitarianism. She has published on Anglo-Polish relations in post-1945 Germany and generated a network of scholars focusing on the United Nations Relief and Rehabilitation Administration (UNRRA). Her upcoming book is *Occupiers, Humanitarian Workers, and Polish Displaced Persons in British-occupied Germany* (2022).

Egor Lykov is a scientific assistant at the chair of architectural theory at the Institute for the History and Theory of Architecture, D-ARCH, ETH Zurich, Switzerland. His research interests include European history, the First World War, national minorities and economic history. He has published on forced migrations in the Habsburg Empire and memory culture. His most recent papers are 'Opfernarrative der "russophilen" Ruthenen und ihr nachhaltiger Einfluss auf gesellschaftspolitische Diskurse' (2018) and 'Die Deportationen der galizischen Ruthenen im Ersten Weltkrieg. Zur Digitalisierung einer Katastrophe' (2020).

Andreas Kossert is head of Documentation and Research at the Stiftung Flucht, Vertreibung, Versöhnung. His research interests focus on the flight and expulsion of Germans from Central and Eastern Europe after 1945 and the history of East Prussia and Masuria, as well as displaced persons in Germany after 1945. He has published extensively in German, Polish and English. His most recent monographs include *Kalte Heimat: die Geschichte der deutschen Vertriebenen nach 1945* (2008), *Damals in Ostpreußen: der Untergang einer deutschen Provinz* (2010) and *Flucht: Eine Menschheitsgeschichte* (2020)

Jill Meißner-Wolfbeisser is an archivist and researcher at the Austrian Frederick and Lillian Kiesler Private Foundation in Vienna. She is currently writing a dissertation on Stefi Kiesler and the exile community of German-speaking literati in New York during the Second World War. She has published particularly on Frederick and Stefi Kiesler and their network. Her research interests include German exile literature, historical network research and Digital Humanities (Digital Editions).

David A. Messenger is professor and chair in the Department of History at the University of South Alabama in Mobile, Alabama. His research interests focus on Spain and its civil war and its subsequent role in the Second World War, with an emphasis on refugees, exiles and foreign policy of the Franco regime and the Western powers in relations to the Spanish dictatorship, as well as on the memory of these conflicts in contemporary Spain. He is the author of three books, is a co-editor of one and has published numerous journal articles and chapters in edited volumes.

Aleksandra Mikulenok is a senior lecturer of the Department of General Education module of North Caucasus branch of Russian State University of Justice, Russian Federation. Her research interests focus on Russian emigration in Eastern Europe between the First World War and Second World War, Soviet-Polish relations (1917–45) and status of ethnic minorities in Eastern Europe. She has published articles on Russian emigration in Eastern Europe in the interwar period. Her most recent book is *Russian emigration in Poland, 1917-1939* (2018).

Bradley J. Nichols is an assistant professor in the Department of History at the University of Missouri. His research focuses on race, resettlement and cultural genocide in the wartime Third Reich. He has published on these topics in several journals and edited volumes, including most recently *German-Occupied Europe in the Second World War* (2019). His current in-progress book manuscript is an integrative study of Nazi Germanization policy based on his doctoral thesis, which won the German Historical Institute's Fritz Stern Dissertation Prize in 2017.

Lennart Onken is a research associate for special exhibitions at the Foundation of Hamburg Memorials and Learning Centres Commemorating the Victims of Nazi Crimes. His research focuses on Jewish history, the history of National Socialism and the concentration camps and their aftermath. His most recent work is the exhibition 'Survived! And now? Hamburg victims of Nazi persecution after their liberation' (2020).

Michał Adam Palacz is a postdoctoral researcher in the School of History, Philosophy and Culture at Oxford Brookes University, UK. He obtained his PhD from the University of Edinburgh in 2016, and his research interests focus on the history of migration and medicine. He is currently working for the Max Planck Society funded project 'Brain research at institutions of the Kaiser Wilhelm Society in the context of Nazi injustices: Brain specimens in institutions of the Max Planck Society and identification of victims', July 2017 to October 2023.

Chelsea Sambells is the head of research for the Holocaust Survivors' Friendship Association in Yorkshire, UK, and research fellow at the University of Huddersfield. Her research focuses on children, humanitarianism and war in the twentieth century. Chelsea's latest project, *Humanitarian Action and Translation*, hosted by the University of Geneva, explores the way language and translation practices facilitated child evacuations to Switzerland and the role of language in multilingual conflict zones today.

Katrin Sippel is a freelance historian and exile researcher and secretary-general of the Austrian Society for Exile Studies (öge) in Vienna. Her main research interest is Portugal as a country of exile and transit for (not only Austrian) refugees fleeing Nazi persecution. She has published on Jewish life in Vienna before and after the annexation of Austria in 1938 and on Austrians in the French *résistance*. Most recent publication is 'Indecent Bathing Suits and Women Who Smoke. Austrian Refugees as Cultural Mediators in the Transit Country Portugal after 1938' in Susanne Korbel and Philipp Strobl (eds), *Cultural Translation and Knowledge Transfer on Alternative Routes of Escape from Nazi Terror: Mediations through Migrations* (2021).

Veronika Weisheimer (née Dyminska) is a doctoral student at the European University Viadrina in Frankfurt (Oder), Germany. Her research interests are migration history and German–Ukrainian relations. Her dissertation project presents a case study of Ukrainian political emigrants in Berlin between 1919 and 1945. She holds a PhD grant from the Heinrich Boell Foundation and was awarded a young talent prize of the Historical Commission of Berlin (2019).

Bastiaan Willems is a Lecturer in the History of War in 20th Century Europe at Lancaster University. His research examines violence and forced migration during the Third Reich and its immediate aftermath. He currently analyses the impact of German intra-ethnic violence on the German late-war society and has published in the *Journal of Slavic Military Studies* and the *Vierteljahrshefte für Zeitgeschichte*. His first monograph, *Violence in Defeat: The Wehrmacht on German Soil, 1944-1945*, was published in 2021.

Miha Zobec is a research assistant at the Research Centre of the Slovenian Academy of Sciences and Arts, Slovenian Migration Institute. His research interests focus on the relation between nation-building processes and migrations and on the history of the family in migration contexts. He has published on the relation between the interwar Yugoslavia and its emigrants, focusing particularly on the emigrants from borderland regions of Julian March and Prekmurje, as well as on the emigrant correspondence and migrations from the village community. His most recent article is 'Creating the Unbound Yugoslav Nation: The Kingdom of Yugoslavia and Emigrants from the "Unredeemed" Julian March' (2021).

Foreword

Andreas Kossert

Sarajevo, October 2021: Walking along the Miljacka riverbank on a beautiful autumn morning reminds me of the Bosnian version of an 'Indian summer'. Hamlets and pencil-like minarets are set picturesquely on the surrounding hills. The capital of Bosnia reveals many layers of history stretching from the Ottoman period, the Austro-Hungarian Empire, interwar Yugoslavia and the socialist era. Only at second glance, the last chapter of war and violence in twentieth-century Europe, which produced a massive scale of *unwilling nomads* in former Yugoslavia, becomes visible, mostly audible, when you are ready to listen. Every citizen of Sarajevo has a personal story of war, violence and displacement, of refugee camps, exile, diaspora and, sometimes, return. The dramatic events took place in the aftermath of the Cold War in early 1990s. At that time, I was a history student, trying to understand the first half of the twentieth century with its complex patterns of nationalism, competing ideologies, concepts of ethnicity and 'race', inclusion and exclusion. All of a sudden, it seemed, history repeated. I remember vividly the difficulties for many, mostly Western, Europeans, to understand what was going on, particularly in Bosnia. Very often, it was sheer disbelief. During spring term 1995, the historian Götz Aly taught a class at Freie Universität Berlin on Forced Migration in Europe. What was supposed to be a history class changed all of a sudden into a disturbing reality show as we witnessed almost live on television this new and final chapter of twentieth-century 'ethnic cleansing' in Europe. The place names mentioned in the news were engraved on my mind: Tuzla, Sarajevo, and ... Srebrenica.

Twenty-six years later, I am visiting those places, which still show many scars. Even the Bosnian landscape tells the story of *unwilling nomads* – destroyed villages, ruins, bullet holes, warning signs for landmines – as an ongoing challenge. This volume, edited by Bastiaan Willems and Michał Palacz, contains fifteen case studies which underline the significance of refugee stories for European history. They chose a transnational focus by implementing a four-dimensional model of 'host society', 'homeland', 'diaspora' and 'other diasporas'. This leads to a fascinating panorama presenting a wide range of different individual experiences and collective patterns. By using a consistently transnational perspective, narrow national and often nationalistic narratives are automatically challenged and questioned. The case studies highlight individual processes and biographies, which help to understand universal dynamics and experiences, that is, with the formation of diasporic communities well beyond Europe.

Unwilling nomads: This metaphor unfolds an enormous dynamism as it reflects various concepts and conflicts. The transnational approach of this volume contextualizes the experience of millions of Europeans and grants them the long-overdue role as 'subjects' of history, not just in numbers but showing the actual dimensions of uprootedness this continent witnessed throughout the last century. This is not to uncritically claim 'victimhood' but to show how they shaped and sometimes changed European societies. *Unwilling nomads* are confronted with sedentary societies that still hold the privilege of having a home. But the latter are the ones who decide the refugees' fate. Refugees depend on their decisions, which determine whether they are welcomed, accepted or denied. After being forcibly displaced and arriving in their host societies, refugees are often confronted with hostile reactions that challenge their identity anew. And this volume asks as well, what follows next: Exile, integration or even assimilation? Until very recently, a very materialistic understanding has dominated the discourse. The writer Reinaldo Arenas experienced his exile in the United States as a constant conflict between *here* and *there*. In an interview for *The New Yorker* in 1983, he was asked if New York was a good place for him to write. He answered that his exile from Cuba was only a physical one: 'Every person who lives outside his context is always a bit of a ghost, because I am here, but at the same time I remember a person who walked those streets, who is there, and that same person is me. So sometimes I really don't know if I am here or there.'[1] For Reinaldo Arenas, the inner ambivalence caused by his uprootedness remains, and he has no means to overcome it. Like him, many refugees live in permanent exile, unable to take root again in new places.

The Cuban intellectual underlines that a refugee does not live in his chosen home but exists as a ghost between two worlds – in both his place of origin and in exile at the same time. His case exemplifies the fact that *arriving* does not necessarily mean being at home. Another refugee, André Aciman, had to leave the Egyptian city of Alexandria as a child. 'What makes exile the pernicious thing it is, is not really the state of being away, as much as the impossibility of ever *not* being away – not just being absent, but never being able to redeem this absence.'[2] It is the transitional nature of being a refugee. Being uprooted means a turbulent and insecure existence in exile and in between. 'It reminds me of the thing I fear most', Aciman continues, 'that my feet are never quite solidly on the ground, but also that the soil under me is equally weak, that the graft didn't take. In the disappearance of small things, I read the tokens of my own dislocation, of my own transiency. An exile reads change the way he reads time, memory, love, fear, beauty: in the key of loss'.[3]

Sarajevo, October 2021: I read this fascinating collection of fifteen new insights on European experiences in this very special city. The fate of Bosnia in the heart of Europe is a constant reminder of how fragile our world is. Some described the twentieth century as the 'century of refugees', which has – as this volume strongly underlines – shaped tens of millions of European biographies. Narratives of displacement and uprootedness provide an important key on how to read Europe. Nowhere becomes this more obvious than in Bosnia. But yet, Bosnia offers another dimension. The streets of Sarajevo are full of new refugees, stranded here from Afghanistan and Syria. Here, the global refugee experience has finally arrived on our doorsteps, whether populists like it or not. The twenty-first century therefore writes yet another chapter in the history of mankind with more refugees and more stories behind anonymous numbers. New images shape a new reality: Croatian special police forces beating refugees mercilessly and pushing them back into Bosnia, refugees dying in cold nights in the forests between Poland and Belarus, people who seek help drowning in the Aegean trying to reach Europe.

The story goes on. Refugees from Afghanistan, Syria, Eritrea and Iran became part of a new European narrative. However, their experience remains the old universal story, unfolded so many times, which the Sarajevo-born American writer Aleksandar Hermon so brilliantly summarized: 'The world is full of people who left the place where they were born just to stay alive, and then die in a place where they never expected to live.'[4] Refugees, expellees, emigrants: they all share this elementary experience of being *unwilling nomads* as told in this book. Yes, sadly, history repeats. But this does not mean that we should get used to it.

Notes

1. Reinaldo Arenas, *Before Night Falls*, trans. Dolores M. Koch (New York: Penguin Books, 2000), 293.
2. André Aciman, 'Editor's Foreword: Permanent Transients', in *Letters of Transit. Reflections on Exile, Identity, Language and Loss*, ed. André Aciman (New York: The New York Public Library, 1999), 9–14, 10.
3. André Aciman, 'Shadow Cities', in *Letters of Transit*, 15–34, 22.
4. Aleksandar Hemon, 'God's Fate', in *The Displaced. Refugee Writers on Refugee Lives*, ed. Viet Thanh Nguyen (New York: Abrams Press, 2018), 91–104, 91.

Acknowledgements

This edited volume grew out of the online workshop 'Unwilling Nomads: The Transnational Consequences of Forced Migration in Europe, 1910–1955', held on 15–16 October 2020. We are most grateful to the participants of this workshop, who had initially been preparing for an in-person conference that was set to take place in May 2020, but who all proved willing and able to change to the new format in the light of the Covid-19 pandemic. We thank Oxford Brookes University for helping us adapt to this new situation and providing us with the platform to host the conference. Early on in the process, we received an Events and Activities Grant from the Social History Society, which, after the physical event was cancelled, was generously reallocated to cover editorial costs for a proposed edited volume. The spirited engagement of the participants with the subject matter and the support of the Social History Society made us confident that the next step, the production of an edited volume, would be possible. We would like to thank Rhodri Mogford, who as history editor at Bloomsbury Academic did a wonderful job guiding us through the publication process, and Nechama Rothschild and Vince Colthurst, whose editorial rigour without exception elevated the different contributions to a higher level. A special thanks goes out to the two anonymous reviewers, as well as to Mary Fulbrook, Stephanie Bird and Stefanie Rauch at UCL, who all made valuable comments on early drafts of this volume. We were incredibly fortunate that all contributors consistently met their deadlines and swiftly incorporated feedback, and we thank Chelsea Sambells and David Messenger for joining this project at its halfway point, helping to bring geographic and chronological balance to the volume. We are also grateful to Andreas Kossert and Pertti Ahonen for offering their time to provide the foreword and concluding remarks, respectively. Finally, we would like to thank our partners, Alison John and Marysia Woźniak, for their constant support and encouragement.

Introduction

Unwilling nomads:
A four-dimensional model of diaspora

Bastiaan Willems and Michał Adam Palacz

The first half of the twentieth century was dominated by all-encompassing armed conflicts, accompanied by mass migration movements. The impact of these movements is virtually unparalleled in European history: only the barbarian incursions into the Roman Empire in the fifth century saw mass movements across the continent that would reshape the fabric of society on a comparably wider scale. Although the two world wars dominate this era, it is critical to note that groups of people did not only leave their homes to flee conflict; an examination of the massive scale of migrations should also actively consider those policies that rested on the premise that the movement of people could bring about shifts in the balance of power. Those people who were uprooted from their homes became 'unwilling nomads', who, as a result of their dislocation, would leave an indelible mark on the political climate of this era.

This makes the refugee experience a subject of key importance within European history. Reconstructing the push and pull factors of the different refugee movements can shed new light on how states, nations and peoples navigated the challenges posed during the first half of the twentieth century. One possible way to do so – the one that will be explored in this volume – is through a transnational lens. There are two main challenges in constructing a broader history of refugee movements. The first is that, naturally, refugees tend to discuss their experiences through a one-dimensional prism of (personal) 'victimhood' and do so in an insular manner. This is hardly surprising, given that they are describing a deeply traumatic event that would permanently alter their lives. Although some refugees show awareness of the hardships faced by other groups, when they reflect on their own time of flight or expulsion they self-evidently focus on their own lived experience. It would be patently unfair to expect such personal accounts to discuss broader socioeconomic developments or comparative models, which, moreover, would draw attention away from the stories they want acknowledged. The second challenge is that host societies are keen to present the integration of refugees as success stories. The strides made with assimilation, the lessons taught by the newcomers to the local population or the added value of introducing new voices to society are too often magnified in order to cater to political agendas. At the same time, unfair and often cynical criticism is also levelled against refugee groups by those segments of the host society that wish to blame these immigrants for the presumed decline of their communities. What both sides of the aisle have in common is that they misrepresent the way refugees were dealt with upon arrival, which are hardly ever points of pride to local policy makers. Refugee experiences tend to lay bare some of the pre-existing strains in host societies, or reveal the less savoury inner workings of state-building – stories that are excluded from the 'national' narratives.

Many of the movements of people this volume discusses have their roots in the drawing of the map of Europe in 1919, although 'Versailles' should certainly not be seen as the 'original sin' of mass population displacement; after all, this new map was the culmination of earlier nation state-building efforts which had already caused the uprooting of innumerable people during the previous decades. The map was an imperfect first draft of today's Europe, but it was nevertheless a map on which for the first time we recognize states and nations we know today. These states were carved out of the Austro-Hungarian Empire, the German Empire, the Russian Empire, and the Ottoman Empire,[1] giving substance to peoples' 'right to self-determination' as championed by US president Woodrow Wilson. Question marks were immediately placed at the validity and feasibility of the new borders,[2] if only because the names of the newly formed states 'Yugoslavia' and 'Czechoslovakia' already betrayed that more than one nation would occupy them. It moreover reinvigorated the idea that successful state-building required the preparedness to 'colour inside the lines' by evicting those who fell outside the new states' ethnic, national, racial or religious norms. Voices arguing in favour of cohabitation in ethnically mixed regions were gradually drowned out by straightforward policies that favoured the violent elimination of minorities as a valid solution to state-building and domestic stability. Some of these beliefs set nations and people on paths that led to genocides, while others led to the forced removals of 'others'. Although the two paths had vastly different outcomes – destruction and annihilation in the case of genocide, expulsion and displacement in the case of forced migration – they both served to remove entire groups of people and as such they were two sides of the same coin.[3] In the context of widespread acceptance to see the removal of groups as legitimate political action, there is a certain arbitrariness as to who becomes the 'victim' and who is the 'perpetrator' in these forced migrations. While refugee groups tend to be styled as victims, it is important to note that some of them had in the years prior to their own expulsion actively facilitated the persecution and forced migration of other groups from the very same regions they now claimed as their lost homes.

Every scholarly work dealing with forced migration needs to address the problem of competing definitions and typologies.[4] It is generally accepted now that the boundary between 'forced' and 'voluntary' migration is often blurry and that the experiences of people on the move can be better represented as a spectrum rather than as a dichotomy.[5] We have therefore adopted a broad category of involuntary migrants that includes all people in Europe whose movement across and within state borders in the first half of the twentieth century was primarily caused by war, persecution and political upheaval. The case studies presented in this volume range from deportees and refugees with limited agency whose displacement was caused by forces beyond their control to political émigrés who consciously chose exile in order to continue their struggle against a repressive regime. The category adopted in this volume does not include migrants whose displacement was mainly induced by economic and environmental factors. However, Chapters 13 and 15 nevertheless demonstrate that in traditional immigration countries, such as Germany and France, the experiences of refugees and displaced persons were often shaped by the host society's attitudes to labour migrants who had previously arrived from the same countries of origin.

The current definition of the refugee as someone who is unable or unwilling to return to their country of origin owing to 'a well-founded fear of being persecuted for reasons of race, religion, nationality, membership of a particular social group or political opinion' was codified in the 1951 United Nations Convention Relating to the Status of Refugees and its 1967 Protocol.[6] The principles of refugee protection were introduced to international law already in the aftermath of the First World War by Fridtjof Nansen (1861–1930), the League of Nations High Commissioner for Refugees. Unlike the current conceptual definition, however, refugees in the interwar period were classified according to nationality, for example, as Russian or Armenian refugees.[7] Both the historical and present classifications do not cover the millions of people who were internally displaced by European empires in the era of the two world wars. This volume focuses on the experiences of different types of forced migrants rather than state policies and international responses, but it nonetheless offers a look at the broader historical context in which the current legal definition of the refugee was born.

The authors of the case studies presented in this volume refer to internees, evacuees, refugees, exiles, émigrés, displaced persons, expellees and so on. Most of these labels were ascribed to victims of forced migration by state and international actors or were constructed *post factum* by historians. The individuals in question would rarely identify with these labels and each group of Europe's 'unwilling nomads' saw themselves as unique and referred to their collective experience by different terms in their respective languages. These, however, do not necessarily correspond to typologies used in the English-language scholarly literature. In Polish, for example, all wartime refugees are referred to as 'political emigrants' (*emigranci polityczni*), even though their displacement was not necessarily caused by political or ideological factors. In turn, ethnic Germans who fled from Eastern Europe after the Second World War are consistently called 'expellees' (*Vertriebene*) rather than 'refugees' (*Flüchtlinge*). On the one hand, adopting national terms would bring scholars closer to the self-identification of victims of forced migration. On the other hand, however, following such labels would undoubtedly lead one back into the 'trap' of national narratives of victimhood which this volume is explicitly trying to transcend. We have therefore decided to use a broad definition of forced migrants which includes the entire spectrum of internally displaced people and those displaced across state borders, ranging from Galician internees in the Austro-Hungarian Empire during the First World War to anti-communist émigrés from Eastern Europe in early 1950s France.

Transnational history and the four-dimensional model of diaspora

Placing the different case studies of this volume within a transnational framework allows us to acknowledge that these events are part of a longer arc of history, thereby tying refugee movements in early-twentieth-century Europe much closer to their causes and consequences. Transnational history explores the movement of people, the formation of socio-economic networks and the exchange of ideas between various parts of the world. Proponents of transnational history focus their research on phenomena that transcended the boundaries of politically defined territories, such as empires, nation states or colonies.[8] The concept of diaspora seems to be particularly helpful in analysing the transnational consequences of migratory movements that connect two or more nation states or geographical areas. The Greek term *diaspora*, meaning 'scattering', was for a long time used in a religious context to refer to the Jews living outside of the Land of Israel, but since the 1990s it has been increasingly applied to other ethnoreligious minorities of migrant origin for whom a material and emotional relationship with the homeland is decisive for their sense of collective identity.[9] Many scholars have so far argued that members of a genuine diaspora are continuously involved in a triadic relationship between the host society, the homeland and the diaspora itself.[10] We would suggest, however, that a narrow definition of diaspora that presupposes an all-embracing bond with the homeland runs the risk of homogenizing the lived experience of individual migrants and their descendants.

All diasporas are, in fact, social constructs rather than primordial communities with a prescribed set of shared values and norms of behaviour. As such, the formation of a diaspora relies heavily on the knowledge of hindsight, as it requires the migrant group in question to settle in a new country. Yet, the first steps the people comprising respective diasporas took were seldom made with the idea that the move from their homes would be a permanent one – many were confident that the situation in their homeland would change, allowing them to return. Often these people were proven correct, and many times their displacement was indeed only temporary in nature. Critically, regardless of the time they spent away from home, their forced scattering created conditions that compelled them to interact with the host society, the homeland and other displaced persons. Thus, even though for large groups of people the experience of forced migration was relatively short-lived, they were still part of a dynamic process that played out on a massive Europe-wide scale. If we compare, for example, forced migration from Galicia and Istria, we see that those involved were initially all citizens of Austria-Hungary, uprooted by the First World War and who all suffered significant hardships during their first years away from home. Yet, while the Istrian evacuees returned home in the later stage of the war, large sections of the Ukrainian refugee groups did not have that option and, as a result of the Russian Revolution and subsequent wars, would eventually settle in Berlin, Vienna and Warsaw. Similar scenarios played out during the Second World War. Dutch, Norwegian and Polish refugees alike fled to Britain, but while for the former two groups this was a temporary experience, for the latter it proved to be the beginning of a decennia-long displacement.

We would therefore argue in favour of a four-dimensional model of diasporic relationships. The first three dimensions ('host society', 'homeland' and 'diaspora') have long been recognized by scholars of migration, but these are often treated in a rigid manner that tends to homogenize the diasporic experience. Rather than suggesting alternative terms, which might have their own limitations, we pose that the relations with 'host society', 'homeland' and 'diaspora' should be seen as a spectrum that varies from one individual to another, changes over time and is mediated by age, gender, psychosexual identity, ethnic background, religious beliefs and socio-economic class. While some refugees continue to identify strongly with their homeland and actively engage with diasporic associations, others consciously adopt a low profile and distance themselves from their compatriots in an attempt to blend in with the dominant society. The relationship with the diaspora is especially complicated for those migrants who were persecuted in the 'homeland' as members of a minority group. In any case, the country of origin and the conditions of displacement typically remain to be points of reference for victims of forced migration for the rest of their lives. Decisions taken in the country of origin continue to affect refugees, even when they are completely settled down in the receiving society, raised their children there, learned the language of the region and familiarized themselves with its habits. Despite participation in the new society (and the gratitude they may very well feel towards a country that offered them shelter), many refugees continue to relate to their large or small homeland even decades after their displacement and they often pass down a hybrid national identity to the next generation of the diaspora.

Finally, we suggest adding a fourth dimension to the triad of 'host society', 'homeland' and 'diaspora': interaction with other diasporas. Members of a particular migrant community are involved in a continuous but evolving relationship with members of other diasporas living within the same country. This type of diasporic relationship can take the form of coexistence, cooperation or conflict.[11] The proposed conceptual model of diaspora can be used by transnational historians as an analytical tool that offers the possibility of looking at the formation of migrant communities as a phenomenon in itself, and not only in relation to the national histories of the respective countries of origin and settlement, as implied by the traditional paradigm of linear assimilation.

The aims of the volume

This volume will demonstrate how the collective experience of refugee groups and the formation of diasporic communities can be analysed through a transnational lens with the help of the proposed four-dimensional model of 'host society', 'homeland', 'diaspora' and 'other diasporas'. Since every diaspora is formed by 'unwilling nomads' with vastly different lived experiences, both on individual and group level, the model is meant to guide – not to govern. The chapters that follow therefore do not necessarily seek to fit respective case studies into our model, but rather focus on one or more of its analytical dimensions. In fact, to gain a deeper understanding of the causes and consequences of European forced migratory movements in the first half of the twentieth century, it makes little sense to study refugee groups in isolation; instead this volume presents fifteen interrelated case studies with the aim of highlighting transnational patterns that challenge the conventional 'national' paradigm in the historiography of forced migration.

Part I introduces different types of forced migrants who were internally displaced or displaced across state borders during the First World War. Serhiy Choliy's opening chapter points out that between 1914 and 1918 organized displacement of people was used in Europe for the purpose of state security. Choliy focuses on the heterogeneous population of Galicia which was divided by both Habsburg and Romanov regimes into potential supporters and suspected enemies and then displaced as conscripts, evacuees or internees. In another contribution dealing with the largely forgotten victims of the Great War, Diego Han focuses on the experiences of Istrian evacuees in their new provisional homes and on their relationship with the local communities. Despite magnanimous efforts by philanthropists and humanitarian organizations to provide relief to the displaced people, the wartime refugee camps were remembered by the evacuees as places of suffering. In turn, Egor Lykov's chapter on Austria-Hungary's displacement and internment of Russophiles from Galicia, Italian irredentists from South Tyrol and Serbophiles from Slavonia challenges previous scholarship on this topic by demonstrating that most internees came from a similar social background and shared the same wartime fate, regardless of their citizenship, ethnicity and political orientation. Their experience of forced migration and internment in the camps of Thalerhof and Katzenau was therefore mediated by educational level and socioeconomic class rather than nationality.

The chapters by Miha Zobec, Veronika Weisheimer and Aleksandra Mikulenok in Part II put the spotlight on the complex relationship between political emigrants and host societies in the interwar period. Zobec focuses on the diaspora activism of Slovene and Croat exiles from Italy in the Kingdom of Yugoslavia. The Julian March émigrés formed a heterogeneous diaspora which was divided by a generational conflict between the old (mostly royalists) and the young (largely anti-fascists). Zobec analyses how this diaspora was instrumentalized by Yugoslav authorities within the dynamic context of Italo-Yugoslav relations in the 1920s and 1930s. Weisheimer's contribution on the political activities of Ukrainian émigrés in Weimar Germany focuses not only on the emigrants' relationship with the host society but also on the construction of Ukrainian identity in exile and the Ukrainian diaspora's complicated relationship with Russian refugees. In turn, the chapter by Aleksandra Mikulenok compares the efforts of Russian diasporic institutions, such as schools and newspapers, to preserve the national identity of emigrants' children in different host societies across interwar Europe. Mikulenok particularly focuses on the Russian diaspora's resistance to assimilatory pressures in Estonia, Latvia and Finland.

Part III focuses on people who were displaced as a result of the rise of fascism in Europe in the 1930s and 1940s. The case studies by Jill Meißner-Wolfbeisser and Katrin Sippel both deal with refugees from Nazism and focus on their day-to-day encounters with culturally alien environments in the countries of asylum. Meißner-Wolfbeisser employs a micro-history approach in her chapter on the librarian Stefi Kiesler who served as a cultural broker for German-speaking refugees in the United States. Although many Central Europeans found a microcosm of their lost homeland in the multicultural space of the New York Public Library, not all émigré writers were able to resume their interrupted careers in the new country. Meißner-Wolfbeisser's contribution therefore challenges conventional narratives on both the reception and the exclusion of European refugees in the United States. In turn, Katrin Sippel's chapter portrays refugee women as agents of cultural change in Portuguese society of the late 1930s and 1940s. Focusing on Portugal as a transit country for Jewish and non-Jewish people escaping from Nazi-dominated Europe, Sippel demonstrates how the arrival of displaced women from Central and Eastern Europe challenged conservative gender norms that were promoted by the *Estado Novo* regime.

The chapter by Chelsea Sambells argues that the failure of the Evian Conference to address the Jewish refugee crisis in 1938, accompanied by international reports of rising violence and persecution of Jews in Nazi Germany, was an unpredictable but critical catalyst that compelled humanitarian agencies to develop innovative methods to protect European refugees, particularly children. Sambells focuses on large-scale transnational child evacuation schemes, such as Britain's famous *Kindertransport* of German Jewish children, Switzerland's evacuation of children from German-occupied Belgium and France, and Sweden's evacuation of Finnish children. In turn, David Messenger's contribution reconstructs the multifaceted experience of Spanish Republican refugees in France. Many of those who escaped from Francoist Spain to France eventually fell into the hands of German Nazis and their collaborators. While prominent Republican leaders were refouled to Spain, both Vichy regime and German authorities in occupied France saw the Spanish refugees as a potential workforce, and most were organized into work groups or sent to Germany as forced labourers. The least fortunate exiles were deported to Nazi concentration camps. Motivated by political conceptions of a lost homeland, shaped by their wartime experiences in occupied France and challenged by the emerging Cold War, Spanish Republicans in post-war France did not have a single journey as refugees, but many. In the last chapter in this part, Bradley J. Nichols demonstrates how forced migrants constructed and contested diasporic identities which were ascribed to them by the host society. Nichols explores how the Nazi regime attempted to consolidate an imagined German diaspora by displacing so-called re-Germanizables from the peripheries to the centre of the Third Reich. These forced migrants from German-occupied Poland, Yugoslavia and Alsace/Lorraine manipulated for their own purposes the racial identities that were assigned to them by Nazi officials. Nichols therefore challenges the traditional understanding of diaspora by following the 'centripetal' direction of forced migration in the first half of the twentieth century.

The case studies in Part IV explore different dimensions of displacement in the aftermath of the Second World War. Samantha Knapton and Lennart Onken both deal with displaced persons (DPs) in British-occupied Germany after the Second World War. Knapton looks at the resettlement, repatriation and 'rehabilitation' of Polish DPs in the British Occupation Zone within the longer arc of Polish (forced) migration to Germany and Britain. Polish DPs and *Ruhrpolen*, the descendants of earlier labour immigrants, formed competing communities within the Polish diaspora in post-war Germany, and while the *Ruhrpolen* dissociated themselves from the newcomers in order to pass as Germans, the DPs mistrusted both the German 'hosts' who exploited them as forced labourers during the war and the British allies who 'betrayed' anti-communist Poles at Yalta. However, as Knapton suggests, the controversy over the resettlement of Polish DPs in Germany was eventually overshadowed by the arrival of German expellees from

Eastern Europe. Lennart Onken's chapter on the self-organization in the Jewish DP camp Bergen-Belsen explores how 'subjectification as a nation' in relation to the Jewish homeland in Palestine was meant to overcome the homelessness and statelessness of Holocaust survivors and prevent their repatriation to their countries of origins in Soviet-dominated Eastern Europe. The application of the four-dimensional model to Onken's case study demonstrates that it is difficult to identify which community served as the 'host society' for Jewish DPs in post-war Germany. In a similar fashion, Cristian Cercel's chapter on the migration of c. 2,500 Danube Swabians to Brazil in the early 1950s challenges a straightforward understanding of both 'homeland' and 'diaspora'. The construction of Danube Swabians as a German diaspora in the interwar period and a putative attempt to reimagine them as an Austrian diaspora after the Second World War demonstrate that diasporic identities can be multi-layered and related to several contested homelands. Cercel moreover hints at the role of international aid organizations in the resettlement of refugees, potentially adding a fifth dimension of the diasporic nexus – a point also raised in the chapter by Sambells. In turn, Aaron Clift explores the relationship between refugees, communists and anti-communists in post-war France within the global context of the emerging Cold War. Clift points out that political conflicts in French society coloured the experiences of refugees who located themselves in relation to societal divisions and manipulated categories, such as communist or anti-communist, which were ascribed to them by French politicians, activists and journalists. At the same time, political events in the refugees' Eastern European homelands influenced the positive or negative appraisals by French anti-communists who constantly compared, characterized and ranked different migrants groups.

This volume concludes with a comparative case study of Polish wartime refugees in Britain and East Prussian expellees in post-war Germany in which Bastiaan Willems and Michał Adam Palacz show the full potential of using the four-dimensional model of diaspora. While the historiography of Polish emigration focuses on the political and military elites who continued their struggle for independence in exile, this chapter offers a de-homogenized account of the Polish wartime diaspora which emphasizes the diversity of experiences and attitudes and includes the stories of hitherto marginalized groups, such as women and Polish Jews. Meanwhile, the East Prussian expellees stressed (and their descendants often continue to stress) their victimization in the winter of 1945 – often deliberately ignoring the years immediately preceding it – and this chapter seeks to put their flight and expulsion from their province in a broader context of German–Slavic hostility and rapprochement. Examining these two seemingly disparate groups from the perspective of their evolving relationship with the host society, homeland, own diaspora and other migrant communities demonstrates the validity of approaching refugee movements in twentieth-century Europe from a transnational perspective.

Taken together, the case studies presented in this volume emphasize the importance of analysing forced migratory movements in the first half of the twentieth century within the longer arc of European history. Deportation, evacuation and flight of millions of people in the aftermath of the First World War often intensified rather than alleviated interethnic conflicts which culminated in mass displacement on an even larger scale during the Second World War. Many of the issues of 1945 and beyond have their roots in the tensions that emerged from the rise of different strands of ethnic nationalism in the late nineteenth century. The proposed four-dimensional model of diaspora demonstrates that, by looking at the experience of involuntary migration as a complex set of evolving relationships with the receiving society, the country of origin, own diaspora and other migrants communities, refugees and other DPs can be studied as subjects of historical significance in and of themselves. The addition of the fourth dimension, that is, the relationship between different migrant communities within the same country of settlement, throws the spotlight on an often overlooked aspect of the European refugee experience in the period of the two world wars. Several chapters in this volume show how the changing perception of refugees was shaped by attitudes towards other migrants living within a given host society.

What is more, by transcending narratives of national resilience and (un)successful assimilation, which presuppose an essentialized and exclusive sense of nationality, this volume reveals that migrant identities in the first half of the twentieth century were hybrid, individualized and constantly reconstructed in response to socio-economic forces and political pressures. The ultimate purpose of this book is therefore to remind the readers time and again about the necessity of looking at the 'unwilling nomads' from a genuinely transnational perspective. In contrast to the proliferating narratives of national victimhood, the case studies collected in this volume ultimately suggest that age, gender, social class, educational level and personal experience of individuals are more important to the understanding of the refugee predicament than a collective ethnoreligious identity.

Notes

1 See especially: Omer Bartov and Eric Weitz (eds), *Shatterzones of Empire: Coexistence and Violence in the German, Habsburg, Russian, and Ottoman Borderlands* (Bloomington: Indiana University Press, 2013).
2 R. M. Douglas, *Orderly and Humane: The Expulsion of the Germans after the Second World War* (New Haven: Yale University Press, 2012), 8.
3 Donald Bloxham, 'The Great Unweaving: The Removal of Peoples in Europe, 1875–1949', in *Removing Peoples: Forced Removal in the Modern World*, ed. Richard Bessel and Claduia B. Haake (New York: Oxford University Press, 2009), 167–74.
4 See, for example: William Petersen, 'A General Typology of Migration', *American Sociological Review* 23, no. 3 (1958): 256–66; Egon F. Kunz, 'The Refugee in Flight: Kinetic Models and Forms of Displacement', *International Migration Review* 7, no. 2 (1973): 125–46 and Sven Tägil, 'From Nebuchadnezzar to Hitler. The Question of Mass Expulsion in History up to World War II', in *The Uprooted. Forced Migration as an International Problem in the Post-War Era*, ed. Göran Rystad (Lund: Lund University Press, 1990), 59–85.
5 Anthony Richmond, 'Reactive Migration: Sociological Perspectives on Refugee Movements', *Journal of Refugee Studies* 6, no. 1 (1993): 7–24.
6 United Nations High Commissioner for Refugees, 'Convention and Protocol Relating to the Status of Refugees', 2010. Available online: https://www.unhcr.org/3b66c2aa10

?fbclid=IwAR3HsZzL8UOgHsmlGQrAKWNYTghqHOdRB387-PF4LgjWxw6xacfkaRmlmYE (accessed 17 August 2021).
7   Ivor C. Jackson, 'Dr. Fridtjof Nansen. A Pioneer in the International Protection of Refugees', *Refugee Survey Quarterly* 22, no. 1 (2003): 7–20. See also: Michael R. Marrus, *The Unwanted: European Refugees in the Twentieth Century* (Oxford: Oxford University Press, 1985), 51–121; Peter Gatrell, *The Making of the Modern Refugee* (Oxford: Oxford University Press, 2013), 52–83.
8   C. A. Bayly et al., '*AHR* Conversation: On Transnational History', *American Historical Review* 111, no. 5 (2006): 1441–64; Patricia Clavin, 'Time, Manner, Place: Writing Modern European History in Global, Transnational and International Contexts', *European History Quarterly* 40, no. 4 (2010): 624–40; Padraic Kenney and Gerd-Rainer Horn (eds), *Transnational Moments of Change. Europe 1945, 1968, 1989* (Lanham: Rowman and Littlefield Publishers, 2004), ix–xix.
9   See, for example: Jana E. Braziel and Anita Mannur, *Theorizing Diaspora: A Reader* (Oxford: Blackwell, 2003); Melvin Ember, Carol R. Ember and Ian A. Skoggard (eds), *Encyclopedia of Diasporas: Immigrant and Refugee Cultures Around the World* (New York: Springer Science+Business Media, 2005); Khachig Tölölyan, 'Rethinking Diaspora(s): Stateless Power in the Transnational Moment', *Diaspora: A Journal of Transnational Studies* 5, no. 1 (1996): 3–36; Khachig Tölölyan, 'The Contemporary Discourse of Diaspora Studies', *Comparative Studies of South Asia, Africa and the Middle East* 27, no. 3 (2007): 647–55; Khachig Tölölyan, 'Diaspora Studies: Past, Present and Promise', *IMI Working Papers* 55 (2011): 1–14.
10 See, for example: Gabriel Sheffer, 'A New Field of Study: Modern Diasporas in International Politics', in *Modern Diasporas in International Politics*, ed. Gabriel Sheffer (New York: St. Martin's Press, 1986), 10; William Safran, 'Diasporas in Modern Societies: Myths of Homeland and Return', *Diaspora: A Journal of Transnational Studies* 1, no. 1 (1991): 91–5; Steven Vertovec, 'Conceiving and Researching Transnationalism', *Ethnic and Racial Studies* 22, no. 2 (1999): 449.
11 Michał Adam Palacz, 'The Polish School of Medicine at the University of Edinburgh (1941–1949). A Case Study in the Transnational History of Polish Wartime Migration to Great Britain' (PhD diss., University of Edinburgh, 2016), 217–23.

Part I

Internees and evacuees during the First World War

Map 1.1 Austro-Hungarian Empire, 1910. © Bastiaan Willems.

1

Population movement, evacuation and internment in Habsburg Galicia during the First World War

Considering the four-dimensional model of diaspora

Serhiy Choliy

The twentieth century saw the emergence and approbation of new technologies, which included population movement as one of the important strategies for internal and external policies.[1] The example of the borderland territory of Galicia – in what is today South-Eastern Poland and Western Ukraine – and the policies of both Habsburg and Romanov regimes there during the First World War was the testing ground for new methods of relocation and internal policies. Taken together, this led to the relocation of different populations and the creation of multiple diasporas which, despite sharing a place of origin, met with different fates that were closely tied to the broader context of the war.

A new political means – population displacement and the organized movement of people for state security – was used during the first decades of the twentieth century and remained an actively used element of political practice during the war. On the eve of the First World War, neighbouring Russia asserted its claim to Galicia, and the local population was to suffer at the hands of both the Habsburg and the Romanov regimes during the war.

Galicia before the First World War

On the eve of the First World War, the territory of Galicia was part of the Austrian half of the Dual Monarchy of Austria-Hungary, ruled by representatives of the Habsburg dynasty, and officially known as 'The Kingdom of Galicia and Lodomeria'. From an economic perspective, Galicia was a peripheral territory of Austria-Hungary. The Galician population mostly consisted of peasants, in a region that was one of the poorest in the Habsburg lands.[2]

Several major ethnic and confessional groups, each having different national interests and foreign policy orientations, inhabited Galicia. The diversity of Galician national life influenced the creation of a unique local microcosm of interethnic relations and cohabitation of the three most important national groups: Jews, Poles and Ukrainians.[3] Poles (mostly Roman Catholics), who inhabited most of the territory of Galicia, especially its Western and Central parts, had the biggest influence and formed a clear majority of the population. They held the main governing offices in Galicia, as well as several leading posts in the empire. From the 1860s on, the central Austrian government used the Polish group in parliament as its ally to achieve internal and external policy goals. In return, Poles were rewarded with greater autonomy in Galicia for decades to come. Poles thus dominated Galician political life; the fact that they made up a large proportion of local landowners meant that they could also influence the economic situation of agricultural Galicia.[4]

The orientations of Polish political parties and groups were quite diverse but united by one common goal – the rebirth of the eighteenth-century Polish state from the Black Sea to the Baltic Sea ('od morza do morza'). Although they mostly declared loyalty to Vienna, they often played a double or even triple game: some even had very close relations with Russian parties and the Russian intelligence service and acted as a hidden enemy of the Habsburg state.[5] Ukrainians (mostly Greek Catholic; also referred to as *Ruthenes* or *Rusyns* in official documents of the time) inhabited the territory of eastern Galicia. Although a national minority in Galicia as a whole, in the compact territory in which they resided, they formed an overwhelming majority. Ukrainians were mostly peasant people, employed in agriculture and living chiefly in villages and small towns. Their political activity only began to increase in the last third of the nineteenth century, simultaneously with the growth of their education level and the self-consciousness of Ukrainians as a separate nation.[6]

After playing an active role in the Austrian revolution of 1848–9 as a Habsburg ally, Ukrainians lost their political influence during the 1870s.[7] The Austrian government decided to make deals with the stronger Poles and left Ukrainians without any significant support. This situation resulted in the emergence of two main directions among Ukrainian politicians. The first, Russophiles (or Muscvophiles), were oriented towards Russia, recognizing the local Ukrainian population as a part of a greater Russian nation and attempting to popularize this idea.[8] Majority of the Russophiles were Greek-Catholic priests of the older generation. A new type of local intelligentsia appeared in the last third of the nineteenth century: these were mostly people who had been educated in lay institutions. Their main political orientation was Ukrainophile: that is, involving the recognition of the local Ukrainian populations of Galicia, Bukovina and Transcarpathia as part of a great Ukrainian nation, divided between Austria-Hungary and Russia.[9]

The third biggest national group of Galicia was formed by Jews ('Hebrews'), who were mostly urban residents, with a high percentage of participation in specific professions, such as trade and arts and crafts. Jews in Austria-Hungary, in contrast to neighbouring countries, were granted rights under the law that were equal to other national and confessional groups. De jure they were equal to all the other citizens of the empire, a policy which made Jews loyal to the existing political order. De facto they were often still discriminated against, although the Jews took an active part in the political life of the empire.[10]

Disparities in governmental structure and the rise of the Ukrainian national movement resulted in the further development of the Polish–Ukrainian conflict in the political, confessional, economic and other spheres. Several bloody incidents took place. Even though by 1914 both parties had come to an understanding known as the *Galizische Ausgleich*, mutual distrust was rising. Both Poles and Ukrainians had an extremist fringe in their political environment, striving to reach their goals at the expense of other national groups.[11]

Another aspect that influenced the instability and emergence of possible dividing lines among the Galician population was the foreign influence of Russia. For the Romanov Empire, the war could become a means to solve important internal problems. The Pan-Slavic rhetoric was employed to assert the Russian Empire's commitment to the territorial unification of all Slavic nations under the rule of the Russian tsar. Long before 1914, a vast campaign of solidarity with 'Russian brothers' abroad had begun. Galician Ukrainians, who were recognized as a part of the Russian nation, Poles, Czechs, Slovaks and South Slavs alike were actively targeted by Russian propaganda and foreign policy.[12]

At the same time, the Ukrainophiles of Galicia were recognized as a direct enemy of Russian Pan-Slavism with no right to a separate state or even autonomy. Galicia was the territory in which the Ukrainian national movement had the best possibilities for development, threatening Russian ideological campaigns of Russification and Pan-Slavism.[13] The Russian authorities also identified the Jewish national community of Galicia as a hidden enemy. Beginning in the 1880s, anti-Semitism became part of official Russian policy, with the organization of pogroms as one of its integral components.[14]

Thus, on the eve of the First World War, the territory of Galicia lay in the sphere of interest of the two major powers of the region, Austria-Hungary and Russia, each with their own stances towards the local national groups. On the other hand, the foreign policy orientation of these groups was often recognized as a threat to national security by both rival states.

The Austrian resettlement activities during the First World War

One of the defining features of the First World War was the creation of mass armies, manned through universal conscription. This was a direct result of the military modernizations of the mid-nineteenth century and was the prerequisite to the formation of millions-strong armies fielded by the most influential participants of the war. The First World War was the first war in which large sections of the population became one of the most important resources for its conduct.[15] The military and civilian mobilization started from the first days of the war. There were three main population relocation activities after the beginning of the mobilization: mobilization of men to the army, the internment of suspected persons and transportation of refugees into the interior.[16]

After the general mobilization was completed during summer 1914, the men of Galicia continued to be mobilized to the army according to the available need by forming so-called March Battalions. By 1916, the Austrian army, due to the lack of human resources, established a special governing body – Chief of the Replacement Body for the Entire Armed Forces, or *Chef des Ersatzwesens für die gesamte Bewaffnete Macht* (CHdE) – which in 1917–18 was managed by Baron von Hazai. His main goal was the development of a more effective system of resource usage in all spheres of life in Austria-Hungary.[17] In 1916, it was estimated that 7.8 million people could be used as soldiers for Austria-Hungary, a great number of people for a country with a population of 52 million: it is worth emphasizing that the male population of Austria-Hungary numbered 25.8 million, with 10.3 million men in the age range of seventeen to forty-five years. As of 1 January 1916, the total losses for the Austro-Hungarian army were estimated to be no less than 4 million. With a monthly contingent of 84,000 men, required for replacement at the front, the Austrian General Staff predicted that by October 1916 all available human resources would be exhausted.[18] Only the active processes of manpower redistribution stabilized the situation. It included the high level of involvement of persons that were previously classified as ineligible for military service, new phases of mobilization and the subsequent return of prisoners of war (POWs) from Russia in 1918. By the end of the war, the general number of those mobilized was estimated at 9 million.[19] As many as 1,383,789 people from the territories of Galicia and Bukovina were drafted into the Austrian army during the war, which amounted to around 15.7 per cent of their 1910 population. In general, no less than 30 per cent of the male population was mobilized for the military purpose, notably almost all men in their productive years (age fifteen to forty-nine). An average of 16.6 per 1,000 of the pre-war population (about 150,000) died in combat.[20]

The second-largest form of displacement undertaken during the war by Viennese authorities was civilian mobilization actions.[21] They were directed at securing public tranquillity by limiting the freedom of those who could be considered as enemies of Austria-Hungary ('enemy aliens') and could help Russia in its military advance, as well as at securing and evacuating those who wanted to leave the war zone. Although the internment of suspected traitors was initiated on the first days of the war, the scale of these actions increased after the first military defeats of Austria-Hungary in Galicia during the summer of 1914.[22] The local population was suspected of welcoming the Russian army, while all Russophiles were suspected of being spies. Mistrust of this kind was soon transferred to all Ukrainians in the Habsburg monarchy, who were often deemed to be a population hostile to Habsburg rule. In the first weeks of the war, all kinds of public activities of Russophiles in Galicia were strictly prohibited. At the same time, the Austrian army, using martial law, sentenced to death and executed many individuals, often simply based on their Russian-like language. The resulting mass hysteria and suspicion led many among the local Galician population to greet the arrival of the Russians. As many as 546 people from Galicia and 46 from Bukovina, mostly Greek Catholic or Orthodox

Ukrainians, were sentenced to death as suspected traitors.[23] All these actions even received the title of 'Ukrainian Betrayal' ('Ukrainischer/Ruthenischer Verrat in Galizien').

One of the most important aspects of the Emergency Ordinances in Galicia was mass internment. Historically, this was one of the first cases of internment on such a massive scale, with relocation and resettlement in specially constructed camps. People who were not sentenced to death, but were suspected of sympathizing with Russia, were typically not left behind the frontline. The success of the Russian army and its rapid occupation of Galicia provoked an avalanche of arrests, and actions, which were often the result of personal antipathy or false denunciation. The arrested were deported by trains to internment camps, the largest being Thalerhof, Spielberg (in Styria) and Theresienstadt (in Bohemia). Some interned persons were kept in smaller camps, located in both Austria and Hungary.[24]

Thalerhof internment camp is infamous as one of the first concentration camps in Europe. Like other camps of this type, it was marked by a high mortality rate, unbearable living conditions, the neglect of internees' needs by the local administration and ignoring of prisoner's civil rights. The core of those imprisoned in Thalerhof was a group of 867 Russophile clergymen from Galicia who were at first simply left in the field. Later, after the first barracks had been constructed, most of the internees were left with neither means of subsistence nor support or medical treatment from local civilian and military administration.

It is difficult to calculate the general number of Galicians interned by Austria-Hungary during the First World War, but historians estimate the number ranges from 10,000 to 60,000 people, with the second figure likely to be the most accurate. War hysteria and the designation of the internees as 'traitors' and 'enemies' were important factors that contributed to the high mortality in camps like Thalerhof, as the local communities had a negative or indifferent attitude towards the internees. Thalerhof and the other camps of this type in Austria-Hungary existed until 2 July 1917, when Emperor Karl I abolished them.

The evacuation of refugees from Galicia was organized at the same time as the internment of the region's 'enemy aliens'. Authorities used similar methods, such as the use of trains to move large numbers of people but pursued a different goal – to move state-friendly local citizens out of a war zone. The passport holders from Austria-Hungary who were abroad, as well as citizens who wished to resettle far from the frontline with Russia, were obliged to move along three established evacuation lines: Boleń-Michałowice-Kraków for western Galicia, Tarnogród-Majdan Sieniawski-Jarosław for central Galicia and Volochysk-Pidvolochysk-Ternopil for eastern Galicia. These citizens first had to be vetted by the local administration and were then resettled or interned. A great number of Galician Jews chose to become refugees to avoid potential repression by the Russian occupation administration, which displayed anti-Semitic tendencies.[25]

During the autumn of 1914, Galician refugees were placed in specially constructed camps in Carinthia, Bohemia, Moravia, Upper and Lower Austria, and Vienna. The displacement of refugees followed the same principle as internment but was relatively better organized and included less violence towards the population. By mid-1915, up to 400,000 refugees from Galicia had been displaced westwards. In total, by the end of the war the number of persons who changed their residence from the eastern to the inner provinces of Austria-Hungary – whether voluntarily or due to coercion – was approximately 1.1 million.[26] Refugees, especially the poorer ones, often had to survive in abject poverty and poor living conditions, either as paupers in big cities or as inhabitants of refugee camps in conditions not much different from those of internees. Wartime shortages, infectious diseases and malnutrition were contributing factors to the high mortality rates among these refugees.[27]

Austrian internal policy during the first year of the First World War can be interpreted as a policy of double standards. The citizens of the Habsburg Empire, which had equal constitutional rights, were divided by war into two categories: loyal and suspected of disloyalty. The first category remained within a legal framework, while suspects were deprived of their rights. Thus, the same policy of displacement worked for each of these categories in quite a different way.

The Russian occupation of Galicia and its population management techniques

The occupation of Galicia was one of the most important goals for Russia in the First World War. This border territory was of little economic importance; rather its significance lay in its strategic and political value. Galicia was the key to the inner provinces of Hungary, as it separated Russia from the passes of the Carpathians, and it was a crucial part of the larger Austro-Hungarian defence system. Galicia could also serve as a symbol for Russian Pan-Slavic propaganda. Its 'liberation from the Austrian yoke' gave Russia millions of local Ukrainians, who were recognized by St. Petersburg as Russians.[28] At the same time, Russian rule in Galicia could also be used as an argument for negotiations with the Polish minority of Russia and as a means for encouraging national movements of Slavic nations within Austria-Hungary. Equally important for the Russian Empire's sustainability was the opportunity to destroy the centre of Ukrainian irredentism and separatism in Galicia.[29]

By 16 September 1914, Russian forces had occupied most of the territory of Galicia and Bukovina, blocked the Austrian fortress of Przemyśl and entered the territory of Hungary. Thereafter, the war on the Eastern front turned into trench warfare, which would last until May 1915, when the Austro-Hungarian army reconquered most of the territory of Galicia.[30] The success of the conquest of Galicia in the summer of 1914 emboldened the Russians to think that the territory's return to Habsburgs' rule would be incredibly unlikely, and they began incorporating Galicia into their empire shortly thereafter. The Russians created an administrative system in the occupied territories that was identical to any other district in Russia. The territory of Galicia and Bukovina received the title 'The Military General-Governorship of Galicia' with Count Georgij Bobrinski as its direct administrator. The territory of the governorship was divided into four provinces (*gubernia*): Lemberg, Tarnopol, Czernowitz and Przemyśl.[31] To further consolidate their rule, the Russians promoted the emigration of administrative staff from Russia to Galicia.[32]

The local population of Galicia was first and foremost treated as a valuable wartime manpower resource. The Russian policy in this sphere aimed to use the local population for its war purposes and prevent the Austrians from doing so. During the first days of the war, Russia introduced several regulations concerning foreigners, whereby citizens of Austria-Hungary and Germany, and later of the Ottoman Empire and Bulgaria, were interned and resettled to a place of internal exile.[33] Such regulations also applied to Russian citizens of non-Slavic nationalities, especially ethnic Germans and Jews. At the outbreak of the fighting on the Austro-Hungarian-Russian border, this fate also befell Austro-Hungarian citizens who were on trips to Russia. Some lucky individuals left the territory of Russia and evaded internment, as in the case of Ukrainian activist Vasyl' Makovsky, who crossed the border with the assistance of smugglers.[34] After the occupation, such regulations were extended to newly acquired territories where reserve soldiers, officers and those fit for military service were subject to internment and resettlement from Galicia or Bukovina.[35]

The obligatory internment of Austro-Hungarian reservists was cancelled due to political reasons for several national groups: Ukrainians, Czechs, Slovaks, Poles, Serbs and later for Italians and Romanians who were recognized as possible allies of Russia in the war.[36] During the first months of the war, the Russian military command organized the release of Austro-Hungarian POWs. Those POWs who came from the occupied Galician territory and showed no hatred of the enemy could be released, the only condition for their release being that they gave their parole of honour and signed a document declaring their refusal to act against the tsar and the Russian state.[37] In the first stage, thousands of POWs were set free without any registration, having been identified only by their spoken language or Orthodox confession.[38]

Russian authorities also commenced internment actions of those who were seen as possible threats to their rule, targeting Austrian administration officials and local political or social activists.[39] They were usually moved from Galicia to the inner provinces of Russia. According to reports of the occupational administration, 1,962 people were evicted from the territory of Galicia and 2,364 were resettled closer to the Russian border during the eleven months of the Russian occupation. Jews were not included in these statistics because they were designated as a hostile population and were evacuated either from Galicia or from the frontline. The number of evacuated Jews was approximately 10,000 people. Austrian officials who had stayed in Galicia after the occupation were also classified as hostile populations but were used as temporary employees in the occupational administration under Russian supervision.[40]

The local population was also obliged to provide hostages, whom the Russians deported and used to guarantee public peace in Galicia and as a safety factor for their military operations and troops. According to reports of the occupational administration, hostages numbered almost 700 people. Often the local administration of the lowest level deported undesirables in the form of hostages or internees without any registration of these actions. Russian reports sometimes failed to differentiate between the categories of 'interned' and 'resettled', which is the main reason why a total of 700 people is likely to be unrealistic.

The following data demonstrates a lack of any system in hostage registration and shows that bribery served as an important method of avoiding internment. During the first days of the Russian occupation, there was a request to provide 250 hostages from Lemberg (Lwów, L'viv), the capital city of Galicia. As a result of subsequent negotiations and direct corruption, this number decreased to 150. Ultimately, the real number of hostages taken from Lemberg was only thirty-seven people – fifteen Jews, twelve Poles and ten Ukrainians.[41] Poles and Ukrainians were settled in Kyiv, where no one took care of them, and they were left starving and destitute. Memoirs and archival sources further indicate that there were 128 Galician hostages of Polish nationality in Kyiv and 554 Galician hostages of unidentified nationality in Poltava. Jewish hostages were settled in Nizhniy Novgorod, much farther from the frontline, and there are no exact data about their numbers.[42] In contrast to official reports, the folk memory among the local population indicates that the number of hostages was significant, especially among the Jewish population. Local leaders, including the highest representatives of local clergy, among them Metropolitan Archbishop Andrzej Sheptytsky, were deported to Siberia; only the Russian Revolution in 1917 allowed these displaced persons to return home.[43]

In May 1915, the united armies of Austria-Hungary and Germany launched an offensive near the town of Gorlice, regaining all of Galicia except its easternmost part around the city of Tarnopol (Ternopil). The result of military defeat was the evacuation of the Russian administration from Galicia during May–July 1915.[44] Having the intention of limiting Austro-Hungarian resources for a possible future conflict, Russian strategists ordered the evacuation of everything that could be used for war purposes or the destruction of those material assets that could not be removed. Human resources, especially men of working age who could have later been mobilized by the Austro-Hungarian army, were also to be evacuated. It created two eastward population flows from Galicia: pro-Russian refugees who were afraid of the return of Austrian administration or had no wish to be mobilized to the Austro-Hungarian army and men of working age plus hostages who were to be interned in Russia. Refugees were evacuated to Kyiv and then Rostov-on-Don, or placed in the neighbouring Russian provinces of Podolia and Bessarabia.[45]

In early 1915, the local Russian authorities in Galicia received orders to register all men between the ages eighteen and fifty who could be used for military service. After military clashes of May 1915, the local authorities had to remove all such men from Galicia as quickly as possible – as with the enforced removal of cattle and stocks of material assets. For this purpose, there were special trains that departed from Lemberg train station each evening; the deported persons had to be settled in neighbouring Volhynia. However, the swiftness of the offensive by the Central Powers and disorganization on the Russian home front thwarted the realization of this project.[46] During the period between May and June 1915, Russian authorities displaced no less than 75,000 people from Galicia. The overall number of refugees and displaced from Galicia to Russia was estimated at 200,000.[47]

The emergence of diasporas and their existence after the First World War

The First World War would permanently shape the foreign policies of European powers. Post-war redistribution of former imperial territories of Austria-Hungary,

Germany, the Ottoman Empire and Russia had nonetheless only a modest impact on the emergence of new diasporas, as most people who were displaced during the war tried to return to their original place of residence. Of course, there were exceptions, as several countries already began the process of national homogenization and ethnic cleansing during or immediately after the end of hostilities.[48]

If we talk about East-Central Europe and Galicia in particular, national homogenization may have been the aim of many of the states that emerged in the 1920s and 1930s, including the Polish state which incorporated Galicia after the end of the First World War. At the same time, the methods of this homogenization differed profoundly from the experiences of the Second World War, which made the return home an acceptable option for most people who were resettled between 1914 and 1918. Even those nations who remained stateless during the interwar period (in the case of Galicia – Jews and Ukrainians) usually choose to return and integrate into newly emerging societies of the interwar European states. Membership in a wartime diaspora influenced the subsequent political activity of only some groups, mostly Ukrainians of Russophile and Ukrainophile orientations in interwar Poland and Czechoslovakia.[49] Both groups used internment martyrdom as an important symbol and an argument in their political struggle and the creation of a group narrative.

Another factor that reinforced the decline of wartime diasporas was the emergence of the Soviet Union as a new geopolitical reality. It narrowed the possible opportunities for those who considered Russia to be the protector of their interests and new homeland, especially the Russophiles and Pan-Slavists. In the short run, the absolute majority of internees and hostages from Galicia as well as POWs returned to Austria-Hungary's successor states. The majority of the refugee population did the same by the end of the Russian Civil War.[50] These are the reasons why Galician diasporas in Russia existed for a very short time and disappeared in the early 1920s.

The most important factor that influenced the fate of those persons who moved or were removed from Galicia during the First World War was their categorization by the host societies, either Austro-Hungarian or Russian. The results of such categorization significantly influenced the fate of each person but did not necessarily correlate with a person's behaviour or political views. The general level of well-being of resettled persons at the early stage of the war as well as the attitude of the population in the area of resettlement varied depending on whether these persons were labelled state-friendly refugees or state-hostile internees. For example, refugees in Russia were often settled in the European part of the empire, while internees in the remote regions of Siberia and the Far East. However, the general shortage of resources, including food and accommodation, started to blur the line between resettled and internees from as early as 1915. Examples of this situation are the Austrian camps of Gmünd (evacuees) and Thalerhof (internees), with practically identical living conditions during the war.[51]

The wartime experiences of resettled people demonstrate that inclusion in this or that category of relocation was often independent of the real political or personal motivations of individual persons. It adds to the image of heterogeneous and diverse experiences of the First World War by members of Galician diasporas and correlates with the four-dimensional model of diaspora, presented in this volume.[52]

Many persons, both of Austrian-Hungarian and Russian descent, were interned or resettled not only against their will but also because of false denunciations or wartime disorganization that depicted them as members of a diaspora group that did not represent their political views or personal motivations. Some tried to avoid the war by fleeing and becoming refugees, either in the Eastern or Western direction. Their main motivation was not to be drafted for military service purposes or live under potentially oppressive occupational administration. Others were falsely accused and interned by the Austrian administration even though they remained loyal to their respective countries. Personal wartime experiences demonstrate this situation. For example, the Ukrainian-born lawyer and Ukrainophile activist Vasyl' Makovskyi, who worked mostly in Buczacz county in Galicia, vacationed in Odessa in the summer of 1914, but decided to return home after the beginning of Russian mobilization. Although the border between Russia and Austria-Hungary had already been closed for civilians, he managed to bypass it via neutral Romania. After coming back to Galicia he was interned as a suspected spy and spent several months in Thalerhof. He was released after the interventions of several Ukrainian deputies to the Austrian parliament and lived in Austria as a refugee until the end of the war.[53]

Another example is Vasyl' Vavryk' (1889–1970). He was a Russophile activist and a student at Lemberg University in 1914. After the beginning of the war, he was interned and spent more than a year in Theresienstadt prison castle and later Thalerhof. In 1915 the Austrian administration drafted him into the army and sent him to the Italian front. After some time spent there as an Austrian soldier, he was captured by the Italian army and became a POW. Later he joined a Russian volunteer formation that fought together with the French and British against Germany on the Western front. In 1917 he immigrated to Russia and stayed there until 1920. He actively participated in the life of the local community of Galician refugees in Rostov and even created a volunteer formation of refugees who took part in the Russian Civil War.[54]

These examples demonstrate important features of Galician diasporas during the First World War. First of all, we should talk about several different Galician diasporas that were created by the bureaucratic machines of the rival empires. These diasporas were often hostile to each other and had different relations with both home and host communities, which reflected their bureaucratic recognition as state-friendly or enemy alien. Second, those small diasporas were often divided internally, depending on personal and political motivations, social background and bureaucratic categorization of their members. As the preceding examples show, there was no actual unity among those people, except the shared will to survive the war. Lastly, the changes in the political and national affiliation of displaced individuals demonstrate the actual fragility of diaspora groups in periods of war and revolution.

Conclusion

Galicia's heterogeneous society was divided during the war into supporters and enemies of competing imperial regimes. From the perspective of the two great empires, the local population became nothing more than a pawn that could be subjected to state-led violence that was wielded to achieve victory in the war. The First World War in this regard demonstrated how the methods of waging war had diversified during the age of modernity: mass displacement, mobilization of mass armies and concentration camps were the inventions that characterized this new epoch, made possible by the technological progress of the nineteenth century. Otherwise natural phenomena, such as population movement, became transformed into a standard means employed in state-led war policy. The First World War can thus be recognized as a model of population movement in the time of late European modernity.

The example of Galicia demonstrates the similarity in the main approaches of both Habsburg and Romanov regimes to the issue of large population masses as a resource during the war. There were few differences in the techniques and means of displacement: mobilization of soldiers, evacuation of friendly refugees, the internment of suspects and their isolation in camps or remote regions of the interior. Organized displacement thus became a strategy that was seen as important for the success of the state's military operations. The First World War demonstrated that displacement of thousands of people could be an effective political method on a local and international level, so much so that it was to become a widely used strategy. At the same time, mass displacement was among those factors that contributed to the following destabilization and collapse of imperial regimes that practised it. The refugee crisis and inability to provide population, secured by resettlement, with appropriate nutrition and housing, increased the internal crises in wartime societies.

Diasporas that were formed as a result of organized displacement from Galicia proved to be a short-lived phenomenon. They were largely constructed through wartime categorization by imperial bureaucrats. That is why such diasporas rapidly disappeared after the collapse of imperial regimes. This categorization had a great influence on the general wartime experiences of diaspora members. Those who were recognized as state-friendly received minor benefits while 'enemy aliens' were treated with hostility. Such divisions among the pre-war population were the main factors that predetermined the interaction with both home and host societies. If we are talking about the interaction of different diasporas among themselves, the official recognition of loyalty was still crucial: internees were usually kept in full isolation and had no opportunity to interact with other groups while refugees were often supported by the host society.

The bureaucratic categorization also had an unintended consequence. There were many cases of persons who were ascribed to one of the resettlement categories against their will and in contrast to their real actions. In some cases, such as with Vasyl' Makovskyi or Vasilii Vavrik, such mislabelling provoked hostility between different members of the newly emerged diaspora of Galician internees. Depending on the case, it took from several months to years for such persons to be re-inscribed to a population group that corresponded to their actual political views. Mistakes and false denunciations often were the factors that predetermined the living conditions, and sometimes even the life or death of individuals, corresponding to the treatment of their assigned group.

After the disintegration of the two rival empires, namely Russia in 1917 and Austria-Hungary in 1918, the Galician diasporas disappeared swiftly. The majority of the civilian internees as well as demobilized soldiers decided to return home to Galicia and settle down in the newly emerged Polish state. At the same time, the Russian Revolution released the POWs and drove wartime refugees to return home, particularly as the threat of possible Habsburg reprisals no longer existed. It was the main reason why wartime Galician diasporas ceased to exist by the early 1920s. The only memories left were the group narratives of expulsion and internment, shaped by national and political activists during the next decades.[55]

Notes

1. An earlier version of this text was published in the online journal *Percorsi storici* in 2014; see Serhiy Choliy, 'War as a Model of Population Movement in the Modern World: The Galician Perspectives in the First World War', *Percorsi Storici* 2 (2014). Available online: http://www.percorsistorici.it/ (accessed 10 January 2018).
2. John-Paul Himka, *Galician Villagers and the Ukrainian National Movement in the Nineteenth Century* (Edmonton: Canadian Institute of Ukrainian Studies, 1988).
3. Tadeusz Dąbkowski, *Ukraiński ruch narodowy w Galicji Wschodniej. 1912–1923* (Warsaw: Instytut Krajów Socjalistycznych PAN, 1985), 27.
4. Andrzej Dziadzio, 'Die Kroatische und Galizische Autonomie: Rechtshistorischer und politologischer Aspekt. Zur Stellung der Rechtsgeschichte in der Erforschungen der Verfassungsgeschichte', in *Zu den gegenwärtigen rechtsgeschichtlichen Forschungen*, ed. Kalman Kovács (Budapest: Eötvös Loránd University, 1987), 25–41.
5. Central State Historical Archive of Ukraine, Kyiv (hereafter CDIAK), fond 361, opys 1, sprava 240, 1–2; Austriacus, *Polnische Russophilen und Masseverhaftungen staatstreuer Ukrainer in Galizien* (Berlin: C. Kroll, 1915), 1–15.
6. Ivan Karpynec, *Halychyna: vijs'kova istoriya 1914–1921 rr.* (L'viv: Panorama, 2005), 12.
7. A. J. P. Taylor, *The Habsburg Monarchy, 1809–1918: A History of the Austrian Empire and Austria-Hungary* (London: Hamish Hamilton, 1941), 67–72.
8. *Otchet' vremennago voennago general'-gubernatora Galicii po upravleniju kraem' za vremja s' 1 sentjabrja 1914 goda po 1 ijulja 1915 goda* (Kyiv: Tipografia Shtaba Kievskogo Vojennogo Okruga, 1916), *Otchet' L'vovskago gubernatora, Prilozhenie #2 K' otchetu vremennago voennago general'-gubernatora Galicii* (Kyiv: Tipografia Shtaba Kievskogo Vojennogo Okruga, 1916), 9.
9. Himka, *Galician Villagers*; Andreas Kappeler, 'Ein "kleines Volk" von 25 Millionen: die Ukrainer um 1900', *Jahrbücher für Geschichte Osteuropas* 5 (1991): 33–43; Myhajlo Lozyns'kyj, *Halychyna v zhyttyu Ukrayiny* (Vienna: Soyuz Vyzvolennya Ukraïny, 1916), 43–6 and 53–60.
10. Ivan Monolatij, *Inshi svoyi: polityčna uchast' etničnyh aktoriv pizn'ohabsburz'kyh Halyčyny i Bukovyny* (Ivano-Frankivs'k: Lileja-NV, 2012), 200–9.
11. Omer Bartov and Eric Weitz, 'Introduction: Coexistence and Violence in German, Habsburg, Russian, and Ottoman Borderlands', in *Shatterzone of Empires: Coexistence and Violence in the German, Habsburg, Russian, and Ottoman Borderlands*, ed. Omer Bartov and Eric Weitz (Bloomington: Indiana University Press, 2013), 8–9; Larry Wolff, *The Idea of Galicia: History and Fantasy in Habsburg Political Culture* (Stanford: Stanford University Press, 2010), 1–7; Alexander Prusin, *The Lands between: Conflict*

in the East European Borderlands, 1870-1992 (Oxford: Oxford University Press, 2010), 12-35; Monolatij, *Inshi svoyi*, 200-9, 316-8 and 329.

12 Falk Schupp, 'Die Bedeutung der Ukraine für den Weltkrieg', *Osteuropaeische Zukunft* 20 (1917): 289-90; Aleksandr Pogodin', *Slavjanskij mir': politicheskoe i jekonomicheskoe polozhenie slavjanskih' narodov' pered' vojnoj 1914 goda* (Moscow: I. D. Sytin, 1915); *Otchet*, 9; Austriacus, *Polnische Russophilen*, 1-15.

13 Josyp Hermajze, 'Materialy do istoriyi ukrayins'koho ruhu za svitovoyi vijny', in *Ukrayins'kyj arheohrafichnyj zbirnyk* (Kyiv: VUAN, 1926), 271-354.

14 Jonathan Dekel-Chen, *Farming the Red Land: Jewish Agricultural Colonization and Local Soviet Power 1924-1941* (New Haven and London: Yale University Press, 2005), 6-7.

15 Horst Haselsteiner, 'The Habsburg Empire in the First World War: Mobilization of Food Supplies', in *War and Society in East Central Europe, Vol. 9: East Central European society in the First World War*, ed. Béla K. Király, Nándor F. Dreisziger and Albert A. Nofi (New York: Columbia University Press, 1985), 87-103; Elena Senjavskaja, *Psihologija vojny v XX veke: istoricheskij opyt Rossii* (Moscow: ROSSPĖN, 1999), 45. The topic of the First World War internment is intensively discussed in contemporary historiography. Here I should mention two seminal volumes devoted to the local and global context of internment: Stefan Manz, Panikos Panayi and Matthew Stibbe (eds), *Internment during the First World War: A Mass Global Phenomenon* (London and New York: Routledge, 2019) and Matthew Stibbe, *Civilian Internment during the First World War: A European and Global History, 1914-1920* (London: Palgrave Macmillan, 2019).

16 Gerald Stourzh, 'Ethnic Attribution in Late Imperial Austria: Good Intentions, Evil Consequences', in *The Habsburg Legacy: National Identity in Historical Perspective*, ed. Ritchie Robertson and Edward Timms (Edinburgh: Edinburgh University Press, 1994), 67-89; *Mobilisierungsinstruktion für die politischen Behörden* (Vienna: Ministerium für Landesverteidigung, 1911), 6-7 and 13-17.

17 *Austrian State Archives - War Archives*, Vienna (hereafter KA), Chef des Ersatzwesens für die gesamte Bewaffnete Macht, Aktenkartons (hereafter ChdE), 2-1/4, 2.

18 KA, ChdE, 127; Wassyl Kutschabsky, *Die Westukraine im Kampfe mit Polen und dem Bolschewismus in den Jahren 1918-1923* (Berlin: Junker und Dünnhaupt, 1934), 233-9.

19 Grigorij Shigalin, *Voennaja ekonomika v pervuju mirovuju vojnu (1914-1918)* (Moscow: Vojenizdat, 1956), 55 and 248.

20 Maciej Krotofil, *Ukraińska Armia Halicka 1918-1920: Organizacja, uzbrojenie, wyposażenie i wartość bojowa sił zbrojnych Zachodnio-Ukraińskiej Republiki Ludowej* (Toruń: Adam Marszałek, 2003), 30; Wilhelm Winkler, *Die Totenverluste der Österreich-Ungarische Monarchie nach Nationalitäten: die Altersgliederung der Toten. Ausblicke in die Zukunft* (Vienna: Seidl, 1919), 3-8.

21 Matthew Stibbe, 'Enemy Aliens, Deportees, Refugees: Internment Practices in the Habsburg Empire, 1914-1918', *Journal of Modern European History* 12, no. 4 (2014): 479-99. Serhiy Choliy, 'The Internment of Russophiles in Austria-Hungary', in *1914-1918-Online. International Encyclopedia of the First World War*. Available online: https://encyclopedia.1914-1918-online.net/article/the_internment_of_russophiles_in _austria-hungary (accessed 30 August 2021).

22 'Spy fever' was a characteristic feature of the war, especially of its first weeks, see Christoph Jahr and Jens Thiel, 'Adding Colour to the Silhouettes: The Internment and Treatment of Foreign Civilians in Germany during the First World War', in *Internment during the First World War*, 41-4.

23 Anna Veronika Wendland, *Die Russophilen in Galizien: Ukrainische konservative zwischen Oesterreich und Russland, 1848-1915* (Vienna: VÖAW, 2001), 540-50; *Talergofskii al'manakh. Propamiatnaia kniga avstriiskikh zhestokostei, izuverstv i nasilii nad karpato-russkim narodom vo vremia vsemïrnoi voiny 1914 - 1917 gg.* (L'viv: Talergofskii komitet, 1924), Vol. 1, 5; Stibbe, *Civilian internment*, 103-16.

24 There were simultaneous events of mass hysteria, directed towards 'enemy aliens' or traitor suspects, in most European states of the time, such as the rise of anti-Semitism in Russia and other countries, see Peter Gatrell, *A Whole Empire Walking: Refugees in Russia during the World War I* (Bloomington: Indiana University Press, 1999), 17; *Talergofskii al'manakh*, Vol. 2, 109-33; Stibbe, 'Enemy Aliens'; Jahr and Thiel, 'Adding Colour'.

25 Central State Historical Archive of Ukraine, L'viv (hereafter CDIAL), fond 146 opys 4 sprava 3366, 63-4 and 66; KA, KM, Karton #2863, 8-9 and 13-16, Annex 1-d.; Volodymyr Zapolovs'kyj, *Bukovyna v ostannij vijni Avstro-Uhorshhyny* (Chernivci: Zoloti lytavry, 2003), 43 and 190-4.

26 Beatrix Holter, *Die Ostjudische Kriegsflüchtlinge in Wien 1914-1923* (Salzburg: 1978), 12-15; Zapolovs'kyj, *Bukovyna*, 43; E. I. Rubinshtejn, *Krushenie Avstro-Vengerskoj monarhii* (Moscow: Izd-vo AN SSSR, 1963), 88; Ivan Semaka, 'Pro vyselenciv', 'Zhytye i dolya vyselenciv na Moraviyi', in *Bazhayemo do Ukraïny*, ed. O. Dobrzhans'kyj and V. Staryk (Odesa: Mayak, 2008), 652-54.

27 Manz, Panayi and Stibbe, *Internment during the First World War*, 6-9; Matthew Stibbe, 'The Internment of Enemy Aliens in the Habsburg Empire, 1914-1918', in *Internment during the First World War*, 68-9.

28 L. Burchak, *Galicija: eja proshloe i nastojashchee* (Moscow: Chitatel', 1914), 30-7.

29 Himka, *Galician Villagers*.

30 Richard Lein, '"Sterb' ich in Polen ...". Strategische und taktische Vorbedingungen der Kriegsführung an der österreichisch-ungarischen Nordostfront 1914', in *Nation, Nationalitäten und Nationalismus im östlichen Europa*, ed. Marija Wakounig, Wolfgang Mueller and Michael Portmann (Vienna and Münster: LIT Verlag, 2010), 387-8.

31 CDIAK, fond 361 opys 1 sprava 79a, 1-48 and sprava 301, 51-133; Otchet' kanceljarij voennago general-gubernatora Galicii. *Prilozhenie #1 K' otchetu vremennago voennago general'-gubernatora Galicii* (Kyiv: Tipografia Shtaba Kievskogo Vojennogo Okruga, 1916), 7, 17; *Prilozhenie #2*, 1.

32 Marzell Chlamtacz, *Lembergs politische physiognomie wärend der Russischen Invasion 3/IX/1914 - 22/VI/1915* (Vienna: Rudolf Lechner & Sohn, 1916), 10-12, 44-6 and 75-95; Himka, *Galician Villagers*, 483-92; Otchet' po L'vovskomu gradonachal'stvu (s' 21 avgusta 1914 goda po den' evakuacii L'vova - 7 ijunja 1915 goda). *Prilozhenie #5 K' otchetu vremennago voennago general'-gubernatora Galicii* (Kyiv: Tipografia Shtaba Kievskogo Vojennogo Okruga, 1916), 5-12 and 19; Ivan Petrovych, *Halychyna pid chas Rosijs'koyi okupaciyi serpen' 1914 - cherven' 1915* (L'viv: Politychna biblioteka, 1915), 14-18, 25, 54-7, 81 and 95.

33 CDIAK, fond 361 opys 1 sprava 1935, 3; fond 1439 opys 1 sprava 1602, 7, 10, 15, 109, 111 and sprava 1756, 18, 21, 37, 173, 121, 245 and 315; fond 1599 opys 1 sprava 130, 19, 71, 104 and 106. According to Peter Gatrell, no less than 200,000 Germans who lived in Russia were displaced due to such regulations, see Gatrell, *A Whole Empire*, 23.

34 Vasyl' Makovs'kyj, *Talerhof: spohady i dokumenty* (L'viv: Dilo, 1934), 1-50.

35 Gatrell, *A Whole Empire*, 16-17; Stibbe, 'Enemy Aliens'.

36 CDIAK, fond 363 opys 1 sprava 77, 1, 27, 99, 305; fond 1439 opys 1 sprava 1602, 11, 46, 126, 133 and 137; Reinhard Nachtigal, *Rußland und seine österreich-ungarische kriegsgefangenen (1914-1918)* (Remshalden: Bernhard Albert Greiner, 2003), 58-9.
37 CDIAK, fond 363 opys 1 sprava 23, 7, 12, 14, 129-30, 154, 160 and 381.
38 CDIAK, fond 361 opys 1 sprava 224, 95 and 119; fond 363 opys 1 sprava 77, 305 and opys 3 sprava 15, 1 -127; *Otchet*, 14, Stibbe, *Civilian Internment*, 243-51.
39 CDIAK, fond 301 opys 1 sprava 3310, 3.
40 Chlamtacz, *Lembergs politische physiognomie*, 109; *Otchet*, 17; *Prilozhenie #1*, 31-32, 43; *Prilozhenie #5*, 5-12 and 19.
41 Józef Białynia-Chołodecki, *Zakładnicy miasta Lwowa w niewoli rosyjskiej 1915-1918* (L'viv: Wschód, 1930), 1 and 9.
42 Białynia-Chołodecki, *Zakładnicy*, 1, 23, 42 and 100-3; *Otchet*, 17; *Prilozhenie #1*, 34.
43 Central State Archive of the Supreme Bodies of Power and Government of Ukraine, Kyiv (hereafter CDAVO), fond 1792 opys 1 sprava 23, 341 and fond 2592 opys 1 sprava 58, 17; Edward Prus, *Władyka Świętojurski. Rzecz o arcybiskupie Andrzeju Szeptyckim 1865-1944* (Warsaw: Instytut Wydawniczy Związków Zawodowych, 1985), 49-56. There were some similarities with other territories, occupied by Russians, se Peter Holquist, 'Forms of Violence during the Russian Occupation of Ottoman Territory and in Northern Persia (Urmia and Astrabad), October 1914–December 1917', in *Shatterzone of Empires*, 334-61.
44 Kratkij otchet' po upravleniju Chernoveckoj guberniej za period' vremeni s' 1 sentjabrja po 7 oktjabrja 1914 g. i s' 17 nojabrja 1914 g. po 1 fevralja 1915 g. b. Chernoveckago gubernatora kamer'-junkera dvora Ego Imperatorskago velichestva Evreinova. *Prilozhenie #3 K' otchetu* vremennago voennago general'-gubernatora Galicii (Kyiv: Tipografia Shtaba Kievskogo Vojennogo Okruga, 1916), 6.
45 CDIAK, fond 361 opys 1 sprava 478-80 and opys 2 sprava 11, 5, 22, 45 and 94-112; Białynia-Chołodecki, *Zakładnicy*, 1; Dmytro Doroshenko, *Moyi spomyny pro nedavnye mynule: 1914-1920* (Kyiv: Tempora, 2007), 51 and 95.
46 CDIAK, fond 361 opys 1 sprava 481, 9 and sprava 552, 1-23, 56-7 and 76; Chlamtacz, *Lembergs politische physiognomie*, 115.
47 Aleksandra Bahturina, *Politika Rossijskoj imperii v Vostochnoj Galicii v gody Pervoj mirovoj vojny* (Moscow: AIRO-XX, 2000), 187-88; *Otchet*, 46; *Prilozhenie #1*, 2, 20, 53; *Prilozhenie #5*, 17; Myhajlo Cehlyns'kyj, *Halyc'ki pohromy: trahichna storinka z zhyttya halyc'kyh Ukrayinciv v chasy evropejs'koyi vijny 1914-1915 rr.* (Cleveland: Robitnyk, 1917), 1-17. There is also alternative data indicating that the overall total of refugees from Galicia was several times higher. Peter Gatrell indicates no less than 400,000 refugees from Galicia alone during 1915, see Gatrell, *A Whole Empire*, 21.
48 Here I should mention the policy of the Turkish state, directed at limiting the influence of the non-Muslim and non-Turkish groups in the Ottoman Empire, and the post-war military conflict between Greece and Turkey that led to practically absolute resettlement of Greeks from Turkey and Turks from Greece in the early 1920s, see Norman Naimark, *Fires of Hatred: Ethnic Cleansing in Twentieth-Century Europe* (Cambridge, MA: Harvard University Press, 2001), 18-49; Anastasia Filippidou, 'The Impact of Forced Top-Down Nation Building on Conflict Resolution: Lessons from the 1923 Compulsory Population Exchange between Greece and Turkey', *Nationalities Papers* 48, no. 1 (2020): 144-57; Akcam Taner, 'The Young Turks and the Plans for the Ethnic Homogenization of Anatolia', in *Shatterzone of Empires*, 258-82.
49 Choliy, 'The Internment of Russophiles'.

50 CDIAK, fond 361 opys 1 sprava 302, 60–71 notices that last Austro-Hungarian refugees left Soviet Russia in 1923. Cf. Hannes Leidinger and Verena Moritz (eds), *In russischer Gefangenschaft: Erlebnisse österreichischer Soldaten im Erster Weltkrieg* (Vienna, Cologne and Weimar: Böhlau, 2008), 273; Stibbe, *Civilian Internment*, 243–51.
51 Manz, Panayi and Stibbe, *Internment during the First World War*, 6–9; Stibbe, 'Internment of Enemy Aliens', 68–9; Stibbe, *Civilian Internment*, 112–16 and 130.
52 See introduction to this volume by Willems and Palacz. Cf. Stibbe, 'Enemy Aliens'; Mark Cornwall, 'Traitors and the Meaning of Treason in Austria-Hungary's Great War', *Transactions of the Royal Historical Society* 25 (2015): 119–23; Daniela L. Caglioti, 'Dealing with Enemy Aliens in WWI: Security Versus Civil Liberties and Property Rights', *Italian Journal of Public Law* 3, no. 2 (2011): 183–8.
53 Makovs'kyj, *Talerhof*.
54 CDIAK, fond 361 opys 1 sprava 302, 60–71. Cf. Vasilii Vavrik, *Karpatorossy v kornilovskom' pohode i dobrovol'cheskoj armii* (L'viv: Stavropigijskij Institut, 1923).
55 Choliy, 'The Internment of Russophiles'.

2

Humiliated and insulted

The multiple categories of Austro-Hungarian civilian internees, 1914–17

Egor Lykov

Historical background

The forced migration of civilians during the First World War was inherently connected to a newly emerging culture of war. This changing nature of war led to the establishment of internment camps in several European countries, including Austria-Hungary, whose approach to and treatment of civilian populations – both their own and foreign populations – differed from those of the other states.[1] The Austro-Hungarian government also persecuted its own citizens living on the internal peripheries of the empire, above all, in Galicia, South Tyrol and Slavonia. Even though the late Habsburg Empire did not acknowledge the existence of nations within the country and hoped to foster supranational forms of patriotism during the First World War, it used national categories for internal security to identify 'suspicious' persons such as the members of the Russophile party in Galicia, Italian irredentists in South Tyrol and Serbophiles in Slavonia. Imperial margins thus became crisis hotspots after the war had broken out; growing Polish, Ukrainian, Russian, Italian and Serbian nationalisms combined with the fragile border situation and the structural weaknesses of the peripheral regions formed a basis for tightening governmental control during the war. This gave the authorities a reason to suspect their own citizens of espionage.[2] 'Suspicious' civilians were brutally removed from the area of operations of the Austro-Hungarian armed forces: in September 1914 from Galicia and Slavonia, and in May 1915 from South Tyrol, and relocated to internment camps in the Austrian interior, especially in Upper Austria, Lower Austria and Styria. The internment camps Thalerhof near Graz (today the airport Graz-Thalerhof) and Katzenau near Linz for Ruthenians (Ukrainians) and Italians, respectively, gained a bad reputation due to the miserable living conditions and high mortality rates, and have played an important role in local memory cultures among the descendants of the survivors.

Current historiography addresses these forced migrations only insufficiently. The current state of research on this subject is described as marginal in Austrian research literature.³ As late as 2010, Austrian historians Georg Hoffmann, Philipp Lesiak and Nicole-Melanie Goll stated that these forced migrations 'had no impact on Austrian history'.⁴ This is also confirmed by the *Lexikon der Vertreibungen* that states: 'The persecution of the Ruthenians as one of the crimes against humanity ordered by the Habsburg war dictatorship is still virtually unknown to the public today and is still awaiting historical elaboration.'⁵ Until then, this topic was only touched upon in the source-based dissertation 'The Russophiles in Galicia. Ukrainian Conservatives between Austria and Russia 1848-1915' by Anna Veronika Wendland, in which a chapter was dedicated to the outbreak of the First World War.⁶ The investigation was limited to the brutal executions and arrests in Galicia, so that the forced resettlement itself was not investigated. Nor did the research deal with cross-national interferences. National historiographies often ignore the achievements of other historiographical traditions and even ignore the sources written in foreign languages, such as Russian, Ukrainian, Serbian, Italian and German. They predominantly focus on the sufferings of one particular national victim group and conclude that it experienced, compared to other nations, the 'worst' treatment.⁷ This requires us to combine several national historiographical traditions and to reflect upon them from a cross-national and intra-imperial perspective.

This chapter aims at describing Austro-Hungarian civilian internment as a system defying the nationally defined analytical framework of previous studies. Investigating the similarities and differences of the governmental internment practices of Italians, Serbs and Ruthenians, this chapter argues that there were almost no differences regarding living conditions, treatment and the release of the internees. The internees shared a similar social background and similar experiences during the internment regardless of their citizenship, ethnicity and political orientation. Notwithstanding the striking similarities, there were slight differences that resulted from a complex process of categorization of single victim groups. Bearing this in mind, this chapter answers the following questions: Who was perceived as suspicious by the Habsburg military government and why? How were the victim groups constituted? What is the relationship between humanity and the economy, that is, the treatment of victims according to their level of local wealth?

Defining the 'suspicious': Growing nationalisms and imperial politics

The legal status of the internees differed considerably from that of the evacuees. Internment refers to 'the deprivation of liberty of political or military opponents organised by the state in the form of accommodation in a specially established camp'.⁸ During internment, the free movement of interned persons was abolished and their civil rights were restricted. Persons who were considered 'suspicious' or 'politically dangerous' were suspected of irredentism and relations with the enemy states. Internment was a measure of repression and a 'universal instrument' against undesired (but not necessarily hostile) population groups.⁹ In the history of other European countries, internment has also been an instrument used against the civilian population of enemy states, for example, in Great Britain, France, Germany, Russia, Romania, Bulgaria and Serbia during the First World War.[10] Austria-Hungary differed in this respect in that internment was carried out not only against enemy aliens but also against its own civilian populations (Ruthenians from Galicia, Italians from South Tyrol and Serbs from Slavonia).[11] Mere suspicion was sufficient as a ground for persecution, and therefore many internees entered the camps without violating the law.

Officials in Vienna saw the Russophile, Italophile and Serbophile political movements as menacing nationalist movements and saw in them a security threat to the monarchy.[12] These groups of Austrian citizens were seen as a channel of influence for belligerent states, prompting Vienna to violently quell these movements. The case of the Russophile movement in Galicia is the most prominent one. The so-called 'Ruthenian question' already engaged the Viennese central authorities in 1883 when the establishment of military rule on the eastern border and the suspension of civil rights in Galicia in the event of war were decided.[13] The Congress of Berlin in 1888 brought about a balance of interests between Russia and Austria-Hungary in the Balkans and thus changed the attitude of the Viennese central authorities towards the Galician Russophiles who were still monitored but were able to continue their political activities. The period from 1888 to 1907 can be described as a period of relaxation in Austria-Hungary's relations with Russia.[14] The attitude of the Austrian government towards the Russophiles tended to depend on Austria-Hungary's relations with belligerent countries and their foreign policies, as well as the internal development logic of the multinational Habsburg monarchy. The years after 1907 (i.e. the years after Russia's devastating defeat in the war against Japan and the consequent shift of focus of its foreign policy to Europe,[15] after the first Russian Revolution and not least after the elections in Galicia, in which the Russophiles gained the majority in the Galician state parliament[16]) led to a tightening of the political course against the Russophiles. The possibility of war against Russia was anticipated in Vienna, and from 1910 onwards meticulous war plans were drawn up in which Galicia was to become the area of operations for the Austro-Hungarian military. The civilian population was to be expelled from Galicia even though this was unconstitutional, as it violated free movement and the ban on expulsion in the Habsburg monarchy. 'All politically suspicious, destitute, useless and unreliable persons' had to be expelled.[17] The same logic and the same procedures were applied to the internment of Serbs in 1914 and that of Italians in 1915.

Even though the preparations for the Great War were begun well in advance, the legal basis for civilian internment was only created retrospectively after the Ruthenians and Serbs had been interned in the summer and autumn of 1914.[18] The admissibility of such expulsions was also discussed in historical research from the perspective of international law. The most conspicuous insight is that the expulsions on the state's own territory did not constitute a breach of international law, and therefore civilian internees, unlike the prisoners of war, received no support from international organizations.[19] Overall, civilian internment in Austria-Hungary epitomized the Habsburgs' military dictatorship (war absolutism) and turned into brutal persecution by the military and unconstitutional restrictions of civil rights.[20] While initial defeats contributed to 'war psychosis' and 'spy hysteria' in the military, the subsequent successes in the area gradually calmed down the cruelty and brutality against their own civilian population.[21] The first transport of the inmates took place from Stanislau to Theresienstadt on 4 July 1914, for example, before the declaration of war by Austria-Hungary against Russia (on 6 August 1914).[22] The Kriegsüberwachungsamt (KÜA) was responsible for the internment of civilians in the Austrian hinterland, an authority that exercised censorship and observed 'suspicious' persons during the war. The aim of the KÜA was to 'provisionally detain large numbers of people of Ruthenian nationality, who were feared to adopt an unpatriotic attitude, from their homes and to bring them to the hinterland'.[23] The desire of the Austrian military to 'protect the Ruthenians from future crime' was fulfilled by a crime – forced migrations and massacres.

The Thalerhof camp is regarded as the endpoint of the internment of the Ruthenians and Katzenau that of the Italians. However, there were many other internment stations such as those in Theresienstadt (Terezín) in Bohemia, and in Kufstein and Schwaz in Tyrol.[24] Camps also existed in the Hungarian half of the empire in Esztergom, Satmar-Nemeti and Miskolc.[25] However, the Thalerhof camp received the most attention in historical research. The decision to construct Thalerhof was poorly thought through. Thalerhof was by no means prepared for the arrival of the inmates in the autumn of 1914 and was only a 'large meadow'. However, the infrastructural conditions for the establishment of an internment camp were technically in place. Thalerhof was located in the hinterland, was uninhabited and had good connections to the railway network, which allowed regular transport to Abtissendorf station.[26] Besides, Thalerhof was the property of the military; large, expandable and easy to guard, which enabled the rapid establishment of an internment camp. The isolation of Thalerhof from the other Styrian settlements was also interpreted in the following way: 'Also, the military authorities rightly surmised that [the internment camp] lay in an area whose local population would not show much compassion or even sympathy for the inmates'.[27]

A change can be observed in the attitude of the Austrian elite towards the internment of the Ruthenians by the terminology used during the war years. In the *Grazer Volksblatt* from 9 September 1914, Thalerhof was called the *Lager der politischen Gefangenen* ('camp of political prisoners').[28] The arrest and internment of the Ruthenians thus had a political reason, whereby the 'harmfulness' of the 'Russophiles' for the Habsburg monarchy not only remained unquestioned but was also increasingly consolidated in the sociopolitical discourse. The same concept can also be found in October 1914, when Thalerhof appeared in the *Grazer Tagblatt* in an article on the migration of the post office Zettling to Thalerhof on 8 October 1914. The newspaper called it the *Häftlings-und Flüchtlingslager* ('prisoner and refugee camp'),[29] leaving little doubt as to the guilt of the arrested persons. Such a picture is consistent with the 'hysteria' in Galicia and Slavonia in 1914 and in South Tyrol in 1915. Until 1917, when the camp was closed, there were no other reports in which Thalerhof was addressed concerning the status of its inmates. It was only after the closing of the camp and the reopening of the parliament that the interned persons at Thalerhof were reframed as victims. The member of parliament from the Czech-radical Party Jiří Stříbrný spoke about 'concentration camps' in this regard.[30] Thus, the innocence of the inmates became a sociopolitical issue, and their status was changed from that of the 'offender' to that of the 'victim' of the military regime. Although the innocence and sacrificial role of the interned Ruthenians, Italians and Serbs were recognized by other parties, there were also critical voices that were fuelled by national contradictions of the late Habsburg Empire. One member of parliament, Tresic-Babicic, a Croat, said that the conditions that became known in Thalerhof are merely a 'pale picture' of what had been done to the camp inmates in south-eastern Europe.[31] This example makes it clear that overcoming the traumatic events of internment, which had cost thousands of lives, was hampered by national differences between the various ethnic groups of the Habsburg monarchy.

The role of profession

The formal justifications of forced migration were manifold and often went into the absurd. Membership in Russian, Italian or Serbian reading societies and contact with the foreign press were the most common reasons for mass arrests. It should be noted that the activities of these associations had nothing to do with politics. The relatives of nationalists and people who fled to Italy, Serbia or Russia, or were living in belligerent countries, were always considered 'suspicious' and arrested. Secret correspondence with relatives living in belligerent countries via Switzerland was also a reason for internment. 'Suspicious statements' are often mentioned as grounds for arrests without any proof. Further reasons for internment included contacts with political enemies (Irredentists, Russophiles, Serbophiles, etc.), agitation, participation in demonstrations and membership in the *Liga Nationale* or the Russophile party. People who were convicted several times were automatically marked as 'dangerous' and deported for safety reasons. Apart from 'dangerous' individuals, the *Kriegsüberwachungsamt* took measures against 'useless' people such as vagabonds, prostitutes and disabled people.[32]

Religious belonging also played an important role when defining 'suspicious' individuals, and therefore members of the Orthodox Church were more likely to be suspected of espionage. In Galicia, the Greek-Catholic denomination was often not distinguished from the Russian Orthodox one. The hysteria went so far that priests were accused of praying for the Russian tsar Nicholas II. The priest Maksym Sandovych was killed only because he was the namesake of a Russophile with whom he was by no means related.

Travelling to Russia was also a reason for internment.[33] Most of the internees were middle-aged people, both men and women. Thirty-five per cent of them were twenty-one to thirty years of age, 24.7 per cent thirty-one to forty and 20.4 per cent eleven to twenty. The professions of the internees were as follows: students (14.70 per cent), civil servants (13.50 per cent), workers (10.50 per cent), teachers (8.70 per cent), craftsmen (8.50 per cent), traders (8.20 per cent), peasants (7.70 per cent), and merchants (7.20 per cent).[34] This structure was more or less characteristic for each national victim group, apart from one significant exception. While there were almost no clergymen among the Roman Catholic Italian civilian internees (about 0.3 per cent), the number of Greek-Catholic Ruthenian priests amounted to up to 12 per cent of civilian internees.

Since fear of peripheral nationalism was a key cause for internment, more middle-class people and those associated with (emerging) intelligentsias were targeted.

The Ruthenians were predominantly Greek Catholic, that is, they had adopted the Church Union with the Pope, which had been enforced by the Habsburg central administration in the eighteenth century. Although the Ruthenians had been largely allowed to maintain the Orthodox rite of the Moscow Patriarchate, the church had been legally subordinate to the pope. The integration of Galicia into Austrian state Catholicism had been a strategy for the region's integration into the Habsburg Empire. However, this measure did not improve the situation of the Ruthenians in a long-term perspective. They were now 'doubly suppressed': from the oppression by the Poles living in Galicia combined with the oppression by the Austrian officials. Due to this precarious position, the Greek-Catholic clergymen fell victim to the Habsburg's military government, as they were perceived as 'infected with Russophilism' (*russophil verseucht*). The mass internment of the Greek-Catholic clergymen to Thalerhof hurt the image of the Habsburg Empire as a Catholic power. The clergymen prepared several petitions to the KÜA and to the Nunciature in Vienna in October 1914, where they complained about bad living conditions and epidemics. This was immediately noticed by the Nunciature, and the Nuncio visited the minister of the interior on 2 November 1914 and demanded a release of the clergymen as soon as possible or by the latest, before Christmas.

The KÜA was well informed about every military crime in internment camps, including the murders of several clergymen by the guards without any reason. However, only the intervention of the Vatican could change the situation. Although the Nunciature insisted on the release of all the priests by Christmas, the investigation by the KÜA took far longer and could only partially concede that demand. There were officially 308 Ruthenian clergymen interned, and only 44 of them were released by 8 February 1915.[35] While the priests themselves and the Vatican considered the clergymen innocent, the KÜA had a different opinion. In its final decision on 8 February 1915, the KÜA concluded that 'a general release of the priests is not feasible, especially since it had been observed that both in Galicia and in Thalerhof it was precisely the Ruthenian clergy who were the worst Russophile agitators'.[36] These hard measures against the Greek-Catholic clergymen harmed Habsburg's relationship with the Vatican, and therefore the Austro-Hungarian government tried to 'avoid public censure from the Vatican'[37] in the future. This might be the reason why hardly any Italian clergymen fell victim to the military regime in the summer of 1915. Unlike their Catholic counterparts, the interned Orthodox priests did not get any help from outside. But it is important to stress that the protection of the Vatican was only limited to a very narrow circle of people. Most importantly, the Vatican only protected its clergymen, but not the believers, and the Greek-Catholic priests never mentioned the sufferings of other internees in their petitions. By trying to obtain exclusive protection rights for themselves, the clergymen ignored the problems of the laypeople.

Concerning the forced migration of the Ruthenians during the First World War, it should be pointed out that many of the internees were faithful and apolitical Austrian citizens who were arrested and deported as a result of 'war hysteria'. Since mere suspicion was sufficient as grounds for forced migration, these people had no possibility of defending themselves against absurd accusations of espionage. The extent of 'war hysteria' was so great that the borders between single national groups, professions, religious beliefs and spies were blurred.[38] Some Ukrainophiles, Germans and Jews, as well as peasants who had no political affiliation, were also interned. This meant that the terror was directed not only against a concrete political movement (Russophile) but also against other political and religious groups and developed several cross-national effects. The Austro-Hungarian military instrumentalized political and national tensions in Galicia, Slavonia and South Tyrol and increasingly took action against the different strata of the Habsburg population in these borderland regions.

At the same time, the Austro-Hungarian military government considered religion an important means of regaining 'healthy Austrian patriotism'.[39] For that reason, churches were built in the internment camps. The church buildings did not exist in every internment camp, and if they were built, it was a drawn-out process. In September 1914, church services at Thalerhof were held in the open, in front of a cross in the courtyard.[40] A small church in Thalerhof was then opened on 18 May 1915 and inaugurated on 1 July 1915. The Greek-Catholic church was built on the initiative of the military commander of Graz, Lieutenant Field Marshal Erwin von Mattanovich, and was consecrated by Prince Bishop Leopold Schuster who also celebrated a pontifical mass there. The building was considered a 'military chapel' and was thus military property.[41] For the Orthodox, a house of prayer was built in a barrack according to all the rules of the construction of an Orthodox church of Byzantine tradition.[42] The Orthodox were worse off in celebrating divine services, as there were no garments for the priests and there was a shortage of gospels and utensils.[43] Although the Greek-Catholic church had been given full equipment with all utensils, it remained closed for a long time because no Greek-Catholic priest could be found.[44] A parish priest was eventually found in September 1915. This was a refugee from Galicia, Iaroslav Karpiak, who was looking for work in Vienna and took up this position in Thalerhof.[45] Since then, permanent Divine Service was celebrated in Thalerhof.[46]

Humanity and economy

The categorization and treatment of the internees were inherently linked to their wealth. The officials always cared about the financial status of internees by making notes: *bemittelt* ('well-off') or *unbemittelt* ('poor'). As a rule, these categories correlated with the internees' class and profession. Thus, students, teachers and peasants tended to be less wealthy than clergymen and civil servants, who continued to receive their salaries. These economic categories influenced the official decisions on arrests, the replacement of internment through confinement and the release of internees. The wealth of the inmates was the most important criterion for their placement in the camps. Thus, the internal correspondence of the KÜA reveals that internment camps substantially differed between one another in terms of comfort and treatment of internees, depending on their solvency. Such camps as Thalerhof and Katzenau were reserved, above all, for the poor, while others, such as the castle of Göllersdorf, were for the people 'who belonged to the better [social] strata'.[47] Göllersdorf was the internment place for Italian and Ruthenian politicians and their relatives, such as the Members of Parliament Almerigo Ventrella and Nicolò Zarotti, and the sister-in-law of the former member of parliament Dmytro Markov with his three daughters. This elite internment station was better equipped than those for the poor people, and the military administration attached particular value to the mild treatment of wealthy internees:

> Starting from the point of view that the purpose of the internments is only the wartime isolation of individuals hostile to the state, unnecessary hardship during their internment should be avoided, given the position these persons will occupy once released after the war, and the detention is structured in such a way that, on the one hand any interaction between internees and the outside world is impossible, but on the other hand guarantees a hygienic accommodation for the internees that prevents an all too great emotional distress among those involved.[48]

Because of this, the internees at Göllersdorf had more freedom compared to the poor internees in other camps, regardless of their national belonging. The internees at Göllersdorf were allowed to purchase food, including alcohol (daily allowance was one beer or a quarter bottle of wine per day), and to smoke within the premises of the internment camp. They spent their days playing games and sports. The poor internees in other camps did not possess these freedoms. In the first year of their internment, the inmates at Katzenau and Thalerhof had no private space in the camp. Also, the internees were not allowed to use sanitary facilities on their own, they were only allowed to visit them collectively during a time that was strictly specified by the camp administration. A gender-mixed group of inmates had to go to the toilet accompanied by the guard, following the command of the guard: *Nieder* ('down!') and *Auf* ('up!').[49] The public display of their bodies was also connected to disinfection procedures during epidemics, which allowed officers to photograph naked women while washing and disinfecting their clothes.[50] In addition to the ban on leaving the camp, there were several prohibitions for the internees within the camp, such as they were not allowed to go through the territory and to visit other barracks.[51] The arbitrarily formed groups of internees were kept apart, which was supposed to stop not only the spread of infectious diseases but also the exchange of ideas among the internees. In Thalerhof, smoking and reading were forbidden until 1915.[52] From the winter of 1915 onwards, the inmates were granted more 'autonomy' and could elect so-called 'room commanders' who took over the functions of guards inside the barracks. The reason for such a decision, however, was not a desire to improve the treatment of inmates, but a fear of the camp administration and the military command of Graz that the guards could be infected with the inmates' epidemic diseases.[53] This innovation however was maintained after the epidemic, which helped the room commanders become intermediaries between the camp administration and the inmates.[54]

The local population was forbidden to enter internment camps, based on considerations of a sanitary nature.[55] Entering the camp was only possible with the permission of the military commander of Graz, Lieutenant Field Marshal Erwin von Mattanovich. The camp commander was also able to issue passports in urgent cases. Access to the camp canteen was strictly forbidden to civilians. Harsh sanctions were imposed on offenders; they were to be arrested or armed force could be used against them.[56]

The internment camp was however visited by members of the nobility. Apart from the noblemen of Ruthenian origin from Galicia, the name of Count Johann Joseph von Herberstein (1854–1944), one of the descendants of the emperor's sixteenth-century ambassador Sigismund von Herberstein, should be mentioned. According to the memories of the interned railway employee Goshovskii, the Count came to Thalerhof in the autumn of 1914 with his wife and children and brought milk, produce, warm blankets and laundry. Because two babies were orphaned in the camp, they were breastfed by the Countess herself. During the rapid spread of epidemic diseases in November 1914, the Count and his family were banned from continuing to visit Thalerhof. But when Goshovskii's daughter was released, she was immediately hired as a maid by Herberstein.[57] It should be borne in mind that these are only individual cases and most inmates did not have any support from outside the camp. However, connections with the locals before and during internment were crucial for life and survival in Thalerhof. In most cases, networking gained through jobs and workplace during internment made it possible to benefit from these contacts, which were inaccessible to other inmates. The railway workers especially built up a strong and broad social network, which (apart from the fact that their professional skills were in demand by the state in the event of war) enabled them to find a much better position in the hierarchy of the interned Ruthenians.

Trade and the necessity to work

The economic situation of the internees varied depending on their profession and social status. The confined situation of the internees was worse than that of refugees, because money was taken from the poor internees before internment and only returned in small instalments, which severely restricted their economic possibilities.[58] There were some salary arrangements for those internees who were economically active before the war. The interned officials and clergy continued to receive their salaries even if they were not in employment at that time.[59] The internees were prevented from changing their residence to find a job. There can be no question of any mobility of the internees (except for work outside the camps). The low support contributions and wages forced the internees to work in inadequate conditions. From that perspective, the state hardly differentiated between the evacuees as 'victims of war' and the internees as alleged 'criminals'.[60]

Even though food in internment camps was regularly distributed, its supply was altogether insufficient, which offered the possibility for trade in goods.[61] Trading in the Thalerhof internment camp was marked by fluctuating price, and the warehouse administration often sold products intended for internees.[62] At the same time, the military command of Graz made permanent offers to lease a market shop in Thalerhof, where the rent amounted to 960 crowns.[63] Given this high rent, the shop was promised high profit. Cafeteria operators were also found shortly. Saleswomen steadily increased the prices of their goods, taking advantage of their monopolistic position vis-à-vis the internees.[64] But the camp administration did not try to prevent this. Only when the facts of the profitable business went beyond Thalerhof, something was done and a trial took place. The cafeteria operators Julie von Duval and Veronika de Thoma, and her managing director Franz Maier, were accused and sentenced for 'shameless exploitation of the internees'. It turned out that they sold the products for twenty times more than the original price.[65] The tenants admitted that the interned women had seemingly been willing to pay this price and even kissed their hands for a kilo of potatoes, which encouraged the tenants to increase the prices more and more. The same notion can also be found in the memoirs of the interned women.[66] A counterexample is the trade in Terezín camp. The Czech inhabitants of the town, Anna Laube and Julianna Kuglerova, made warm clothes that were sold at fair market prices.[67] The trade in Terezín was so favourable for the internees that Laube also received orders from internees from Vienna and Thalerhof.[68] Thus, trade was not only characterized by the exploitation of the internees. However, it must be taken into account that not all goods could be sent to the camps because of short shelf life and robbery in post offices. This only promoted the flourishing price gouging.

The court case against the tenants of the shop did not bring any improvements to the trade situation in the internment camps as a whole. According to memoirs, it was not possible to buy products locally in the camps from 1916 onwards. This led to the smuggling of products into the camp by soldiers.[69] The maintenance of the internment camps made the monarchy's precarious supply situation more difficult.[70] The people who received products from their home countries were in a better position as they were able to resell them.[71] Profit margins were often very high. An example is an incident of a priest who bought 100 postcards for 40 hellers in total and immediately sold them for 70 hellers each.[72] Against this background, it can be said that speculation in the internment camps was a reflex of the time, involving not only the camp administration and canteen tenants but also the inmates themselves.

The poor internees also had to work, but their jobs were different in nature. In Thalerhof, the construction of barracks was the main occupation for adult male internees during the first year of internment.[73] In Tyrol, the interned Ruthenians and Italians were primarily used for river regulation work on the Drava river.[74] The internees of the camps Kufstein and Schwaz worked in road construction, river regulation and agriculture until the dissolution of the camps in 1916.[75] The employment for women consisted of doing the laundry and cleaning streets inside and outside the camps. In Terezín, women were engaged in gardening and fieldwork.[76] The increasing activity of women working outside the camps led to the abandonment of children in the camps.[77] There are reports that the internees were employed in demeaning jobs. This was particularly true of clergymen who were forced to load horse manure with their bare hands. Anecdotal evidence suggests that internees were treated poorly and sometimes even beaten on their way to work.[78] However, there was also subsistence work in the internment camps that was aimed at the needs of the individual internees. This included the production of straw shoes and handwork in all the camps where straw sacks, upholstery and soap were made by internees themselves for their own consumption.[79]

On the one hand, the work of internees, accompanied by the guards, entailed several risks in terms of occupational safety, protection and insurance.[80] On the other hand, the work outside the camp also offered some opportunities. During work, materials (wood, etc.) were smuggled into the camps, from which the products necessary for survival were subsequently manufactured.[81] The adaptation of the internees to the prevailing employment conditions in the internment camps determined in many respects the survival (or a better life) within the camps. Also, personal networks were important for survival. The effort to improve camp life is said to have served to stimulate the work of the camp inmates. This also required the establishment of close relationships with the camp administration.[82]

The qualifications and work experience of the internees were of particular importance for their employment, as it was easier for skilled workers to find a suitable place for work. This is particularly true for the railway employees, of whom 1,600 seasonal workers were accommodated in Tyrol and 4,300 in Salzburg, who were assigned to Gmünd in 1915.[83] Goshovskii was a professional railwayman before his internment at Thalerhof. After his confinement in Groß-Florian von Deutschlandsberg at the end of March 1917, he was immediately able to find a job at the local railway station.[84] A high level of professional qualification made it much easier for internees to find a job. At the same time, it took into account the skills and work experience of individual displaced persons and the work needs on site. This gradually alleviated the tragic consequences of forced migration.

Conclusion

Regarding the outbreak of the First World War, historical research speaks of a 'sleepwalker' thesis, according to which the unleashing of the First World War was due to mutual misunderstandings and false information.[85] This thesis can also be applied to the forced migration of 'internal enemies' in the First World War. The obvious overvaluation of the Russophile, Serbophile and Italian irredentist movements, the deliberate spreading of false rumours and the 'spy hysteria' led to mass arbitrary extermination and groundless deprivation of liberty of large parts of the population by the Austro-Hungarian military and local civilians. The inability of the military government to find another non-violent solution to the national and political conflicts in Galicia, Slavonia and South Tyrol led to macabre consequences for the fates of individuals and families, to the alienation and uprooting of the Habsburg-loyal peoples, including the 'promoted' nations such as Poles and Ukrainians, and the shredding of the Austro-Hungarian territory.

Civilian internees became unwilling nomads in their home country. Overall, civilian internment during the First World War revealed how the late Austro-Hungarian monarchy dealt with otherness and national, political and religious minorities at that time. Thus, the violence towards internees and continuous surveillance were considered valid solutions for 're-educating' the people who did not conform to the Habsburg's supranational idea of patriotism. The relationships of internees with the host society, homeland and among and between the respective diasporas were restricted by martial law. The military selected the internment places according to the attitudes of the locals towards the internees and made use of common clichés about the affected ethnic groups among the German-speaking population. This strategy proved, indeed, highly effective since the locals were, as a rule, hostile towards the internees. Not only was there little to no contact with the local population, the military also prohibited any contact with the internees' home regions, which exacerbated their poor economic situation. At the same time, the state authorities were aware of miserable living conditions in the vast majority of internment camps created in 1914 and 1915, yet directed more attention towards the wealth of internees when improving the sanitary conditions, food supply and regulations. For that reason, the creation of various (political, social and economic) categories of internees transcended the boundaries of mere ethnic belonging and predominantly focused on the assumed social and political role that the internees would play in post-war society. Only the wealthy social strata of civilian internees were considered deserving of better treatment and better living conditions while the poor – the vast majority of the internees – had to suffer from worse treatment, epidemic diseases and insufficient food supply. For the poor internees, the informal personal and professional networks were crucial for their survival and constituted the only realm of their lives not entirely controlled by the military authorities. These links defied the national boundaries and decisively contributed to overcoming the difficulties inherent in the state-supported system of civilian internment.

Notes

1 Matthew Stibbe, 'Civilian Internment and Civilian Internees in Europe, 1914–20', *Immigrants & Minorities*, no. 26 (2008): 49–81, 50.
2 Cf. Klaus Bachmann, *'Ein Herd der Feindschaft gegen Rußland'. Galizien als Krisenherd in den Beziehungen der Donaumonarchie mit Rußland 1907–1914* (Vienna: Böhlau, 2001); Anton Holzer, *Das Lächeln der Henker. Der unbekannte Krieg gegen die Zivilbevölkerung 1914–1918* (Darmstadt: Primus, 2008); Anna Veronika Wendland, *Die Russophilen in Galizien. Ukrainische Konservative zwischen Österreich und Rußland, 1848–1915* (Vienna: VÖAW, 2001), 490 and 499.
3 Nicole-Melanie Goll, '"Russophile" Zivilinternierte aus Galizien im Lager Thalerhof bei Graz im Ersten Weltkrieg', in *Update! Perspektiven der Zeitgeschichte. Zeitgeschichtetage 2010*, ed. Linda Erker et al. (Innsbruck: Studienverlag, 2012), 29–33, 30.
4 Georg Hoffmann, Nicole-Melanie Goll and Philipp Lesiak, *Thalerhof 1914–1936. Die Geschichte eines vergessenen Lagers und seiner Opfer* (Herne: Schäfer, 2010), 7.
5 Detlef Brandes, Holm Sundhaussen and Stefan Troebst (eds), *Lexikon der Vertreibungen. Deportation, Zwangsaussiedlung und ethnische Säuberung im Europa des 20. Jahrhunderts* (Vienna: Böhlau, 2010), 568.
6 Cf. Wendland, *Die Russophilen*.
7 Cf. Jörg Echternkamp, 'Introduction. Camp Systems, International Law and Humanitarian Action', in *Wartime Captivity in the Twentieth Century. Archives, Stories, Memories*, ed. Anne-Marie Pathé and Fabien Théofilakis (New York and Oxford: Berghahn, 2016), 25–9. Becker calls this phenomenon the 'languages of captivity'. Cf. Annette Becker, 'Introduction. Languages of Captivity: Bodies and Minds Behind the Barbed Wire', in *Wartime Captivity in the Twentieth Century*, 79–83.
8 Hoffmann et al., *Thalerhof*, 22f.
9 Ibid., 23 and 68.
10 Stibbe, 'Civilian Internment', 50.
11 Cf. Brandes et al., *Lexikon der Vertreibungen*, 305–7. Nicola Fontana and Mirko Saltori, 'Trentino', in *Katastrophenjahre. Der Erste Weltkrieg und Tirol*, ed. Hermann J. W. Kuprian and Oswald Überegger (Innsbruck: Wagner Innsbruck, 2014), 479–508; Oswald Haller, 'Das Internierungslager Katzenau bei Linz. Die Internierung und

Konfinierung der italienischsprachigen Zivilbevölkerung des Trentinos zur Zeit des Ersten Weltkrieges' (Diploma thesis, University of Vienna, 1999).
12 Goll, '"Russophile" Zivilinternierte', 29.
13 Wendland, *Die Russophilen*, 531–32.
14 Marija Wakounig, 'Dissens versus Konsens. Das Österreichbild in Russland während der Franzisko-Josephinischen Ära', in *Die Habsburgermonarchie 1848-1918, Vol. 6: Die Habsburgermonarchie im System der internationalen Beziehungen, Part 2*, ed. Adam Wandruszka (Vienna: VÖAW, 1993), 436–90, 438–41.
15 Hermann J. W. Kuprian, 'Zwangsmigration', in *Katastrophenjahre*, 217–40, 218.
16 Denis Akhremenko (ed.), *Zabytaia tragediia rusinov: natsional'naia politika Gabsburgov v gody Pervoi mirovoi voiny* (Briansk: Istorichaskoe soznanie, 2016), 32.
17 Goll, '"Russophile" Zivilinternierte', 29f.
18 Brandes et al., *Lexikon der Vertreibungen*, 566; Hermann J. W. Kuprian, 'Flüchtlinge, Evakuierte und die staatliche Fürsorge', in *Tirol und der Erste Weltkrieg*, ed. Klaus Eisterer and Rolf Steininger (Innsbruck: Studienverlag, 1995), 277–305, 279.
19 Gerhard Hirschfeld (ed.), *Enzyklopädie Erster Weltkrieg* (Paderborn: Ferdinand Schöningh, 2008), 289.
20 Goll, '"Russophile" Zivilinternierte', 29 and Kuprian, 'Flüchtlinge', 285.
21 Hans Hautmann, 'Kriegsgesetzte und Militärjustiz in der österreichischen Reichshälfte 1914-1918', in *Justiz und Zeitgeschichte. Symposionsbeiträge 1., 1976-1993*, ed. Erika Weinzierl et al. (Vienna: Jugend und Volk, 1995), 73–85.
22 Brandes et al., *Lexikon der Vertreibungen*, 566.
23 Goll, '"Russophile" Zivilinternierte', 29.
24 Kuprian, 'Zwangsmigration', 225.
25 *Talergofskii al'manakh. Propamiatnaia kniga avstriiskikh zhestokostei, izuverstv i nasilii nad karpato-russkim narodom vo vremia vsemïrnoi voiny 1914–1917 gg.* (L'viv: Talergofskii komitet, 1924), Vol. 2, 108–112.
26 Goll, '"Russophile" Zivilinternierte', 31; Hoffmann et al., *Thalerhof*, 24.
27 Brandes et al., *Lexikon der Vertreibungen*, 566.
28 *Grazer Volksblatt* (10 September 1914): 4.
29 *Grazer Tagblatt* (24 October 1914): 4.
30 *Arbeiterwille* (16 June 1917): 5.
31 Ibid., 4.
32 Austrian State Archives, Vienna (hereafter ÖStA), KA, KÜA 282, 285.
33 Wendland, *Die Russophilen*, 540; Hoffmann et al., *Thalerhof*, 20. Vasilii Vavrik, *Terezin i Talergof. K 50-letnei godovshchine tragedii Galitsko-russkogo naroda* (Moscow: Soft-Izdat, 2001), 6 and 9; Nina Pashaeva, *Ocherki istorii russkogo dvizheniia v Galichine* (Moscow: Imperskaia traditsiia, 2001), 141.
34 Author's estimation based on ÖStA, KA, KÜA 282, 285.
35 ÖStA, HHStA, 816 Interna; ÖStA, KÜA 284.
36 ÖStA, HHStA, 816 Interna.
37 Matthew Stibbe, *Civilian Internment during the First World War. A European and Global History, 1914-1920* (London: Palgrave Macmillan, 2019), 104.
38 Hoffmann et al., *Thalerhof*, 21.
39 ÖStA, HHStA, 816 Interna.
40 *Talergofskii al'manakh*, Vol. 3, 7.
41 *Grazer Volksblatt* (19 July 1915): 2.
42 Cf. Mihailo St. Popović, 'Kirchenraum, Choreographie, Funktion des Raumes', in *Die Liturgie der Ostkirche. Ein Führer zu Gottesdienst und Glaubensleben der orthodoxen*

und orientalischen Kirchen, ed. Basilius J. Groen and Christian Gastgeber (Freiburg: Herder, 2012), 47–60; *Talergofskii al'manakh*, Vol. 4, 121.
43 *Talergofskii al'manakh*, Vol. 4, 114.
44 *Grazer Volksblatt* (19 July 1915): 2.
45 *Talergofskii al'manakh*, Vol. 3, 9.
46 Pashaeva, *Ocherki*, 145.
47 ÖStA, KA, KÜA 283.
48 Ibid.
49 *Talergofskii al'manakh*, Vol. 1, 79–80.
50 *Stenographische Protokolle über die Sitzungen des Hauses der Abgeordneten des österreichischen Reichsrats im Jahr 1917* (Vienna: k.u.k. Hof-und Staatsdruckerei, 1917), 246.
51 *Talergofskii al'manakh*, Vol. 4, 111.
52 Ibid., Vol. 3, 8.
53 Ibid., Vol. 4, 114.
54 Ibid., 115.
55 *Grazer Volksblatt* (10 September 1914): 4.
56 Ibid., 2.
57 *Talergofskii al'manakh*, Vol. 3, 6.
58 *Stenographische Protokolle*, 245.
59 Kuprian, 'Zwangsmigration', 225; *Talergofskii al'manakh*, Vol. 2, 116 and Vol. 3, 9.
60 Kuprian, 'Zwangsmigration', 235.
61 *Talergofskii al'manakh*, Vol. 3, 8.
62 *Stenographische Protokolle*, 564.
63 *Grazer Volksblatt* (27 August 1915): 8 (29 August 1915): 15 and (31 August 1915): 8.
64 *Talergofskii al'manakh*, Vol. 3, 32 and Vol. 4, 110.
65 *Grazer Tagblatt* (19 July 1916).
66 Vavrik, *Terezin*, 17.
67 *Talergofskii al'manakh*, Vol. 2, 113.
68 Ibid., Vol. 2, 129.
69 Ibid., Vol. 3, 11.
70 Hoffmann et al., *Thalerhof*, 112.
71 Ibid.
72 *Talergofskii al'manakh*, Vol. 4, 60.
73 *Grazer Volksblatt* (10 September 1914): 4; Hoffmann et al., *Thalerhof*, 31.
74 *Grazer Volksblatt* (10 November 1914): 8.
75 Kuprian, 'Zwangsmigration', 225.
76 Vavrik, *Terezin*, 12; *Talergofskii al'manakh*, Vol. 2, 113.
77 Cf. Matthias Egger and Joachim Bürgschwentner, 'Kriegsfürsorge', in *Katastrophenjahre*, 153–75, 169.
78 *Stenographische Protokolle*, 246.
79 Hoffmann et al., *Thalerhof*, 60.
80 Ibid., 115.
81 *Talergofskii al'manakh*, Vol. 2, 127.
82 Ibid., Vol. 3, 19.
83 Kuprian, 'Zwangsmigration', 223.
84 *Talergofskii al'manakh*, Vol. 3, 6.
85 Christopher Clark, *Die Schlafwandler. Wie Europa in den Ersten Weltkrieg zog* (Munich: DVA, 2013).

3

Between suffering and displacement

The case of the Istrian *Evakuirci*

Diego Han

Introduction

The First World War, with its unprecedented reach, changed European society forever. As a result of deeper socio-economic processes, such as industrialization and the gradual massification of politics, the conflict took some unexpected directions, turning into a new kind of war that only a few were able to foresee, which would eventually impact the lives of millions of people.[1] In this context, the Istrian peninsula, in what is today northern Croatia and which was relatively far from the front lines, also suffered consequences of war, especially its southern part. The city of Pula's transformation into the main military port of Austria-Hungary ensured that the entire area became of crucial strategic importance, while decisions taken by the government would also trigger several catastrophic economic and social consequences from which the peninsula took decades to recover. Among these decisions, the most important was one taken in May 1915, a few days after the Kingdom of Italy entered the war against Austria-Hungary. According to this decision, all of the non-essential civil population south of the Lim channel-Raša channel line were to be evacuated and transferred into the empire's mainland.[2] The reasons behind these decisions were mostly of a military nature, although humanitarian motives played their part too. On the one hand, the military authorities wanted to diminish the number of civilians as much as possible so that military operations could be implemented without undesired interference, while on the other hand the inner parts of the empire were considered to be safer for these civilians. However, the situation soon proved to be much more complicated than what officials expected, which turned the evacuation into a tragedy.

This chapter aims to analyse the history of these people, who in the Croatian historiography are referred to as *evakuirci* (the evacuated), through the four-dimensional approach proposed in the opening chapter of this volume. Accordingly, special attention will be paid to the examination of their lives in displacement, on how they dwelled in their new provisional homes and on their relationship with the local communities as well as on their bond with their homeland during their evacuation.

Furthermore, the humanitarian organizations that tried to take care of the displaced people will also be studied, with a special focus on the first months of the evacuation. During this period there were no official governmental organizations established to assist the evacuated, and so aid was instead primarily carried out by single political representatives, clergy members and volunteers. In order to be able to get a better insight into the way *evakuirci* internalized their experience of displacement, attention will be put majorly on their own writings about the evacuation.

Pula – from obscurity to military port

When discussing the destiny of the Istrian *evakuirci*, it is necessary to start from the city of Pula. Today, Pula is the biggest urban centre of the region, but after the fall of the Roman Empire and during the Middle Ages and the Modern period it was a scarcely inhabited city of negligible importance. Even in the past, the city has long been described as a paradoxical contrast between its glorious antique past and the abandoned and decayed present.[3] The short-term Napoleonic administration in the early nineteenth century did not bring any significant improvement, which, given that Pula only counted 900 inhabitants at that time, is hardly surprising.[4] Pula's role only started to change when the peninsula came under the Habsburg rule after Napoleon's fall. A few decades later, Venice, which at the time was the main military port of the Habsburgs, faced the real possibility of falling to the newly established Kingdom of Italy, prompting a search for a new suitable naval base.[5] In this search, the Austrian authorities became interested in the Istrian city, but the final decision was only officialized in 1853 when Pula was confirmed as the new main naval military base.[6] The path which transformed a small semi-abandoned city into one of the most important places of the empire was neither easy nor straightforward. First of all, Pula was a rather insignificant town even in the Istrian context and did poorly economically. Additionally, there was no infrastructure to justify the decision, and the surrounding area was known for its malaria problems.[7] However, despite his own initial opposition, the Danish admiral serving under the Imperial flag, Hans Birch Dahlerup, managed to convince the Viennese court and Emperor Franz Joseph that Pula was a suitable location for the new base. In fact, regardless of all the inadequacies, the city had a lot of potential, starting from its strategic position from which it was easier to defend the commercial ports of Trieste and Rijeka, to the very deep and spacious gulf which could perfectly suit all the navy's needs.[8] Moreover, the nearby Fažana channel was ideal for defending the base and could serve as a second anchorage.[9]

In only a few decades, all these advantages transformed a small backward town into a lively Central European and Mediterranean city with a population of 60,000 people. However, this metamorphosis meant that the city was now also a crucial target for any potential enemy, which despite an agreement signed in 1882, turned out to be the Kingdom of Italy.[10] With its declaration of war against Austria-Hungary in 1915, Pula found itself dragged into the vortex of war which will eventually cause the tragedy of the *evakuirci*.

The war and the evacuation

The history of the evacuated people from the territory of southern Istria has long been a marginal topic in historiography[11] and only gained importance as the Great War's centenary was approaching.[12] Yet, the evacuation was a crucial event that influenced both the economic and the sociopolitical life on the peninsula for decades. When the full-scale war erupted in August 1914, Pula, as the empire's main naval base, underwent a full mobilization. The civilians were informed about the evacuation process as early as the 7th of the same month. Only those who could gather enough supplies for a three-month period (and could prove it) were permitted to stay, while all others had to leave.[13] However, leaving the city was forbidden for all the people who could contribute to the war effort, from the workers in the Arsenal to those employed in the city's gas plant.[14] However, even though the announcement was removed from the public notice boards on 8th of August, as many as 6,000 people had already left Pula.[15] Three days later, the authorities made another proclamation announcing a new evacuation, this time with many more details about the procedure. Yet, this proclamation was also not comprehensive, as it still did not mention a deadline for leaving the city and continued to present evacuation as a voluntary decision. Nevertheless, before the end of the month, 26,000 people left Pula, finding a new temporary home in the northern part of the peninsula or in other cities like Trieste and Monfalcone. For most of the *evakuirci* their absence from home lasted until winter, when many decided to ask the authorities for permission to return as they were not really prepared to stay away for such a long period and were lacking warm clothes, supplies and money. Fortunately, as the situation near Pula was stable, the authorities accepted their plea.[16]

These first evacuations were used by the local command as a test for eventual full removal of civilians from Pula, and so from autumn 1914 to spring 1915 important preparations were carried out in order to be as ready as possible in case of a large-scale evacuation of the city. Some towns in the northern part of the peninsula were asked to help but most protested stating that their economic conditions were barring them from accepting refugees. Seeing the objective problems in transferring the population in those parts of the region, the authorities turned their attention towards the possible alternatives. Thus, they decided to move these people to other regions of the empire, where refugees coming from different frontline areas had already been displaced during 1914.[17]

Eventually, the moment came for the population of southern Istria to be evacuated on 23 May 1915, when the Kingdom of Italy officially declared war on the Austro-Hungarian Empire. The declaration of war did not come as a surprise, as this information had been circulating between the diplomatic channels for weeks. In anticipation of the conflict, the military command had already given a compulsory order of evacuation for all civilians living south of the line Barbariga-Vodnjan-Valtura, in early May, including the northern territories of the city of Rovinj and the village of Kanfanar.[18] In just a few days, 60,000 people left their homes and were transferred by train to the inner parts of Upper and Lower Austria, Hungary, Moravia and

Bohemia.[19] From the very first day, it became clear that the whole process was due to become a very painful and exhausting experience. For example, the authorities had predicted that around 8,000 people would have to leave the city of Pula per day, but they did not know when that number would be reached. Because of this problem, many would go to the train station fully packed for the journey, only to be told to return to their homes once the maximum number for that day had been reached. Understandably, this approach created an enormous level of stress and nervousness among the population, so that the military command decided to put all those who could not be evacuated into the nearby Hotel Riviera in order to avoid sending them home for the night.[20] Moreover, the wagons in which they travelled were designed to transport cattle, so they were very uncomfortable. The hygienic conditions were bad and spaces very cramped, while one of the biggest difficulties was represented by the necessity of satisfying one's physiological needs.[21] From time to time the trains would stop, which meant that those who had money could go and get some food and drinks. However, getting out of the carriage was a potentially ill-fated decision as the trains had a very tight schedule which they strictly followed. Unfortunately, many young children who exited the wagons got lost in the confusion and were separated from their families, with only the lucky ones able to rejoin them within the next months.[22] The only category of evacuees that seemed to be excited by this chaos was the youth. To them, this represented the possibility to get out of their normal provincial routine and the chance to go and live in new places which up to then they had only known from stories.[23]

The train journey typically lasted two or three days, depending on the convoy's destination. However, their voyage was not over as the first big stop was usually used to redirect the various groups towards their final destination. For the Istrian evacuees the junction at Wagna, a small place near Leibnitz in today's Austria, was the point from which they were directed further towards Hungary, Moravia and Bohemia.[24] The continuation of the journey meant new inconveniences for many of the evacuees, especially for those of Italian ethnicity. Even though they were Austro-Hungarian subjects, their cultural background meant that local communities welcomed them with insults and threats, often mistaking them for prisoners of war coming from the Kingdom of Italy. The negative psychological effects of such encounters were understandable but could not be forgotten by the evacuees despite the fact that the locals would generally change their approach once they were told who these people really were.[25] At this point, it is also interesting to note that the Italian Istrian population was seen by the Austro-Hungarian authorities as a possible fifth column in the event of a potential Italian ground attack, and thus more than 200 'irredentists' and suspects were interned even before and during the first months of the war.[26] At first, the worst conditions were felt by the *evakuirci* which had been evacuated to Hungary, where they could not get used to a very different climate and a language that did not permit them to understand the local population, which still saw them as unwanted foreigners. To solve these problems, the authorities decided to send these people back to Styria and Lower Austria, or at least to transfer them further to Moravia or Bohemia.[27] Only after this last move were most of the evacuees sent to the places where they would spend the majority of the wartime.

Life as evacuees

Help and support

Based on the periodization proposed by the Italian historian Paolo Malni, it is possible to divide the Austro-Hungarian politics towards the evacuees into three phases – the urgency phase (1914/1915), the stabilization phase (1915/1917) and the reforms phase (1917/1918).[28] The first phase includes the evacuation period with the organization of the transportation and the lodging of the transferred population, starting with the first arrivals from Bukovina and Galicia from the Eastern front. In this period, it was decided that all those who could financially provide for themselves could freely settle wherever they wanted, excluding the territories that were considered war zones (Istria, Galicia, Bukovina, South Tyrol, etc.), where the evacuees would have been seen as a bother to the war efforts. All the others had to be relocated into specific camps where the state was responsible for their sustenance.[29] Another very important difference between these two groups lay in the financial support they were granted by the authorities. For example, those who were living outside the camps were given 90 hellers per day, while those in the camps did not get any funding as the state deemed that they were paid in kind by food and supplies.[30] Besides, it is important to note that in this initial phase the authorities believed that any form of help was a charitable effort, rather than a right.[31]

At the state level, there were different committees that had to put into action the official policy of the monarchy, such as the Auxiliary Committee for the Refugees from the South, an institution promoted by Archduchess Marie Josephine, or the War Auxiliary Committee from Pula, which organized direct aid for the evacuees and was under the direct control of the Central Committee in Vienna.[32] What was also very important was the help and the support the evacuees received from local politicians and the church. As for the latter, a key role was played by Trifone Pederzolli, the bishop of Poreč and Pula, who constantly encouraged his clergy to collect any financial and material help that could be sent to those who were staying far away from their homes.[33] Moreover, the bishop embraced his role by visiting the camps on many different occasions in order to provide spiritual support for the members of his dioceses.[34] The clergy also tried to work together with the civil authorities by warning them of the awful conditions in which the evacuees were living and by asking them to improve them.[35] Meanwhile, the civil authorities were mostly acting through the efforts of the local representatives in the pre-war Imperial Council[36] such as Ivan Cukon and Matko Laginja. The evacuees frequently wrote to their representatives themselves about the harsh conditions in which they were living, begging them for help. In their letters one can read all about the roughness of their lives and their daily problems, from food shortages to tragic testimonies of their loved ones passing away. For example, in a letter written by Blaž Ikić and Mate Biban from Glaubendorf to the representative Vjekoslav Spinčić, the two men openly beg him to assist them to return home because where they are staying they have nothing to eat and are suffering a lot. Furthermore, they have lost their children, and if they are not helped, they 'are also going to die'. Additionally, Ikić and Biban try to explain how at home they could at least work in the fields and thus help the cities of Pula and Vodnjan.[37]

The camps

According to Malni, the second phase was characterized by a sort of stabilization.[38] It started at the beginning of 1915, lasting until 1917 when the first large-scale returns of *evakuirci* were organized. As the belligerent sides accepted that the war was not going to end anytime soon, the authorities switched their focus towards the evacuees. New efforts were made to improve hygiene and education in the camps by opening new field hospitals, kindergartens and sanitary facilities, while the evacuees outside the camps were given the possibility of visiting the local doctors. Free movement was still forbidden, so in order to exit the camps a special pass was needed, but at least the authorities had agreed on reconnecting family members that were housed at different sites.[39]

When discussing the stabilization phase, it has to be noted that all the improvements were made because of the catastrophic conditions in the internment camps.[40] From the very beginning, the preparation of these camps was not organized according to the number of evacuees that were arriving on a daily basis, which caused numerous serious problems. For example, at the beginning of 1915 the Ministry of War had estimated that around 30,000 people from the Austrian Littoral would have to be evacuated, plus probably 40,000 people from the Tyrol region. However, as soon as May of 1915, the number of evacuees had reached the astonishing level of 120,000 people, which consequently created severe logistical difficulties.[41] The camps were initially constructed to house evacuees from Bukovina and Galicia,[42] but once the Central Powers managed to counterattack on the Eastern front, these provisional shelters became the new homes of the Istrian refugees.[43] The evacuees from the Austrian Littoral were located in some of the biggest camps, such as Wagna, Pottendorf, Gmünd and Steinklamm-Rabenstein.

The majority of the evacuees were put in the camp of Wagna, a place carved into the collective memory of those who had the misfortune to stay there during the war. It was built in just a few weeks between October and November of 1914, when the first evacuees coming from Poland were housed there.[44] According to its first plans, the camp's capacity was meant to be for 10,000 people, divided into 25 barracks counting 400 places each. However, as early as December 1914 the decision was made to double its size. In the spring of 1915, the camp already housed over 12,000 people, which urged authorities to expand the camp with new barracks, field hospitals and better infrastructure. By doing so, the capacity of the camp was increased to 20,000 people. Electricity, a water supply network and a sewage system were also introduced in the course of 1915. With these improvements the authorities wanted to show the public that the empire was taking good care of its subjects, but the reality was somewhat different.[45] First of all, the camps were not only refugee centres but also places of control. The internees could not leave the camp without an official permit and had to follow a very strict daily schedule.[46] Privacy was also a big issue. Upon arrival, evacuees had to take showers and go through a disinfection process, which meant undressing in front of a large number of people and standing in line naked to wait for their turn. Moreover, the privacy problem in barracks containing 400 people requires little further explanation.[47] Despite the fact that barracks designed for 160 people were later constructed, accessibility to the various services still remained a big problem.

The first evacuees from Istria were transferred to Wagna in the spring of 1915. This group of approximately 21,000 people mostly consisted of Italians, since the Croats and Slovenes of Istria were generally placed in Gmünd and Steinklamm-Rabenstein. Upon their arrival in the camps, they were divided into smaller units consisting of ten to twenty barracks and three to four kitchens. Every unit had an administrative deputy who took care of the organization of the accommodation and the hygienic conditions, while at the same time serving as an intermediary between the evacuees and the camp authorities. Every barrack also had its commander and his/her deputy, which were both elected directly by the evacuees.[48] Despite the vast majority of *evakuirci* being housed in the bigger barracks, the camp had also other types of accommodation built to suit the members of the upper classes. The so-called *Intelligenzbaracke*, colloquially referred to as 'villas', were meant for the clergy, doctors, teachers and professors, of whom many had been brought into the camp in order to carry out specific jobs.[49] They stayed in smaller apartments with private bedrooms and kitchens, with the possibility of cooking their own meals.[50] To increase the quality of life, the camp administration tried to organize some kind of entertainment for all the evacuees, such as dance recitals, theatre plays and prize games, which however had little impact on the morale of those in the camp.[51]

As for other camps, the Istrian Italian population was also present in larger numbers in Pottendorf, while, as already mentioned, the Istrian Croatian population stayed mostly in Gmünd, Steinklamm-Rabenstein and Bruck an der Leitha.[52] If Wagna became the symbol of suffering for Istrian Italian evacuees, the same was valid for the Istrian Croatian evacuees in Gmünd. This camp was established in 1914 and served at first as a place where Russian prisoners of war were kept.[53] However, as the conflict was aggravated, the authorities decided to also construct some wooden barracks where the evacuees could stay.[54] Their number rose exponentially during the year 1915 so that by spring there were already 26,000 Ukrainians and 10,000 Croats and Slovenes from the Austrian Littoral in the camp, which reached 53,000 people in September.[55] Similar to what happened in Wagna, after some time Gmünd too got its electricity system and a water supply network, a post office was opened, as well as a school and a field hospital. From the very first steps inside the camp, the procedure reflected the one in the other sites so that the evacuees would first go through a disinfection and showering process, after which they would be assigned to their barracks according to family, national and geographical criteria.[56] Not surprisingly, Gmünd also had its 'elite' barracks, but their number was just forty from a population of 50,000 people.[57]

Diseases and famine

Despite the attempts of the authorities to offer some kind of comfort and entertainment to the evacuees, these camps were still seen as terrible places. The government was trying to show how the camps were suitable places to live, but the reality was almost diametrically opposite as food shortages and catastrophic hygienic conditions were their main characteristics. The huge number of people gathered in a cramped place from all over the empire created a breeding ground for diseases, especially those with high epidemic potential. Epidemics were already spreading through the camps since late 1914, when diphtheria, typhoid fever, scarlet fever and measles appeared.[58] Obviously, for the Istrian evacuees, the worst period came after their arrival in Wagna, Gmünd and the other camps during the second part of 1915. In Wagna between October 1915 and the end of January 1916, 1,092 people died from disease.[59] Even worse, 84 per cent of those who died were younger than 10 years old, of which 300 died before reaching their first year.[60] The main cause of death for the children was measles, especially during the epidemics of October/November 1915, when, on average, five children passed away per day.[61] Their bodies and immune systems were too weak for the harsh conditions in which they were living, a state worsened by the constant food shortages. Understandably, this high child death rate resulted in a strong distrust towards physicians, and the mothers often preferred to hide their children rather than hand them over to the hospital staff.[62] In the same period, between thirty and sixty people died daily in Gmünd, and in November this number reached ninety people per day.[63] In Wagna, stories soon started to circulate among the evacuees, which alluded that doctors were deliberately killing their patients in order to diminish their numbers in the camp. The authorities tried to stop this ongoing tragedy by improving the conditions in the field hospitals and by introducing fresh milk as a supplement to children's meals. These measures helped to improve the situation, but the death rate among children still remained higher than during pre-war time.[64]

Yet, what remained constant during the whole period was malnutrition. It affected almost every social layer, and its chronicity caused desperation among the evacuees.[65] Still, at first, the authorities tried to organize a good quality diet, made of two meals per day. Even if the dinner was always based on a variation of polenta combined with cheese, coffee or salad, the lunch was more diverse and consisted of potato dishes, bean soups, meat, rice and so on.[66] Sadly, this menu was hardly ever implemented. In the first period of the evacuation, private companies ran the supply chain and in the name of profit often sent smaller quantities than stipulated by the authorities. Furthermore, employees frequently stole food, and large amounts of it were also thrown away because they had become unusable. In fact, the food in Wagna during 1916 was so bad that even the representative of the War Auxiliary Committee, Špiro Peručić, was shocked when he saw that the evacuees' main dish had turned into a 'waterish cabbage soup'.[67] When Peručić visited one of the camps' kitchens, he was informed that 40 per cent of potatoes and 20 per cent of cabbage were typically unusable. Another example came from Gmünd, where the diet consisted almost exclusively of fodder and beet soups, cabbage and potatoes, while meat was a privilege that was given only once a week.[68] Still, not all the evacuees received the same treatment. The inhabitants of the *Intelligenzbaracke* were given their supplies directly and could prepare their own meals in their private barracks. However, it seems that in other camps, such as in Pottendorf, the situation was way better, primarily due to larger food rations.[69] In general the food provision problem was one of the main issues and it got worse depending on the course of the war. This situation led to frequent demonstrations and riots in the camps, such as on 4 October 1917, a serious clash occurred between the evacuees and the gendarmerie when in Wagna, leaving an eleven-year-old boy dead.[70] This event led to some concrete changes in the camp as Wagna's administrators decided to introduce new intermediaries that could communicate with both the evacuees and the camp authorities. At the same time, they also replaced the gendarmerie with security personnel chosen directly from among the evacuees or war invalids. Finally, from then on, all illegal activities were made punishable according to a regular civil penal code such as for any free Austrian citizen, thus replacing the previous practice based on martial law.[71]

Homecoming

The third and final phase of Malni's periodization starts in early 1917, that is, during the period of the evacuees' harshest protests and the attempts of Austria-Hungary's new emperor, Karl I, to improve their conditions. The first important move was the reopening of the Imperial Council in spring 1917, which led to the creation of the Commission for Refugees later that year.[72] By reopening the Council, the emperor wanted primarily to achieve a normalization of the political life in the empire and consequently gain more support from the various national groups that had suffered under the military dictatorship. However, this decision created even more problems for the new ruler, who faced even harsher criticism and complaints about the living and working conditions.[73] Similarly, despite the potential of the Commission for Refugees and the special new law that was now regulating the status of the evacuees, life in the camps was changing at a pace that the vast majority deemed too slow.[74] At this point, the only thing the evacuees wanted was to return to their homes. As the war continued, the military and civil authorities at last concluded that the conditions were suitable for part of them to return to their households, especially those who lived in the rural areas north of the city of Pula. This was only possible because during late 1916, the situation on the Italian front was stable and the possibility for a massive breakthrough by the Italian troops towards Pula was difficult to imagine. Most importantly, the economy was suffering from a lack of workforce, particularly in the agricultural sector, which caused the authorities to decide that it was better for at least a part of the *evakuirci* to return to their homes and contribute to the war economy. In 1916 the military command in Pula, in agreement with the supreme military command, made the decision to allow the population from the territories of Kanfanar, Savičenta, Barbana, Golaš, Krmed and Krnica to return, while others had the possibility of being transferred to the northern part of the Istrian peninsula. However, those who accepted the latter proposal had to give up their right to aid from the state, which caused many to nevertheless remain in the camps throughout 1916 and 1917.[75] Repatriation efforts were once again halted until 1917 and the defeat of the Italian troops at Caporetto, after which the first large returns took place to the city of Rovinj and other rural areas.[76] Still, many evacuees remained in the camps, where their conditions again worsened at the beginning of 1918, at the same time as a wave of anti-war protests was shaking the empire. The workers of Pula's Arsenal joined the demonstration, demanding for their families to return. These men, who had to stay in the city due to their significance to the war effort, had not seen their relatives for years, and thus on 22 January 1918, they went on strike. The return of their families was not the only demand of the strikers, as they also called for higher wages and the right to get appropriate work suits and footwear.⁷⁷ The strike ended on 27 January when they were promised a 30 per cent wage rise from October 1918 and the return of their families.⁷⁸ As a consequence, 5,000 people from Pula gained permission to go back, most of them farmers who were needed to revitalize the land that was decaying after years of neglect.⁷⁹ In August 1918, 15,000 people from the territory of Pula were still away from their homes, and their status was only solved during that autumn. On 7 October, the Austrian-Hungarian authorities finally gave the evacuees permission to return, only a month before the truce was signed between the Kingdom of Italy and the dying empire. Nevertheless, due to the financial and political situation of the empire, not even the end of the war meant that all the evacuees could go back home, a problem that was only solved in February 1919 when the new Italian authorities declared an act of full repatriation for all the evacuated people, with which the last formal obstacle to their return disappeared.⁸⁰ Once the evacuees were finally able to overcome all the logistical and bureaucratic obstacles preventing their return, they eventually found themselves under the rule of the Kingdom of Italy, whose troops had invaded the Istrian peninsula soon after Austria-Hungary signed its capitulation on 3 November 1918. For the Istrian Italian population, especially for its urban and intellectual element, this understandably represented a positive outcome of the war, while for their Slavic counterpart a new era of political and cultural struggle was just beginning. Still, for the majority of the *evakuirci*, the most important thing was to be home at last.

Conclusion

The First World War caused unprecedented sociopolitical changes on a global scale. Besides forever altering the concept of war itself, it also transformed the role of the civil population, dragging them into its vortex of destruction. Even if at first the evacuation of a part of the Istrian population seemed to follow a clear military and humanitarian logic, it soon became clear that most of the evacuees became and continued to be displaced without a concrete logistical reason. The fact that a lot of them had already returned home in 1916 only corroborates this statement. Besides, it is important to note that many of these people were transferred not only due to military reasons but also because of a precise political decision. The Istrian evacuees were transferred to faraway camps under the direct orders of the military authorities in Pula, who did not want any kind of disturbance during the conflict. However, many problems happened because of the dynamic of the evacuation, especially in its first phase and before mid-1916. From the very beginning the whole process was extremely unpleasant. While the long journey in catastrophic hygienic conditions added concrete health problems to the already difficult situation, these escalated when epidemics caused a high death rate among the evacuees. Another issue was the initial neglect shown by the authorities towards the way these people were divided into the camps, often leading to families scattered across different sites. Understandably, with time this dissatisfaction grew into open demonstrations, which forced the authorities to improve their conditions during 1916 and 1917. Still, these reforms were wholly insufficient and came too late to be fully implemented. Regardless of the fact that Austro-Hungarian authorities wanted to exhibit these camps as the reflection of their care towards their subjects, camps such as Wagna and Gmünd soon became known as synonyms for the suffering of the civilian population during the Great War, and as places from where many would never return.

The experience of the Istrian *evakuirci* does not fit neatly within the four-dimensional model as proposed in the introduction of this volume. First of all, not all *evakuirci* were transferred to internment camps, as those who could provide for themselves were relatively free to temporarily settle in non-war zones and survive by any means they could come up with. This is important because a study of the experience of this group of people would give much more information about their relationship with the host society in everyday life. Also, by being mostly held in camps according to ethnic principles, the possibilities for the *evakuirci* to interact with other diasporas were quite low and not sufficient for a broader analysis of the phenomenon, as it could have been, for example, for those who were staying outside of the camps the whole time. Nevertheless, their relationship with the host society can be studied through a lens focused on the way the authorities treated them and tried to somehow alleviate their struggles. On the other hand, what can be traced quite well even by concentrating only on the group that was confined in the camps is their relationship with the homeland and their own diaspora. For example, as demonstrated in this chapter, a clear diversification was present among the evacuees, as the majority lived in cramped barracks with very basic and precarious hygienic facilities, while the higher-class minority was enjoying such privileges as private kitchens. However, what these two groups had in common was that their ties with the homeland were based on a strong and pervasive nostalgia. These bonds were made even more intense by the fact that many evacuees had close family members, mostly men, who stayed in the region in order to contribute to the empire's war effort, which caused even more discomfort and suffering to both those who had to leave and those who stayed behind. Eventually, the evacuation process entered into the local collective memory as a symbol of pain and misery, which was only overshadowed by the even worse horrors that hit the region during the Second World War.

Notes

1 Eric Hobsbawm, *L'età degli imperi 1875–1914* (Bari: Laterza, 2005), 354–5.
2 Andrej Bader, *Zaboravljeni egzodus 1915–1918* (Ližnjan: Općina Ližnjan, 2011), 32.
3 Miroslav Bertoša, 'Pulska luka u doba Venecije', in *Zbornik iz povijesti pulske luke*, ed. Mladen Černi (Pula: Lučka uprava, 2006), 46–7.
4 Darko Dukovski, *Povijest Pule* (Pula: Istarski ogranak društva hrvatskih književnika, 2011), 104–7.
5 Branko Perović, 'Luka Pula austrougarskog doba', in *Zbornik iz povijesti pulske luke*, 86.
6 Ibid., 89.
7 Dukovski, *Povijest Pule*, 112.
8 Branko Perović, 'Strateški značaj Pule kao glavne ratne luke Austro-Ugarske Monarhije', in *Mornarička knjižnica i austrijska/austrougarska mornarica u Puli*,

ed. Bruno Dobrić (Pula: Sveučilišna knjižnica, 2005), 59; Perović, 'Luka Pula austrougarskog doba', 91.
9 Dukovski, *Povijest Pule*, 113.
10 David Stevenson, *La grande guerra* (Milano: Rizzoli, 2004), 46.
11 Only one broader work completely dedicated to this topic has been written in the twentieth century, that is: Joso Defrančeski, *C. i Kr. ratni logori, 1914-1918* (Osijek: Štamparija Antun Rott, 1937).
12 For more information about the bibliography dealing with the Istrian peninsula during the Great War see: Mihovil Dabo and Milan Radošević, 'Prilog bibliografiji o Prvome svjetskom ratu u Istri', in *Usjeni Velikog rata*, ed. Mihovil Dabo and Milan Radošević (Pula: Istarsko povijesno društvo, 2019), 33-58.
13 Paolo Malni, *Fuggiaschi. Il campo profughi di Wagna 1915-1918* (San Canzian d'Isonzo: Editore Consorzio Culturale del Monfalconese, 1998), 11.
14 Bader, *Zaboravljeni egzodus*, 29.
15 Sandra De Menech and Marina Leghissa Santin, 'Pola e Rovigno. L'esodo negli anni della Prima guerra mondiale', in *Un esilio che non ha pari*, ed. Franco Cecotti (Gorizia: Libreria Editrice Goriziana, 2001), 199.
16 Ibid., 201-3.
17 Ibid., 202-3.
18 Davor Mandić, 'Pulski Hrvatski list (1915-1918.) - zapisi o "evakuircima" s područja Pomorske utvrde Pula', *Časopis za suvremenu povijest* 42, no. 3 (2010): 785; Malni, *Fuggiaschi*, 23.
19 Samanta Paronić, *Logori smrti. Potresna stvarnost barbarskih i proštinskih 'evakuiraca' (1914-1918)* (Pula: Gea Idea, 2015), 28.
20 Bader, *Zaboravljeni egzodus*, 48. For a further example, see: Ita Cherin, 'L'esodo degli abitanti di Rovigno nel periodo di guerra 1915-1918. Testimonianze di Rovignesi sfollati a Pottendorf-Landegg', *Atti* 8 (1978): 373-7.
21 Marta Manzin, 'La popolazione dell'Istria nei campi d'internamento austriaci (1915-1918)', *Atti* 29 (1999): 595-6.
22 Bader, *Zaboravljeni egzodus*, 55; Manzin, 'La popolazione dell'Istria', 596.
23 Manzin, 'La popolazione dell'Istria', 595; Cherin, 'L'esodo degli abitanti di Rovigno', 374-5.
24 Malni, *Fuggiaschi*, 33.
25 For more information, see: Paolo Malni, 'Evacuati e fuggiaschi dal fronte dell'Isonzo. I profughi della Grande guerra in Austria e in Italia', in *Un esilio che non ha pari*, 113; Cherin, 'Testimonianza di Rovignesi sfollati a Wagna (1915-1918)', *Atti* 2 (1972): 350-6; Manzin, 'La popolazione dell'Istria', 596; Bader, *Zaboravljeni egzodus*, 67-70.
26 Franco Cecotti, 'Internamenti di civili durante la Prima guerra mondiale. Friuli austriaco, Istria e Trieste', in *Un esilio che non ha pari*, 76; Bader, *Zaboravljeni egzodus*, 39.
27 Mandić, 'Pulski Hrvatski list (1915-1918)', 787.
28 Paolo Malni, 'Oggetti da amministrare: l'Austria di fronte alla questione profughi (1914-1918)', in *Usjeni Velikog rata*, 182.
29 Ibid., 185.
30 Mandić, 'Pulski Hrvatski List (1915-1918)', 79; Malni, *Fuggiaschi*, 50.
31 Malni, 'Oggetti da amministrare', 183.
32 Paronić, *Logori smrti*, 73.
33 Stipan Trogrlić, 'Porečki i pulski biskup Trifun Pederzolli i istarski iseljenici (evakuirci), 1915-1918', in *Usjeni Velikog rata*, 200-1.

34 Ibid., 202–4; Paronić, *Logori smrti*, 84–6.
35 Trogrlić, 'Porečki i pulski biskup Trifun Pederzolli', 204–5.
36 The Imperial Council had been suspended at the beginning of the War, only to be re-established in 1916.
37 See for example: Bader, *Zaboravljeni egzodus*, 71–2, 87, 97 and 162–5; Paronić, *Logori smrti*, 78–83.
38 For more information about the Austrian-Hungarian internment camps and a comparative perspective on this topic in general, see for example: Matthew Stibbe, 'Enemy Aliens, Deportees, Refugees: Internment Practices in the Habsburg Empire, 1914-198', *Journal of Modern European History* 12, no. 4 (2014): 479–99; Julie Thorpe, 'Displacing Empire. Refugee Welfare, National Activism and State Legitimacy in Austria-Hungary in the First World War', in *Refugees and the End of Empire. Imperial Collapse and Forced Migration in the Twentieth Century*, ed. Panikos Panayi and Pippa Virdee (New York: Palgrave Macmillian, 2011), 102–26; Stefan Manz, Panikos Panayi and Matthew Stibbe (eds), *Internment During the First World War: A Mass Global Phenomenon* (London and New York: Routledge, 2019).
39 Malni, 'Oggetti da amministrare', 187–8.
40 Pieter M. Judson, *The Habsburg Empire. A New History* (Cambridge, MA and London: Harvard University Press, 2016), 278.
41 Bader, *Zaboravljeni egzodus*, 47.
42 Manzin, 'La popolazione dell'Istria', 599.
43 Josip Vretenar, 'Evakuacija i zbjeg civila iz Austrijskog primorja u Prvome svjetskom ratu', in *Usjeni Velikog rata*, 221; Paronić, *Logori smrti*, 33.
44 Malni, *Fuggiaschi*, 14.
45 Ibid., 14–15.
46 Judson, *The Habsburg Empire*, 277; Malni, 'Evacuati e fuggiaschi dal fronte dell'Isonzo', 125; Manzin, 'La popolazione dell'Istria', 604–5;
47 Manzin, 'La popolazione dell'Istria', 603–4.
48 Paronić, *Logori smrti*, 34.
49 Malni, *Fuggiaschi*, 57.
50 Ibid., 76–7.
51 Ibid., 71.
52 Malni, 'Evacuati e fuggiaschi dal fronte dell'Isonzo', 123.
53 Bader, *Zaboravljeni egzodus*, 77.
54 Paronić, *Logori smrti*, 39–40.
55 Bader, *Zaboravljeni egzodus*, 78; Paronić, *Logori smrti*, 40.
56 Paronić, *Logori smrti*, 40–2.
57 Bader, *Zaboravljeni egzodus*, 81.
58 Malni, *Fuggiaschi*, 78.
59 Dean Krmac, 'Wagna: la strage degli innocenti istriani (ottobre 1915–gennaio 1916)', in *Istra u Velikom ratu. Glad, bolesti, smrt*, ed. Petra Svoljšak (Koper: Histria Editiones, 2017), 113.
60 Ibid., 115.
61 Dean Krmac, 'Un'evenienza funesta della Grande guerra istriana: l'epidemia di morbillo nel campo profughi di Wagna (autunno 1915)', in *Usjeni Velikog rata*, 237.
62 Paronić, *Logori smrti*, 43; Manzin, 'La popolazione dell'Istria', 618.
63 Bader, *Zaboravljeni egzodus*, 89.
64 Malni, 'Evacuati e fuggiaschi dal fronte dell'Isonzo', 127.
65 Malni, 'Oggetti da amministrare', 193.

66 For a detailed insight in the camp's menu, see for example: Malni, *Fuggiaschi*, 74.
67 Bader, *Zaboravljeni egzodus*, 138.
68 Ibid., 85; Paronić, *Logori smrti*, 43
69 Malni, *Fuggiaschi*, 77.
70 Paronić, *Logori smrti*, 38-9. In some other sources the boy was reported to be twelve, see: Malni, *Fuggiaschi*, 141.
71 Malni, *Fuggiaschi*, 147.
72 Malni, 'Oggetti da amministrare', 194; Mandić, 'Pulski Hrvatski List (1915-1918)', 806.
73 Judson, *The Habsburg Empire*, 285-6.
74 See for example: Bader, *Zaboravljeni egzodus*, 162-6; Malni, *Fuggiaschi*, 133 and 151.
75 Paronić, *Logori smrti*, 89.
76 Malni, *Fuggiaschi*, 152; De Menech and Leghissa Santin, 'Pola e Rovigno', 212; Bader, *Zaboravljeni egzodus*, 159.
77 Mandić, 'Pulski Hrvatski List (1915-1918)', 810.
78 The wage rise was meant to follow a future improvement of the Austrian-Hungarian position in the war, see ibid., 811.
79 Milan Radošević, 'Epidemija svraba u Puli 1918/1919: prilog poznavanju (po)ratnih socijalnih i zdravstvenih prilika u gradu', in *Istra u Velikom ratu*, 211; De Menech and Leghissa Santin, 'Pola e Rovigno', 214-5.
80 Paronić, *Logori smrti*, 98-9.

Part II

Political emigrants in the interwar era

Map 4.1 Kingdom of Yugoslavia, 1930. © Bastiaan Willems.

4

Salvaging the 'unredeemed' in Italy

The Kingdom of Yugoslavia and the Julian March émigrés

Miha Zobec

Introduction

The aftermath of the Great War,[1] which in East-Central Europe 'failed to end' in 1918,[2] provoked massive upheaval with intense political, social and ethnic violence which particularly affected the imperial borderlands.[3] On the ruins of empires, new nation states were established. Eventually, the consolidated states, functioning as 'properties' of their titular nations, the 'national majorities', aimed at national homogenization of territories under their sovereignty. Borderlands were considered to be particularly sensitive as the states believed the ethnic 'others', the 'national minorities', might function on these territories as a fifth column for their 'national homelands'. Therefore, the states sought to use all the means necessary to nationalize these territories, even by force. In fear of their existence, borderland minorities often sought shelter in their 'national homelands', in so doing, becoming part of the latters' nation-building projects.[4]

Economic downturn and forced Italianization of the Julian March/Venezia Giulia[5] region (former Austrian Littoral), annexed to Italy with the Treaty of Rapallo in 1920, provoked massive emigration of Slovene and Croat population. The majority of emigrants relocated to the neighbouring Kingdom of Serbs, Croats and Slovenes (from 1929 on the Kingdom of Yugoslavia; hereafter I will refer to the state simply as Yugoslavia) while their preferred overseas destination became Argentina. Political oppression undertaken by the Italian fascist regime united politically engaged emigrants in opposition to the Italian domination over the annexed region. The fascist authorities were concerned about the emigrant activism which was drawing attention to the minority problem in the region and was therefore undermining the fascist propaganda of a successfully incorporated Julian March.[6] In addition, the émigrés networked extensively with the anti-fascist clandestine movement within the region, thereby causing direct threat to the fascist rule. Consequently, the fascist regime struggled to crush émigré activities.

Conversely, Yugoslavia considered the Julian March emigrants part of its constitutive Serbo-Croat-Slovene nation (according to the state-proclaimed ideology, Serbs, Croats and Slovenes were merely tribes of a single Yugoslav nation) and, besides managing immigration of Julian March co-nationals on its territory, aimed at instrumentalizing emigrants' activities to its own political ends, namely achieving national and ideological unity and countering separatist and autonomist tendencies. However, the problem concerning the emigrant movement, namely the issue of Julian March and border delimitation on the Upper Adriatic, was largely alien to the Serb ruling elite which directed its geopolitical interests to the Balkans and the Danube basin.[7] Moreover, as an economically and politically weak state, Yugoslavia refrained from border revisionism.[8] The emigrant political movement, therefore, was recognized by the Yugoslav government only when relations with Italy were tense. At that time, Yugoslavia exploited emigrants' resentment towards the fascist regime and their philo-Yugoslavism in order to foster internal stability and to exert pressure on Italy. Nevertheless, emigrants' protests against the 'unfair' border agreement hindered rapprochement with Italy, one of the foremost economic partners of Yugoslavia. The eventual establishment of cordial relations between Yugoslavia and Italy in the second half of the 1930s led to the final obscuring of the emigrant movement.

The émigré elite linked their organizations' emigrant activism to the issue of settling the borders in the Adriatic. Therefore, this chapter starts with an outline of the competing territorial claims laid out by Italian and Slovene nationalists. Second, it will examine émigré activism and its relation to Yugoslav state policies through the lens of the Italian diplomatic service which, thanks to its well-developed system of espionage, delved deep into the functioning of emigrant associations.[9] Certainly, the diplomatic sources should not be taken at face value as the views of the Italian ambassador reflected Italian foreign policy which treated Yugoslavia as an inferior neighbour and tended either to downplay émigré activism or exaggerate with it, depending on Italo-Yugoslav relations. In addition, the diplomatic material will be corroborated by sources pertaining to Julian March emigrant politicians as well as by the emigrant newspaper *Istra*.

Emigrant activism can be divided into three phases. In the first phase, activism was only gaining ground and could not count on the support of the Yugoslav regime. The second coincided with King Aleksandar's dictatorship[10] which was allegedly introduced in order to overcome the political crisis provoked by the murder of Stjepan Radić in 1928, a political leader with the largest backing in Croatia. At that time emigrant political engagement became useful to the regime, acquired widespread irredentist appeal and in fact reached its apogee. Following Aleksandar's death, emigrant activism declined. The ensuing economic crisis and especially a new rapprochement with Italy led to the eclipse of the movement in Yugoslavia and its transfer to the Julian March emigrant communities in the United States and Argentina.[11] Furthermore, the émigré activists could count on their transnational ties with Italian anti-fascist émigrés who helped to engender support in the struggle against oppression but did not support the irredentism advocated by the émigré elite in the mid-1930s.

Could the experience of the Julian March emigrants be framed within the diaspora model proposed by Willems and Palacz in the introduction? At first glance, the sheer cause for diaspora formation was missing as the émigrés relocated to their 'homeland', and therefore host society and homeland were ostensibly one and the same in this case. Nevertheless, obstacles related to the integration of the émigrés into the host society as well as their activism for the Julian March demonstrate that their experience was in reality not so dissimilar to one of the other diasporas discussed in the volume. Even though they moved to the land they called 'homeland', the émigré elite constantly discouraged the emigrants from assimilating into Yugoslav society so as not to lose their 'defining cause'. In addition, even though Yugoslavia in general figured as their homeland, many emigrants opposed the royal regime and envisioned a different homeland, a socially transformed Yugoslavia, even if they never produced a definitive political programme for achieving this. Moreover, even though the emigrants came 'home', many natives still considered them to be foreigners. Consequently, the case of the Julian March émigrés confirms the assumption put to the foreground in the present volume that homeland cannot be defined in terms of an objective area, but should rather be conceived as a socially imagined place. In short, it is difficult to place the emigrants' experiences within the homeland/host society dichotomy and categorize their modes of political engagement, because each classification would impose certain restricted visions upon their actions. Instead, it seems more worthwhile to examine the political claims and practices advanced by these emigrants.

The minority exiles from the Julian March were far from exceptional in interwar Europe. Political divisions among emigrants as well as co-optation into the motherland's political framework were widespread. Alignment with authoritarian politics was not limited to Yugoslavia, either.[12] Yet, while the activism of the Julian March émigrés has been examined,[13] processes regarding their incorporation into the Yugoslav sociopolitical system remain under-researched. The aim of this chapter is to place the émigré political movement within Yugoslavia's nation-building efforts and therefore shed some new light on the connection between state-building processes and associational life in interwar Yugoslavia, namely, to show that the Julian March emigrants' associations in Yugoslavia formed part of the state's 'voluntary associations' and that these became, as Petrungaro and Giomi claim, 'an additional tool for the Yugoslav state- and nation-building projects'.[14] Yet, while these emigrants were located in a Yugoslav political context, their activities were defined by the position of the 'unredeemed territory', which suggests the importance of studying extraterritorial dimensions of Yugoslav nation building.

How does the Julian March diaspora fit into the frame of anti-fascist exiles, so numerous in interwar Europe?[15] Like anti-fascists, the Julian March emigrants composed a diverse community, ranging from the irredentist émigré elite to socialist youth. Yet, while the anti-fascists targeted the ideological nature of the regimes, the Julian March émigré elite's primary agenda was irredentist, demanding the annexation of Julian March to Yugoslavia. However, as they were engaged in opposing fascist discrimination against national minorities and had contacts with the Italian anti-fascists, it is difficult to label them as solely anti-Italian, and therefore it seems more reasonable to think about the movement in terms of anti-fascism.

Between the young and the old: Emigrant associations and the Julian March issue till the royal dictatorship

As in other parts of Europe which underwent imperial dissolution, the Upper Adriatic region witnessed territorial disputes which surfaced in the aftermath of the Great War. European forces had long contested the control of the Adriatic shores.[16] In the period following the conflagration, the 'Adriatic question' was to become the bone of contention between Italy and Yugoslavia. Despite the treaties of Rapallo and Rome (singed in 1920 and 1924, respectively) which determined the state borders and settled some sensitive issues (such as the issue of the Italian minority in Dalmatia), the question of control over the Adriatic continuously obstructed bilateral relations and thus made rapprochement increasingly difficult.

On the eve of the Great War, Italian nationalism became ever more aggressive in demanding the incorporation of not only Trieste and Trento but also Dalmatia and Istria into Italy.[17] By the end of war, irredentists felt that Italian territorial aspirations were unfulfilled. The idea of a 'mutilated victory', fuelled by the belief that Italy should have acquired (redeemed was the nationalist slogan) the territory promised by the London Treaty[18] and the town of Rijeka/Fiume, gained immense support among the Italian public. Ultimately, nationalists found the expression of their desires in fascist foreign policy, founded on the belief that Yugoslavia suffered from both internal and external instability and could therefore easily surrender to Italian expansionism.[19] According to Italian military reports, Yugoslavia was perceived as 'a thorny alliance of nations which would have collapsed if peoples had not been united in their hatred towards Italy'.[20] Besides, many Yugoslav neighbours were revisionist and therefore sought to expand their territory at the cost of Yugoslavia. It was believed that Italy could wisely take advantage of Yugoslav instability, thereby destabilizing and gradually ruining the country.[21] Therefore, the gateway to control the Adriatic ('our gulf'), seen by the fascists as necessary for establishing the Italian Mediterranean Empire, would be open.[22]

The territory of the former Austrian Littoral had been promised to Italy by the Entente and was subsequently occupied by the Italian army. Yugoslav representatives, basing their arguments on ethnic criteria, worked on retrieving this territory. Among the most fervent advocates of the incorporation of the occupied territory to Yugoslavia were refugees coming from this contested region. In fact, the first emigrant organization with clear political aims was established immediately after the armistice had been signed. The purpose of the Office for the Occupied Territory (*Pisarna za zasedeno ozemlje*), a semi-official organization which derived from the National Council (*Narodni svet*, an authority which emerged with the collapse of the Austro-Hungarian Empire) in Ljubljana, was twofold. First, with the view of demonstrating the predominantly Slav ethnic composition of the territory occupied by Italian forces, it published propaganda pamphlets for the Paris Peace Conference. These pamphlets depicted the former Austrian Littoral as 'Our Alsace-Lorraine', alluding to the French re-conquest of the territory which had been annexed to Germany in 1871.[23] Relying on ethnic criteria, members of the Office for the Occupied Territory argued that by virtue of self-determination, the region should be incorporated into Yugoslavia.[24] Second, they initiated espionage activities with intelligence centres in Trieste and Gorizia which sought to collect data regarding the demeanour of Italian authorities towards Slovenes and Croats and to spur national activism among co-nationals.[25] Spying activities on the territory that was to become Italian were later continued by other organizations with similar aims. In addition, they were accompanied by paramilitary activities undertaken by the units of Orjuna (*Organizacija jugoslovanskih nacionalista*, Organization of Yugoslav Nationalists),[26] which coordinated the organization of underground subversion against Italian occupation. Needless to say, the Italian authorities were infuriated by these activities and used them as a pretext for exerting additional pressure on the Slovene and Croat population.

Signing of the Treaty of Rapallo provoked demonstrations across Yugoslavia with massive protests in Ljubljana, Zagreb and Belgrade.[27] The condemnation of the Rapallo Treaty was eventually transformed into an annual commemoration. With the escalation of fascist discrimination against the Julian March minorities, commemorative events often converted into protests against fascist policy, with student youth playing an ever more important role in them. Nonetheless, during the protests in Ljubljana on the eighth anniversary of Rapallo Treaty,[28] the Yugoslav Queen Bee (*Jugoslovanska matica*) organization, which aimed at raising awareness of the stranded Yugoslav minorities,[29] noticed a decline in engagement and lack of support for the 'enslaved' or 'unredeemed brothers' as those belonging to Slovene and Croat minorities were designated in the official Yugoslav ethnopolitical discourse.[30] Initial zeal for 'liberating the unredeemed brothers' that was present at the time of the Rapallo Treaty had clearly subsided.

The emigrants flowed to Yugoslavia in distinctive waves, creating thus a complex and diverse reality. The first wave was composed of state employees who left the Julian March during the Italian occupation. As a result of the shortage of public officials – most of the German-speaking Austrian bureaucracy had fled after the collapse of the Habsburg Empire – they entered the Yugoslav workforce with relative ease.[31] Consequently, by the end of the 1920s, they were already integrated into society, and they preferred to look at the Julian March with nostalgia rather than with manifest discontent. On the other hand, new immigrants, driven from their homes by economic decline and the fascist discrimination that was becoming ever harsher after the introduction of dictatorship in 1926, fervently opposed the Italian oppression.[32] The fascist policy of denationalization outlawed the ethnic press and dissolved Slovene and Croat associations as well as their cooperatives and saving banks, thereby undermining their economic foundations. Moreover, the persecution carried out by the political police and the Special Tribunal (*Tribunale speciale per la difesa dello stato*), aimed at intimidating the masses by punishing the resistance, pushed young anti-fascists and their families to seek shelter in Yugoslavia.[33]

They were among the thousands who fled from the Julian March throughout the interwar period. The exact number of emigrants is difficult to assess because of unreliable and incomplete statistics provided by Italy and the countries of immigration.[34] Yet, most scholars consider the figures provided by the emigrant umbrella organization Union of the Yugoslav Emigrants from the Julian March (*Zveza jugoslovanskih emigrantov iz Julijske krajine*)[35] to be accurate. These figures set the emigration from the Julian March at around 100,000, of whom 70,000 emigrated to Yugoslavia, 30,000 relocated to South America and around 5,000 to France and Belgium.[36] The same number of Julian March emigrants in the South Slavic state was also confirmed by the Italian sources.[37]

Many immigrants who arrived by the late 1920s were not welcomed by the host society, even though they regarded Yugoslavia as their homeland. Often seen by natives as those who were depriving them of jobs, they called them *Lahi* (a derogatory word for Italians), or even fascists.[38] Moreover, most immigrants considered a strong Yugoslavia to be an ultimate bulwark against Italian expansion and were therefore decisively philo-Yugoslav as opposed to Slovenes who were in favour of autonomism or Croats who pushed for federalization. The writer Vladimir Bartol, himself an emigrant (his family moved from Trieste to Ljubljana in 1919), captured well not only the immigrants' character traits, which were shaped by the different sociopolitical context of their lives before departure, but also their political attitude:

> These refugees brought their distinctive temperament, their breadth of mind, and their dreams of a big and powerful Yugoslav state that was to prepare everything for the liberation of their land and their enslaved co-nationals. . . . In contrast to Ljubljana's petit bourgeois man, each Littoral co-national, even the most simple-minded one, was aware what the unification of Yugoslav nations had brought and what significance the state of one's own had. As a result, they were decidedly in favour of state-building and were upset by domestic intrigues which they felt compelled to criticize and which within their wider state-political concept they viewed as petty. Their inclination to state-building, however, encountered misunderstanding among the natives. They blamed them for ambitiousness, elbowing and political opportunism.[39]

Among the immigrants there was, however, a stark contrast in views over how the Yugoslav state ought to be organized and how the issue of Italian oppression of the Julian March minorities should be addressed. An essential distinction stemmed from the generational gap setting apart the perceptions of the young and the old. The young had been active in youth organizations and, upon their dissolution, some of them vowed to continue an uncompromising struggle against fascism, waging their fight in clandestine associations. They felt overwhelmed by the collapse of the Austro-Hungarian Empire and post-war instability but also animated by the Russian Revolution. They perceived the established bourgeois culture as a 'dusty museum exhibit'.[40] As their arrival in Yugoslavia coincided with the economic depression, they perceived themselves as belonging to a generation devoid of real opportunities and therefore standing 'in front of the closed door'.[41] Consequently, their political interests were socially motivated, with several members being involved in leftist politics. As they considered the regime of King Aleksandar to be related to Italian fascism, they believed that struggle against fascism had to be waged in Yugoslavia as well. Among the ranks of the old, on the other hand, there were representatives of the nationalist bourgeois elite from the Julian March who had been fond of pan-Slavism even before the war. Faithful to the Yugoslav ruling elite, they openly embraced unitarism (the belief that Slovenes, Croats and Serbs were merely tribes of a single Yugoslav nation) and centralism.⁴²

Obviously, not every emigrant was engaged in the émigré political movement. In fact, only a minority vowed a relentless struggle against the Italian annexation. In many cases, emigrant political involvement depended on the possibility of improving unfavourable economic conditions. Therefore, many migrants joined the emigrant political organizations in order to cope with precariousness.⁴³ Moreover, some emigrants were simply indifferent to the discrimination against Julian March minorities, while others even cooperated with the Italian consular infrastructure.⁴⁴ Besides the character traits that determined emigrants' behaviour, constrictions imposed by citizenship often restricted their engagement. Yugoslavia's 1928 Citizenship Law facilitated acquisition of citizenship to persons of 'Serbo-Croat-Slovene descent'.⁴⁵ Naturally, citizenship was not only a prerequisite for obtaining a job in the public sector but was also necessary for participating in the state's welfare programmes. Therefore, during the period of economic crisis, obtaining Yugoslav citizenship was of vital interest to the emigrants. However, Yugoslavia did not allow double citizenship, and those emigrants who opted to become Yugoslavs automatically lost their Italian citizenship. As Italy required Yugoslav citizens to obtain visa to cross the border, the acquisition of Yugoslav citizenship by the Julian March emigrants very often meant the loss of contact with their dear ones in the 'enslaved region', in addition to a host of other problems, such as the discontinuation of studies. In short, the instrument of citizenship, along with Italian restrictions on entering the country, diminished emigrant engagement.⁴⁶

Yet, even though the mechanism of citizenship discouraged many diasporic activism, some émigrés persisted in salvaging the 'enslaved brothers'. Perceiving the associations that had been set up by the older emigrants as inadequate, the young began searching for a more suitable way to express the ideas of youth activism which they had developed before departing.⁴⁷ In the end, they founded an umbrella organization, called *Orjem*, or Organization of the Yugoslav Emigrants (*Organizacija jugoslovanskih emigrantov*), which linked local emigrant organizations across Yugoslavia. The organization was avowedly opposed to the fascist discrimination in the Julian March but it dissociated itself from Yugoslav politics.⁴⁸ Despite the association's efforts to present itself as an apolitical organization, authorities of King Aleksandar's dictatorial regime perceived *Orjem* as not suitable for the Yugoslav sociopolitical framework.⁴⁹ Given that the royal regime expected the citizens to actively celebrate King Aleksandar's rule, it is no surprise that *Orjem* was not accepted by the government.⁵⁰

Even though *Orjem* failed to achieve its aims, it paved the way for the formation of an umbrella emigrant organization in the future. Moreover, its essence as a youth movement reinforced youth activism that was antagonistic to the perspectives of traditional émigré elites. Because of their links to the court, the old generation of emigrants eventually managed to secure their dominance, but they never held complete sway over the Julian March diaspora. The issue of the political purpose of emigration and its relation to the 'problem' of the Julian March remained fields of competition.

The old in power: Seeking King Aleksandar's support for the Julian March

Despite the inability of the emigrant youth to acquire governmental support, the Italian ambassador to Belgrade noticed that Yugoslav authorities relied on the Julian March emigrants to stir up feelings of Yugoslavism. These sentiments were coupled with resentment towards Italy, which became ever more pronounced after the 1929 and 1930 trials undertaken by the Special Tribunal against anti-fascist clandestine organizations. With the Trieste trial in 1930, these organizations in Julian March suffered an almost deadly blow with four members receiving death sentences and several others incarcerated.[51] The Julian March diaspora transformed the Trieste trial into a *lieu de mémoire* around which the community gathered not only in Yugoslavia but even in the Americas. The trial echoed also in the international press, most notably in Yugoslav-friendly Czechoslovakia.[52] The Italian ambassador to Belgrade noted that the persecution of Slovene and Croat anti-fascists reinforced Yugoslav unity against Italy.[53] Furthermore, he noticed that even Serbs, who had previously allegedly considered Slovenes to be 'submissive and uncombative', began to show concern for the 'Slovene issue' after the Trieste trial.[54]

Policies carried out by Yugoslav authorities converged with ideas of the émigré politician Ivan Marija Čok, a lawyer and one of the leaders of Slovene nationalist liberals in Trieste, who fled to Yugoslavia after his arrest in 1928. Subsequently, he aspired to leadership of the emigrant movement. Čok had become acquainted with the Belgrade elite during the Paris Peace Conference, where he served as the Yugoslav expert for ethnic issues and could therefore easily win governmental support for the emigrant movement. In 1929, when Italo-Yugoslav relations were tense, Čok considered that the royal regime could use the united organization of Slovene and Croat emigrants to counter Mussolini's expansionism.[55]

The royal dictatorship readily exploited emigrants' philo-Yugoslavism and resentment towards Italy. Preoccupied with the Croat discontent, the authorities deployed the most bellicose emigrants to Croatia in order to redirect Croat opposition to Serb hegemony into resistance against Italy.[56] The emigrant organization therefore fostered internal stability by mitigating Croat pressure for federalization.

Thanks to governmental intervention, the centre of emigrant activities was transferred from Ljubljana (where proximity to Italy made the situation sensitive) to Zagreb (and later to Belgrade). It was therefore not a coincidence that the foundational meeting of the new emigrant umbrella organization, called the Union of the Yugoslav Emigrants from the Julian March (*Savez jugoslovenskih emigranata iz Julijske krajine*, the Union), directed by Čok, took place in the Croat capital in 1931. The Italian ambassador believed that the emigrant movement became part of the state machinery of Yugoslav nationalist organizations, directed by King Aleksandar. Allegedly, organizations such as the association of war veterans called National Defense (*Narodna odbrana*) were directly subordinated to the king. Inspired by anti-liberalism and heroism of the Serb war sacrifice, National Defense blamed parliamentarism for Yugoslav instability and therefore praised the royal dictatorship which, as it hoped, would engender Yugoslav spiritual unity.[57] Čok was an ally of the king and formed part of National Defense's governing board. Therefore, the statements of the Italian ambassador regarding the subjugation of the Union to the royal dictatorship, although they might appear somewhat exaggerated, are not unfounded, especially considering the fact that freedom of association was at that time curtailed in Yugoslavia and that the abovementioned organizations were tightly surveilled and tied to the court.

Čok worked tirelessly to present the issue of Julian March as a problem which concerned all of Yugoslavia. Even though the economic crisis hampered the Union's activism, the annual Rapallo commemoration was transformed into a mass manifestation at which representatives of powerful organizations, such as the Sokols,[58] the Adriatic Guard[59] and National Defense, played an important role.[60] These organizations had their branches throughout the country. The breadth of the Union's activity disturbed Italian diplomatic representatives, who pressed Yugoslav authorities to suppress Čok's activities and called for the dissolution of the Union.[61]

However, the existence of the Union was not just threatened by external factors. The association also struggled to overcome internal divisions which challenged its purported unity. Throughout the entire period of its existence, from 1931 to 1940, the Union was directed by Čok and could count on firm support of the émigré elite who was chiefly opposed by the younger emigrants. The surveillance of emigrant associations, exercised by the governing board of the Union and the Yugoslav authorities, further fuelled the clash between the young and the old. As it turned out, the governing board was also responsible for prison sentences imposed on members of communist-leaning associations of emigrant youth in the Slovene part of Yugoslavia.[62]

Generational divisions further shaped diverging attitudes towards solving the Julian March issue. With the outbreak of the Spanish Civil War and the advent of the Popular Front, the young increasingly linked the problem of the Julian March with the international anti-fascist struggle.[63] The governing board, on the other hand, openly championed irredentism and the annexation of the Julian March to Yugoslavia in isolation. Basing his arguments on the ethnic composition of the territory as well as on traditional geopolitics, Čok considered that Yugoslavia ought to combat advancing Italian, Hungarian and German revisionism with its anti-revisionist campaign. Relying on propagandism, he claimed that Yugoslav revisionism was, in contrast to the one exercised by greater powers, just, because it supposedly relied on the ethnic criteria and not on imperialism. Professing Yugoslav nationalism at the 'antirevisionist' meeting in Belgrade in 1933, he claimed that 'Yugoslavia is where Yugoslav hearts beat'.[64] Despite the Union's successful penetration into Yugoslav society and its circles of power, it is difficult to claim that the mobilization of Yugoslav nationalist associations encouraged Yugoslavia's kin-state politics, hence its engagement for stranded Yugoslav minorities. After all, it was only during King Aleksandar's regime that rallies of state-wide associations took place. Notwithstanding Čok's efforts, it seems that the 'unredeemed' Julian March never really acquired appeal by the Yugoslav ruling elite. Beset by a record of mistreating national minorities on its own territory and an unfavourable position in international relations (it had disputes with virtually all of its neighbours, apart from Greece), Yugoslavia did not raise complaints in the League of Nations about the treatment of the Yugoslav minority in fascist Italy.[65]

The shift in Italo-Yugoslav relations and the decline of diaspora engagement in Yugoslavia

The Union reached its apogee at the congress in Maribor in 1934 (one of the annual congresses at which the organization's programme was publicly proclaimed), its greatest and most publicized manifestation, when the governing board affirmed the association's irredentist programme. Consequently, it even further alienated the young from the organization.[66] Subsequently, a sharp decline of associational activities followed.[67] The downfall of the Union was intrinsically linked with the shift in the equilibrium of European powers which drew Yugoslavia closer to Italy. Italy, preparing for a war in Ethiopia, did not want to face difficulties in the Adriatic. France, Yugoslavia's main ally, also sought closer relations with Italy in the wake of German rearmament, while the impact of the Great Depression on the French economy likewise increased the importance of Italy as one of Yugoslavia's foremost trading partners. In addition, the Yugoslav prime minister Milan Stojadinović was an admirer of Mussolini, leaving him more open to the idea of rapprochement.[68] All of these factors worked in favour of revitalized diplomatic engagement between the two countries, which culminated in the 1937 Treaty of Friendship, and which inevitably came at the expense of the Union.[69]

The Union criticized the Yugoslav government for not raising awareness among its citizens about the situation of Yugoslavs in the Julian March and requested that the treaty of Italo-Yugoslav partnership would stipulate the protection of the Slovene and Croat minorities.[70] Despite their hopes, the Stojadinović-Ciano Treaty which institutionalized the partnership between Italy and Yugoslavia, did not contain any provisions for minority protection.[71] Ciano only promised Stojadinović that Italy would solve the minority issue treating it as a question of its 'internal affairs'.[72] Italy demanded Yugoslavia to abstain from supporting emigrant associations. The diplomatic rapprochement between the neighbours finally eclipsed the activity of the Union. As the Italian ambassador to Belgrade noted, the Yugoslav Ministry of Interior began to carefully monitor the activities of the Union, banning all the protests against Italy.[73]

Irreconcilable political divisions, skilfully hidden beneath manifested unity, were present until 1940, when the Union was officially banned by governmental decree. However, not even the approaching war could hinder Čok's endeavours to 'liberate' the 'enslaved' Julian March. When the occupiers conquered Yugoslavia in April 1941, Čok formed the Yugoslav Committee from Italy (*Jugoslovanski odbor iz Italije*) with the help of the émigré Ivan Rudolf and support of the British Secret Service. With the outbreak of the war, they fled from Yugoslavia. Collaborating with the Yugoslav government-in-exile (Čok later with Tito's partisans), they searched for volunteers among the Julian March Slovenes and Croats drafted to fight for Italy in the Middle East. Their plan was to involve these soldiers in the fight which aimed at annexing the Julian March to Yugoslavia.[74]

Throughout the whole period of its existence, the Union worked for the 'redemption' of the Julian March. Its unrestrained irredentism, engendered by the conviction that this sort of 'anti-revisionism' was merely based on ethnic criteria, was in fact a continuation of previous endeavours for the incorporation of the region into the frame of Yugoslavia which allegedly did little to internationalize the issue. Referring to the right of self-determination, politicians affiliated with the Office for the Occupied Territory, aimed at raising awareness concerning the 'enslaved brothers' at the Paris Peace Conference and across the political spectrum of the newly founded state. Čok's endeavours were more far-reaching, gaining the attention of the ruling elite and thus transforming the movement into an organization recognized by the state.

In order to internationalize the issue, Čok continued cooperating with Italian anti-fascist organizations as well as with numerous Yugoslav emigrants. Despite the Italian anti-fascists' sympathy towards the persecuted ethnic minorities on Italian territory, divergence of views over border revision prevented eventual agreement. While the Union set irredentism as its primary objective, only a handful of Italian anti-fascist organizations in France were in favour of border revisionism. Italian anti-fascists supported revision in the context of a general social rearrangement and were not willing to embrace the idea of annexation of the disputed territory into Yugoslavia at all costs.[75]

Faced with the dwindling support of Italian anti-fascists, the émigré elite decided to internationalize the issue by strengthening the networks with Julian March emigrants in Argentina who shared a similar experience of victimhood. Čok willingly accepted the request of these emigrants to publish articles about the plight of the minority in the newspaper of Julian March emigrants in Argentina.[76] In addition to the engagement in Argentina, the minority issue of Yugoslavs in the Julian March reverberated among the Yugoslav emigrants in the United States who had emigrated already before the First World War.

Conclusion

The ongoing discrimination against the Julian March minority transformed many emigrants into a community that was united in its condemnation of the Italian policy towards the annexed region. However, diverging political viewpoints divided the emigrants. In the struggle to achieve primacy over the representation of the emigrant movement, the old elite obviously fared better as it could count on the support of the Yugoslav government. In fact, this support was so decisive that it is impossible to imagine the elite's dominance over the movement without state's backing. The elite's programme was pretty much in line with King Aleksandar's identity politics which aimed at transforming Yugoslavia into a state of an indivisible Yugoslav nation. Mobilization campaigns aimed at involving a plethora of Yugoslav-wide associations in what was believed to be the struggle to liberate the 'unredeemed' seem to prove that Yugoslavia wanted, at least in the time of dictatorship, to present itself as a strong state which, like other European powers, nurtured bonds with its stranded minorities. However, no matter how profound Yugoslav sympathies for the 'unredeemed' might appear, they could not conceal the fact that the state was in no position to address this issue in the way revisionist powers did at that time. As an economically deficient state, Yugoslavia had to prioritize its economic interests over the nation-building project, the process which in the Yugoslav case was in itself very complex. The feeling of territorial loss which permeated the public in border revisionist states such as Hungary did not affect Yugoslavia's population evenly and the authorities could therefore justify economic arguments without losing popular appeal.

What can the case of the Julian March émigrés tell about Yugoslav nation-building policies? The fact that the issue of émigrés was inherently linked to Yugoslav policies towards the stranded minorities suggests that it is misleading to examine Yugoslav nation-building processes solely within the context of a territorial-bounded state. Even though Yugoslavia had no revisionist claims, the authorities thought of the Yugoslav nation in terms of an ethnic community stretching beyond its territorial borders.[77] When and for what purposes did the Yugoslav authorities stand for the 'unredeemed'? The evidence suggests that the state supported the issue of Julian March in order to achieve national homogenization and impede the processes which might hamper royal authoritarianism.[78] Ultimately, however, diaspora policies increased tensions which they aimed at alleviating: instead of creating a nationally unified polity, they intensified fractures and alienated the Julian March emigrants. While the Serbs did not identify with the issue of the 'unredeemed', Croats and Slovenes did not share Yugoslavism, championed by the Julian March émigré elite. As the emigrants faced problems in obtaining citizenship and could therefore not become fully involved in the Yugoslav sociopolitical framework, they lost trust in the state which supposedly supported them.

The issue of the Julian March émigrés has been traditionally examined from the viewpoint of national historiography, emphasizing their continuous struggle against the fascist oppression of minorities. Yet, contextualizing émigrés endeavour in Yugoslavia's nation-building project demonstrates how state's policies were interwoven with the ambitions of the emigrant elite and how the latter managed to dominate the movement thanks to governmental intervention. The movement was in fact far from unique: it formed part of the 'culture of exile' which in the interwar period encompassed anti-fascists and minority activists across the globe. Transnational connections which the Julian March diaspora maintained with other dissident exiles allow the examination of the cross-fertilization of ideas which crystallized in the movement's activism. This perspective which promises to yield new insights still awaits to be properly applied.

Notes

1 This work was supported by the Slovene Research Agency (ARRS) under Grant Z5-1880 'Minorities, Diasporas and the Subversives: Extraterritorial Control Over the Slovene Emigrants during the Interwar Period'. The author would like to thank Francesca Rolandi, Sabine Rutar and the editors of this volume for their insightful comments on earlier drafts of this chapter.
2 Robert Gerwarth, *The Vanquished. Why the First World War Failed to End, 1917–1923* (New York: Penguin Random House, 2016).
3 See Omer Bartov and Eric Weitz, 'Introduction: Coexistence and Violence in the German, Habsburg, Russian and Ottoman Borderlands', in *Shatterzone of Empires. Coexistence and Violence in the German, Habsburg, Russian and Ottoman Borderlands*, ed. Omer Bartov and Eric D. Weitz (Bloomington: Indiana University Press, 2013), 1–9.

4 Cf. Rogers Brubaker, *Nationalism Reframed: Nationhood and the National Question in the New Europe* (Cambridge: Cambridge University Press, 1996), 5; Harris Mylonas, *The Politics of Nation-Building. Making Co-Nationals, Refugees and Minorities* (Cambridge: Cambridge University Press, 2012).
5 The 'Julian March' is the English translation of the Slavic designation *Julijska krajina* for the Venezia Giulia region, which was annexed to Italy in November 1920. It referred to the territory including Trieste, Gorizia, Istria and parts of the Dalmatian coast. See Maura Hametz, *Making Trieste Italian, 1918-1954* (Woodbridge: Boydell Press, 2005), 87.
6 See Anna Maria Vinci, *Sentinelle della patria: il fascismo al confine orientale* (Rome: Laterza, 2011), 168.
7 Lavo Čermelj, 'Kako je prišlo do prijateljskega pakta med Italijo in Kraljevino SHS l. 1924', *Zgodovinski časopis* 9 (1955): 194.
8 See Mylonas, *The Politics of Nation-Building*, 147.
9 See Andrej Vovko, 'Organizacije jugoslovanskih emigrantov iz Julijske krajine do leta 1933', *Zgodovinski časopis* 32 (1978): 471.
10 The dictatorship was imposed by King Aleksandar's coup d'etat in 1929. The king dissolved all political parties and ruled by decree until 1931 when he introduced a new constitution. A governmental party was now allowed but all political life was still directed by the king and prime ministers appointed by him. The dictatorship ended with Aleksandar's assassination in Marseilles in 1934. For a detailed study of Yugoslavia during King Aleksandar's dictatorship, see Christian Axboe Nielsen, *Making Yugoslavs. Identity in King Aleksandar's Yugoslavia* (Toronto: University of Toronto Press, 2014).
11 On activism in the United States, see Aleksej Kalc and Mirjam Milharčič-Hladnik, 'Prvi tržaški proces in Slovenci v ZDA', *Annales, Series Historia et Sociologia* 25 (2015): 925-36; in Argentina see Miha Zobec, 'Creating the Unbound Yugoslav Nation: The Kingdom of Yugoslavia and Emigrants from the "Unredeemed" Julian March', *Nationalities Papers* 49 (2021): 1-20.
12 Xosé M. Núñez Seixas, 'Unholy Alliances? Nationalist Exiles, Minorities and Anti-Fascism in Interwar Europe', *Contemporary European History* 25 (2016): 597-8.
13 See for instance Aleksej Kalc, 'L'emigrazione slovena e croata dalla Venezia Giulia tra le due guerre ed il suo ruolo politico', *Anali za istrske in mediteranske študije* 6 (1996): 23-61; Vovko, 'Organizacije jugoslovanskih emigrantov'.
14 Stefano Petrungaro and Fabio Giomi, 'Voluntary Associations, State and Gender in Interwar Yugoslavia. An Introduction', *European Review of History/Revue européenne d'histoire* 26 (2019): 7.
15 Cf. Hugo García, 'Transnational History: A New Paradigm for Anti-Fascist Studies?', *Contemporary European History* 25 (2016): 566.
16 For the contest over Adriatic, see Borut Klabjan, '"Scramble for Adria": Discourses of Appropriation of the Adriatic Space Before and After World War I', *Austrian History Yearbook* 42 (2011): 16-32.
17 Fabio Capano, 'From a Cosmopolitan to a Fascist Land: Adriatic Irredentism in Motion', *Nationalities Papers* 46 (2018): 979-80.
18 The London Treaty was the secret treaty signed by Italy and the Entente by which Italy entered the war. Assuming the victory against Central Powers, the Entente promised Italy parts of Tyrol, northern Dalmatia, the entire Austrian Littoral (without the port of Rijeka and island of Krk), Dodecanese Islands, parts of Carniola, protectorate over Albania and a part of the Ottoman Empire in the event of its partition.

19 See Luciano Monzali, 'Attilio Tamaro, la questione adriatica e la politica estera italiana (1920–1922)', in *Attilio Tamaro e Fabio Cusin nella storiografia Triestina. Atti del convegno nel ricordo di Arduino Agnelli*, ed. Silvano Cavazza and Giuseppe Trebbi (Trieste: Deputazione di storia patria per la Venezia Giulia, 2007), 117–41.
20 Historico-Diplomatic Archives of the Ministry of Foreign Affairs, Rome (hereafter ASDMAE), Affari politici 1919–1930, b. (box) 786, Promemoria sulla situazione balcanica, 5 November 1921, 13–14.
21 Ibid.
22 Marco Bresciani, 'Conservative and radical dynamics of Italian Fascism: an East (European) perspective (1918–1938)', in *Conservatives and Right Radicals in Interwar Europe*, ed. Marco Bresciani (London and New York: Routledge, 2020), 84.
23 Dinko Puc and Slavko Fornazarič, *Naša Alzacija-Lorena* (Ljubljana: Pisarna za zasedeno ozemlje, 1920).
24 Ferdo Seidl, *Kod naj se potegne pravična državna meja med Jugoslavijo in Italijo?* (Ljubljana: Odsek za zasedeno ozemlje, 1919).
25 Dušan Nećak, 'Pisarna za zasedeno ozemlje', *Kronika, časopis za slovensko krajevno zgodovino* 20 (1972): 104–5.
26 Orjuna was a paramilitary organization defending Yugoslav unity linked to Pribičević's Democratic Party. It enjoyed strong backing in Slovenia where it had a record of relentless suppression of political opponents that was akin to the fascist use of violence. See Stevo Đurašković, 'Ideologija Organizacije jugoslovanskih nacionalista (Orjuna)', *Časopis za suvremeno povijest* 43 (2011): 225–47.
27 For the protest in Ljubljana, see 'Protesti proti nasilju v Santi Margheriti', *Jutro* (16 November 1920): 1; for the protest in Belgrade: 'Nezadovoljstvo u Slovenačkoj', *Pravda* (16 November 1920): 1.
28 'Krvave rapalske manifestacije v Ljubljani', *Jutro* (13 November 1928): 2.
29 Janez Stergar, *Sedem desetletij ljubljanskega Inštituta za narodnostna vprašanja* (Ljubljana: Inštitut za narodnostna vprašanja, 1995), 9.
30 'Kriza Jugoslovanske matice v Mariboru', *Jutro* (13 November 1928): 3.
31 See Piero Purini, 'Le metamorfosi etniche di Trieste nel periodo 1914–1919', *Annales, series historia et sociologia* 12 (2002): 349–50; Albert Rejec, 'Odgovori na vprašalnico', in *Domovina, kje si? Zbornik ob stoletnici rojstva Alberta Rejca*, ed. Branko Marušič (Gorica: Goriška Mohorjeva družba, 1998), 37.
32 Purini, 'Le metamorfosi etniche di Trieste', 349–50.
33 Maura Hametz, 'Quotidian Intimidation and Mussolini's Special Tribunal in Istria and the Eastern Borderlands', *Acta Histriae* 26 (2018): 1125–43; Vovko, 'Organizacije jugoslovanskih emigrantov', 451.
34 Kalc, 'L'emigrazione slovena e croata', 28; Piero Purini, 'Raznarodovanje slovenske manjšine v Trstu. Problematika ugotavljanja števila neitalijanskih izseljencev iz Julijske krajine po prvi svetovni vojni', *Prispevki za novejšo zgodovino* 38 (1998): 39–40.
35 See Lavo Čermelj, *Life-and-death Struggle of a National Minority: the Jugoslavs in Italy* (Association for the League of Nations: Ljubljana, 1936). Slovene translation in *Slovenci in Hrvatje pod Italijo* (Ljubljana: Slovenska matica, 1965), 186.
36 Purini, 'Le metamorfosi etniche di Trieste', 40; Kalc, 'L'emigrazione slovena e croata', 28–9.
37 Rolf Wörsdörfer, *Krisenherd Adria, 1915–1955. Konstruktion und Artikulation des Nationalen im italienisch-jugoslawischen Grenzraum* (Ferdinand Schöningh: Paderborn, 2004), 283.
38 Lavo Čermelj, *Med prvim in drugim tržaškim procesom* (Ljubljana: Slovenska matica, 1972), 39.

39　Vladimir Bartol, 'Nekaj opažanj o zgodovinskem čutu in tipologiji dobe', in *Zakrinkani trubadur: izbrani članki in eseji*, ed. Drago Bajt (Ljubljana: Slovenska matica, 1993), 308.
40　Bartol, 'Nekaj opažanj o zgodovinskem čutu', 312; Ivo Brnčić, *Generacija pred zaprtimi vrati: izbor esejev in kritik* (Ljubljana: Cankarjeva založba, 1954), 12; Vekoslav Španger, *Bazoviški spomenik: pričevanje* (Koper: Društvo za negovanje rodoljubnih tradicij TIGR Primorske, 2014), 29.
41　Brnčić, *Generacija pred zaprtimi vrati*, 14.
42　Kalc, 'Ľemigrazione slovena e croata', 39; Andrej Vovko, 'Delovanje Zveze jugoslovanskih izseljencev iz Julijske krajine v letih 1933–1940', *Zgodovinski časopis* 33 (1979): 96–7.
43　Wörsdörfer, *Krisenherd Adria*, 288.
44　'Potegnimo ostro črto med zvestobo in nezvestobo', *Istra* (13 February 1932): 6.
45　As opposed to applicants of other nationalities, people of "Serbo-Croat-Slovene" origin were not obliged to spend ten years in Yugoslavia before applying for citizenship. See article 12 of the Citizenship law of the Kingdom of Serbs, Croats and Slovenes: 'Zakon o državljanstvu kraljevine Srbov, Hrvatov in Slovencev', *Uradni list mariborske in ljubljanske oblasti* (19 November 1928): 741.
46　Provincial Archives in Nova Gorica (hereafter PANG), f. 1133 Engelbert Besednjak, b. 19, Letter of *Primorsko akademsko starešinstvo* (Primorje academic seniority) to the Minister of Interior Anton Korošec, 8 May 1936.
47　Lado Božič, 'V kolikšnih težavah je nastala organizacija Orjem', *Primorski dnevnik* (15 July 1976): 4.
48　Vovko, 'Organizacije jugoslovanskih emigrantov', 453.
49　Lado Božič, 'Imeti smo hoteli sicer politično, a nestrankarsko organizacijo', *Primorski dnevnik* (16 July 1976): 4.
50　Christian Axboe Nielsen, 'Policing Yugoslavism. Surveillance, Denunciations and Ideology during King Aleksandar's dictatorship, 1929–1934', *East European Politics and Societies* 23 (2009): 35.
51　Milica Kacin Wohinz, 'Prvi tržaški proces', in *Primorski upor fašizmu: 1920–1941*, ed. Milica Kacin Wohinz and Marta Verginella (Ljubljana: Slovenska matica, 2008), 169–74.
52　J. Goričar, *Bazovica: 6. IX. 1930: odmevi tržaškega procesa v inozemskem časopisju* (Maribor: H. Sax, 1931).
53　ASDMAE, Affari politici 1931–1945, Jugoslavia, b. 1, Situazione della Jugoslavia nell'anno 1930, 11.
54　ASDMAE, Affari politici 1931–1945, Jugoslavia, b. 14, fascicolo Egilberto Besednjak, On. Besednjak = notizie, 20 February 1931.
55　Rejec, 'Desetletno delovanje primorske emigracije', 252; Massimo Bucarelli, *Mussolini e la Jugoslavia, 1922–1939* (Bari: Edizioni B. A. Graphis, 2006), 174–9.
56　ASDMAE, Affari politici 1931–1945, Jugoslavia, b. 10, Movimento irredentista giuliano, 30 January 1931.
57　John Paul Newman, *Yugoslavia in the Shadow of War. Veterans and the Limits of State Building* (Cambridge: Cambridge University Press, 2015), 216–18.
58　For the Sokol movement in interwar Yugoslavia, see Pieter Troch, 'Interwar Yugoslav State-Building and the Changing Social Position of the Sokol Gymnastics Movement', *European Review of History: Revue européenne d'histoire* 26 (2019): 60–83.
59　For the Adriatic Guard and its relation to Yugoslav politics, see Igor Tchoukarine, 'The Contested Adriatic Sea: The Adriatic Guard and Identity Politics in Interwar Yugoslavia', *Austrian History Yearbook* 42 (2011): 33–51.

60 ASDMAE, Affari politici, 1931–1945, Jugoslavia, b. 38, Manifestazioni irredentistiche per ricorrenza trattato Rapallo, 25 November 1933.
61 ASDMAE, Affari politici 1931–1945, Jugoslavia, b. 38, Manifestazione contro Rapallo del 12 Novembre. Mio colloquio con Jevtich, 4 December 1933.
62 Kalc, 'L'emigrazione slovena e croata', 41.
63 'Emigracija u novoj situaciji', *Jadranski koledar* (1937): 17–19.
64 'Govor Dra Ivana Marije Čoka na zboru u Beogradu', *Istra* (9 June 1933): 2.
65 PANG, f. 1133 Engelbert Besednjak, b. 17, 'Avdijenca na Dedinju dne 3. oktobra 1934' (Audience of Engelbert Besednjak with the King Aleksandar).
66 Lado Božič, 'Trenja v ljubljanskem "Taboru" so odraz podobnih razmer drugod', *Primorski dnevnik* (14 July 1976): 4.
67 Vovko, 'Delovanje Zveze jugoslovanskih izseljencev', 96.
68 Bucarelli, *Mussolini e Jugoslavia*, 326; Teodoro Sala, 'Priprave na sporazum Ciano-Stojadinović. Vpliv na Julijsko krajino', *Prispevki za novejšo zgodovino* 40 (2000): 136.
69 'Jugoslavija in Italija', *Slovenski list* (5 February 1937): 1.
70 ASDMAE, Affari politici 1931–1945, Jugoslavia, b. 80, Sezione di organizzazione e di propaganda della Lega delle associazioni jugoslave fra fuoriusciti in Jugoslavia, 'L'attività nazionale difensiva e l'attività per la liberazione dei fratelli in schiavitù sono una questione d'onore per tutti i jugoslavi!', Lubiana, ottobre 1935.
71 Kalc, 'L'emigrazione slovena e croata', 42; Sala, 'Priprave na sporazum Ciano-Stojadinović', 139.
72 Milan Stojadinović, *Ni rat ni pakt. Jugoslavija između dva rata* (Buenos Aires: El Economista, 1961), 461.
73 ASDMAE, Affari politici 1931–1945, Jugoslavia, b. 80, Fuoriuscitismo in Jugoslavia, 26 November 1936.
74 Gorazd Bajc, *Zapletena razmerja: Ivan Marija Čok v mreži primorske usode* (Koper: Društvo TIGR Primorske, 2000), 98–110.
75 'Talijanski antifašizam i Julijska krajina', *Istra* (13 April 1934): 5.
76 PANG, f. 1133, b. 5, Letter of Ivan Marija Čok to Engelbert Besednjak regarding the request of Viktor Kjuder to publish articles concerning the Julian March in the newspaper Novi list, Belgrade, 25 November 1933; 'Pozdrav predsednika emigrantskih udruženj iz Julijske krajine v Jugoslaviji bratom v Južni Ameriki', *Novi list* (6 January 1934): 1.
77 Cf. Francesco Ragazzi, *Governing Diasporas in International Relations. The Transnational Politics of Croatia and Former Yugoslavia* (London and New York: Routledge, 2017), 13.
78 Cf. Myra Waterbury, *Between State and Nation. Diaspora Politics and Kin-State Nationalism in Hungary* (Basingstoke: Palgrave Macmillan, 2010), 32.

Ukrainian emigration in the Weimar Republic and its role in German foreign policy

Veronika Weisheimer

At the beginning of the 1920s, hundreds of thousands of Eastern European refugees and political emigrants arrived in the major cities of Western and Central Europe. The dramatic events of the First World War, the resulting collapse of empires and civil war[1] and the new European order forced the old aristocratic and new democratic elites to flee and search for safety in exile. The newly emerged Ukrainian political elite, who had established a sovereign Ukrainian state between 1917 and 1920, shared this fate. Berlin became one of the most important exile centres, where the Ukrainian exile community came into contact with the Weimar Republic political establishment. After its defeat in 1918, Germany lost its position as a major European power and tried to regain this status despite the restrictions mandated in the Treaty of Versailles. Eastern Europe remained a region of geopolitical and strategic importance, even if it could not be compared with its previous form, having undergone widespread changes in its political regimes, borders and power constellations. The émigrés, stuck in between the new reality of life in exile and the longing to return to active politics, were welcomed to participate in both official and clandestine German endeavours in Eastern Europe. This chapter aims to investigate the networks operating between German political circles and Ukrainian exiles as well as the self-identification process of the Ukrainian diaspora during the Weimar Republic.

From revolution to exile

The starting point of the discussion is March 1917, when mass demonstrations led to the abdication of Tsar Nicholas II which triggered the revolution in Russia. Eastern Europe, which was already a battlefield during the First World War, now suddenly became a stage for a civil war taking place across the territory of the former Russian Empire. After the collapse of the Austro-Hungarian Empire in November 1918, much of Central and Eastern Europe devolved into armed conflicts between smaller nation states which proclaimed their independence. For millions of people living in this part of Europe, hostilities only ended at the beginning of the 1920s, meaning that their wartime experience lasted over seven years. The variety of players involved, the fluid change of front lines and rapid border changes turned the whole process into a complicated quagmire. Besides the *Red* Bolsheviks and the *White* Romanov loyalists fighting for power in Saint Petersburg, there was a multitude of smaller national political groups as well as foreign interventionists.

The Russian Revolution also had ramifications for the territory of Ukraine, or, more precisely, the region where Ukrainians constituted the majority of the local population. Between 1917 and 1920, the Ukrainian political elite established and tried to maintain a sovereign Ukrainian state with its capital in Kyiv. The Ukrainian National Republic was established in March 1917, and marked by its socialist political platform and legislation, it constituted a nationally minded, patriotic political entity. It was interrupted by the proclamation of the Ukrainian state (April till December 1918), an authoritarian regime led by the Ukrainian aristocrat and former tsarist General Pavlo Skoropadskyi (1873–1945) under the military auspices of the Central Powers (see Figure 5.1). Furthermore, the Western Ukrainian National Republic was founded in November 1918, but it was quickly forced to merge with the Ukrainian National Republic in January 1919 due to setbacks in fighting the conflict against Poland. The existence of a Ukrainian state was constantly being challenged as there were many players interested in gaining control of Ukrainian territory. So, the government in Kyiv had to fight both foreign and domestic enemies and consistently lost control over different parts of the country. In order to maintain its

Figure 5.1 Pavlo Skoropadskyi with his officers and members of the Ukrainian government, Kyiv, spring 1918. Soon after the proclamation of the Ukrainian state, pictures like these started featuring in the German press to illustrate the close ties between the two countries. © N/A Public domain.

regime, the Ukrainian government was forced to search for cooperation and support from international partners. After the formation of a Polish–Ukrainian alliance in April 1920, the hostilities between Poland and Bolshevik Russia took a new turn. Ultimately, this step signified the end of Ukrainian statehood: by the end of 1920 the Ukrainian authorities had lost power entirely. The Ukrainian delegation was not allowed to take part in the negotiations which led to the Treaty of Riga and the new Soviet-Polish border. In March 1921, Ukraine was ultimately divided between Poland and Bolshevik Russia, with small parts of its territory going to Romania and Czechoslovakia.

The Ukrainian political elite aimed to maintain Ukraine as a sovereign and independent state but were aware that this was near insurmountable task that would be impossible to achieve without international recognition and support. The Entente Powers tended to support the restoration of monarchist Russia with its imperial borders and were therefore not interested in self-proclaimed nation states in the borderlands. Germany and Austro-Hungary took the opposite position and supported the so-called *Randstaaten* (peripheral states) along the Eastern front. The Central Powers sought to both destabilize the Russian Empire from the inside and to expand their influence across a wider swath of Central European territory. For this reason, they supported the national aspirations of ethnic minorities, which were hitherto suppressed in Russia. German–Ukrainian cooperation began with the Treaty of Brest-Litovsk on 9 February 1918 (not to be confused with the similarly named treaty with Bolshevik Russia signed 3 March 1918) and was the first international recognition of Ukrainian statehood. However, the Ukrainian Republic did not supply Germany and Austria-Hungary with food and commodities as defined in the treaty. Their cooperation culminated in a coup on 29 April 1918 with the proclamation of a Ukrainian state ruled by *Hetman*[2] Pavlo Skoropadskyi. On 14 December 1918, closely after the end of the First World War and with the withdrawal of the German army from Ukraine, Skoropadskyi was forced to abdicate and the previous republic was re-established. As the Central Powers withdrew from the territories they occupied in Eastern Europe, Ukraine lost its main international support. The attempts by the new Ukrainian government to establish contacts with the Allied powers failed to bring any results, largely because they did not recognize Ukraine's claim to national sovereignty. This is in stark contrast with their recognition of the successor states of the Habsburg Empire, for example, Poland or Czechoslovakia. This differentiation was probably due to more stable and reliable governments in these new nation states and their unwillingness to cooperate with the Central Powers.

The failure to establish an independent Ukrainian state, and their subsequent persecution under the Bolshevik regime, forced Ukrainian political, military and intellectual elites to flee to Western and Central Europe. By doing so, they joined the enormous wave of Eastern European migrants who largely emanated from the former Russian Empire. Similar to the huge groups of *White* refugees, which also predominantly consisted of members of the Russian aristocracy, the Ukrainians also realized the necessity of establishing a national political exile. Compared to the enormous Russian émigré movement,[3] the wave of Ukrainian political emigration was relatively small: only about 100,000 Ukrainians moved to the various European countries, while the majority were Ukrainian soldiers interned in Poland, Romania and Czechoslovakia.[4]

During the 1920s, three main centres of Ukrainian political exile formed in Central European capitals: Berlin (conservatives and later nationalists), Prague (intellectuals, students and demobilized soldiers) and Warsaw (former military and political figures from the Ukrainian National Republic). However, Central Europe was not a traditional destination for Ukrainian migration. Previous migration movements, such as that of Ukrainian peasants in the late nineteenth century, were often oriented towards more remote destinations, such as the United States, Canada or the Russian Far East.[5] Among Ukrainian citizens who had previously lived in the Austro-Hungarian Empire there was some familiarity with Central Europe, but to those who had previously lived under Russian rule this was an entirely new experience.

However, the level of influence this exile group had upon the other Ukrainian emigrants and their interaction with local politicians and state institutions was of exceeding importance than the actual number of Ukrainian emigrants in each city. The elites from each Ukrainian state managed to escape from Ukraine and were able to create new political centres in exile. The government-in-exile of the Ukrainian National Republic was based in Paris until its leader, Symon Petliura, was assassinated in 1926, whereupon it moved to Warsaw. The Western Ukrainian government-in-exile was located in Vienna till its dissolution in 1923. Pavlo Skoropadskyi maintained his political activities from Berlin and positioned himself as an exile leader, even though he had abdicated and had no claim to represent a government-in-exile. Due to this, each host country was predominated by a different political movement. This meant that the Ukrainian émigré spheres of influence were also divided geographically. There were some smaller Ukrainian émigré groups in other countries too; however, their influence was either negligible, they lost political influence during the early years in exile or they functioned as satellites of more important groups.

Constructing Ukrainian identity

The short period of fighting for national independence between March 1917 and November 1920, as well as the proclamation of the Ukrainian state, had important symbolic meaning for the development of Ukrainian political life and national self-identification. For the first time in its history, the necessity of a modern Ukrainian nation state was articulated. Moreover, this was the first attempt to unite the Ukrainian population, which was hitherto divided between Russian, Polish and Habsburg influence for several centuries. The eruption of Ukrainian political activity in 1917 was rushed and complex: within a short timeframe, a wide variety of political parties, movements and leaders had emerged. Some of them had historical roots in the cultural and political activity of the Ukrainian intellectual elite in Russia and Austria-Hungary during the second half of the nineteenth century. Most of the political groups were, however, represented by revolutionary new-borns.

After the civil war ended in 1921, Ukraine continued to exist in many forms: as Soviet Ukraine, which joined the Soviet Union on 30 December 1922, as a part of Poland, Czechoslovakia and Romania and finally Ukraine as a utopian conception in the minds of the political exiles. So, the starting point for most of the émigré's thinking about the homeland was the short phase of Ukrainian sovereignty and statehood. Political independence was considered to be the ultimate achievement for the exiled political elites who continued to pursue it despite the impossibility of the task, so the desire to manifest this non-existing homeland endured. Instead, it lived on in the form of political parties in exile and in the parallel societies of the Ukrainian diaspora, which maintained a strong nation-building character.[6] The variety of political platforms present in the different exilic communities led to conflicts between the emigrants and further complicated the relationships with the authorities in the host nations, as each political group considered itself to be the most influential representative of the Ukrainian movement. However, there was one common feature shared by all political groups possessed at the beginning of their existence in exile. It was the desire to restore an independent state at the first possible opportunity, even though many factors made it impossible to realize.

In the 1920s, when the Eastern European political landscape stabilized, the temporary nature of life in exile became permanent. This also affected the political mission of the different émigré groups, inasmuch as politicians could no longer return to Ukrainian territory. Their goal of restoring a Ukrainian state had to be postponed and turned from a concrete political aspiration to something that solely manifested itself as a long-term desire. As time went by and the power constellations in the region crystallized, mainly between the Soviet Union and Poland, the Ukrainian émigrés could not expect open support for their independence projects. Nevertheless, they managed to continue their political activity in restricted form, did not dissolve their diaspora organizations and did not relinquish their aspirations. The Ukrainian émigrés during the interwar period created their own communities, which made significant contribution to the development of Ukrainian studies, academia, political thought and the nation-building process. Especially important in this regard are the contributions made by historians, cultural scientists and intellectuals, who continued their work at Ukrainian free universities-in-exile in Prague, Warsaw and Berlin. There were several Ukrainian institutions of higher learning in Czechoslovakia (for cultural, technical and economic studies). The most important one was the Ukrainian Free University in Prague (established in Vienna in 1921, transferred to Prague in the same year). In 1926, the Ukrainian Scientific Institute in Berlin was established, and in 1930, a Ukrainian Scientific Institute in Warsaw expanded the network.

German views on the émigrés

After the end of the First World War and the signing of the Treaty of Versailles, German foreign policy perspectives became extremely limited. Even though it affected German policy towards Ukraine, the newly established Weimar Republic did not want to lose its influence in the region. Therefore, contact between Ukrainian politicians and German authorities had to go through unofficial channels. Relations continued through the old connections with Skoropadskyi, although he no longer represented Ukraine in an official capacity. Until its closing in 1923, Germany tolerated the embassy of the Ukrainian National Republic in Berlin, even if it could not be officially acknowledged. With the civil war lasting till 1920, the Polish–Bolshevik war between 1919 and 1921, and the defeat of the *White* forces in Ukraine in 1920, new changes to Germany's Eastern European policy were necessary, as Poland and the Bolsheviks proved themselves to be the new key regional players. The general attitude of German political elites and society towards Poland was marked by negativity, disrespect and hostility. The new Polish state, to which some formerly German territory now belonged, was regarded as a *Saisonstaat* (temporary state), and the main goal of the Weimar Republic's Poland policy was to prohibit its successful development, political stability and economic growth.[7] In this regard, Bolshevik Russia was considered to be less dangerous for Germany, and the possibility of international cooperation and added pressure on Poland was taken into consideration. As Germany was afraid of the spread of Bolshevism and was loyal to the *White* movement, it was not regarded as a long-term political partner. The Soviet Union, similar to Weimar Germany, had been abandoned by the major European players and had to seek its own international recognition. The two states surprised the world with the signing of the Treaty of Rapallo on 16 April 1922 during the Genoa Conference, which initiated diplomatic relations and economic cooperation between the two nations. The next decade was marked by German-Soviet friendship, which would subsequently be supplemented with secret military cooperation. For Germany, the establishment of the new Eastern European partnership signified a foreign and domestic political achievement as it helped to improve the economic situation and to stabilize the war reparation payments.[8]

Thus, Ukraine became a factor of German relations with both Poland and the Soviet Union, but attention to the Ukrainian question was primarily paid with regard to the Polish case. Concerning the Ukrainian Soviet Socialistic Republic, it was regarded as an integral part of the Soviet Union. In February 1923, German authorities allowed the Soviet Ukrainian diplomatic mission to seize the property of the embassy of the Ukrainian National Republic in Berlin and to occupy its building.[9] Furthermore, Germany did not intend to use the Ukrainian emigrants to exert pressure on Kyiv or Moscow and avoided public contact with them. The role of the Ukrainian factor in the Polish context was the complete opposite, as Germany tried to use the voices of ethnic minorities to destabilize the domestic situation in Poland. For this endeavour, it supported several non-Polish political organizations, including those representing German and Ukrainian minorities, and provided them with financial assistance. This clandestine influence was intended to affect the political situation in Warsaw as well as in the Polish borderlands, and the participation of the Ukrainian emigrants in Berlin was supposed to be mobilized for this destructive mission.[10]

The Ukrainian emigrants, however, were not used as instruments of the German authorities. Germany passively supported the activities of those Ukrainian politicians lobbying for the restoration of Ukrainian sovereignty. The long-term idea of establishing an independent Ukrainian state as a German partner in Eastern Europe still had priority. For Ukrainian politicians in exile, who could not expect strong, quick and financially reliable support from Ukrainians under Polish and Soviet rule, the possibility of getting recognition, income and support from a powerful international partner was a lucrative option. An important feature of this cooperation was its unofficial character, since Germany did not want to reveal the double-sided nature of its foreign policy in Eastern Europe. Most correspondences between Ukrainian and German actors occurred through personal contacts and friendships. Even if there were several cases of institutional cooperation, they were coordinated through the strong personal connections of the players involved. The emigrants were a useful information channel about the local situation, a method for influencing specific groups of people, and an integral part of a future project for a potential new order in Eastern and Central Europe.

Ukrainian activities in Berlin

Each host country had a different stance towards the Ukrainian diaspora. In Poland and Czechoslovakia, where Ukrainians formed a significant population group in their eastern borderlands, Ukrainians were classified as both citizens and foreigners and therefore the Ukrainian question simultaneously affected domestic and foreign politics. The foreign policy matter in this regard was the attitude towards the Soviet Union, to which a major part of Ukrainian lands belonged. The absence of an autochthon Ukrainian community within Germany made German–Ukrainian relations less complicated. Ukrainian émigrés did not have a *local* group of supporters and could only focus their political activities towards the small diaspora and the Ukrainian population outside Germany.

Starting in 1919, Berlin became a unique place on the map of Ukrainian political emigration. Representatives from every political group either tried to foster their activity here or stayed and settled down. Although everyday life in Germany was not easy, having been shaken by revolution, poverty and hardship, it still seemed bearable for those emigrants whose homeland had been ravaged by war. They hoped to get support from Germany, as it was still a European global player. The first group to appear in Berlin was the political elite from Skoropadskyi's Ukrainian state, which fled after the *Hetman* abdicated on 14 December 1918. Besides Pavlo Skoropadskyi himself, the most important representatives were his adjutants Ivan Poltavets-Ostrianytsia, Hnat Zelenevskyi and Oleksandr Kryha. However, they rejected further cooperation with their former leader. The *Hetman* adjutants founded a Cossack organization in Berlin in 1920 and invited Skoropadskyi to head it, but the former *Hetman* turned down his colleagues' proposition and set his own course.[11] Skoropadskyi benefited from his personal contacts with German politicians who provided personal support for him and his family. After a two-year stay in Switzerland between the summer of 1919 and 1921, Skoropadskyi returned to Berlin and settled down at his villa in Wannsee, where he lived until the end of his life in 1945. Upon his return to Germany, Skoropadskyi was head of a conservative Ukrainian émigré group, whose ideological platform was based on a monarchist concept developed by Viacheslav Lypynskyi, the *Hetman's* ambassador to Vienna in 1918. The only former adjutant who did not give up his political aspirations was Ivan Poltavets-Ostrianytsia, who sought to cooperate with German and Russian far-right groups in Munich. In 1926, he proclaimed himself as the *Hetman* of Ukraine. Nevertheless, he did not find many supporters among the Ukrainian emigrants and was not a factor of significance for German authorities. Other former colleagues of Skoropadskyj refused to pursue their political careers in exile. Hnat Zelenevskyi founded a community of former Ukrainian officers in Berlin, but it was politically insignificant. Oleksandr Kryha (better known under his German name Alexander von Kryha) worked as an inventor, creating the Kryha encryption machine (1926), the main competitor to the Enigma machine. Both broke off contact with Skoropadskyi after 1920.

The second group can roughly be defined as politicians affiliated with the Ukrainian National Republic. The main centre for this group was the Ukrainian embassy in Berlin, which remained active until February 1923 and was considered to be the most successful and stable representation of the Ukrainian government abroad. In the early 1920s, new personalities joined this Ukrainian community. Volodymyr Vynnychenko, one of the leaders of the coup against Skoropadskyi in December 1918, remained in Berlin after his failed attempt to collaborate with the Bolsheviks. After spending some years in Germany working as a writer and remaining politically inactive, he moved to France.[12] Jevhen Petrushevych, the former leader of the Western Ukrainian National Republic, arrived in Berlin in 1923, from his exile in Vienna. Nevertheless, he failed to find any German support and spent the rest of his life in emigration without any significant political success.[13] Andrii Makarenko and Fedir Shvets, political figureheads of the Ukrainian National Republic, also tried to apply for financial assistance from the German government, but did not become long-lasting partners.[14] The third significant group which formed in Berlin in the late 1920s were the Galicia-based nationalists represented by Jevhen Konovalets. Nevertheless, the left-wing politicians did not gain any favour with the German authorities. All in all, it was primarily the right-wing conservative and nationalist groups who were supported by the German authorities, and thus they dominated the Ukrainian scene.

Probably the most important achievement for both the German and Ukrainian side was the foundation of the Ukrainian Scientific Institute at the Friedrich Wilhelm University in Berlin in 1926. The research institute, which was chaired by four cultural studies professors, was officially apolitical and aimed to build a bridge between the Ukrainian and German academic worlds by providing Ukrainian students with access to German academia. Its unofficial aim, however, was to support the anti-Polish activities of Ukrainian students and intellectuals from Western Ukraine and to compete against Prague as the centre of the Ukrainian intellectual exile.[15] The institute was financed by the German Foreign Office and the Prussian Ministry of Culture and Education. It was also responsible for selecting Ukrainian students who were awarded scholarships. For the Ukrainian political scene in Berlin and for fostering Ukrainian contributions to science and culture, it was a notable success. Strong ties here can be traced back to one specific exile group: every professor at the institute was either a member or supporter of the former *Hetman's* conservative movement, and the initiator and the spiritual father of this project was Pavlo Skoropadskyi.[16]

Due to his previous position as Ukraine's national leader, Skoropadskyi had the best chances of becoming the iconic symbol of the Ukrainian diaspora in Berlin. Even if he was not particularly popular among the Ukrainian population at the time of his escape, there were many loyal intellectuals, middle and upper-class businessmen and aristocrats who could provide him with long-lasting support. His noble origin, military career and connections to the aristocracy in Russia, Germany and other European states meant that he was incredibly well-positioned to start a new life in exile. The most influential connections, which were established during the German cooperation with the Ukrainian state of Skoropadskyi in 1918, lasted through the coming decades. Whereas other Ukrainian political refugees had to struggle for attention, Skoropadskyi could often rely on his friendship network to further his private and political aims. His friends and allies were influential politicians of the Weimar Republic who had prominent careers dating back to before the First World War. Wilhelm Groener was one of the German military leaders on the Eastern front during the First World War and the leader of the German occupation of Ukraine in 1918. During the Weimar Republic, he acted as the minister of transport (1920–23) and the minister of defence (1928–31). Werner von Alvensleben served as the representative of the German emperor to Skoropadskyi in 1918. He did not have any official political position in the 1920s, acted though as a sort of grey eminence between the German army, secret service, Foreign Office and the president's office. With both Groener and Alvensleben, Skoropadskyi had strong friendships, established in 1918. Skoropadskyi was personally funded in the form of a generous honorary pension, which was awarded to him monthly starting in 1926 personally by Paul von Hindenburg.[17] However, his conservative émigré organization did not benefit from any state support and was privately financed by Skoropadskyi himself.

From the German perspective, Skoropadskyi was not perceived as a partner for immediate action, but rather seen from a long-term perspective. The German authorities did not want to endanger the established friendship with the Soviet Union, but at the same time had not given up completely on regime change in Moscow. This issue became more pressing after Vladimir Lenin's death in 1924, when the power constellation within the Soviet regime became uncertain. If the Soviet regime were to fall, Skoropadskyi was expected to seize power in Kyiv.[18] His conservative political views met with agreement among the members of German nobility, many of whom had managed to retain high political and military positions in the Weimar Republic. The Germans did not look to re-establish the Russian monarchy (as the *White* Russian elites intended), but did show interest in the restructuring of Eastern Europe on a democratic basis and in gaining prospective partners. Therefore, Skoropadskyi was considered for various possible roles, both as the leader of a sovereign Ukrainian state and within a 're-established' Russian Empire.

Despite the fact that Skoropadskyi represented a Ukraine free of Soviet rule, Moscow did not consider him a grave threat. The power constellation in Moscow also stabilized when Joseph Stalin assumed power and expelled his rivals, and the notion of a new Eastern European order quickly vanished from Western European discussions. Nevertheless, it did not mean backsliding or indifference towards Skoropadskyi, as he was still consulted in questions concerning Ukraine. For emigrants, he played a significant role in building social and institutional connections and was instrumental in holding the Ukrainian diaspora in Berlin together. This made him the most influential person of interwar *Ukrainian* Berlin, whose name was affiliated with a wide network of Ukrainian organizations: the political organizations, the publishing house *Ukrainske Slovo* (The Ukrainian Word), the welfare organization for Ukrainian refugees in Germany, the association of Ukrainian emigrants *Hromada* (Society), the aforementioned scientific institute and even the Ukrainian Orthodox parish (founded in the late 1930s).

The right-wing nationalist movement within the Ukrainian emigration, originating from Western Ukraine and led by Jevhen Konovalets, gained favour with the German Ministry of Defence and was better suited for German ambitions and involvement in mutual actions against Poland. In the early 1920s, Konovalets developed the Ukrainian Military Organization, which consisted mostly of Ukrainian soldiers who had been interned in Poland and Czechoslovakia after the end of the civil war. During the 1920s, its members participated in special German armed forces training courses in Munich.[19] In 1929, nationalist elements proclaimed the Organization of Ukrainian Nationalists (OUN), which later became the most powerful force in Ukrainian exile. As the leader of the right-wing movement, Jevhen Konovalets could also gain support for his terrorist actions in Poland.[20] At the civic level, Germany offered clandestine financial support to the Ukrainian National Democratic Alliance, a party representing the Ukrainian minority in the Polish parliament. In this regard, the role of facilitator was played by Jevhen Petrushevych, the former dictator of the Western Ukrainian National Republic who lived in exile in Berlin. Nevertheless, it was the only German political action in which he was involved.[21]

Tension between Ukrainian and Russian diasporas

Even though the Ukrainian diaspora became an integral part of multi-ethnic and multicultural interwar Berlin, it did not develop any significant political cooperation with other national groups. It was often linked to the much larger Russian emigration, or even erroneously considered to be part of it, which led to much irritation among Ukrainians. Ukrainian emigrants expressly distanced themselves from the Russian movement, and articulating the difference between the Ukrainian and the Russian nations became a constant part of the emigrants' rhetoric, political discourse and cultural studies research. This tension, which arose from the Ukrainian population's experience under the Russian rule, as well as from the emancipatory character of the civil war, was transferred into exile. Adding to this tension was the fact that *White* Russian groups also did not recognize Ukrainian sovereign aspirations and simply considered the territory part of *Great Russia*.

Even if political cooperation between exile groups came to nought, the private connections between Russian and Ukrainian families, former colleagues and friends still existed. Due to their entangled background, interaction between these groups never completely ceased. Both Ukrainian and Russian emigrants were stateless persons who possessed the so-called Nansen passports, and even though their lack of status as 'Ukrainian refugees' was an additional cause of frustration, the two groups shared the same legal limitations.[22] As a result, their daily lives inevitably overlapped. They both interacted as congregants of the Russian Orthodox parish in Berlin, as far as a Ukrainian parish was founded only shortly before the Second World War. Many aristocratic families maintained their connections during their emigration despite conflicting political views, and they were members of both Russian and Ukrainian cultural clubs and welfare organizations.

For some emigrants who previously identified as subjects of the Russian Empire, life in exile meant making a decision of consequence, whether one identified themselves with the Ukrainian or Russian diaspora and, by proxy, the Ukrainian or Russian state. Some attempted to use their ethnic and social background to interconnect these two diasporas, while others identified themselves not by ethnicity or origin, but through their participation in political life during the civil war and its aftermath. Pavlo Skoropadskyi is a striking example of this: born as a successor to a Ukrainian aristocratic family, socialized as a Russian general, advanced to the head of an independent Ukrainian state and finally emigrated as a part of the Ukrainian exile movement. In emigration, Skoropadskyi's stance towards Ukrainian independence fluctuated: in the early 1920s he promoted the *Great Trinity* concept, which called for the Ukrainian, Russian and Belarussian nations to build a democratic confederation in Eastern Europe, whereas in the 1930s he became an advocate for an independent Ukrainian state and retracted his old views. Skoropadskyi fostered only private friendships with Russian emigrants; the notion of common political action with the *White* general Pyotr Wrangel, which circulated in 1920 and awoke great interest in Britain, was fruitless. In 1919 and 1920, Skoropadskyi, who lived at that time in Switzerland, negotiated with the British Foreign Office about a possible common action in Southern Ukraine. The British Army intended to support the *Whites* in the Russian civil war. The idea was to create a joint action between Skoropadskyi and general Pyotr Wrangel. Nevertheless, this idea failed, as far as the White forces suffered huge losses in 1920 and retreated.[23] Skoropadskyi's wife, born Aleksandra Durnovo, herself a Russian aristocrat, shared the Ukrainian-oriented views of her husband, but at the same time maintained strong relationships with her relatives and friends in the *White* Russian diaspora. Another individual with a Russian-Ukrainian background was Vladimir Korostovets, a journalist and cultivator of unofficial Ukrainian and Russian emigrant networks, connecting them with German officials as well as British and American businessmen in Berlin. Viacheslav Lypynskyi, a Skoropadskyi movement ideologue, also belonged to the group of self-identified Ukrainians: born as a Polish Catholic nobleman, he had declared himself a Ukrainian patriot even before the First World War.

Legacy for National Socialist Germany

The case of German–Ukrainian relations during the 1920s illustrates the Weimar Republic's ambivalent policy towards Eastern Europe and demonstrates the importance of both official and unofficial political channels. German political influence was limited due to its defeat in the First World War and the predominance of a negative attitude towards its neighbour Poland. The Weimar Republic nonetheless still intended to profit from the regional specifics, from the local ethnic tensions to the unstable political situation. Hence, the exile leaders represented only a fraction of the spectrum of Ukrainian political thought in the interwar period; the variety of political options popularized by the Ukrainian émigrés in Germany had both its advantages and disadvantages. For Ukrainians, the plurality of political movements in exile was evidence of a freedom that could not be achieved at home. On the other hand, this broad spectrum prohibited the Ukrainian diaspora from consolidating into one political block, as various rival political groups fought against each other for influence over the Ukrainian diaspora. This diversity led to further tensions and exacerbated generational conflicts. This fact was also somewhat disadvantageous for the host nation Germany, as there was no single Ukrainian political leader who had authority over the entire Ukrainian community. For better or worse, Germany remained a land of hope for all Ukrainian factions. Poland and the Soviet Union adopted hostile and repressive attitudes towards Ukrainians, and France did not show any interest in the Ukrainian question. Germany, on the other hand, proved to be the only powerful state that appreciated the key Ukrainian position in Eastern Europe, and therefore had a vested interest in supporting the different émigré groups.

The important role of Ukrainian emigrant influence upon German foreign policy can be proven by the fact that the National Socialist regime continued using the established connections and patterns of cooperation, even though their roots extended into the Weimar Republic and even the German Empire. The German foreign policy of the 1930s was marked by hostility towards communism and the Soviet Union and a rapprochement with the authoritarian regime in Poland. Despite these changes, the Ukrainian diaspora maintained its social position and did not suffer any large-scale repressions. During the first years of National Socialist rule, Germany was compelled to conceal its already well-known connections with Ukrainian nationalists, even though both groups had many ideological similarities. At the beginning, the conservative movement of Skoropadskyi and its international network received most of the Germans' attention. In 1930, Skoropadskyi sent his ally Vladimir Korostovec on a mission to London to establish contacts between the Ukrainian émigrés and British government and industry. Between 1932 and 1934 he published *Investigator*, a journal focusing on the Ukrainian question and the Skoropadskyi movement. He also made important contacts within British conservative circles, which were particularly interested for the new regime in Berlin.[24] The Ukrainian Scientific Institute remained an important research centre for Ukrainian topics, and its head Ivan Mirchuk (1933–45) maintained good relations with the National Socialists. The institute was responsible for a large number of academic publications on Ukraine, its history, geography and language. At the same time, it did not become an instrument of German propaganda and conducted research of academic quality till the end of the Second World War.[25] The Ukrainian nationalists received more attention and were given more opportunities in the late 1930s when German policy towards Eastern Europe and particularly towards Poland took a radical turn. The closer the Second World War came, the more the connections intensified. In 1938, the Ukrainian Institution of Trust in the German Reich was founded, and Mykola Sushko, a figure within nationalist circles, became its head under German supervision. The agency's mission was to coordinate state help for Ukrainian emigrants; however, it became an obvious instrument of control over the Ukrainian diaspora in Germany.[26]

Despite the regime change, Germany remained a stable partner for Ukrainian émigrés with permanent interest on the Ukrainian question. This provided for continuous development of the diaspora for over twenty years, till the new generation of Ukrainian DPs, refugees and emigrants replaced them and created their own diaspora after 1945. The Ukrainian emigration of the interwar period made an outstanding contribution to the development of Ukrainian political thought, culture and society, of which the legacy can even be found today. The émigrés sought to create and maintain a Ukrainian self-identity in foreign social environments. Paradoxically, it would become even more complicated to preserve Ukrainian traditions and roots in the homeland, as the Soviet regime and interwar Poland drastically repressed and damaged Ukrainian culture, language and identity. On the other hand, the interwar émigrés articulated and brought the topic of Ukraine to an international discourse, so that the existence of one more European nation would not be forgotten.

Notes

1 The term 'civil war' will be used instead of the traditional formulation 'Russian civil war' as the conflict between 1917 and 1921 was a multi-ethnic and multinational civil war, as Karl Schlögel and other historians have formulated; see Karl Schlögel (ed.), *Russische Emigration in Deutschland 1918 bis 1941. Leben im europäischen Bürgerkrieg* (Berlin: Akademie-Verlag, 1995).
2 Hetman, derived from the German word *Hauptmann*, is a Ukrainian traditional term defining the elected leader of the Zaporozhian Cossacks.
3 In 1920, there were about 500,000 Russian refugees in Germany alone. See Karl Schlögel, 'Berlin: "Stiefmutter unter den russischen Städten"', in *Der große Exodus. Die russische Emigration und ihre Zentren 1917 bis 1941*, ed. Karl Schlögel (Munich: C.H. Beck, 1994), 235–6.
4 Volodymyr Kubijovych, *Encyclopedia of Ukraine*, Vol. 1 (Toronto: University of Toronto Press, 1984), 821. Gregor Prokoptschuk places their number at 150,000 (see Gregor Prokoptschuk, *Ukrainer in München und in der Bundesrepublik*, Vol. 2 (Munich: Verlag Ukraine, 1959), 5). The approximate number of Ukrainian emigrants per country was as follows: 20,000 in Czechoslovakia, 30,000 in Poland, 15,000 in Germany (Frank Golczewski, 'Die ukrainische Emigration', in *Geschichte der Ukraine*, ed. Frank Golczewski (Göttingen: Vandenhoeck & Ruprecht, 1993), 233 and 236; Prokoptschuk, *Ukrainer in München*, Vol. 2, 5). Nevertheless, the political elite was only a small part of the aforementioned groups.
5 Kubijovych, *Encyclopedia of Ukraine*, Vol. 1, 818–21.
6 Frank Golczewski, 'Die ukrainische und die russische Emigration in Deutschland', in *Russische Emigration in Deutschland 1918 bis 1941*, 77 and 81–2.
7 Hans-Christof Kraus, *Versailles und die Folgen* (Berlin: be.bra, 2013), 44–7.
8 Peter Krüger, 'A Rainy Day, April 16, 1922: The Rapallo Treaty and the Cloudy Perspective for German Foreign Policy', in *Genoa, Rapallo, and European Reconstruction in 1922*, ed. Carole Fink, Axel Frohn and Jürgen Heideking

(Cambridge: Cambridge University Press, 1991), 53-7; Werner Benecke, *Die Ostgebiete der Zweiten Polnischen Republik: Staatsmacht und öffentliche Ordnung in einer Minderheitenregion 1918-1939* (Cologne: Böhlau, 1999), 62.

9 Frank Golczewski, *Deutsche und Ukrainer 1914-1939* (Paderborn: Ferdinand Schöningh, 2010), 420.
10 Benecke, *Die Ostgebiete der Zweiten Polnischen Republik*, 62-76.
11 'Z informacijnoho bjuletenia №1 dyplomatychnoho viddilu posolstva UNR v Nimechchyni pro dijalnist posolstva ta ukrainsko-nimecki vidnosyny', 26 October 1920, in *Ukrainski dyplomatychni predstavnytstva v Nimechchyni (1918-1922). Dokumenty i materialy*, ed. Vasyl Danylenko and Nataliia Kryvets (Kyiv: Smoloskyp, 2012), 329.
12 Volodymyr Troshchynskyi, *Mizhvoienna ukrainska emihraciia v Jevropi jak isotrychne i sotsialno-politychne javyshche* (Kyiv: Intel, 1994), 99-121.
13 Golczewski, 'Die ukrainische Emigration', 231-2.
14 Ibid., 232.
15 Political Archive of the German Foreign Office, Berlin (hereafter PAAA), R 35713, E369671-E369672, Correspondence from Herbert von Dirksen (German Foreign Office) to the German ambassador in Prague, 29 April 1926.
16 Carsten Kumke, 'Das Ukrainische Wissenschaftliche Institut in Berlin zwischen Politik und Wissenschaft', *Jahrbücher für Geschichte Osteuropas* 43, no. 2 (1995): 221-9.
17 PAAA, R 30766, K033094, Correspondence from Otto Meissner to Gustav Stresemann, 26 October 1927. The sum of the pension was RM 1000 every month, which was extremely high. For comparison, a university professor could earn about RM 450 in a month.
18 PAAA, R 35713, E369699-E369700, Memorandum of the central office of the Hetman organisations, 1926; PAAA, R 84273, IV Ru 3451, Correspondence from Werner von Alvensleben to Herbert von Dirksen, 4 June 1927.
19 Golczewski, 'Die ukrainische Emigration', 234.
20 Werner Benecke, '"…ein allerdings zur Zeit sehr schwacher Verbündeter Deutschlands". Das Auswärtige Amt und die ukrainische Minderheit in der polnischen Republik 1922-1930', *Zeitschrift für Ostmitteleuropaforschung* 49 (2000): 235.
21 Ibid., 228-34.
22 Nansen passports, introduced in 1922 and named after Fridtjof Nansen, were documents which the League of Nations provided for stateless refugees, predominantly from the former Russian Empire. Since the League of Nations did not recognize the Ukrainian National Republic, Ukrainian refugees were recorded as Russians.
23 PAAA, R 84244, K510031, Correspondence from Wipert von Blücher to Herbert von Dirksen, 15 October 1920; PAAA, R 31505k, E498315-E498319, Anonymous notes (German Foreign Office), 26 October 1920.
24 Volodymyr Potulnyckyi, *Dyplomatiia Pavla Skoropadskoho* (Charkiv: Akta, 2014), 166 and 175.
25 Kumke, 'Das Ukrainische Wissenschaftliche Institut in Berlin', 237-53.
26 Golczewski, *Deutsche und Ukrainer 1914-1939*, 760-71.

6

Protecting the national identity of Russian emigrants and their children in interwar Eastern Europe

Aleksandra Mikulenok

After the 1917 revolution in Russia, there was a mass drift of its citizens out of the country. Initially, the major emigration flow headed west, towards countries that shared a land border with Russia, such as Finland, Estonia, Latvia, Lithuania, Poland and Romania. The Versailles Treaty, as well as the constitutions of these countries, de jure guaranteed the protection of national rights of minorities living on their lands, including the right to education in their native language. However, many of these legislative guarantees were not enforced. Policies pursued by local governments led to a phenomenon known as 'denationalization' (from French 'denationalisation' – the loss or suppression of national characteristics[1]). Children were most susceptible to this process, as the emigrants themselves soon fully realized. The issue was first brought up in the Russian emigrant press in 1921.[2] In April 1923, at the All-emigrant Congress regarding primary and secondary schools, a report was heard announcing a rapid annual growth in the rate of denationalization as well as the need to fight it. It was emphasized that denationalization among pre-schoolers had reached a critical level. Children whose parents valued the language of the host country were most susceptible to it. That was true for France, Germany and Great Britain. However, in Slavic countries, in spite of all the measures undertaken by the host countries aimed at assisting the native language of emigrants, a corruption of the Russian language had taken place because of its morphologic relation to Slavic languages. According to the migrants' view, European countries were conventionally divided into three groups, depending on socio-economic and legal living conditions of emigrants:[3]

(1) Limitrophe countries (from Latin 'limitrophus' – adjacent[4]). Russian minorities in limitrophe countries, such as Estonia, Latvia and Finland, had national minority status that was protected by law, which made it possible for them to seek their rights via the courts.
(2) The second group consisted of Slavic countries, such as Bulgaria, Yugoslavia and Czechoslovakia.

(3) The third group was comprised of France, Germany and Great Britain. Denationalization in these countries was most obvious. The reason lay in a relatively small ratio of Russian-based schools to the number of emigrant children.[5]

The 1924 Bureau of Education Congress, which touched upon the issue of dealing with denationalization, emphasized that its different causes required different ways to fight it.[6] Measures aimed at fighting denationalization were divided into school-based and out-of-school methods. It was accepted that in countries where there were Russian schools, children would be less susceptible to denationalization. In countries where there were no Russian schools, the members of the Congress stressed the need to set up nursery schools (for children from one to seven years old), children's clubs, summer camps, children's parties commemorating remarkable days in the Russian culture, children's assemblies and small libraries.[7] A number of ways to fight denationalization were proposed:

(1) Communicating to the child in their native language. Especially important was the child's ability to speak Russian. Upon selecting a babysitter, priority was to be given to a Russian-speaking candidate.
(2) Singing Russian songs with the child from an early age. Singing classes in a Russian church or conventional choir was considered to be very useful. Among other things, they made the children well organized and nationalized their life.
(3) Daily prayer. It contributed to the fighting against denationalization and acquainted children with Orthodoxy from early ages.
(4) Reading Russian literature regardless of genre.
(5) Paying special attention to studying national history.
(6) Developing a love of art. An emphasis was placed on Russian folk dances.
(7) Acquainting the child with various religious and non-religious holidays, such as Christmas, Easter, Russian Culture Day, Day of the Russian Child and Intransigence Day.[8]
(8) Extracurricular classes in Russian language and literature for refugee children who went to local schools.

The most common cause for denationalization was identified as the lack of specialized preschools and schools. A need for nursery schools for children age four and older was stressed. The reason for that supposedly lay in the fact that most parents spent all day at work. Therefore, children were left to themselves and all their spare time was spent outside among local peers. This, in turn, took away any prospect of receiving an education in Russian-speaking schools due to their lack of knowledge of basic Russian grammar, which was necessary in order to apply for a place in one of them.[9]

Initially, Russian expatriate communities sought to deal with denationalization by opening Russian schools. In later years many of them would close due to a lack of financial support, insufficient teaching staff and because parents opted to send their children to local schools. It was because of these reasons that efforts to halt denationalization focused on offering extracurricular Russian classes for children who went to local schools. This proved fairly effective in dealing with denationalization. However, another issue later came to light – children's fatigue – which led to irregular attendance and a high 'turnover' of pupils. Furthermore, the strictness of these classes led to a gradual aversion to the Russian language and literature and later to anything Russian. Proposals were made to alter the curriculum, making it more game-like and with a focus on self-development. At times the classes consisted of reading assignments of literature with a tutor or one of the parents, following a retelling of the read passage. A big contribution to dealing with denationalization was also made by illustrated periodicals or paintings depicting Russian nature, daily routine or history, as well as periodical magazines for children in the Russian language. Best known among these was the magazine *Murzilka*, which was established in 1924. In Warsaw, the first weekly illustrated magazine named *Sverchok* (a Russian word for 'cricket') for children ages between six and ten was published from June 1933 onwards. The issues consisted of short stories, fairy tales, poems, fables, various illustrations, games, riddles and charades.[10] Many migrants, however, left these magazines unread. To combat 'denationalization', from 1922 onwards the Russian House in Warsaw hosted a number of children's celebrations, such as Nativity plays and so-called Children's Mornings. The celebrations began with a play, followed by poem recitals, singing, dancing and games.[11]

Russian emigrants also tried to use foreign examples to prevent denationalization. For instance, they saw how the Poles, after losing their sovereignty in 1795, had succeeded in keeping their national identity, despite the fact that the country had been partitioned by Russia, Prussia and Austria-Hungary. Poles actively instilled their culture in their children by setting up private schools and extracurricular classes. Another example was that of the Czechs, who saved their cultural traditions and national identity by teaching the Czech language and by distributing Czech magazines and books and also thanks to an operating organization known as 'Falcon',[12] which held annual meetings in Prague since 1862.[13] Yet, for Russian emigrants, it was challenging to maintain their heritage. More often than not, parents preferred to send their children to state schools. For instance, in interwar Poland having a Polish education did not just give an advantage upon entering a university or college; it was a prerequisite to be accepted, since many private schools did not have the right to award graduation certificates, and without one of these it was impossible to apply for a place at university or college. All Russian-speaking schools were private and consequently had to be paid for by parents or caretakers, but only a minority of Russian emigrants could afford them, even though grants and scholarship programmes for gifted children were available. Since the language of studies in primary and secondary state schools was Polish, many emigrant parents were worried about the growing denationalization of their children.[14] They were unsatisfied with the insufficient number of Russian-language classes taught at local schools. For instance, in Lwów, a city in the southeast of interwar Poland (today Lviv in Ukraine), Russian-language classes were available in neither state nor private gymnasia. In Prague's secondary schools, the number of academic hours for the Russian language was the same as for Latin – thirty. It was for this reason that parents appealed to the Benefit Union seeking help in organizing extracurricular classes for children ages six to nine. Apart from that, an alternative way of dealing with progressing denationalization was put forward – exclusively sending children to Russian seminaries (student residences), where the Russian language, history, geography and literature were taught in addition to the regular Polish curriculum.[15] Despite difficult material and legal position emigrants tried to help each other, establishing a system of charity for children was based on the Imperial charity system, but which had been done away with in the newly established Soviet Union.[16] One of these organizations, the Russian Emigrant Children Aid Committee, started to operate in Poland in April 1923 and was founded with the aim of satisfying the needs of internee children and emigrants. It was responsible for providing financial and first aid, as well as providing nutrition and clothing for the children. Besides that, it hosted concerts, games and poetic nights for them in the winter, and organized so-called children's playgrounds in the summer. They were fairly effective for pre-schoolers and schoolchildren, which was why the events took place annually and exclusively with Russian-speaking staff.[17] It was pointed out that by the end of the summer, children could understand Russian speech and speak the language.

In East European countries (Estonia, Finland, Latvia, Lithuania), the Russian-speaking population was assisted by two types of organizations in the 1920s and 1930s: those established by newly arrived emigrants and those set up by members of established national minorities.[18] For example, in Poland these were the Russian Stewardship Committee for Emigrants in Poland, the Committee for Aid to Children of Russian Emigrants, the Union of Russian Students-Emigrants in Poland, the Union of War Disabled People, the Society of Emigrant Lawyers, as well as the organization of the Russian national projects: the Russian Charitable Society, the Orthodox Metropolitan Charitable Society and various charitable societies in different cities of Poland. In Latvia it was the Aid Committee, and the International Union for Aid to Children. In Estonia it was the 'Drop of Milk' society, and the Committee of Russian emigrants in Estonia. The main purposes of their activity were providing material and legal assistance to Russian emigrants, finding jobs, organizing educational institutions and so on. These were specifically engaged in the issue of helping the younger generation, including helping them in the completion of their education. For example, in Poland, this was handled by the Committee for Aid to Children, which was created in April 1923 at the Russian House in Warsaw and was at the Russian Board of Trustees for Emigrants but was independent in terms of interacting with all institutions and organizations.[19] The main purpose of the organization was to provide assistance to children in need from families of Russian officers and soldiers interned in prisoner of war camps. With the liquidation of the camps after the end of the First World War, their activities extended to the children of all Russian emigrants.

To achieve the main goal of the committee (to provide comprehensive assistance to the children of Russian emigrants), Polish authorities allowed them to acquire the necessary funds and property for this purpose. The affairs of the committee were managed by the General Meeting of the members of the committee and the board elected by it, and the accounts were checked by the Audit Commission. The organization received funding, not from the Polish state but from membership fees, income from property, organized evenings, concerts, lectures, voluntary donations and sums received from other public and charitable organizations. So, the main income in the 1930-1 academic year came from donations, charitable events and church fees. And in the 1932-3 academic year, 60 per cent of the annual income came from the assistance of other organizations: the International Committee to Help Children, the Nansen International Office for Refugees, the Zemsko City Committee (Zemgor) and the Russian Children's Day Foundation.[20]

The funds were mainly used to provide individual financial assistance to sick and weak children in the form of benefits for enhanced nutrition, distribution of clothes, linen and shoes. To attract additional funds, a search system for 'godparents' was set up for children in need. To this end, so-called 'photo cards' were distributed that featured the neediest children, who had been selected through the use of questionnaires. Such photo cards appeared for the first time in the early 1930s during the trip of the chairman of Zemgor A. I. Konovalov to the United States. The cards had data of the specific children about their lives and needs. Thanks to such cards, 128 children from Estonia, Latvia, Poland and Finland received assistance in the form of payment for their upkeep in a boarding school, stays in summer camps and payment for treatment.[21]

In addition to individual assistance, material aid was also provided to children's institutions. In correspondence with other organizations, it was repeatedly noted that an important task for the committee was the organization of an orphanage in Warsaw, consisting of a nursery, a kindergarten and a shelter. Under its umbrella it was supposed to organize a boarding school for children from other areas who studied at primary schools and the Russian gymnasium in Warsaw. By creating a Russian-language space for socialization in a nursery-school gymnasium, the organization thereby tried to preserve a nationally determined living environment for children. For example, it was noted that 'the absence of a kindergarten entails the denationalization of children who have to spend all their time on the street and among children who speak Polish, deprives parents of the opportunity to send their children to Russian primary schools, since they do not receive the basic knowledge necessary for admission to such a school'.[22] The committee organized and supported an orphanage, transferred money to pay for manuals and textbooks, and partially compensated the education of low-income students in a Russian primary school in Warsaw. Particularly important, given the shortage of books in Russian, was the opening and maintenance of a children's library, which initially numbered about 3,000 books.

Originally, 'playgrounds' were meant for schoolchildren and from 1929 onwards for children of both genders ages four to fourteen.[23] Their purpose was twofold: strengthening the health of children and combating progressive denationalization. The curriculum included gymnastics, marches, active games and singing. In addition, children learned songs and read works of Russian writers.[24] Apart from that, all children had a light breakfast, consisting of cocoa or tea and an open sandwich with butter. The playground was open from 10.00 am until 2.00 pm daily, except for holidays, until the start of the school term in autumn. On hot days, children were allowed to play in water and sunbathe at the local beach. To develop their general knowledge, trips to the zoological gardens and outside the town were arranged. The playgrounds sadly did not have enough space for everybody. Consequently, priority was given to families in need where denationalization was most prominent. The playgrounds had an extremely positive impact, not only because of their general healthy effect on children but also due to the fact that they united them and did not let them forget their native language. It was stressed that children who did not speak any Russian at all, acquired it after attending playgrounds daily during the summer.[25]

Russian Culture Day

To strengthen the ties between their children and their native culture, Russian emigrants also established a number of holidays, most importantly Russian Children's Day and the Russian Culture Day (RCD). Commemorations were to coincide with the birthday of the famed author Alexander Pushkin, as he was seen as the founder of the Russian literary language, but most children did not know who he was, or any of his works. The RCD first took place in 1924 in Estonia. It was initially called Enlightenment Day, and it was established by A. K. Janson, the Russian national secretary at the Public Education Ministry of the Republic of Estonia. The holiday coincided with the 125th anniversary of Pushkin's birth.[26] On this day, a solemn Divine Service took place with a procession of the cross, a festive performance in the theatre, dances in the square and games for children.[27] The event itself was very successful, so in November 1924, at a congress in Prague on the problem of denationalization, a representative of the Pedagogical Bureau in Estonia made a proposal to organize a similar holiday in other countries. In 1925, the holiday was held in thirteen countries (Bulgaria, Belgium, Germany, Latvia, Lithuania, Poland, Turkey, Finland, France, Czechoslovakia, Switzerland, Estonia and Yugoslavia), and since 1926, it became an annual event with a constantly increasing number of participating countries. In addition, it was customary to exchange postcards, specially issued for this day between the committees organizing the holiday in different countries, Russian cultural and educational organizations, and students.

The Pedagogical Bureau in Prague sent out 1,000 appeals for all Russians to organize Russian Culture Day in different countries in 1925. It was also printed in almost every Russian-language newspaper, and significant preparatory work was carried out to organize and hold the holiday.[28] However, there were initially also cases of refusal to conduct the RCD, for example, in the United Kingdom and the United States. But by the early 1930s, the RCD day was observed in almost every country where Russian emigrants resided.[29] The programme consisted of generally observed components, but, depending on the financial capabilities of the event organizers, specific local initiatives could be included too. It was obligatory to hold a collective Divine Service for the well-being of Russia on the RCD and to have a plate or mug collection for the needs of emigrants. This was followed by an entertainment programme, which was opened by the national anthem of the resident country and the national anthem of the Russian Empire and all emigrants: 'If our Lord is glorious in Zion . . .', an opening speech by the organizers, and only after that did the cultural and entertainment events begin. However, as the emigrants themselves noticed, quite often the holiday programme was almost completely duplicated for the following years.

Various one-day newspapers (e.g. *The Day of Russian Enlightenment*, *The Russian Culture Day*, and *The Russian Day*) and brochures with the programme of the holiday were published specially for this day. In Prague, a detailed programme of the holiday was developed with activities of recitation of poetry, singing of romances and dancing, and the day ending with charity lotteries. Entry to the event was usually free, but everyone could make a donation, for which they received a badge.[30] Despite the fact that the RCD, as a rule, was celebrated on the birthday of A. S. Pushkin,[31] it was always timed to coincide with other events too: a memorable date (the anniversary of the death or birthday of the writer – A. S. Pushkin, N. V. Gogol, I. S. Turgenev, N. A. Nekrasov) or dedicated to ancient Russian cities such as Moscow, Novgorod or Pskov. For example, the 'Moscow' report was so popular that it was read about twenty times in different European countries.[32] And, according to M. Raev, 'a real cult of Pushkin has developed in the Russian diaspora'.[33]

Almost immediately since the inauguration of RCD, namely from 1926, there was a tendency to 'stretch out' the holiday. It manifested itself in that the dates varied from 16 May to 24 June, and depended only on the organizers. However, the need to celebrate the RCD at the same time in all countries of residence of emigrants was repeatedly noted. The reasons were that, according to the Organizing Committee of the Russian Culture Day, this would have an additional positive impact on the emigrants and contribute to their greater cohesion. Therefore, the question of the date of the RCD was included in the programme of the Congress of the Pedagogical Bureau on 1–3 July 1928.[34] Nevertheless, despite all the efforts made, the Bureau was not able to achieve unity in the conduct of the RCD. In Germany it was held on 6 June, in Denmark on 8 June, in Danzig in early July, in Belgium in the autumn.[35] In addition, there was no unity within the countries themselves. In Estonia, in the countryside, the holiday was held on the first Sunday of June, according to the decree of one of the Delegate Congresses of the Union, and in Yuryev (Tartu) and Reval it was held in autumn.

In Poland, the RCD in 1930 was held in Vilno on 9 June, in Lwów on 14 June and in Warsaw on 15 June, although the Parisian newspapers wrote that the RCD was held simultaneously. In Belgrade, the RCD was celebrated twice – the first date was timed to coincide with the birthday of Alexander Pushkin, and the second – to the day of the Baptism of Rus in 988. This was due to the fact that, in the opinion of some emigrants, the religious component of the holiday would make a more significant contribution to the fight against denationalization.[36] Postcards with the images of either children or one of the greatest Russian writers were specially published for this day, which were usually exchanged between the committees of the RCD, Russian cultural and educational organizations and students in different countries. For example, in 1934, postcards dedicated to the RCD were published with the image of N. V. Gogol.[37] And since 1927, special postcards with the emblem of the resurrection of Russia were issued by order of the Pedagogical Bureau. The executor of all 'emigrant' postcards was the famous Russian artist Ivan Vilibin.[38]

At the initiative of the Pedagogical Bureau, reports on the celebration of the holiday were drawn up annually; calendars were issued indicating anniversaries, to coordinate the actions of the RCD Committees and experiences were exchanged regarding its organization. Therefore, in order to draw up the most accurate and objective reports, the Pedagogical Bureau asked for programmes, posters, photographs, 'souvenir newspapers' for the RCD, newspaper articles and other sources mentioning it.[39] However, it cannot be said with certainty that these reports were in great demand and were of interest directly to the emigrants themselves. The nature of the celebration also varied, with the programme often having an elite, academic flavour in Western European countries, whereas in Eastern European states with their larger Russian populations, events were often of a more populist nature.

In 1925, the RCD was celebrated twice in Latvia – on 8 June and 20 September. This was due to the fact that in June only one emigrant organization – the Young Emigrant Society – had organized festive events. Therefore on the initiative of the secretary of the RCD Committee in Czechoslovakia – I. N Zavoloko, a second celebration was organized. The largest RCD celebration took place in Riga. Festivities began on the evening of 19 September with a Divine Service in the main émigré church – Ivanovskaya in the Moscow suburb, but there was not enough space for everybody. After the end of the service, leaflets with the RCD programme were handed out at the cemetery gate. The festivities continued the next day with a liturgy in Latvian. The solemn programme began at one o'clock. All tickets were sold out a few days before the event. At the same time, there were five different entertainment venues in Riga which were open until 8.00 pm. A concert performance was organized in the Russian House, which ended at 1.00 am. Interestingly, the repertoire not only consisted of works by generally recognized classics, such as A. S. Pushkin, I. A. Krylov, M. Yu. Lermontov, but also of the Soviet writer Maksim Gorky.[40] In 1930, an exhibition of paintings was timed to coincide with the RCD in Riga, in which, along with famous Russian artists, fifty-three young talents were also selected to participate in the exhibition.[41] In Finland, in 1925, the holiday took place on 7 June and was arranged only in Helsinki, until the outbreak of the Second World War. It was a great success among the Russian-speaking population. The event was designed for 1,500 people, but there were many more guests, as Russians came from all over the area. The festival was opened by the initiator of the organization of the RCD in Finland – Aleksandr Fen (chairman of the special committee for Russian affairs in Finland). The programme of the event itself consisted of a performance by a Russian choir, reports on the importance of Russian culture and the role of A. S. Pushkin in its development, recitation of poetry, performance of folk music and singing of romances and opera arias. There was no admission fee. In addition, all the children present at the celebration received gifts in the form of a box of chocolates with the image of the poet. In the lobby of the hall, a charitable sale of event programmes and postcards with the image of A. S. Pushkin was arranged to support the poet's grandson, who lived in Narva (Estonia) and was in a difficult financial situation.[42]

In Poland, the celebration in 1925 took place in many cities. In Warsaw, the organizers were the Russian Charitable Society in Poland, the Russian Academic Group and the Russian Gymnasium in Warsaw. The celebration began on 8 June with a solemn prayer service. In the Russian House, the 'Children's Morning' was organized for students of Russian schools, with gifts in the form of books and sweets. In the evening, a literary and musical concert was held, which was attended by about 1,000 people. There were many Poles among them. In the opinion of the emigrants themselves, the evening was isolated and boring; the musical numbers were bad, with the exception of some performances. The emigrants thought that the reason for such an unsatisfactory conduct of the RCD in Warsaw was the fact that the organizers were Polish citizens of Russian nationality.[43] However, the Russian Charitable Society did not agree with this opinion, arguing that in May all refugee organizations were informed about the upcoming celebration of the RCD and the need to organize it. But not a single refugee organization took the initiative in this matter; therefore the Russian Charitable Society took on this role. In addition, meetings were regularly held to organize the holiday, but with the exception of some organizations, nobody attended those meetings.[44]

In Lwów, the holiday was more successful than in Warsaw. The ceremonial part consisted of a speech by L. B. Mandelstam on the importance of the RCD and the role of Russian culture in the life of Russia. The festive programme itself consisted of the recitation of works by Russian writers and the performance of musical pieces. After the official part, dances were arranged until the morning. In the south-eastern Polish town of Ostroh, the situation was somewhat different – local authorities expressed dissatisfaction with the organization of the holiday and banned it three days before the event. This was explained by the fact that the local headman did not like the programme of the celebrations. It was originally planned to hold the festivities for two days – 7 and 8 June. On the first day, a children's party was to be organized with concerts, performances and various forms of entertainment. On 8 June the main event would be held, with mass entertainment and a small entrance fee, and the traditional organization of a lace gathering and the sale of the one-day newspaper *Russian Culture*, whose proceeds were to go to a cultural and educational fund. Russian public organizations tried to have the ban lifted: all representatives of the Russian-speaking population in the Sejm and the Senate, the Central Russian Organization in Warsaw were notified, appropriate statements were made in the émigré and Polish press, and protests were sent to the Ministry of Internal Affairs. But despite these efforts, only a prayer service and a collection of cups were allowed to take place. Therefore, the children's holiday was postponed to 14 June, and on 7 and 8 June, Russian feature films were shown in the cinema (in which it was planned to hold a festive concert) at the lowest possible price as a sign of solidarity towards the Russian-speaking population. The collection was held throughout the day, all donors were given badges and rosettes with national colours. At 1.00 pm, a solemn prayer service was held in the Russian House, after which 'tea cups' were organized. However, despite the difficulties in organizing the RCD, the festive hall was overcrowded and could not accommodate everyone. The concert programme consisted of performances by a choir, a symphony orchestra and theatrical performances. It is curious that the refusal of the Ukrainian troupe of A. I. Ulykhanov to perform in the RCD was the reason for its boycott by the Russian, Polish and Jewish public, which led to the dissolution of the troupe.[45]

From 1926 onward, the RCD was celebrated not only in cities but also in the provinces. Nevertheless, in the countryside of Galicia different Ukrainian and Belarusian groups managed to prevent it from taking place, and in 1927 the RCD was held only in Lwów.[46] By 1930, the RCD was celebrated in the Pechersk Territory (in Estonia), where the festivities took on the character of a national celebration. In Lithuania, the RCD was celebrated in many cities, while in Finland the festivities were held only in Helsinki. However, despite the fact that the RCD was an apolitical holiday, it still depended on political events taking place inside the country. In Poland in 1935, the RCD was postponed to the end of October in connection with the mourning for the deceased Marshal Józef Piłsudski.[47] The event was quite successful, following an initiative by the Bureau of Education to host similar ones in other countries, which was published in Russian printed press abroad in 1925. By 1925 the celebration had already taken place in thirteen countries (Bulgaria, Belgium, Germany, Latvia, Lithuania, Poland, Turkey, Finland, France, Czechoslovakia, Switzerland, Estonia and Yugoslavia), and since 1926 it became annual with the number of participant countries constantly growing.[48] On the day the organizing committees from different countries, Russian cultural educational organizations and students were supposed to exchange greeting cards, which were custom designed for the day.[49]

The Day of the Russian Child

The idea of holding the Day of the Russian Child originated in Prague in 1928. It was based on 'White Chamomile Day', which existed in Russia since 1910. In pre-revolutionary times, it was customary to sell chamomile or any other white artificial flowers on this day, and all the money raised went to the needs of children with tuberculosis. 'White Chamomile Day' and 'The Day of the Russian Child' were timed to coincide with the Annunciation – 25 March (7 April according to the new style). However, the main goal of this day had changed for Russian emigration. It was to combat the progressing denationalization, to find funds for the needy and to draw attention to the moral and material situation of children living in emigration. This was why the celebration was settled to commemorate the Annunciation Day in spring. The day was meant to focus on the problems of emigrant children and to start fundraising by means of distributing one-day newspapers, organizing charity lottery and concerts, as well accepting donations in a way of mugs or plates, and so on.[50] There were several ways to raise funds for the needs of children – church plates and cup collections, through subscription lists, through the publication of one-day newspapers, the organization of charity lotteries, performances, children's parties under the motto 'Children to Children' and so on. The success of the Day of the Russian Child contributed to the presence in many countries of temporary and permanent committees of the Day of the Russian Child, coordinating their activities with the Central Committee, which was located in Prague.[51]

Since 1934, an annual magazine dedicated to the Day of the Russian Child has been regularly published. All authors who were asked for assistance in preparing the journal willingly cooperated with the editorial board. All the profits from the sale of the circulation went to the needs of immigrant children. Publishing costs were fully covered by paid advertisements and voluntary donations. The cost of one copy of the magazine, regardless of its volume and number of circulations, remained unchanged at 25 cents.[52] For the most part, the Day of the Russian Child was timed to coincide with the Annunciation; however, in New York and in some other cities of the United States it was celebrated on the third Saturday of October. All funds received from the collections on this day were sent to the Central Fund of the Russian Culture Day, which distributed them among the countries in need.[53]

In many countries, the Day of the Russian Child began with a prayer service in the church and festive speeches. Often parish councils directly initiated the organization of the holiday. As a rule, the theme of the Day of the Russian Child in different countries was similar and depended only on the material resources and desires of the organizers. The programme included dance sketches; these were either ballet scenes or staging of Russian folk dances, declarations of poems and performances of string orchestras. Various productions of 'live pictures' were also very popular, for example, dedicated to the tragic death of the royal family. After the festive programme, various events were organized for adults and children, such as dances, charity lotteries and buffets. The admission fee was usually 3 francs.[54]

Conclusion

To many Russian expatriate organizations, the problem of denationalization among emigrant children in the interwar period was an acute one. According to Russian expatriates, 'the first generation of children did not know either their native language, or culture or history'.[55] However, among the expats, two groups were prominent: people who assimilated in their host country and those who were anxious about growing denationalization. It was the latter who made efforts to fight it by organizing various cultural and educational events aimed at preserving their national identity. Nevertheless, denationalization spread and progressed depending on the environment of the refugees and their financial status. And despite measures to keep their national identity throughout emigration, refugees could not prevent assimilation and, consequently, denationalization.

In addition, there was an acute question about where to get funding to fight denationalization, so they needed comprehensive assistance from the governments of the host countries, but for a number of reasons, this was not always possible. For example, in Yugoslavia, Czechoslovakia, Bulgaria and a number of other countries, this problem was solved mainly by governments, while in Poland, Finland, Latvia, Lithuania and Estonia this was achieved mainly by private organizations. In addition, the difference between states bordering Russia and other European countries was that the former also consisted of an indigenous Russian-speaking population, who had tried to preserve their national identity. However, by the mid-1930s, the scale of denationalization did not decrease, rather it increased: Russian children did not know the language, culture or history of Russia. There are a number of reasons why emigrant communities failed to combat denationalization. Younger generations either remembered practically nothing about their homeland or would only hear about it from their parents and relatives but never visited those places. They only had an abstract idea of Russia, while living in another country with a completely different culture and language. They were Russians, Ukrainians, Belarusians, but at the same time they did not quite understand what it meant to be Russian, Ukrainian or Belarusian. Moreover, they did not always understand the Russian culture and what the Russian spirit was, did not understand what Russian writers were writing about and did not know about national dress and customs, or only vaguely imagined what they were like. In addition, many parents deliberately sent their children to state schools rather than to national ones. This was primarily due to the fact that their children lived in another country with a different language, and in order to obtain higher education or a good job, it was necessary to know the language of the host country, so the process of denationalization was almost impossible to stop. Therefore, even though speaking about denationalization and the methods of dealing with it that were unsuccessful at that time, it is necessary to take into account the realities of this and understand that in some cases denationalization was a conscious choice of parents and children.

Notes

1. D. N. Ushakov (ed.), *Tolkovyy slovar' russkogo yazyka*, 4 vols (Moscow: State Publishing House of Foreign and National Dictionaries, 1935–40). Available online: http://dic.academic.ru/dic.nsf/ushakov (accessed 1 October 2020).
2. *Golos emigranta* (21 July 1921): 8–10.
3. L. I. Petrusheva, 'Rol' jemigrantskih obshhestvennyh organizacij v sohranenii nacional'nyh kul'turnyh tradicij. Den' russkogo rebenka (konec 1920-h — 1930-e gg.)', in *Sotsialno-ekonomicheskaya adaptatsiya rossiyskikh emigrantov (konets XIX-XX v)* (Moscow: IRI Publ., 1999), 141; State Archive of the Russian Federation, Moscow (hereafter GARF), f. 5785, op. 1, d. 30, l. 261–3.
4. Ushakov, *Tolkovyy slovar' russkogo yazyka*.
5. Petrusheva, 'Rol' jemigrantskih obshhestvennyh organizacij', 141–2; GARF. f. 5785, op. 1, d. 28, l.35: The resolution of the first congress about child, 1925.
6. The Bureau of Education Congress was created in 1923 by V. Zenkovsky, V. Svetozarov, P. Dolgorukov and A. Bem. The main aim of this organization was cultural and educational activities, communication with migrants' school in different countries, helping to save Russian culture, language and traditions and also printing books in the Russian language.
7. GARF, f. 5785, op. 1, d. 30, l. 261–3: Information about the aims and tasks of the Bureau of Education.
8. GARF, f. 5785, op. 1, d. 28, l. 35: Resolution of the first congress about children, 1925.
9. GARF, f. 5864, op. 1, d. 14, l. 26: Letter to the metropolitans' charity society, 1926.
10. GARF f. 10243, op. 1, roll (katushka) 27, frame 0335: Documents about Poland (box 7), 1 January 1935.
11. *Za svobodu!* (13 March 1922): 120; GARF, f. 5864. op. 1. d. 5. l. 106 and d. 22, l. 72–3: The report about the International Committee for Helping Children, 1929.
12. 'Falcon' or 'okolstvo'.
13. GARF f. 5785, op. 3, d. 42, l. 1: The article about The Day of the Russian Child in Russian emigrations' newspapers, 20 February 1939.
14. GARF f. 5785, op. 2, d. 69, l. 37: The article about Russian refugees' children in Russian emigrations' newspapers, 8 September 1929.
15. Ibid.; Petrusheva, 'Rol' jemigrantskih obshhestvennyh organizacij', 108.
16. Elizabeth White, *A Modern History of Russian Childhood: From the Late Imperial Period to the Collapse of the Soviet Union* (London: Bloomsbury Academic, 2020), 27–9, 33–8, 41–3, 49, 56.
17. GARF f. 5864, op. 1, d. 14, l. 23–6: The correspondence with different refugees' organizations located in Poland and the United States, 1926.
18. V. A. Obolensky and B. M. Sarach (eds), *Russkiy al'manakh* (Paris: B.M. Sarach, 1931), 438–42.

19 N. A. Kovalevskaya, 'Dejatel'nost' Komiteta pomoshhi detjam russkih jemigrantov v Pol'she (1923–1935 gg.)'. Available online: http://www.rusnauka.com/35_OINBG_2012/Istoria/1_122731.doc.htm (accessed 1 October 2020).
20 GARF f. 5785, op. 2, d. 69, l. 12: Article about Russian refugees' children in Russian emigrations' newspapers, 1929.
21 Z. S. Bocharova, *Russkiy mir 1930–kh godov: ot rastsveta k uvyadaniyu zarubezhnoy Rossii* (Moscow: AIRO-XXI, 2014), 249.
22 Ibid.
23 GARF f. 5785, op. 2, d. 69, l. 12: Article about Russian refugees' children in Russian emigrations' newspapers, 1929.
24 GARF f. 5864, op. 1, d. 14, l. 26 and 57: The correspondence with refugees' organizations located in Poland and the United States, 1926.
25 Ibid., l. 57: The correspondence with different refugees' organizations located in Poland and the United States, 1926.
26 GARF f. 5850, op. 1, d. 39, l. 40: Reports, information, articles about The Russian Culture Day in Poland, 1924; G. A. Kuzina, 'Znachenie "Dnej russkoj kul'tury" v zhizni rossijskoj jemigracii pervoj volny Tekst', in *Kultura Rossiyskogo Zarubezhya*, ed. A. V. Kvakin and E. A. Shulepova (Moscow: Rossiyskiy institut kul'turologii, 1995), 46.
27 S. K. Kudryashova and V. E. Deryuga, 'Nacional'nye prazdniki kak istochnik sohranenija russkoj kul'tury v uslovijah jemigracii', *Innovatsii v nauke* 12, no. 2 (2012). Available online: http://cyberleninka.ru/article/n/natsionalnye-prazdniki-kak-istochnik-sohraneniya-russkoy-kultury-v-usloviyah-emigratsii (accessed 29 December 2021).
28 Kuzina, 'Znachenie "Dnej russkoj kul'tury"', 46–7.
29 N. A. Tsurikov, *Den' russkoy kul'tury: kratkiy otchet o prazdnovanii v 1926 godu* (Prague: Pedagogical Bureau, 1927), 12; GARF, f. 5850, op. 1, d. 37; *Za Svobodu!* (7 July 1925): 147.
30 GARF f. 5850, op. 1, d. 27, l. 40: Reports, information and articles about 'Russian Culture Day' in Lithuania, 6 June 1926.
31 Ibid.
32 GARF f. 5850, op. 1, d. 40: Articles about 'Russian Culture Day' in Estonia, 1928–32.
33 M. Raeff, *Rossiya za rubezhom: Istoriya kul'tury russkoy emigratsii: 1919–1939* (Moscow: 1994), 93.
34 GARF f. 5785, op. 1, d. 20, l. 77: The correspondence with different refugees' organizations about the 'Russian Culture Day', about school-books for Russian schools, and about refugees' children, 5 June 1928.
35 GARF f. 5850, op. 1, d. 26, l. 10: Reports, information and articles about 'Russian Culture Day' in Latvia, 1930.
36 GARF f. 5785, op. 1, d. 20, l. 70: The correspondence with different refugees' organizations about the 'Russian Culture Day', about school-books for Russian schools, and about refugees' children, 25 May 1928.
37 GARF f. 5913, op. 1, d. 40, l. 2 and 23: Copy of Astrov's article about 'Russian Culture Day', 6 June 1930.
38 GARF f. 5850, op. 1, d. 30, l. 145: Reports, information and articles about 'Russian Culture Day' in Poland, 1927.
39 For a RCD example from Latvia, see GARF, f. 5785, op. 1, d. 4., l. 56: Minutes of meetings of the presidium of the Bureau of Education (original documents and copy), 1923–5.
40 Ibid.
41 GARF f. 5785, op. 1, d. 26, l. 87: The League of Nation's bulletin (in French), 1931.

42 L. I. Petrusheva, 'A.L. Boehm i den' russkij kultury: A.L. Bem i gumanitarnye proekty russkogo zarubezh'ya', *Proc. of the International Research Conference. 16-18 November 2006* (Moscow: Russkiy put', 2008), 276-7.
43 *Za Svobodu!* (7 July 1925): 3.
44 GARF f. 5850, op. 1, d. 30, l. 3-7: Reports, information and articles about 'Russian Culture Day' in Poland, 1928-32.
45 Ibid., l. 17 and 48: Reports, information and articles about 'Russian Culture Day' in Poland, 1926.
46 Ibid., l. 124 and 247: Reports, information and articles about 'Russian Culture Day' in Poland, 1927.
47 GARF f. 5913, op. 1, d. 40, l. 40: Copy of Astrov's article about 'Russian Culture Day', 6 June 1930.
48 Ibid.
49 Ibid.
50 Petrusheva, 'Rol' jemigrantskih obshhestvennyh organizacij', 138.
51 GARF f. 5785, op. 3. d. 30, l. 2-5: *The Day of the Russian Child* (May 1938).
52 Ibid.
53 Ibid.
54 GARF f. 5785, op. 1. d. 60, l. 42-101: Journal articles about 'Russian Culture Day' and 'Day of the Russian Child', 1932-3.
55 *Za svobodu!* (11 April 1925): 3.

Part III

People on the move in fascist Europe

7

Stefi Kiesler

A librarian as 'Intellectual Refugee Service'

Jill Meißner-Wolfbeisser

Stefi Kiesler was widely known among the writers who had escaped from Nazi Germany to New York[1]. The wife of the avant-garde artist-architect Frederick Kiesler, Stefi was a librarian, writer, journalist, translator and artist. In the framework of German exile literature she played an important role primarily as a cultural mediator and networker; nevertheless only few people today have heard of her. Building a bridge between homeland and host society, she helped refugees by using her contacts to American publishers, newspapers and universities. But she also tried to alleviate their everyday existential problems: she procured places to sleep with German-speaking people, wrote letters of application or just made sure that friends would get a warm meal on a regular basis. So, who was Stefi Kiesler, the 'intellectual refugee service for German scholars and novelists',[2] as Manfred George, editor-in-chief of the German Jewish exile newspaper *Aufbau*, called her?[3] This chapter will not only present Kiesler as a central figure in the exile community of German literati during the Second World War but will also introduce the public library as an important meeting point and trace the different fates of selected émigré writers from Central Europe. The four-dimensional model of diaspora explained in the volume's introduction will function as a guideline for the following case study.

Biographical outline

Stefi Kiesler was born as Stephanie Frischer on 18 July 1897 in Skoczów (then Austria-Hungary, today Poland) as the third and youngest child of Ernestine (born Glasel) and Philipp Frischer.[4] Not much is known of her early years, as few documents have survived. The Frischer family was Jewish and supposedly middle class, and as a young adult Frischer moved to Vienna, where she would meet her future husband – reportedly at the Café Museum, an important meeting point for young artists and architects in the 1910s. Some sources suggest she was a student of philology at the University of Vienna; others mention an apprenticeship in bookselling. Stephanie Frischer and Friedrich

Kiesler (later Frederick Kiesler)[5] got married on 19 August 1920 at the Stadttempel, Vienna's main synagogue at Seitenstettengasse. The Kieslers' poor bohemian studio apartment in the attic of a building in Vienna's eighth district (Daungasse 1) was a popular meeting place for various creative people and intellectuals, including the art historian couple Erica Tietze-Conrat and Hans Tietze, the writers Franz Theodor Csokor and Albert Ehrenstein, as well as the actress Elisabeth Bergner.[6] Due to the sparse sources, the Kieslers' Vienna period still represents a large blind spot in research.[7]

From the autumn of 1921 the Kieslers repeatedly spent several months in Berlin. Frederick Kiesler's stage design for Karel Čapek's robot drama *R.U.R. (Rossum's Universal Robots)* brought him the artistic breakthrough in the spring of 1923.[8] As a result he got to know leading avant-garde artists and architects, such as Theo van Doesburg, Hans Richter and Ludwig Mies van der Rohe. Further documented contacts in Berlin are Herwarth Walden and the network around the gallery Der Sturm, as well as the writer Alfred Döblin. When Frederick Kiesler was commissioned to organize the *Internationale Ausstellung neuer Theatertechnik* (International Exhibition of New Theatre Techniques) in 1924, he took the opportunity to bring the European avant-garde to Vienna and deepen his contacts. Subsequently Josef Hoffmann invited him to Paris to design the Austrian theatre section at the 1925 international arts and crafts exhibition (*Exposition Internationale des Arts Décoratifs et Industriels Modernes*). Both Kieslers immediately felt at home in Paris and were welcomed with open arms in artistic circles. They spent a lot of time with Theo and Nelly van Doesburg, Tristan Tzara and the American composer George Antheil.[9] Obviously the Kieslers soon decided not to return to Vienna, but to stay in Paris. In this creative environment Stefi Kiesler appeared as an artist for the first time. In a letter to Tristan Tzara in autumn 1925, she wrote: 'I have a new direction in art !! . . . It beats all previous art !! . . . Surpasses Picasso !!! . . . The real collectivism found !!! . . . Montparnasse in the brightest uproar ! 15 art critics go insane every day !!'[10] This 'new direction in art' involves geometric typewriter images, which she called 'Typoplastics'. They are abstract works, consisting of letters and punctuation marks, composed on her typewriter.[11]

Due to his startling work in Berlin, Vienna, and Paris, Frederick Kiesler was invited by Jane Heap, editor of the avant-garde magazine *The Little Review*, to curate with her an international theatre exhibition in New York. With several hundred works of art and great plans, the Kieslers boarded the SS Leviathan (United States Lines) for New York on 19 January 1926. At that time they still intended to return to Paris a few weeks later. Both the cooperation with Jane Heap at the *International Theatre Exposition* (27 February to 21 March 1926) and the first impressions of New York were a big disappointment for the Kieslers. Years later Stefi spoke to the journalist Vera Craener of an 'intellectual desert': 'You cannot imagine the orgies materialism celebrated and how sad it was for the spiritual. One knew absolutely nothing about modern art, this was something that lay beyond the ocean, and authors like Kafka and Werfel had never been heard of here, even in good publishing houses.'[12] The mood and the financial situation of the Kieslers were bad. The supposedly progressive 'New World' proved to be a great disappointment and less open to visionary architecture and modern art than expected. Soon the Kieslers found themselves faced with a dilemma: on the one hand they did not have the financial means to make a living in New York, on the other hand they could not afford to buy tickets for a ship back to Europe.

In this difficult situation Stefi Kiesler ended her artistic work and accepted a position in the New York Public Library in August 1927. A newspaper article on the occasion of the twenty-fifth anniversary of her service has said in retrospect:

> Steffi's career . . . begins with the position of a 'clerk'. Because that's all you can become if you don't have any 'American experience' and especially if you haven't graduated from the local librarian school. For a year she dutifully writes addresses and sticks stamps, and since she does it with tremendous speed and true devotion – 'I couldn't lose my job under any circumstances, because that was the only money we had' – this strange bird with the 'foreign accent' comes to the attention of the highest authority. She is advised to catch up on the training necessary for a career as a librarian and is also entrusted with the work of the German and French departments in the lending office on 42nd Street, the so-called 'Central Circulation', which had been greatly reduced by the war.[13]

Probably around 1930 Kiesler was given responsibility for the German and French literature departments in the Central Circulation.[14] While working, she caught up on her American librarian training. For about thirty years – until her retirement in 1958 – Stefi Kiesler provided a regular household income as a librarian, thus securing a livelihood for herself and her husband, who was recognized as a visionary artist and architect but could not achieve commercial success.

In September 1935, the Kieslers moved into a penthouse at 56 Seventh Avenue, which quickly became a meeting place for the avant-garde. Having moved frequently since arriving in New York, the Kieslers finally found a real home where they would spend the rest of their lives. At times they harboured exiles there, for example, the French artist Marcel Duchamp lived with them for a year. The Kieslers also took care of the children of friends from Europe, for example, Alfred Döblin's son, Peter, or Max Ernst's son, Jimmy.[15] Stefi's calendar diaries provide detailed information about all meetings and activities of the Kiesler couple. Between 1930 and 1952 she noted down who they met, which plays they saw, which exhibitions they went to, which parties they were invited to, and so on. In the early 1940s, the contacts with Surrealist artists are particularly striking. In this creative environment Stefi Kiesler became artistically active again and contributed two collages for the exhibition *The Imagery of Chess* in the Julien Levy Gallery (12 December 1944 to 31 January 1945): *A Chess Village* and *Is Chess a Martial Game?*.[16] Stefi Kiesler's literary oeuvre is far more extensive than her artistic work, although hardly anything was published. It includes short stories, translations and journalistic articles. For example, an English translation of Egon Friedell's novel *Die Rückkehr der Zeitmaschine* (The Return of the Time Machine) and Alfred Döblin's *Märchen vom Materialismus* (Fairy Tale of Materialism) have been preserved, as well as an attempt to translate Marcel Duchamp's *Boîte verte* (Green Box). In the 1940s she worked on an extensive anthology of dreams in literature, a project that might also have come about through the exchange with the surrealists. However, the anthology was never completed and published.[17]

In 1958, Stefi Kiesler retired from the New York Public Library. But instead of actually retiring, she became active in the German Jewish newspaper *Aufbau*. The *Aufbau* had been founded as the club newspaper of the German Jewish Club, which had celebrated its tenth anniversary in December 1934 with a twelve-page magazine. The German Jewish Club was later renamed the New World Club and the club newspaper crossed the threshold of serious printed matter in November 1939 at the latest. The period of Manfred George as editor-in-chief from 1939 to 1965 is regarded as the heyday of the *Aufbau*, which became a gathering place for émigré journalists during the Second World War, including Hannah Arendt, Martin Buber, Heinrich Eduard Jacob, Thomas Mann, Hertha Pauli, Alfred Polgar and Will Schaber. The demand for a connecting German-language medium increased among the diaspora from Germany and Austria. Many exiles sent letters to the editorial staff, in which they reported their personal strokes of fate and which were then printed in the newspaper. 'In a sense, the emigrants wrote their newspaper themselves.'[18] The *Aufbau* provided information on events, English courses and organized excursions. After the end of the war, the newspaper helped bring together many families scattered all over the world through search advertisements. Stefi Kiesler took over editorial activities and wrote literary, theatre and film reviews. She worked at the *Aufbau* until shortly before her death on 3 September 1963, and thus dedicated over three decades and half of her life to migrants, refugees and displaced people. She herself never set foot on European soil again after 1930.[19] Although she had been an American citizen since 1936, she would always feel a deep connection with her homeland. In a letter to W. Green from the American Federation of Austrian Democrats, dated 14 April 1943, Kiesler wrote: 'I am certainly more than a friend of Austria, I am a born Austrian.'[20]

A librarian as language and cultural mediator

What did Stefi Kiesler's work in the New York Public Library exactly entail, and in what condition did she take over the German-language collection around 1930? A public library always reflects historical and social processes. During the First World War, the United States was in conflict with Germany and Austria-Hungary, and consequently German-language literature and culture were considered hostile. In the New York Public Library, the book holdings were reduced, and there were little or no new acquisitions in the German Department. When Stefi Kiesler took over responsibility, she found a decimated, neglected and outdated selection of books. With a lot of heart and soul, she slowly rebuilt and updated the collection. As a native Austrian, it was of particular concern to her that 'hardly any important Austrian name is missing'[21] in the German-language collection, including Franz Werfel, Stefan Zweig, Karl Kraus, Albert Ehrenstein and Friedrich Torberg. As she wrote in her article 'Österreich in der Public Library' (Austria in the Public Library), Kiesler even made it her task to 'do some pioneering work and, so to speak, "en passant" to clarify the difference between German and Austrian authors in terms of literary history'.[22] She complained that 'there is still no good history of Austria and none of literature in English' and that the

Americans 'returned from Vienna and Salzburg enthusiastically, wearing dirndls and short lederhosen, but never with a Nestroy or Altenberg book'.[23]

As 'Foreign Language Specialist', Stefi Kiesler's tasks included selecting, reviewing and purchasing German and French-language books.[24] She was also assigned to the information service daily from 11.00 am to 1.00 pm. This included help with the general selection of books, the search for special literature, explaining the catalogue and classification system and also help with filling out the form to apply for new user cards. As a foreign-language specialist, her main task was to enable people with poor or no English skills to use the library. She was supposed to help Europeans to get to know American customs and traditions as quickly and efficiently as possible. This was done mainly by purchasing books about America in German and French, buying translations of American standard literature, creating simple reading lists and providing information about language courses in library branches and other institutions. She was also supposed to support American readers with more or less good language skills in selecting literature.

Stefi Kiesler's work changed abruptly with the arrival of the first political refugees from Europe in the 1930s. On 1 June 1945 – shortly after Hitler's suicide and the capitulation of the Germans – she described this change in retrospect and in dramatic intensification in her article 'Meet Me at the Library':

> Up to 1933 readers were mostly Americans. . . . Foreign language circulation collections were used by firmly rooted immigrants for pleasurable reading. French chefs read Dumas and Ohnet, German house wives Marlitt and Courths-Mahler, Russians and other nationals similar gems. But in 1933 the national-socialist snake reared its poisonous head with the Hitler mask – and a change took place – so rapid and fantastic that even Fifth Avenue and 42nd Street felt the impact of its rattle. . . . We, in the Library, were wakened from our sweet twilight sleep. We had been so accustomed to readers who told us 'You know, for months I planned to come and look this up', whatever 'this' was. And now, crowds of pale, nervous looking people came, almost with luggage in hand, voicing their request haltingly, often in a more than faulty English – disclosing that they had just arrived – and were already in desperate need of – books.[25]

According to Kiesler, the public libraries were one of the first places to go for exiles in New York.[26] Kiesler herself upgraded her role from simple librarian to language and cultural mediator; her bread-and-butter job thus turned from a mere duty to a social obligation. According to her own account, she had often tried in vain to familiarize her customers with sophisticated literature in the first years, presumably also in order to justify these purchases to her superiors. With the diaspora from Germany and Austria more and more people interested in literature from the educated middle class came and asked for precisely these books.

The role of public libraries – and librarians like Stefi Kiesler – for refugees, exiles and (forced) migrants will subsequently be looked at with regard to the four-dimensional model of diaspora. Stefi Kiesler's remarks and various exiles' memories will serve as sources in the search for possible answers.

Host society: The library as meeting ground and school

As a librarian, Stefi Kiesler presented the newcomers with their library card as an 'entrance ticket' to a new language and culture. At the same time, the library also formed a bridge to the homeland left behind and the familiarity of the mother tongue. Kiesler was convinced that with the arrival of large numbers of immigrants and refugees, the primary task of public libraries was to enable the newly arrived 'intellectual access to history and culture'.[27] The best way for the library to introduce foreigners to the United States was

> by having as many good translations of American standard works as possible in our foreign language departments. . . . Because I am of the opinion that it is not the study of these books in the original text that accelerates the Americanisation of the future citizen, but that he is much more likely to penetrate the spirit of the country if he can read about it in his mother tongue.[28]

Consequently, for Kiesler the cultural introduction was just as important, if not more important, than the linguistic one. This may have had something to do with her own experiences as a migrant from Europe, because letters from the early days in New York show that the Kieslers had some difficulties in understanding the 'American Way of Life'. In addition, the Kieslers did not know a word of English when they arrived. A few years later, Stefi Kiesler remembered how she found support and comfort in the library, where she first encountered the familiarity of the German language and then the possibilities to connect on a linguistic and cultural level with the host society: 'The library helped me the first year of my stay in America to be happy and this brings unforgettable thanks on my part.'[29]

An article by Mary Kelly, entitled 'The Refugee Is Taking Notes' and published in *The Christian Science Monitor* in September 1943, has been preserved in Stefi Kiesler's papers. It probably served as an inspiration for her own article 'Meet Me at the Library' two years later, in which she took down anecdotes from her own daily life in the New York Public Library. In both texts the European refugees are described as very interested in their host society's history and culture and determined to quickly learn the new language and integrate. Kelly writes from the point of view of an American:

> There is so much to learn about America, and they [the refugees] want to begin at once. They are going to live here for the duration at least. Perhaps always. Since most of them are from Germany and Austria, they are eager to learn the truth about us. They want first-hand impressions, so they sit down to read what Americans say about America. Travel books, regional novels, sociology – anything that will help. Probably their first request is an easy English grammar, although it is amazing how many of them read English.[30]

In terms of individual fates, a typescript by the German journalist Kurt Pinthus reports on his experience of arriving in the United States in 1937 'without any knowledge of the English language, without money, without books, even without notes'.[31] Pinthus recalled not only that he was amazed to find all his publications at the library but also that a colleague of Stefi Kiesler at the New York Public Library recommended him to the director of The New School for Social Research, Alvin Johnson, who hired him as a lecturer and thus gave him the opportunity to make a living in his host country. Pinthus wrote: 'I think I am a typical case of a newcomer whose physical as well as intellectual being has been saved by this country – particularly with the aid of a Public Library which enabled me to continue my literary work immediately after my arrival over here'.[32] After finding a first foothold at The New School for Social Research in New York, he worked for the Theatre Collection at the Library of Congress in Washington, D.C. and finally taught Theatre History at Columbia University. In 1967 he returned to Germany and settled at Marbach, the birth town of Friedrich Schiller and home to the German Literature Archive (Deutsches Literaturarchiv Marbach), where he worked during his final years.

Homeland: The library as repository of language and culture

The public library serves as a substitute for the private book collection left behind, especially for refugee writers, scientists, artists and intellectuals. Stefi Kiesler, who had also had to leave her book collection behind in Vienna and Paris – albeit under completely different circumstances – emphasized this aspect of the public library with foreign-language departments in her article 'Österreich in der Public Library': '[Raoul] Auernheimer once said so nicely that he is less mourning the loss of his own private library, since he actually found it again in New York in the Public Library'.[33] In the case of published writers and scholars, it was not only the loss of their own library in general but also of their own works in particular. Here, too, Kiesler was able to help as a librarian: 'How happy you are when writers can borrow their own works that have been burned in Europe and they themselves no longer have a single copy.'[34]

Refugees from Europe often arrived in New York without means and without orientation, also with regard to their own identity and further life planning. The German-Czech writer and journalist Hans Natonek, for example, recalled the difficult early days in a letter to Kiesler dated 4 May 1962:

> First encounters when you arrive lost in New York (1941) are memorable. 'Are you in the end identical with the famous writer Hans Natonek?' were your first words in the library. I felt so strange, so 'down and out' in America after many years of fleeing, – I hardly knew who I was any more. The deeper the impact of your words (with a slight Viennese accent.) Oh vanity of writers, so worried about their little identity![35]

Natonek also described this encounter, which was so moving for him, in a German-language typescript that has been preserved in his estate in Albany, New York, and was translated into English as 'In Search of Myself' and published in a small edition in 1943:

> Then Mrs. Kiessling [sic] led me into the huge catalogue room and pulled a box out of the wall, which consisted of nothing but boxes. She flipped through the cards. I did not know what she was looking for. 'Here', she said, 'this is you'. I was a bit moved and confused because I didn't expect to find my name and some titles here – a faint trace. I felt as if I was looking into a half-extinguished mirror; my past lay before me like stripped skin; yet it was a part of my self, a piece of my lost identity.[36]

Natonek described Stefi Kiesler as a person endeavouring to remind the traumatized and disoriented writers of their old identity and their creative ability and thus to reawaken their spirits. The lost feeling of control over their path in life could perhaps be restored, so that the exiles could continue their earlier work and find the courage to actively take their lives into their own hands again. The shift in Kiesler's own role from being a mere librarian to becoming a pivotal point for the exiles in New York represents such a process of reinterpretation in favour of self-empowerment. After a few years in New York, Natonek moved with his future wife Anne Grünwald to Tucson, Arizona, where he remained until his death in 1963. He became an American citizen and returned to Europe only once, in 1957. Natonek continued to write, tried to switch to English, but failed and never published another book. 'Neither the American nor the German book market showed any interest in the writer Hans Natonek.'[37] While the book market has pursued commercial interests and only supported authors who appealed to a broad audience, in libraries other aspects counted, too: as a locus of memory, they have kept works by now largely forgotten authors like Natonek.

In search of his own work, Friedrich Torberg also turned to Stefi Kiesler.[38] In November 1942 he wrote to her from California looking for a copy of his novel *Die Mannschaft* (The Team), as a passage from it was to appear in an anthology of Central European writers. Kiesler procured the book as quickly as possible from the holdings of the New York Public Library and sent it to Torberg with the following comment:

> Since it is a library book, it cannot be sold and since you do not have a card for our lending library, I am taking it in my name. My very private and very discreet advice is that you simply lose it and replace the price. We charge $1.75 for a lost German book because we cannot make individual prices.[39]

In a letter dated 26 December 1942, Torberg expressed his gratitude as well as his fear that the only copy of his book accessible to him might have been lost in the Christmas hustle and bustle of the post office. 'I will guard this book like the apple of my eye (as a one-eyed man would guard his eyeball)', he promised and added: 'If I manage to get hold of a second copy, yours will be at your disposal again. By then you will unfortunately have lost it.'[40] The library appears here as an all-encompassing repository of written culture that carefully preserves rarities. Nevertheless, in this case it was more important for Kiesler to make his work accessible to the creator himself than to the general readership.

In contrast to Natonek, Torberg was able to build on his earlier success after the Second World War and returned to Vienna in 1951. One of his most important works today is his collection of anecdotes, published in 1975, *Die Tante Jolesch oder der Untergang des Abendlandes in Anekdoten* (The Aunt Jolesch, or, the Decline of the West in Anecdotes), in which he devoted himself to a lost culture, in this case the Jewish coffee house world of the Danube Monarchy and its successor states. This Jewish educated middle class of the Austro-Hungarian Empire, which Stefi and Frederick Kiesler were also part of and which made such an enormous impact on the society of *fin-de-siècle* and interwar Vienna, was extinguished all of a sudden with the National Socialist takeover and the Second World War. Those who could escape scattered all over the world and many never returned to their homeland. The importance of making an effort to retain lost cultures was also stressed by Kurt Pinthus. In the aforementioned typescript he wrote:

> The Public Library should collect the books destroyed by the Fascists in all European countries, books which are no longer available, not even from or through the authors themselves. For I think this should be one of the great tasks of this young and wonderful country, to save the documents of the decaying European cultures, as once Italy preserved the cultures of ancient Hellas and Rome and thus achieved her own flourishing Renaissance.[41]

Diaspora: The library as village fountain and café

From Kiesler's point of view, the public library functioned as a place of encounter both with members of the host society and with old acquaintances from the homeland, as she described in her article 'Meet Me at the Library':

> Eminent university professors met unexpectedly friends and students they hadn't seen for years at the catalogue room; actors encountered their former directors and producers; they met in the entrance, the stairways, the reading rooms. At my desk they left messages for appointments, manuscripts to be called for, letters for friends. The Library gradually extended far beyond the book circle and became the meeting grounds for friend and foe, scholar and businessman. 'Meet me at the Library' is convenient and easy. It was *Studierstube* and the *Café*, the rendezvous of mind and body.[42]

In Kiesler's stylization the library combines the intellectual prestige of the university and the creative aura of the theatre as well as the homeliness of the Viennese café. The library is characterized as a vibrant place of human interaction on the one hand and a school/study room (*Studierstube*) on the other.

In his obituary of Kiesler in the *Aufbau*, the German American journalist and caricaturist Ludwig Wronkow wrote that '[h]er table at 42nd Street became a village fountain where writers and journalists met. They met here, as they had once met in the coffee houses'.[43] Recollecting his own positive experiences two decades earlier, he stylized the library, usually known as an emotionless place of knowledge, into a room full of warmth and conviviality. The journalist Vera Craener found similar words in her article on the occasion of Stefi Kiesler's twenty-fifth anniversary of service:

> At the small table in the lending desk of the Public Library on 42nd Street, where she has her headquarters and holds a kind of literary consultation hour every

day from 11 a.m. to 1 p.m., her friends meet: writers and artists, academics and intellectuals. Here they talk about new books, art exhibitions and dance evenings. Here you can find out who has just been appointed to a professorial chair, who is writing a radio play for the 'Voice of America' and who will soon have something in the 'Commentary'. If there was coffee, too, you would have something like the 'Romanisches Café'[44] right here in the heart of New York City.[45]

Thus, Craener made a comparison with the European café as a regular meeting place for the educated middle class and the bohemian in her laudatory speech for Stefi Kiesler. She presented her as a hub around which – as at the regulars' table (*Stammtisch*) of Karl Kraus or Peter Altenberg in *fin-de-siècle* Vienna – an interested audience gathered. Accordingly, a visit to the library was not only about books and intellectual exchange but also about plain personal interaction and gossip. There was no entrance fee like in a museum or theatre, and there was no obligation to consume as in restaurants or bars. With the increasing number of Central European exiles, the German and French Departments of the New York Public Library increasingly developed into a place with functions similar to those of a café thanks to the Austrian librarian. In 'The Refugee Is Taking Notes', Mary Kelly confirmed that '[e]xtending its influence beyond the book circle, the public library has often been the meeting ground for old friends from the days of a happier Europe'.[46]

Other diasporas: The library as multicultural microcosm

Of course, not all refugees that came to the United States in consequence of the fascist takeover in Europe and the Second World War were from Austria and Germany; there were many other nationalities that foregathered in places like New York City, each individual with his or her own (tragic) story and reason to leave home. But regardless of their background, suddenly they were all 'in the same boat'. They all had to start from scratch, learn a new language and figure out how to continue with their lives. The New York Public Library offered not only books from the German and French collections headed by Stefi Kiesler but also held volumes in many other languages. It thus turned into a multicultural gathering place for people from all over the world. Although this paper has focused on Kiesler as a case study, there are a lot of similar stories that still need to be told. Mary Kelly mostly referred to Austrian and German refugees in her article, but also mentioned others:

> No two days at the library are alike, and no two refugees are alike. There are sometimes as many as 27 nationalities represented at a single branch. There was the woman from Holland who loved outdoor life. One day as she came into the library, a bowl of tulips ('bulbs from Holland!') met her eyes, which filled promptly with tears. Then there was the Frenchwoman who came in after the news that the French fleet had been scuttled. . . . 'Now we can sing the Marseillaise again', she said fervently. . . . Another library user, this time an Italian, reflected the relief of his countrymen in the United States on the day immediately following the

announcement by Solicitor General Francis Biddle that Italians are not 'enemy aliens.' He came into the library with an outstretched hand: . . . 'Ah! It is so different now. . . . We are friends.' . . . 'It rips into your emotions some days', remarked a librarian at one of the liveliest branches.[47]

Conclusion

In addition to Kurt Pinthus, Hans Natonek and Friedrich Torberg, Stefi Kiesler supported many other well-known as well as forgotten writers, such as Alfred Döblin, Oskar Maria Graf, Albert Ehrenstein, Annette Kolb, Erika Mann and Ernst Toller. Stefi Kiesler, a migrant herself, could well understand the exiles: the disorientation and the perceived loss of their own identity, the difficulties with the foreign culture and language and the existential fear due to the difficult financial situation. Kiesler helped wherever she could. For example, it is thanks to her and Friderike Zweig's commitment, that the Viennese writer Albert Ehrenstein was not buried in an anonymous mass grave. Ehrenstein had arrived in New York in 1941 and had not been able to gain a foothold in America. He died impoverished and lonely in 1950 after a stroke paralysed him and deprived him of speech.[48] In the summer of 1949 Kiesler had been working together with Ehrenstein on German translations of short stories by the English writer A. E. Coppard, offering them to Swiss publishers.[49] And when the German playwright and political activist Ernst Toller committed suicide in his New York hotel room on 22 May 1939, Kiesler was concerned that he would be memorized and esteemed. The very next day she attended a meeting of several writers who were trying to organize a memorial service.[50] Stefi Kiesler was also involved in associations of exiled writers in New York, such as the German American Writers' Association, which was newly founded in 1938.[51] She was in close contact with the American-European Friendship Association, the PEN Club and the American Guild for German Cultural Freedom. Vera Craener emphasized that the right person was in the right place, a migrant who stood up for other migrants: 'For she not only speaks the language of the newly arrived, but also understands their worries and problems, and the esteemed little librarian, to whom readers always turned only when they were looking for a particular book or needed sources for their work, now became a famous social aid centre overnight.'[52] This creates an image of Kiesler as a 'receptionist' who helped refugees integrate into American society: listening to them patiently, giving them something to eat and helping them find work. The example of Stefi Kiesler shows that librarians can play an important' mediating role in terms of integration and demonstrates the potential that public libraries have for bringing cultures together.

Notes

1   The spelling of the name varies between 'Stefi' and 'Steffi' in the preserved documents. The former is used in official documents such as the American Certificate of Citizenship, the latter is common to her and her friends. For the purpose of

consistency, this text uses the variant 'Stefi' throughout. In quotations, the respective spelling is retained.
2. Vera Craener, 'Jubiläum ohne Fanfare', *Aufbau* (9 January 1953): 6. (Translated from German.) – Original: 'geistige Refugee Service für die deutschen Gelehrten und Schriftsteller'.
3. Stefi Kiesler's estate is the main source of information. It comprises twenty-seven archive boxes and contains photographs, correspondence, diaries and calendars, various manuscripts and typescripts as well as research material for her 'Dream Book'. It is held as a crypton estate in the Austrian Frederick and Lillian Kiesler Private Foundation in Vienna (hereafter ÖFLKS).
4. My diploma thesis provides a first overview of Stefi Kiesler's life and work (in German). Cf. Jill Meißner, 'Stefi Kiesler (1897–1963): Künstlerfrau – Vermittlerin – Literatin' (diploma thesis, University of Vienna, 2013). Available online: http://othes.univie.ac.at/24950/1/2013-01-14_0502865.pdf (accessed 24 September 2020).
5. Born Friedrich Jacob Kiesler in Chernivtsi on 22 September 1890, he later changed his name in the United States to Frederick John Kiesler. For the purpose of consistency and to avoid confusion, this text uses 'Frederick Kiesler' throughout.
6. Erica Tietze-Conrat's diaries, edited by Alexandra Caruso, provide some rare insights into the Kieslers' network and activities in Vienna, cf. Alexandra Caruso (ed.), *Erica Tietze-Conrat: Tagebücher*, 3 vols (Vienna: Böhlau, 2015); Dieter Bogner and Gerd Zillner, 'The Kieslers and the Tietzes. New Insights into the Close-knit Network of 1920s Vienna', in *Frederick Kiesler: Face to Face with the Avant-Garde*, ed. Peter Bogner, Gerd Zillner and Frederick Kiesler Foundation (Basel: Birkhäuser, 2019), 83–96.
7. Almost no sources from their time in Europe have been preserved in the papers of Stefi and Frederick Kiesler, the same applies to the first years in the United States due to the frequent changes of residence. Only from about 1930 on, calendars, correspondence etc. provide information.
8. Until 1925 there are no documents of Stefi Kiesler's activities preserved. She probably supported her husband during these years in the first place. For more information on life and work of Fredrick Kiesler see Gerd Zillner, Peter Bogner and Dieter Bogner (eds), *Friedrich Kiesler. Architekt Künstler Visionär* (Munich, London and New York: Prestel, 2016).
9. Cf. Laura McGuire, 'Frederick Kiesler and Theo van Doesburg. Influence and Elaboration', in *Frederick Kiesler: Face to Face with the Avant-Garde*, 151–64; Mauro Piccinini, 'George Antheil, Kiesler's First American Friend. "Wild Bird" Meets "Face of the Future"', in *Frederick Kiesler: Face to Face with the Avant-Garde*, 193–205.
10. Bibliothèque littéraire Jacques Doucet, Paris, Fonds Tristan Tzara, Stefi Kiesler, letter to Tristan Tzara, undated [1925]. (Translated from German.) The letter itself has the character of an artwork, which explains its unusual punctuation.
11. Cf. Dieter Bogner, 'Stefi Kiesler: Avant-Garde from the Typewriter', in *City of Women: Female Artists in Vienna. 1900–1938*, ed. Stella Rollig and Sabine Fellner (Munich, London and New York: Prestel, 2019), 199–202. How many works of this kind Stefi Kiesler created can no longer be reconstructed, unfortunately. Three were published in the avant-garde magazine *De Stijl*, five originals are part of the collection of the Yale University Art Gallery.
12. Craener, 'Jubiläum ohne Fanfare', 5. (Translated from German.)
13. Ibid., 6. (Translated from German.)

14 The Central Circulation is the well-known main building of the New York Public Library on Fifth Avenue/42nd Street, now Stephen A. Schwarzman Building.
15 Cf. Jimmy Ernst, *A Not-So-Still Life* (New York: Pushcart Press, 1992), 179.
16 Cf. Larry List (ed.), *The Imagery of Chess Revisited* (New York: Isamu Noguchi Foundation and Garden Museum/George Braziller, 2005). The collages are now part of the collection of the Philadelphia Museum of Art.
17 The German émigré publisher Kurt Wolff, who founded Pantheon Books in exile in New York in 1942, was a good friend of Stefi's and interested in publishing her dream anthology.
18 Elke-Vera Kotowski (ed.), *Aufbau. Sprachrohr. Heimat. Mythos. Geschichte(n) einer deutschjüdischen Zeitung aus New York 1934 bis heute* (Berlin: Hentrich und Hentrich, 2011), 19. (Translated from German.)
19 Unlike his wife, Frederick Kiesler travelled to Europe several times during the 1940s, 50s and 60s. Interestingly, he never returned to Vienna, but repeatedly visited Paris and took vacations in Southern France and Italy.
20 ÖFLKS, LET 2471/0, Stefi Kiesler, letter to W. Green, 14 April 1943.
21 Steffi Kiesler, 'Österreich in der Public Library', *Austro American Tribune* (November 1943): 7. (Translated from German.)
22 Ibid. (Translated from German.)
23 Ibid. (Translated from German.)
24 Cf. ÖFLKS, LD 6464/0 and LD 6464/1, Position Description: Stefi Kiesler, Foreign Language Specialist, 1951.
25 Steffi Kiesler, 'Meet Me at the Library', *Aufbau* (7 June 1945): 32.
26 Cf. Jill Meissner-Wolfbeisser, '"Meet Me at the Library". Explorationen über Steffi Kiesler und die Rolle der öffentlichen Bibliothek im Exil', in *Frauen und Exil, Vol. 11: Grenzüberschreitungen. Migrantinnen und Migranten als Akteure im 20. Jahrhundert*, ed. Kristina Schulz, Wiebke von Bernstorff and Heike Klapdor (Munich: text+kritik, 2019), 191–205.
27 Quoted from Craener, 'Jubiläum ohne Fanfare', 6. (Translated from German.) – Original: 'den geistigen Zugang in die Geschichte und die Kultur'.
28 Ibid. (Translated from German.)
29 ÖFLKS, TXT 6907/0, Steffi Kiesler, Organization and development of a French and German collection of circulating books with special attention to the problems of the Central Circulation branch, typescript, New York, 1930.
30 ÖFLKS, CLP 7273/0, Mary Kelly, 'The Refugee Is Taking Notes', *The Christian Science Monitor* (11 September 1943): 7.
31 ÖFLKS, TXT 7438/0, Kurt Pinthus, untitled typescript ('I think I am a typical case of a newcomer ...'), undated, 1.
32 Ibid.
33 Kiesler, 'Österreich in der Public Library', 7. (Translated from German.)
34 Ibid. (Translated from German.)
35 ÖFLKS, LET 2754/0, Hans Natonek, letter to Stefi Kiesler, 4 May 1962. (Translated from German.)
36 Quoted after Steffi Böttger, *Für immer fremd. Das Leben des jüdischen Schriftstellers Hans Natonek* (Leipzig: Lehmstedt, 2013), 138. (Translated from German.)
37 Ibid., 180. (Translated from German.)
38 The correspondence was first printed in: Susanne Blumesberger, 'Bibliothekarin im Exil. Beruf oder Berufung?', in *Österreichische Bibliothekarinnen auf der Flucht. Verfolgt, verdrängt, vergessen?*, ed. Ilse Korotin (Vienna: Praesens, 2007), 68–71.

39 Austrian National Library, Department of Manuscripts and Rare Books, Autogr. 1196/23-1, Stefi Kiesler, letter to Friedrich Torberg, 4 December 1942. (Translated from German.)
40 Ibid., Autogr. 1196/23, Beilage 2, Friedrich Torberg, letter to Stefi Kiesler, 26 December 1942. (Translated from German.)
41 ÖFLKS, TXT 7438/0, Pinthus, untitled typescript, 3–4.
42 Kiesler, 'Meet Me at the Library', 32.
43 Ludwig Wronkow, 'Helferin in der Not. In Memoriam Steffi Kiesler', *Aufbau* (13 September 1963): 31. (Translated from German.)
44 The 'Romanisches Café' was a popular meeting place for intellectuals and artists in Berlin during the 1920s.
45 Craener, 'Jubiläum ohne Fanfare', 5. (Translated from German.)
46 Kelly, 'The Refugee Is Taking Notes', 7.
47 Ibid.
48 Cf. Friderike Maria Zweig, *Spiegelungen des Lebens* (Frankfurt am Main: Fischer, 1985), 212.
49 Since both spent the summer in the New York area, this project is relatively well documented through their correspondence. In Stefi Kiesler's estate, five texts have been assigned to this project: 'Der grüne Enterich' (Original: The Green Drake), 'Freda Listowell schwindet ins nichts' (Ahoy, Sailor Boy!), 'Judith' (Judith), 'Adam, Eva und Gabriel' (Adam and Eve and Pinch Me) and 'Im Silberzirkus' (Silver Circus). They are each available in several versions, some with handwritten corrections; furthermore, a letter of rejection from the *Neue Zürcher Zeitung* dated 16 October 1949 has been preserved.
50 ÖFLKS, MED 853/0, Toller's suicide on 22 May 1939 is recorded in Stefi Kiesler's diary ('2.30 Toller hangs himself'), on 23 May 1939 she noted: '9 p.m. Joe [= Joseph Freeman?], [Oskar Maria] Graf, [Manfred] Georg / [Ferdinand] Bruckner for meeting (Toller / funeral)'.
51 In the first mailing, this association listed Thomas Mann as honorary president, Oskar Maria Graf as first chairman, Ferdinand Bruckner as second chairman, Manfred George as secretary and Stefi Kiesler as treasurer. Cf. ÖFLKS, MED 7200/0.
52 Craener, 'Jubiläum ohne Fanfare', 6. (Translated from German.)

8

The catalysts of 1938

European child evacuations as humanitarian innovation

Chelsea Sambells

The year 1938 was a watershed in terms of how European nations addressed and defined their positions towards persecuted refugees. Germany's *Anschluss* of Austria in mid-March, the failures of the Evian Conference in July, the Munich Agreement and subsequent occupation of the Sudetenland in September and October, and finally, the violent pogrom against German and Austrian Jews (*Kristallnacht*) in November 1938 created an unprecedented number of new 'stateless' refugees who could not rely on international laws for protection. As a result, individual nations were forced to confront and, importantly, balance four critical factors: restrictive federal legislation and policies towards refugees, the urgent needs of the persecuted individuals, the realistic capacity of local charities to support vulnerable groups upon resettlement and the public pressure (often conveyed in the press and media) to ensure swift, comprehensive action.

Concerns about the type of refugees who could be relocated dominated the discussions among government officials and humanitarian activists across the United States, the United Kingdom and Europe. But the permanent resettlement of thousands of individuals was to be avoided at all costs, as refugees were perceived as a permanent national burden and costly economic drain.[1] Instead, persecuted and stateless *child* refugees were soon identified as an easier group to relocate. They were not a threat to job markets that had been decimated by the economic depression; they were more malleable than adults and could quickly learn local languages and customs, and, importantly, children were more able to win the hearts of sympathetic citizens and generate large sums of humanitarian donations. It was also understood that because of all these reasons, children could also easily relocate back to their countries of origin once stability returned to Europe.

It is within this context that various nations, including the UK, Sweden and Switzerland, began to find original, innovative methods to protect vulnerable groups and refugees, particularly children. Large-scale temporary child evacuations quickly became a new inventive method to protect Europe's most vulnerable members of society. Britain's famous *Kindertransport* of German Jewish children, Sweden's evacuation of Finnish children and Switzerland's evacuations of Belgian and French children meant that hundreds of thousands of children were resettled to foreign nations during a devastating war and despite the absence of a coordinated global migration framework. This chapter will argue that the failures of the international community to achieve a coordinated diplomatic solution, accompanied by international events of rising violence of persecution in Europe, were unpredictable but critical catalysts in 1938 that compelled governments and humanitarian agencies to provide innovative forms of protection.

The catalysts of 1938

After Adolf Hitler came to power in January 1933, it took the Nazis only a few months to systematically exclude German Jews from everyday life. For many, emigration thus became a means of escape. Although Nazi Germany had not yet planned to exterminate all its Jews, its core aim was to drive them out of Europe, even if it meant to Palestine.[2] However, increasing expropriation and exclusion from work impoverished many German Jews, who then lost the means to emigrate. In 1933, emigrants from Germany retained 75 per cent of the value of their assets but by 1938 that was reduced to just 5 per cent.[3] Wider attitudes to German Jewish immigrants also affected their relocation. Of the approximately half a million Jews in Germany in 1933, 37,000 emigrated in the first year alone. Although the United States was a popular destination for Jewish immigrants in the nineteenth century, nearly 73 per cent of those 37,000 Jewish emigrants in 1933 remained within Europe; only 8 per cent travelled as far as the United States as a result of the country's strict immigration policies.[4] Economic uncertainty, growing international instability and the lack of international laws to protect persecuted groups meant that German Jews had very few practical options other than to relocate to nearby nations with familial and professional connections.

Receptive nations also had their own prejudices and legislative restrictions. Officials in Great Britain perceived Jews as 'alien' and whose immigration, if not restricted, would threaten homogeneity and national stability.[5] After 1933, the British government relied on the Jewish community to meet the maintenance costs of Jewish migrants; as the crisis grew, this measure evolved into limited support for only temporary stays of Jewish refugees, before their onward emigration to Palestine or other parts of the empire.[6] Nations that were declared neutral during the Second World War, including Sweden and Switzerland, had their own restrictive and anti-Semitic refugee policies. Despite their accessible geographic locations for those fleeing Nazi persecution, both Sweden and Switzerland defended their borders from refugees for fear of upsetting their internal economies. For the British Mandate of Palestine, Jewish immigrants from Germany were welcomed but only upon the condition that Reichsmarks were transferred to Palestinian banks. This *Ha'avarah* (Transfer) Agreement was, understandably, heavily criticized for its preference for wealthy Jewish immigrants.[7]

These types of attitudes in the 1930s exacerbated the refugees' plight and seldom offered robust asylum or support to persecuted peoples.

In mid-March 1938, the refugees fleeing the German *Anschluss* of Austria provoked the world's attention to confront the rising humanitarian crisis that was unfolding in Europe. The international community faced two critical challenges at this stage: first, to overcome the deeply entrenched prejudice within federal immigration policies to such an extent that states could offer sanctuary to persecuted individuals and, second, to resolve the perceived threat that the mass exodus and expulsion of refugees, regardless of their religious or ethnic identities, posed to receptive countries. Put plainly, both the quality and quantity of refugees were obstacles to immigration within individual states in the 1930s.[8]

Unfortunately, these challenges could not be resolved by turning to either the League of Nations or international law. During the interwar period, the League of Nations had fallen victim to infighting, micropolitics and general unwillingness to take risks.[9] Germany had withdrawn from the League in 1933 and did not recognize its authority. Other legal mechanisms that would have forced world powers to accept refugees, such as the international laws that protected basic human rights for civilians, were not created until the Geneva Convention of 1951. Thus, the global community in the late 1930s was not legally compelled to take action. Refugees were entirely at the mercy of individual governments.

US president Franklin D. Roosevelt believed a solution could be found through the formation of a new organization. Roosevelt's Intergovernmental Committee for Political Refugees, based in London, invited thirty-two countries to attend a conference from 6 to 15 July 1938 at the glamorous spa town of Evian, France.[10] These chosen democratic nations were tasked to find solutions that would facilitate the migration of refugees from Nazi Germany (including recently annexed Austria). US secretary of state Cordell Hull, who penned the proposal to attendees, claimed that the current humanitarian crisis required 'speedy cooperation if widespread suffering is to be averted'.[11] The ultimate goal was to establish a permanent organization to facilitate a long-term strategy for alleviating 'political' refugees. In order to appeal to reluctant participants, the committee made it clear that the cost for resettlement would be borne by 'private organisations'. This was typical since the interwar period, when humanitarian groups had distinguished themselves for their altruism by fundraising for refugees and other vulnerable groups displaced by war, such as children. Additionally, the committee specified that countries would *not* be 'expected or asked to receive a greater number of immigrants than is permitted by its existing legislation'.[12] With these details conveyed, representatives of relevant local or national charities were also invited to share in the proceedings, and the costs, of the refugee burden.

The Evian Conference – the first global attempt to resolve an international refugee crisis through diplomacy – was a failure. In fact, the conference seemed to have the opposite effect, as many of the participating nations used it to add further limits to their intake of refugees. Even before the conference began, the American and British governments came to a private understanding that neither would pressure the other to revise its immigration laws during deliberations.[13] Echoing most participants, Britain's delegates offered unreserved sympathy to refugees while rejecting any changes to

British refugee policies as it would be economically untenable to do so, especially as the Reich continued to deprive emigrants of any 'means of subsistence'.[14] Smaller European nations, such as Switzerland and Sweden, proposed to help only if others were willing to take on the majority of the burden. Swiss delegate Heinrich Rothmund argued that countries with significant immigrant populations, such as the United States, should absorb large numbers of refugees so that European nations could restrict their role as solely 'transit countries'.[15] This was also echoed by Sweden's delegate Gösta Engzell who explained that although Sweden had a 'most liberal' admissions policy for immigrants, Sweden was not a state of immigration. Instead, Engzell pronounced, immigrants must be relocated beyond European borders.[16]

Within days of the Evian Conference ending, the international press reflected the contradictory and ineffective results that came to characterize this global meeting. The *Manchester Guardian* wrote that '[t]he most disappointing feature of the Conference was the lack of practical offers from any nation to take any large number of refugees', which it claimed was chiefly the failure of the British and French governments.[17] The *New York Post* declared that the US government might have been able to liberalize its immigration quotas but that, ultimately, mass immigration would have to be directed to 'undeveloped states', such as Mexico and other countries in Central and South America.[18] Notably, the Dominican Republic was the only state to offer practical resettlement of a small number of Jewish refugees.[19] The sole accomplishment of the Evian Conference was the creation of the London-based Intergovernmental Committee for Political Refugees Coming from Germany (IGCR). Although its goals were to help countries develop safe opportunities for refugee resettlement, members did not provide the IGCR with funding or authority to function commensurately with the tasks it was intended to complete. During the following years, the IGCR was ultimately ineffectual and criticized as a 'face-saving organization' for reluctant, bickering democratic nations.[20]

Shortly following the Evian Conference, another two significant events intensified the refugee crisis. In late September 1938, British prime minister Neville Chamberlain signed the Munich Agreement following several negotiations with Hitler about the issue of Sudeten Germans in Czechoslovakia. Just a few days later, on 1 October 1938, German troops were allowed to march across the border into Czechoslovakia. Anticipating the German takeover, over 25,000 people, mostly Czech, had already fled a month previously from the Sudetenland into Czech areas.[21] Their fears were quickly validated; the Gestapo and SS, supported by the new government in Prague, suppressed communists and Social Democrats, and of course Jews. By May 1939, the number of Jews in the Sudetenland fell from 20,000 to less than 2,000.[22]

Just weeks later, Germany held violent nationwide pogroms from 9 to 13 November 1938, called *Kristallnacht*. This event has been distinguished by historians as an intensely brutal precedent in the discrimination of German Jews and, in many ways, a turning point towards even more systematic, bureaucratic violence.[23] These overwhelmingly violent riots certainly drew the shock and condemnation of the world and terrified Jews in Germany and German-occupied lands. In Vienna alone, some 680 Jews committed suicide in the days following the pogroms, especially as further anti-Jewish measures were soon announced.[24] Tens of thousands of Jewish men were arrested and put in concentration camps, while synagogues were destroyed and religious observances strictly limited. Full cultural exclusion was also a reality; Jews were banned from theatres, cinemas, concerts, sports and bathing facilities.[25]

Children, significantly, were now at risk. After nearly a dozen men burst into fifteen-year-old Susan Sinclair's family's home in Nuremberg, she remembers, 'They pulled me out of bed and tore my nightdress to shreds.... There were roars of laughers from these young men, who seemed as if they were drunk'.[26] Similarly, a German Jewish schoolgirl, Hedy Epstein, headed to class the morning of 10 November and was humiliated by the principal who turned to her and said, 'Get out you dirty Jew'.[27] Such traumatic accounts were widespread following *Kristallnacht*. Children who had previously been protected by their parents and families were now persecuted victims themselves and, following *Kristallnacht*, all Jewish children were excluded from German classrooms.[28] Jewish parents frantically tried to find ways to send their children away from Germany, even unaccompanied.[29] Distant familial relations and sympathetic friends, religious networks and other humanitarian agencies were all approached by desperate parents attempting to save their children.

Despite the fierce violence that characterized *Kristallnacht*, it was not the decisive turning point that forced governments to liberalize their refugee policies, even for children. In fact, no European nation unconditionally opened their doors to child refugees following *Kristallnacht*.[30] However, the collective events of 1938 (the *Anschluss*, the Evian Conference, the Munich Agreement and occupation of the Sudetenland, and *Kristallnacht*) were critical catalysts that provoked a remarkable reaction among humanitarian organizations. These charitable agencies, networks and altruistic individuals were tasked to find new, innovative methods to offer coordinated action for persecuted populations. Although Jewish refugees were clearly at risk, these agencies embraced other vulnerable populations they deemed worthy of saving, particularly children, as war and genocide soon spread across Europe.

Children as an innovative solution: The Kindertransport

The challenging task to save refugees in late 1938, even children, was not an easy undertaking. In Britain, various meetings in Whitehall in November 1938 confirmed that PM Chamberlain would not put pressure on Germany to change its treatment of Jews.[31] Therefore, the only solution lay in relocating persecuted populations beyond German borders. Ministers turned initially to the United States as a solution. British foreign secretary Lord Halifax suggested that part of the unused British quota for immigration into the United States be used for refugees from Germany. This was rejected by the Americans as it was legally impossible to transfer one country's quota to another sovereign country.[32] The British also hoped that the United States would offer a quota transfer on refugees. But this was deemed unlikely as President Roosevelt signed an executive order in November that cancelled the expiration of visas for 12,000–15,000 German visitors that were currently within the United States.[33] Ministers then raised the possibility of sending refugees (or unaccompanied children) to the British Mandate of Palestine or British Guiana. However, because the British government had argued that Palestine could not be used to resolve the refugee problem during the Evian Conference, it was again deemed impossible despite the events of *Kristallnacht*.[34] Historian Louise London argues that British Guiana was considered the most hopeful option among government officials, but even Prime Minister Chamberlain had to reiterate to colleagues that 'any proposed colonial settlement was unable to meet the immediate need for large-scale refuge'.[35] Put simply, the British government quickly ran out of practical ideas that resolved the immediate refugee issue.

However, humanitarian agencies stepped up to the urgent refugee crisis with innovative proposals. First, the proposal for relocating German Jewish children up to the age of seventeen years old to Britain for temporary periods was first put forward by a member of the British Jewish elite, Wilfred Israel (1899–1943), to the Council for German Jewry. On 15 November, this proposal was put to Prime Minister Chamberlain by Viscount Samuel, a member of the Council for German Jewry, who claimed that no public funds would be spent on children, and that their residency in Britain would be temporary.[36] Another idea was offered by *Yishuv*, the pre-State Jewish community in Palestine, whereby 10,000 Jewish refugee children from Central Europe would be resettled in Palestine. However, this led to infighting among the Foreign and Home Offices which could not reconcile such a scheme with overarching government policy.[37] Ideas were then considered about helping elderly, rather than young, refugees, on the basis that ageing groups were equally as worthy of humanitarian protection. However, this was also rejected due to the pressures from Jewish refugee organizations, which placed greater emphasis on the value of children and which had already offered a practical solution via the Council of German Jewry's proposal.

Ultimately, these various innovative ideas helped to clarify the British government's position. First, it was clear that *children* to the age of seventeen were the best group to target for humanitarian resettlement, as this could swiftly generate positive publicity for government action, significant donations from the public and practical support from key humanitarian actors. Secondly, relocating refugee children to other parts of the British Empire or the United States was politically untenable or impossible; thus, children would need to be relocated to Britain itself. Thirdly, concerns for children's welfare (including the upsetting experiences of resettlement abroad, or relocation back to their original countries) were secondary to the perceived political and economic necessity to ensure such child refugees remained a *temporary*, not permanent, burden.

These considerations resulted in Britain's famous *Kindertransport*, which carried out the (initially intended as temporary) evacuation of 10,000 child refugees from Germany, Austria, Poland and Czechoslovakia within nine months. To achieve this, a new, non-sectarian organization was created called the Refugee Children's Movement (RCM). This organization was equipped with enough bureaucratic strength to sustain the scope of the child evacuees and the large budget required to carry out the evacuations.[38] Although it mostly benefitted Jewish children (mostly from intact families), some children were also from mixed marriages or were the children of converted Jews.[39] As a result, the RCM included support from both Jewish and non-Jewish religious groups, including Roman Catholics, nonconformists and members of the Church of England. It is also noteworthy to highlight that although the scheme was publicly endorsed by individuals like Lord Samuel and Lord Gorell, the

Kindertransport's various operational tasks fell to accomplished and intelligent women, including Dorothy Hardisty, Lola Hahn-Warburg and Elaine Laski.[40]

Private and governmental funding for the *Kindertransport* adapted as the situation unfolded. Funds were initially raised privately; sponsors had to guarantee £50 for each evacuee to cover the costs of the children's train fares, hostels, clothes and the salaries of a matron and cook, or to subsidize children living with foster families.[41] Government promotions, including the Lord Baldwin Fund,[42] along with campaigns (whereby schools and networks raised money for 'adoptions' of evacuees) were supported by community collections from shops, offices, cinemas and events including balls, concerts and even boxing tournaments.[43]

The British government also changed its attitude towards funding. Public pressure in July 1939 compelled the British government to review its policy as set out during the Evian Conference. Although the RCM covered the costs of maintaining, educating and training the children, others expenditures had not been included, such as the children's transportation to Britain, guarantees for unsponsored children and administrative costs for rent, utilities and taxes of RCM offices.[44] Once the war was declared, it became clear that refugee children would not return to Europe. As a result, the British government agreed to pay half the cost of children's maintenance and administration and, ultimately, became responsible for three-quarters of the welfare, maintenance and administration costs for all needy refugees.[45]

As the majority (estimated 7,500) child evacuees were Jewish, this sparked debate among humanitarians about whether they should be hosted exclusively by Jewish foster families.[46] Orthodox rabbi Solomon Schonfeld, of the Chief Rabbi's Religious Emergency Council, went to great lengths to ensure that Hasidic children were selected (even travelling to Europe to persuade Hasidic parents to allow their children to join transports to Britain). Schonfeld ensured these Jewish evacuees were then hosted by Orthodox families, hostels or in his own mother's home.[47] However, in the end, and despite disagreement from some parents, many children were hosted by other religious groups and not exclusively by the Jewish community in Britain.

Experiences among child evacuees varied. There are abundant testimonies from *Kindertransport* evacuees who portray British host families as loving, nurturing and warm. This has led to recasting the *Kindertransport* as a narrative of rescue, salvation, altruism and integration. However, in recent years there have been more critical analyses of the Kindertransport and evacuee experiences.[48] Instances of food deprivation, maltreatment (including being exploited for domestic labour and caring responsibilities), physical and even sexual abuse have also been recorded.[49] Clearly, the impact of evacuees' losing their identities, homes, families and countries requires greater scrutiny, especially given the portrayal of the *Kindertransport* within British narratives, museums and commemorations as overwhelmingly positive.[50]

The last evacuation under the auspices of Britain's *Kindertransport* took place on 1 September 1939, just two days before Britain declared war on Germany.[51] Thus, British efforts were exclusively designed to succeed only during peacetime and were limited and conditional. However, these efforts were nonetheless innovative; the *Kindertransport* forced competing agencies with overlapping rivalries to collaborate their efforts through the RCM. Meanwhile, the British government's initial attempts to avert a permanent national burden by sending evacuees to the United States, Palestine or British Guiana were ultimately abandoned in the face of overpowering and innovative proposals by humanitarian networks, charities and individuals. Although the *Kindertransport* has become disproportionately mythologized in British national memory,[52] and now reflects a strong flavour of British exceptionalism in the history of wartime child evacuations, it was able to offer – for a limited time and with very restricted parameters – a novel solution to a global refugee crisis.

War, neutrality and child evacuations: Sweden and Switzerland

As war gripped Europe in September 1939, followed by the German occupation of Western Europe in mid-1940, the threats against civilians became increasingly indiscriminate. Bombings targeted cities, making the rural populations safer. Food rationing, especially in Nazi zones of occupation, allowed black markets to thrive, while lower-income households suffered malnutrition and disease. Political violence escalated against Jews, Roma and Sinti, the disabled, homosexuals, Jehovah's Witnesses and many others. The need for swift, humanitarian intervention was desired by nearly every segment of European society.

Humanitarian networks within Sweden and Switzerland, which were both neutral throughout the Second World War, distinguished children as their priority groups for intervention. They would not threaten the job market, they would generate humanitarian donations from sympathetic citizens more easily than adult refugees, and they were less difficult to relocate. Moreover, children's vulnerability to wartime attacks (such as bombings) and their deteriorating health and education (especially for those under German occupation) sparked calls for immediate assistance. While the financial burden to evacuate children lay chiefly with humanitarian agencies, the success of the operations depended entirely on the cooperation with neutral governments which could issue the necessary visas for immigration, even temporarily.[53] But unlike Britain's *Kindertransport*, such negotiations were now conducted against a backdrop of total war.

The pre-war attitudes to immigration in Sweden and Switzerland were extremely restrictive. Sweden's Aliens Act of 1937 aimed to grant protection to political refugees, but ultimately excluded Jewish refugees the right to be recognized under its remit.[54] At the Evian Conference, Swedish delegates persistently claimed that Sweden could not become a repository for refugees and instead called on larger nations (namely the United States) to absorb the majority of immigrants. Even when Denmark pushed for a joint Nordic approach on refugees, Sweden would not liberalize any of its policies.[55] For example, at the outbreak of the Second World War, there were only 5,000 refugees in Sweden (which would increase to 200,000 by 1945).[56]

Due to its proximity to German borders, Switzerland likewise guarded itself from Jewish refugees, especially after 1933.[57] Switzerland even went so far as to occasionally repatriate refugees from Germany (and Austria after the *Anschluss*), violating a concept of international law.[58] By 1938, Switzerland's severe anti-refugee policies had clearly failed, causing the Swiss to create the infamous J-stamp for Jewish passports, a procedure the Nazi authorities also adopted.⁵⁹ When Swiss delegate, Heinrich Rothmund, spoke at the Evian Conference in 1938, he argued that Switzerland should operate as a transit country so that immigrants could be permanently relocated to the United States.⁶⁰ Similar to Sweden, Switzerland was averse to the economic risks involved with absorbing refugees.

However, both Sweden and Switzerland's attitudes changed as their neighbours were drawn into war and their neutrality was threatened. For Sweden, the Winter War (beginning on 30 November 1939 between Finland and the Soviet Union) posed an immediate threat: if Finland collapsed, Sweden would have to defend itself against Soviet aggression and thereby jeopardize its neutral status. For Switzerland, which bordered three Axis nations, the Wehrmacht's invasion of France in the spring of 1940 caused concern that refugees could overwhelm its borders, compromise its neutrality and thus force the Swiss into war.⁶¹

Underpinning these 'neutrality concerns' were the rising calls from outspoken humanitarian groups and sympathetic government officials who argued against Swedish or Swiss passivity under the guise of 'neutrality'. In Sweden, parliamentarians were known for challenging anti-Semitism in debates, while Swedish voluntary refugee committees advocated the slogan 'Finlands sak är vår' (Finland's cause is ours).⁶² Switzerland, despite its anti-Semitic national policies, was also the home of the famous Red Cross movement since the 1860s. It thus prided itself in its humanitarianism and often advocated for international laws, practices and standards.⁶³ Following the occupation of northern France in 1940, outspoken Swiss humanitarians, such as Odette Micheli, queried government officials about how to help French children by way of evacuations.⁶⁴ The immunity of the Red Cross, further supported by the political neutrality of its homeland, meant that Swiss agencies often had great success and scope in their activities. With its convenient geography in the centre of Europe, Switzerland was therefore in an extraordinary position to offer humanitarian relief during the Second World War.

Both neutral nations confronted the war in similar ways. Within just weeks of the Winter War in December 1939, the newly established Central Aid for Finland began evacuations of Finnish children to Sweden. As Finnish fathers were drafted and mothers were alone to care for their children, these evacuations were promoted as an opportunity for children to enjoy a temporary stay in Sweden. They were financed by Swedish host families, while travel on boats and trains was subsidized by the Swedish government.⁶⁵ Approximately 8,000 children were transported during this brief three-and-a-half-month period, and by June 1940, most of the children had returned to Finland.

Swedish officials viewed these child evacuations as a suitable opportunity to counteract criticisms against Sweden's self-mandated position as a non-belligerent, neutral country.⁶⁶ As Sweden received an ultimatum from Germany that it could not support Denmark or Norway, lest it also wished to be attacked, Sweden had very few practical options to maintain good relations with its Nordic neighbours. Historian Ann Nehlin argues that these child evacuations were critical to creating good relations, whereby Finland would continue to fight against belligerents so that Sweden could retain its neutral status.⁶⁷

Child evacuations resumed during the Continuation War, during which Finland sided with Germany against the Soviet Union. Although only 2,000 children were initially selected, a total of 40,000 Finnish children were evacuated over the three years.[68] These child evacuations, although fraught with challenges and difficulties, were effective because of the adaptability of all parties, particularly the Swedish government, to negotiate and persist. For example, when friction arose between competing committees regarding the number of children to be evacuated, the Swedish government reconsidered that certain targets should be prioritized. Also, supporting Finland during the Continuation War was more complex than during the Winter War, because Finland's alliance was with Nazi Germany. As a result, Sweden was careful not to damage its credibility and carefully reduced its public promotion of child evacuations.[69] Finally, many Finns were understandably hesitant to send their children away for long periods. Finns often requested sponsorships to Finnish war orphanages and/or monetary donations from Swedish philanthropists and organizations.[70] They even asked if only sick and 'feeble' children could be evacuated instead.[71] However, Swedish government officials were persistent, particularly during the Continuation War, and insisted on the evacuations as politically necessary. Officials proclaimed the evacuations would 'have a substantial effect in strengthening the bonds between the two countries'.[72] Soon after, Finnish reluctance lessened, and the child evacuations to Sweden were gradually seen more favourably. Although the stays were initially temporary, many children remained for the duration of the war and, by 1945, over 70,000 Finnish children had been hosted in Sweden.[73]

Similarly, Switzerland quickly mobilized to protect its neutrality through inventive humanitarian measures that involved elaborate child evacuations. Following the German occupation of France in June 1940, a coalition of Swiss charities began various initiatives. These included 'sponsorships' (in the form of monthly stipends) for destitute French families, establishing dozens of Swiss-run children's homes for Jewish and orphaned children across Western Europe, and finally, the mass evacuations of children from southern, unoccupied Vichy France.[74] This coalition had operated similar child evacuations during the Spanish Civil War, so the leftover funds and networks were absorbed into the new initiative. Also, the language and proximity of the children to Swiss borders were important considerations. French children were accessible (unlike Finnish and Greek children who were deemed 'too far away'[75]) and they could communicate with French-speaking Swiss families, making foreign children more attractive to host.

In November 1940, the coalition began evacuating small convoys of French children from the unoccupied zone to Switzerland for three-month periods. Children (between the ages of four and fourteen years old), who were deemed indigent, sickly or malnourished, were selected by local Red Cross doctors in France. Evacuees were sent to Lyon (in the southern French zone) for processing before making the 150-kilometre journey to Geneva. From there, they were sent onwards to various parts of French-speaking Switzerland, usually around the region of Lake Geneva. The Swiss people and youth networks raised enormous funds from individuals and businesses, all of which reinforced that hosting child evacuees was 'the Swiss thing to do'.[76] This national sentiment was a cornerstone of the evacuations – Switzerland's role, according to the Swiss people, was to help the children of Europe.

The increasing popularity of the evacuations was alarming for government officials, particularly Switzerland's chief of police (and head of immigration), Heinrich Rothmund. Rothmund swiftly created visas for evacuees, which both streamlined and enforced the strict three-month duration. But these visas excluded 'non-Aryan'(Jewish) children and French-born children of immigrants (many of whom were Jewish and had fled Germany and Austria in 1938).[77] This was because Vichy France could withdraw its naturalization at any time, and Rothmund feared that such evacuees would not be permitted to return to France; meaning that Switzerland to have to provide for them, perhaps indefinitely.

But Switzerland's strict neutrality also facilitated the expansion of the evacuations into German-occupied northern France (Pas-de-Calais) and occupied Belgium. For over a year, from February 1941 until May 1942, the commanders of the Military Administration allowed French children (from Dunkirk, Calais and Boulogne) and Belgian children to be evacuated to Switzerland (see Figure 8.1). They justified this because of Switzerland's neutrality; children would not be politicized or turn against the Nazi regime. In fact, they affirmed to colleagues in Berlin, such child evacuations would pacify local parents and thereby increase local labour production. The military commanders argued that these humanitarian measures could offer a better form of control over their zone of occupation. Unfortunately for these children, Hitler disagreed with his commanders' arguments and terminated the evacuations to Switzerland in May 1942.[78]

Nonetheless, the evacuations continued to be extremely popular among the Swiss; everyone, from children to adults, businesses to charities, bankers to diplomats,

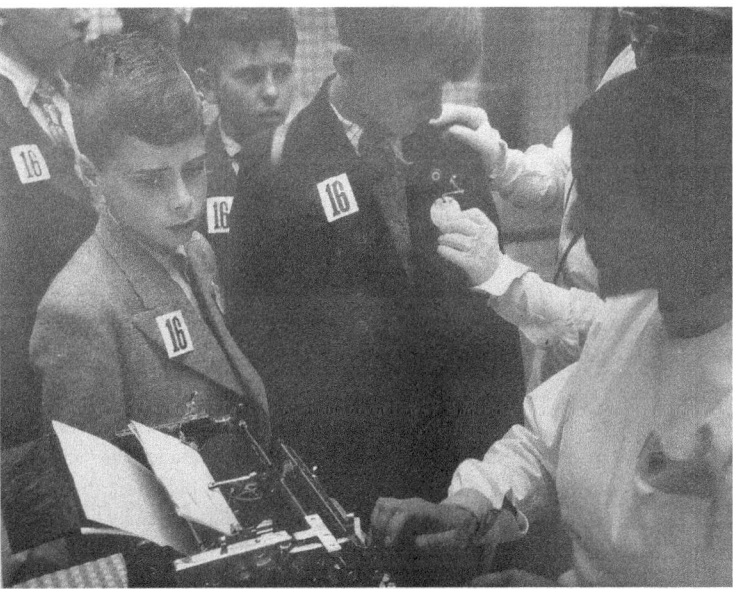

Figure 8.1 A convoy of Belgian children arrives in Switzerland, 1942. © Swiss Federal Archives (CH-BAR) J2.15-02#1969/7#408B, Belgische Kinder Kommen, 1942.

knew about these evacuations, even if they did not host children themselves. The Swiss (many of whom felt guilty about being neutral) supported these evacuations as a way to actively participate and support victims of war. In January 1942, the Swiss government united all operations under the Swiss Red Cross (SRC) to form *Kinderhilfe des Schweizerischen Roten Kreuzes* (Swiss Red Cross Children's Relief). It was also stipulated that the Swiss government had total control over the new *Kinderhilfe*. Although unusual, this arrangement reflected the concern that Switzerland's overtly humanitarian actions would be unfavourable to belligerent nations and jeopardize their neutral status. Similar to Sweden, Swiss officials found themselves monitoring and occasionally modifying the press coverage and propaganda about the evacuations in order to portray Switzerland as absolutely impartial. Offers were made to Axis governments to offer 'holiday stays' for German and Italian children as a method to balance the scales.[79]

With the rising persecution of Jews across Europe, Swiss Jewish groups and other concerned citizens began to question whether Jewish children were included in the evacuations. This caused a maelstrom of negative press in the spring of 1942, and various Swiss Jewish organizations lobbied Rothmund to include at least 200 Jewish children within every three-month stay.[80] Rothmund, reluctantly, declared in late April 1942 that 'French, Jewish children from non-occupied France can be admitted to convoys, provided that they benefit from a return visa and provided that their proportion remains reasonable (around two per cent)'.[81] This 2 per cent offer was not generous (no more than 103 Jewish children may have benefitted from this policy[82]), but it did indicate that even Switzerland's strictest officials could be forced to modify immigration policies.

By the summer of 1942, the overwhelming number of refugees fleeing Nazi persecution compelled Swiss officials to close their borders to all refugees, including child evacuees in August. The decision was harshly condemned by SRC officials, especially those on the Board of the *Kinderhilfe*; it remains controversial in Switzerland today. After the Allied invasion of Europe in June 1944, when the tide of war shifted considerably, the Swiss reopened their borders to refugees. The temporary child evacuations were restarted and by 1949, Switzerland had hosted an additional 100,000 children from all over Europe, including Germany, Austria, Hungary, Poland and England. In total, Switzerland hosted 160,000 children, the majority of whom were French.[83]

Sweden and Switzerland's chief priority was to maintain their neutrality in war. By carefully adapting to shifting wartime demands (both domestic and foreign), this priority was achieved by offering humanitarian assistance. Swedish officials were able to mitigate any challenges that arose during the humanitarian operations, as the evacuations of Finnish children allowed Sweden to compensate for the lack of military support while simultaneously bettering its own name. Likewise, for Switzerland, the evacuations reinforced its humanitarian image, while offering tangible relief to neighbours in a way that would not undermine belligerents or its own strict refugee policies. From each government's perspective, child evacuations were not motivated by a humanitarian impulse, but a highly politicized and calculated intervention that ensured political security and national resilience within the broader context of war.

Conclusion

By late 1938, it was no secret that the global community categorically failed to protect the discriminated and persecuted peoples of Central Europe, regrettably just months before war and genocide gripped the world. The *Anschluss*, the invasion of the Sudetenland and *Kristallnacht* typified Germany's aggression and created tens of thousands of refugees, while the Munich Agreement and the Evian Conference signified that the international community would neither confront Germany nor actively find solutions to save refugees caused by German aggression.

Children, remarkably, became the solution that either accommodated restrictive refugee legislation or eluded them altogether. But there was a constant push-and-pull between humanitarian groups and governments to implement this creative solution. Targeting *only* children for evacuation circumvented the immigration issue that precluded adult refugees from similar support, but it was not a long-term solution to a global crisis. Child evacuees generated significant financial donations but, even so, British, Swedish and Swiss governments had to financially support the evacuations in one form or another as they unfolded. The intended *temporary* duration of the children's stays (which was ultimately only possible in the Swiss case) meant that these evacuees would not become permanent burdens to the state. However, this failed in practice, as demonstrated in both post-war Britain and Sweden; while children were perceived as malleable entities that could relocate and adapt quickly, host families were the opposite. Many forged lifelong relationships with foster children and, in the case of Finnish evacuees in Sweden, ended up in bitter, post-war custody battles.[84] Clearly, there were great discrepancies between the initial intentions of the evacuations and their ultimate reality, regardless of the remarkable compromises and standardized practices that were negotiated between the highest levels of government and the most determined humanitarian activists.

Children who were evacuated for temporary durations to Britain, Sweden and Switzerland to an extent defy some of the categories seen among other refugee groups. While other migrants and displaced persons may choose to share their identities and customs with new communities, child evacuees (and child refugees more broadly) were often unable to remember or articulate their traditions, customs and even their names. While children were *perceived* to be able to adapt to their new host societies more easily than adults, historians, such as Rebecca Clifford, are currently reversing this perception.[85] In fact, some child refugees only gained a sense of belonging within their original diasporas and communities decades later. These renewed desires to return to the past were often a result of events in their adult lives, such as the death of a (biological or adoptive) parent, or the birth of their own child.[86] Others explored their own pasts by educating themselves about the Second World War and Holocaust, as a way to map their own experiences within the broader histories of the time. This sometimes led to confronting repressed memories or deconstructing protective myths that refugees and survivors told themselves to ward off upsetting thoughts and memories.[87] But such research highlights the traumatic legacies of child evacuees' experiences, and also allows us to confront the misguided perceptions that governments and humanitarian actors held towards children, even when creating elaborate evacuation plans, they claimed, for their benefit.

Notes

1. Anti-immigrant attitudes developed and/or intensified in many Western nations in the 1920s, and these attitudes continued to overshadow discussions about refugees in the 1930s. For the UK, see Louise London, *Whitehall and the Jews, 1933–1948* (Cambridge: Cambridge University Press, 2000); for Sweden, see H. Lindberg, *Svensk flyktingpolitik under internationellt tryck 1936–41* (Stockholm: Allmänna förl., 1973); for Switzerland, see Independent Commission of Experts Switzerland – The Second World War (hereafter ICE), *Switzerland and Refugees in the Nazi Era*, Vol. 17 (Bern: Chronos Verlag, 1999), and for a discussion of immigration among those nations who attended the Evian Conference in July 1938, see Dennis Ross Laffer, 'The Jewish Trail of Tears, the Evian Conference of July 1938' (PhD diss., University of South Florida, 2011).
2. Richard Evans, *The Third Reich in Power* (London: Penguin, 2005), 557.
3. Laffer, 'The Jewish Trail of Tears', 306.
4. Evans, *The Third Reich in Power*, 555; George Tindall and David Shi, *America, A Narrative History*, 5th ed. (New York: Norton & Company, 2000), 896.
5. London, *Whitehall and the Jews*, 281–2.
6. Ibid., 25–57.
7. Rebecca Boeling and Uta Larkey, *Life and Loss in the Shadow of the Holocaust: A Jewish Family's Untold Story* (Cambridge: Cambridge University Press, 2011), 144.
8. On government restrictions, see Tindall and Shi, *America*, 895–6; London, *Whitehall and the Jews*, 42–4; Laffer, 'The Jewish Trail of Tears', 270.
9. Laffer, 'The Jewish Trail of Tears', 65–72.
10. Geneva, Switzerland had initially been chosen to host the conference, but declined on the grounds that it might lead to increased pressure to host a permanent agency in Switzerland, see ICE), *Switzerland and Refugees in the Nazi Era*, 41.
11. *Tampa Tribune* (25 March 1938): 1 and 9, quoted in Laffer, 'The Jewish Trail of Tears', 75.
12. Ibid.
13. Laffer, 'The Jewish Trail of Tears', 101.
14. Ibid., 167.
15. ICE, *Switzerland, National Socialism and the Second World War. Final Report* (Zürich: Pendo Verlag GmBH, 2001), 164.
16. Laffer, 'The Jewish Trail of Tears', 226.
17. 'After Evian', *Manchester Guardian* (16 July 1938): 12.
18. Ludwig Lore, 'Behind the Cables', *New York Post* (16 July 1938): 10.
19. There were around 500 Jews resettled in the Dominican Republic during the war. See Marion Kaplan, *Dominican Haven: The Jewish Refugee Settlement in Sosúa, 1940–1945* (New York: Museum of Jewish Heritage, 2008).
20. Laffer, 'The Jewish Trail of Tears', 304.
21. Evans, *Third Reich in Power*, 678.
22. Ibid., 678.
23. Michael Burleigh, *The Third Reich: A New History* (London: Pan Books, 2001), 323.
24. Ibid., 331.
25. Michael Kater, *Culture in Nazi Germany* (London: Yale University Press, 2019), 138.
26. Imperial War Museums, London, interview 17177, reel 1, Susan Sinclair, interview by Lyn Smith, 25 November 1996.
27. Ibid., interview 12397, reel 1, Hedy Epstein, interview by Lyn Smith, 12 December 1991.

28 Kater, *Culture in Nazi Germany*, 138.
29 German parents placed advertisements in the *Manchester Guardian* and other British newspapers to urgently appeal to potential foster parents to host their children. Julian Borger, '"I Seek a Kind Person": The Guardian ad that Saved My Jewish Father from the Nazis', *The Guardian* (6 May 2021). Available online: https://www.theguardian.com/media/2021/may/06/guardian-200-ad-that-saved-jewish-father-from-nazis (accessed on 10 December 12021).
30 Baumel-Schwartz, *Never Look Back*, 52.
31 London, *Whitehall and the Jews*, 101.
32 Baumel-Schwartz, *Never Look Back*, 55.
33 Ibid., 51.
34 Ibid., 53.
35 London, *Whitehall and the Jews*, 101.
36 Baumel-Schwartz, *Never Look Back*, 53.
37 Ibid., 55.
38 At one stage in early 1939, five different organizations relocated children from Germany to the UK (the B'nai Brith Council for Refugee Children, the Children's Inter-Aid Committee, the Movement for the Care of Children from Germany, the Women's Appeal Committee and the Chief Rabbi's Religious Emergency Council).
39 'Kindertransport', in *Holocaust Encyclopedia*, ed. United States Holocaust Memorial Museum (30 September 2021). Available online: https://encyclopedia.ushmm.org/content/en/article/kindertransport-1938-40/ (accessed 10 December 2021).
40 Baumel-Schwartz, *Never Look Back*, 76–7.
41 Ibid., 91.
42 Ibid., 92.
43 Over 2,500,000 USD had been pledged in advance of the first radio broadcast, see 'Baldwin Broadcast Appeal for Refugees', *Jewish Telegraphic Agency* (9 December 1938): 7.
44 Baumel-Schwartz, *Never Look Back*, 94–5.
45 Ibid., 95.
46 'Kindertransport', in *Holocaust Encyclopedia*.
47 Baumel-Schwartz, *Never Look Back*, 82.
48 See, for example, Paul Weindling, 'The Kindertransport from Vienna: The Children Who Came and Those Left Behind', *Jewish Historical Studies* 51 (2020): 16–32 and 'Tagungsbericht: Forward from the Past: The Kindertransport from a Contemporary Perspective, 25.06.2013 London', *H-Soz-Kult* (11 August 2013). Available online: https://www.hsozkult.de/conferencereport/id/tagungsberichte-4972 (accessed 10 December 2021).
49 Charlotte Ingle, 'Ten Thousand Children: Rethinking Childhood Experiences of Family Life Among Kindertransportees' (Undergraduate Diss., University of Bristol, 2018), 16–20.
50 Amy Williams, 'Memory of the Kindertransport in National and Transnational Perspective' (PhD Diss., Nottingham Trent University, 2020), 181.
51 'Kindertransport', in *Holocaust Encyclopedia*.
52 Andrea Hammel, 'The 1938 Kindertransport saved 10,000 Children But It's Hard to Describe it as Purely Success', *The Conversation UK* (22 November 2018). Available online: https://theconversation.com/the-1938-kindertransport-saved-10-000-children-but-its-hard-to-describe-it-as-purely-a-success-107299/ (accessed on 10 December 2021).

53 Chelsea Sambells, 'Convenient and Conditional Humanitarianism: Evacuating French and French Jewish Children to Switzerland during the Second World War', *Nottingham French Studies* 59, no. 2 (2020): 174–90.
54 Mikael Byström, 'When the State Stepped into the Arena: The Swedish Welfare State, Refugees and Immigrants 1930s–1950s', *Journal of Contemporary History* 49, no. 3 (2014): 608.
55 Ibid., 609.
56 Ibid., 610.
57 Jacques Picard, *Die Schweiz und die Juden* (Zurich: Chronos, 1994), 17–18.
58 ICE, *Final Report*, 164–5.
59 Ibid., 129.
60 Ibid., 164.
61 Documents diplomatique Suisse (hereafter DODIS), 47423, *Notice du Délégué du Conseil fédéral aux Œuvres d'Entraide internationale, E. de Haller, pour le Chef du Département politique, M. Pilet-Golaz*, 15 September 1942.
62 Byström, 'When the State Stepped into the Arena', 611; Aura Korppi-Tommola, 'War and Children in Finland during the Second World War', *Paedagogica Historica* 44 (2008): 447.
63 Many organizations and international bodies, including the International Committee of the Red Cross, International Labour Organization and the League of Nations, established themselves in Geneva during the interwar years.
64 Swiss Federal Archives, Bern, Papers of the Federal State Since 1848 (hereafter CH-BAR), E2001D 1968/74 BD 16 D.009 14, *Hospitalisation français*, 27 November 1940.
65 Ann Nehlin, 'Building Bridges of Trust: Child Transports from Finland to Sweden during the Second World War', *War & Society* 36, no. 2 (2017): 152.
66 Ibid., 136.
67 Ibid.
68 Ibid., 143.
69 Ibid., 142.
70 Korppi-Tommola, 'War and Children in Finland', 448.
71 Nehlin, 'Building Bridges of Trust', 148.
72 Swedish National Archives, The Committee for Finnish Summer Children, Minutes of board meeting, 9 May 1941, quoted in Nehlin, 'Building Bridges of Trust', 148.
73 The permanent relocation of children led to lengthy post-war custody battles. As a result, many Finnish parents were often unable to retrieve their children from Sweden. Children who did return to Finland had the rare experience of growing up in both cultures and even retaining both languages, an unusual phenomenon that has complicated and strengthened Finnish attitudes to their neighbours. See Korppi-Tommola, 'War and Children in Finland', 445–55.
74 Chelsea Sambells, 'Saving Foreign Children from "Moral Decay": Switzerland's Children's Homes During the Second World War', *The Journal of the History of Childhood and Youth* 11, no. 1 (2018): 5–26.
75 CH-BAR, E2001D 1000/1552 BD187, *Motion Reinhard*, 19 March 1942.
76 CH-BAR, E2001D 1000/1552 BD 187, *Croix-Rouge Suisse, Secours aux Enfants: Circulaires et imprimés des commissions*, 12 March 1942.
77 Ibid., *Croix-Rouge Suisse, Secours aux Enfants*, 23 May 1941.
78 Chelsea Sambells, '"Children Are to Be Regarded as Propaganda": Contradictions of German Occupation Policies in the Child Evacuations to Switzerland, 1941–1942', *European History Quarterly* 51, no. 1 (2021): 76–97.

79 DODIS, 47331, *Département politique Berichterstattung*, 7 January 1942.
80 Serge Nessi, *La Croix-Rouge Suisse au secours des enfants 1942–1945* (Geneva: Éditions Slatkine, 2011), 174 and Antonia Schmidlin, *Eine andere Schweiz: Helferinnen, Kriegskinder und humanitäre Politik 1933–1942* (Zurich: Chronos Verlag, 1999), 240.
81 CH-BAR, E2001D 1968/74 BD 16, *Hospitalisation en Suisse d'enfants français*, 29 April 1942.
82 Sambells, 'Convenient and Conditional Humanitarianism', 183.
83 Nessi, *La Croix-Rouge Suisse*, 237.
84 Korppi-Tommola, 'War and Children in Finland', 445–55.
85 Rebecca Clifford, *Survivors, Children's Lives after the Holocaust* (London: Yale University Press, 2020).
86 Sarah Moskovitz, *Love Despite Hate: Child Survivors of the Holocaust and their Adult lives* (New York: Schocken Books, 1983).
87 Clifford, *Survivors*, 179–97.

9

'And Without a Hat!'

Refugee women in the transit country Portugal after 1933

Katrin Sippel

Introduction

The notion of the 'otherness' of refugees in comparison to the local population is a recurring topic in scientific works about refugees in Portugal as well as in refugees' own memoirs and testimonies.[1] The following research on the cultural transfer from refugees to locals in Portugal during and after the Second World War is based on newspaper and magazine articles published in Lisbon in the period between 1937 and 1946. Two of these featured articles specifically related to this topic: The *Mundo Gráfico* (Graphic World)[2] presented fashion novelties and changes in women's habits in society, while the *Boletim mensal* (Monthly Bulletin) of the female youth group *Mocidade Portuguesa Feminina* (MPF, Female Portuguese Youth)[3] criticized those heavily. In this chapter, I will provide an overview of refugees in Portugal and the Portuguese host society, in particular the role of women, in the 1930s and 1940s as well as of the changes which refugees induced in the area of fashion, habits and morals.

Refugees in Portugal

After Hitler's assumption of power in Germany in 1933, refugees from National Socialism started to arrive in Portugal. Many more followed after the annexation of Austria and the November pogroms in 1938. The largest influx of refugees occurred after the capitulation of France in June 1940. Those who had sought refuge there were subsequently forced to move on and tried to get a passage overseas from the port of Lisbon. The number of refugees who passed through Portugal is estimated at 60,000–80,000 persons.[4] This wide margin is due to the fact that many immigrated illegally, and that counts by government agencies and aid organizations were incomplete.[5] More than 90 per cent of these refugees were Jewish, of which the vast majority consisted of assimilated Jews. Most of them only attended the synagogue on High Holidays. To accommodate them, the Lisbon Jewish community rented big halls for Yom Kippur services in the years 1940 and 1941. It also extended the Lisbon synagogue which after the war was too vast, as nearly all the refugees had left.[6] Although most refugees did not keep kosher, the offers were also for observant Jews. In October 1940, the *Cozinha Económica* (soup kitchen) of the Lisbon Jewish community served 500 kosher meals daily,[7] and in the beach town Ericeira north of Lisbon, one of the places of *residência fixa* (assigned residence), to which refugees were sent once Lisbon had become 'overcrowded' after the fall of France, a kosher abattoir was established.[8]

The refugees in Portugal would send food parcels to their families and friends left behind in Nazi-occupied countries.[9] Among the Austrians, there were several conservative and a few leftist political refugees. Many of them were Jewish. The refugees' memoirs show nostalgia for the lost *Heimat*. Some refugees were politically active while in Portugal. Hans Rott, for instance, liaised with Otto von Habsburg-Lothringen about an Austrian exile government,[10] while Carl-Ludwig von Habsburg-Lothringen negotiated with Hungarian politicians about the foundation of a Danube federation.[11]

Despite their large numbers, the Jewish refugee presence in Portugal was not meant to be permanent, and very few opted to stay there. They regarded their stay merely as a period of transit, as did the Portuguese authorities. Hardly any refugee wanted to settle in Portugal. It was too close to Nazi-occupied France and fascist Spain, many lived in fear of a German invasion during the war. Portugal was too poor and too backward, the socio-economic differences too big, which did not make it attractive as a country of exile. The Portuguese people were considered to be friendly, welcoming and interested, but the authorities wanted to avoid foreign influences and established laws that made it difficult to settle down for non-Portuguese citizens. Their integration was not intended, as the government did not wish for them to stay. Most refugees therefore did not care about adapting to local customs or trying to blend in with the host society. They just behaved as if at home and by doing so would change the host society.

Throughout the war, the corporatist authoritarian *Estado Novo* regime under Antonio de Oliveira Salazar maintained its neutrality and pursued a seesaw policy between the Allies and the Axis powers.[12] The country's asylum policy was liberal in the years before the Second World War, very restrictive after it began and more generous again when the Allied victory was in sight.[13] Nevertheless, Portugal still presents the magnanimous welcoming and 'salvation' of refugees as a success story. It is true that many thousands were saved by being allowed to cross the borders; however, for some, those borders were not opened. In the archives of the Foreign Ministry, many visa applications can be found which had been rejected because the applicants were Jews. 'No – Jew!' is written in red on their files.[14]

Portugal in the late 1930s and early 1940s

The refugees came to a place which was very different from their familiar environment. In 1932, Antonio de Oliveira Salazar had been appointed prime minister and soon consolidated his rule. He later coined the famous phrase *orgulhosamente sós* (proudly alone). Indeed, during his tenure the Iberian country lived in a kind of 'splendid isolation'.[15] Or, as the writer José Rodrigues Miguéis put it, 'O mundo ficava longe' (The world was far away).[16] 'It would be patently unfair to expect [the refugees'] personal accounts to discuss broader socioeconomic developments or comparative models' – the editors of this volume write in their introduction. However, the memoirs and reports of several persons who had been refugees in Portugal nevertheless show that they had a good understanding of the social situation in their host country. The Portuguese isolation from the rest of the world left them puzzled. Gretchen Wohlwill[17] wrote in her memoir that she could not understand the submissiveness of the women and the locals' limited horizons.[18] 'Not only . . . the common people . . . , also the middle classes vegetate in a certain apathy. "Provincial" is the word that serves well to characterize Lisbon.'[19]

In the former Jewish refugee Ilse Losa's[20] semi-autobiographical novel *Under Strange Skies*,[21] a German exile calls Portugal a quiet and backward country.[22] To a foreign cosmopolitan protagonist of the book, the city of Porto is 'phlegmatic',[23] 'village-like'[24] and 'extremely provincial'.[25] Stefan Zweig's estranged wife, Friderike Zweig-Winternitz,[26] stayed in Lisbon and Estoril in the autumn of 1940 and travelled through the country.[27] In her 1964 memoir, she spoke very positively about the Portuguese people, their patience with foreigners and their warmth. Lisbon to her is a 'Weltstadt', a cosmopolitan city, but she observed:

> A strange country . . . the past can be felt everywhere, also in the political realm. A sterile standstill . . . a lost grandeur in the middle of an unstoppable new world that Portugal does not accept. Therefore, also the clinging to what she, in reality, no longer owns, the colonies, trying in vain to feign an empire. . . . Were we in Europe or was this a strange country between the times?[28]

Women in Portugal

One of the most striking differences between Portugal and Central Europe was the status of women. In 1930, about 70 per cent of women in Portugal compared to 53 per cent of men were illiterate.[29] Only widows, divorcees and women whose husbands lived abroad were allowed to vote, provided they had a secondary school degree or a university education.[30] Professional activity by women was frowned upon by the Salazar regime, which feared it would lead to the disintegration of families.[31] The government set minimum wages which were lower for women. Female teachers were not allowed to wear make-up and had to ask the Ministry of Education for permission to marry.[32] The motto and the three pillars of Salazarism were *Deus, Pátria, Família* (God, Fatherland, Family). The education policy of the *Estado Novo* aimed at building a new society that followed these principles. In 1937, Salazar established two organizations for female citizens: the *Obra das Mães para a Educação Nacional* (Mothers' Work for National Education) encouraged young women to become wives and concentrate on household, family and education of 'the future men of Portugal'.[33] Membership in the youth group

MPF was mandatory for all Portuguese girls between the ages of seven and fourteen and voluntary until the age of twenty-one, or twenty-five for students.[34]

The MPF provides a good example of the prevailing ideas and ideals about and for women at that time. Its five cornerstones were (1) moral and religious education (the exaltation of faith and Christian virtues), (2) nationalist education (love for the nation, the rural, maritime and colonial ideal), (3) family and household education, (4) physical education (order and discipline) and (5) studies and culture (taste for arts, literature and science).[35] The MPF girls ought to be sensible, chaste and restrained in their relationships with boys. While love was important, the bond of marriage had to be consolidated by children – the more, the better.[36] The family was the 'nucleus of society'. Healthy, happy, united and disciplined families were synonymous with a strong, cohesive, obedient nation.[37] Wives and mothers were supposed to be obedient, loyal, docile, tender, vigilant and ready to sacrifice everything for their family.[38] They should be educated in order to avoid monotony in the marriage, but not have a know-it-all attitude.[39] Spiritual beauty was what mattered most for an MPF member. As appearance reflected inner beauty, readers of the MPF magazine were constantly reminded to dress, do their hair and behave in society in a simple and modest manner. Luxury and flamboyance in dress, arrogance and vanity, artificial make-up, but also neglect of one's appearance were heavily criticized.[40] The magazine recommended physical exercise to maintain a slender figure, add elegance to the movements and remain resilient to illness. The exercises suggested included walks with the baby carriage or running around with small children. Horse riding (side saddle), fencing, volleyball, basketball, tennis, swimming, cycling, skating and walking were considered physically and morally healthy. Building up muscles, however, was not considered feminine.[41]

The experience of the refugees in Portugal laid bare, for refugees and locals, the very unjust society as far as gender and class were concerned. In her novel, Ilse Losa depicts a small bourgeois Portuguese family consisting of a couple, their eleven-year-old daughter, the mother's mother and the mother's unmarried sister who as a milliner is mainly responsible for earning the household income. Still, the only man in the family has to grant the women permission to go to the theatre or the cinema. 'At the most, they were allowed to attend mass on their own.'[42] The wife serves her husband lunch and dinner while standing behind his chair and only eats after he has finished.[43]

Refugees' perceptions

Female refugees were shocked by the submissiveness of the Portuguese women. Zweig-Winternitz noted:

> It is a sad and almost biblical image when small caravans cross the barren fields, the man on the donkey, the woman on foot, loaded with bags, barefoot, careworn, in spite of all the feminism in the rest of the world. In the south of the country the women still wore black scarves, pulled down over the forehead. In the cafés on

Rossio Square, only men can be seen. The nobler a woman, the more hidden she was, and probably still is today, because this remains a country of the past.[44]

The Jewish heiress and art collector Peggy Guggenheim had the same impression. She was aghast at the public invisibility of female Portuguese, except for peasant women on the market, 'and a few whores'. In Cascais, the homes seemed to her 'hermetically sealed, their walls closing up the lives of all the women, who were not allowed on the streets'.[45] Margit Morawetz from Innsbruck, the daughter of a Jewish banker, was eighteen years old when she arrived in Lisbon with her mother in 1940. In her memoir, she wrote: 'At the time, young, middle-class Portuguese women were not permitted to go out by themselves. By custom they had to be accompanied by siblings or other family members. I, on the other hand, felt perfectly free to come and go.' The landlady's daughter, about Margit's age, who 'spent most of her day on the windowsill', was envious.[46]

In a 1995 interview, Ruth Arons[47] recalled a pre-war episode. The lawyer's family from Berlin had recently arrived in Lisbon. Ruth's mother came to pick her up from school and, while waiting, sat down on a bench on the Avenida. The next day, a schoolmate came over to Ruth to ask her why her mother had been sitting on a bench, and without a hat![48] Marion Kaplan states that only prostitutes did not cover their heads at that time in Lisbon.[49] Yvette Davidoff,[50] who was also Jewish and originally from Vienna, arrived in Portugal as a young woman with her mother. She remembered her first day in Lisbon:

> we entered a café and suddenly there was a queue of men staring at us! And my mother said: 'There will be a demonstration!' Later, people told them: 'Don't go to cafés, you can't do that here, it's only for men. . . . [W]e could not do anything, not even go to the cinema on our own! You don't do that here!'[51]

The seventeen-year-old French girl Denise Hahn went to a park with her sisters in Porto, and they 'quickly understood that this was unacceptable behaviour for proper folks'.[52] A German refugee girl in Ilse Losa's novel complained about Porto: 'A girl cannot go out into the street after dinner unless she wants to be taken for a whore.'[53] In 1939, the US State Department distributed a leaflet among its diplomats in Lisbon advising them not to speak to Portuguese ladies without their husbands being present or having been formally introduced, and to stay away from Portuguese women in general in order to avoid complications.[54] In contrast, Central European women are described as

> ordinary bourgeois women who went to the market, did their shopping and worked without maids to help in the house. These women participated actively in their children's literary and artistic education. They spoke several languages, played the piano, sang, appreciated opera and ballet and were discerning about what was going on politically in the war and its dramas. They talked openly about the war atrocities they knew of, expressed their views on the most recent moves by the allies that were broadcast on the radio for all to hear.[55]

The use of public space

The female refugees challenged traditional gender roles. They started to have an influence on 'the daily rituals' as well as fashion and the role of women in society as a whole.[56] The cafés in Portugal were traditionally meeting points for men. Ilse Losa describes a café in Porto: 'As was customary at that time, no female element was present, except two heavily made-up whores . . .'[57] Now, foreign women were sitting there, wearing neither hats, gloves, nor stockings. Their presence shocked the 'sociedade patriarcal salazarista' (patriarchal society of Salazarism).[58] Another novelty introduced by the refugees was to sit outside in the sun instead of inside the cafés: 'enforced idleness, tight living quarters and appreciation of the sunny climate' are given as reasons for frequenting the cafés and their terraces.[59] The writer Alves Redol, in his novel *O Cavalo Espantado*, describes how in 1939 on the Carmo square, 'at the request of refugees without sun to warm them in life', tables were put outside.[60]

The locals' attitude

Portugal's 'exacerbated nostalgia of the past' and the closure of the country influenced the perception of the refugees by the locals. The foreigners were associated with a temporal dimension 'linked to progress, comfort and a carelessness towards tradition'.[61] Ruth Arons recalled that depending on age, class and sometimes gender, the Portuguese found the refugee women's behaviour either outrageous or fascinating.[62] For some Portuguese, the refugees seemed to be inhabitants of a different planet. In June 1940, the *Diario de Coimbra* reported that wherever a foreigner appeared, he or she was instantly surrounded by half a dozen curious locals staring at him or her.[63] A German refugee in Losa's novel complains about being made fun of for not wearing stockings: 'as if we were clowns'.[64] In the novel *O Cavalo Espantado*, a Polish refugee says to her husband: 'We seem to be in the zoo.'[65] The *Pastelaria Suiça*,[66] a popular meeting point of refugees in central Lisbon, was called *Bompernasse* by the Portuguese (an allusion to the mondain Paris suburb of Montparnasse), and also as one could see 'good legs' there (*bom* for good, *pernas* for legs). The foreign women used to wear short skirts or dresses, local men came to stare, newspaper boys even tried to get a glimpse from below.[67]

In the small *residência fixa* beach town Figueira da Foz, the locals were dumbfounded when blond refugee women with short skirts and headscarves smoked in the streets.[68] In Ericeira, elderly ladies reportedly went on 'excursions' to watch refugee women. They were shocked by couples that kissed in public or lived together without being married.[69] The parson of Ericeira described the foreign women in an alarming sermon as dishonest, and the men, an old accusation against Jews, as assassins of Jesus, urging the locals to stay away from them.[70] Nonetheless, many activities were organized together. At picnics and parties the locals tried to drink more than the foreigners but usually failed.[71] The ladies' choice practised by the refugee women caused quite a stir.[72]

At odds with the law due to morality issues

How did the role of gender influence experiences of refugees in Portugal? One can diagnose, in Marion Kaplan's words, 'a flattening of gender roles rather than an extreme role reversal: both men and women stood in consulate lines, both applied to aid organizations, both waited and worried in cafés, and both had lost homes, homelands, and their places in society'.[73] Gender mattered a lot, as women were more in the focus of attention than men and their behaviour was faster judged as inappropriate, with severe consequences. The journalist Eugen Tillinger reported that a father of four had left his wife and children for a young refugee: 'The Dutch girl was arrested and accused of immoral behaviour. She is in Caxias prison waiting for a visa to return to her country.'[74] According to the journalist and screenwriter Jan Lustig, another girl was accused of prostitution and deported to assigned residence in the spa town Curia.[75] Lustig also reported in October 1940 the arrest of two refugee girls because they had worn trousers on the Figueira beach and had been seen with a gentleman in a cabriolet. They, too, were accused of disturbing public morality and of prostitution. No lawyer was permitted to defend them.[76] Salamon Dembitzer, in his autobiographical novel *Visum nach Amerika*, writes that a female refugee was arrested because a married Portuguese man had fallen in love with her.[77] The fate of these unfortunate women remains unknown.

Fashion

The writer Otto Zoff's assessment of Lisbon women was unflattering: 'Everything is crude, unattractive, provincial. The women look as though women farmers had decided to organize a Paris-themed fancy-dress ball.'[78] Bourgeois women in Portugal had to wear gloves, hats and stockings unless they wanted to break the rules of good manners.[79] The refugee women wore, for example, sleeveless blouses or dresses of much lighter and flashier colours, sometimes with ornaments or large buttons instead of jewellery they no longer owned.[80] They also 'introduced the use of slacks and even shorts'.[81] Their hair was arranged in ponytails, pinned up or with scarves around their heads, mainly because they lacked money for the hairdresser.[82] The *penteado à refugiada* (refugee-style hairdo), according to different sources either a short cut or a pinned-up hairstyle, became popular with Portuguese women,[83] as well as turbans.[84]

The attire of the male refugees was not very different from that of the Portuguese males, but it was noticed that they often did not wear hats,[85] and complaints were made that they wore open shirts without ties.[86] There are reports of protests by the locals, for example, if somebody wore sandals in a restaurant.[87] Some refugees lent their dresses, brought from Western or Central Europe, to Portuguese haute couture ateliers that copied them, sometimes in exchange for a new dress.[88]

Among the almost 1,900 Austrians identified so far by the research project on refugees in Portugal, there were milliners, tailors and dressmakers. Some of them practised their profession while in Portugal. Franziska and Ludwig Rosenbaum[89] established an illegal dress-making workshop in the home of the prominent Jewish Levy family in central

Lisbon. Another refugee woman made undergarments for ladies, while her husband repaired shoes.[90] The teenager Margit Morawetz also went into the dress-making business: 'Through word-of-mouth I became the dressmaker of the refugee crowd.' She specialized in pleated skirts from pre-cut and pre-pleated material prepared by another emigrant woman. 'My reputation as a good dressmaker grew among the refugees and pretty soon I was busy enough to support Mother and me.'[91] The changes in fashion were well noted in the press. An article in the *Mundo Grafico* magazine is entitled 'Lisboa a capital da moda': 'Lisbon became the capital of fashion with the war . . . you don't have to look for dresses in Paris any more. They come by train – naturally on their living models.'[92] The caption of a photograph in the article reads: 'Portuguese women are already used to not wearing hats. This new habit reveals us new hairstyles.'[93]

The swimsuit issue

During their stay in Portugal, which sometimes lasted many months, as visas and naval tickets overseas were scarce and expensive, the refugees visited the beaches. Thus arose a special 'problem' for Portuguese morality, especially concerning the bathing suits in two parts, bikinis *avant la lettre*, which were considered scandalous.[94] The Ministry of the Interior, in its 'zeal for morality', wanted to safeguard a 'minimum of decency'.[95] It issued a decree with detailed rules on how to dress at the beach which was posted in the beach resorts.[96] Penalties were set and some foreigners, including the Duke of Windsor's male secretary, were fined by the beach patrol.[97] Male bathing suits had to cover the torso and especially the nipples.[98] Women had to wear bathing suits with an over-skirt. The cleavage should not be 'exaggerated'. Bathing suits that became transparent in the water were prohibited. Girls up to ten and boys up to twelve years were exempt from these norms, except in cases of precocious development.[99] Marta Feuchtwanger wore her two-piece bathing suit at Estoril beach. When she spotted a man approaching her, she thought he might be interested in her, something she would have considered 'much easier', but instead, he identified himself as a police officer, told her that her bathing suit constituted a 'crime' against morality and fined her.[100] Also, Peggy Guggenheim recalled that 'we were always being taken up by the police for wearing what they considered indecent bathing suits. As they could not speak French or English they used to measure the outstanding parts of our bodies, make scenes, and then proceed to fine us.' Her partner, the German painter Max Ernst, was required to wear a shirt on the beach.[101] For those who were not sure whether their bathing suits were in compliance with the rules, the MPF commercialized its own line of officially approved bathing suits.[102] Without much success: in several articles the magazine of the MPF warned its members against the two-part bathing suit,[103] or praised girls and women who dressed properly.

Food, outdoors, sports and the body

The refugees are said to have introduced yoghurt and pizza, whiskey, the habit of drinking beer rather than wine,[104] and the very popular *Bola de Berlim*, a larger version of the *Berliner Pfannkuchen*, filled with an egg-yolk-based cream. The Portuguese were bewildered by the refugees' habit of going out for walks and considered them stupid for not accepting offers of lifts from the drivers of passing cars.[105] The love for nature and open-air exercise was new to them.[106] At the same time, sports activities established bonds between locals and foreigners. In the spa town of Caldas da Rainha, another place of *residência fixa*, an Italian refugee gave boxing classes, and a Russian with the nickname 'Papa Urso' founded the male gymnastics group 'Os Ursos Brancos'[107] and furthermore taught foreigners and locals judo, ping-pong, snooker and singing.[108] Some refugees in Caldas played tennis at the *Clube do Parque*. Very soon, the *Caldenses* began to practise this sport as well;[109] thus, sports became a strategy for living together.[110]

Another change the refugees brought to Portugal was 'the habit of taking showers, washing hair frequently, taking care of the skin with facials that included masks made with natural products such as eggs, rose water, honey and lemon, mixed with almond oil that was also used for massaging the face or the body'.[111] Salomon Dembitzer described the bathtub in a pension in Porto that had apparently not been used in years, and the stir caused when the newly arrived refugee couple wanted to take a bath.[112] The actor and writer Leon Kane mentioned in his autobiographical novel that bathing in the pension was only allowed in the morning, lodgers had to pay for an extra bath taken in the evening.[113] Several women refugees had taken courses in sewing or cosmetics prior to their forced emigration, in order to be able to earn an income. Of a list of nine refugees still in Lisbon in 1949, two were specialists for cosmetic massages.[114]

Conclusion: Influences and changes

Unlike in other European refugee hubs like London and Paris, refugees in Lisbon and Porto had little opportunity to develop a distinct exile culture.[115] The cultural impact of refugees was a different one. 'The risk of contamination of young Portuguese by the mundane habits of the refugees was a real menace.'[116] Ilse Losa witnessed that 'all of a sudden, one could see Portuguese girls from the so-called old Lusitanian families [traditional upper-class families with pedigree] sit in the cafés with feigned nonchalance and a hairstyle *à la Refugié*, smoking and arguing loudly or loiter in the foyers during intervals of theatre performances'.[117] They also started to talk with their hands.[118] Eugen Tillinger wrote in the *Daily Mirror* in 1940:

> Lisbon clerical circles are worried about the 'bad influence' that many lady refugees coming from Paris, Brussels and Warsaw may have on Portuguese morals. They note that the Portuguese women are wearing more and more makeup and that, which is worse, they are copying fashions in hats and shoes worn by the foreign ladies. On top of this, they are starting to smoke in public.[119]

Portuguese men were not pleased to observe how their wives and daughters imitated the dress and hairstyle of the refugees.[120] Not only private persons but also the authorities noticed the changes in their society and tried to hold back these modern touches whenever they can. In vain, the seeds were sown and some of them would bear fruit in a short time, particularly at seaside resorts, where... life was more relaxed. Before the end of the war some Portuguese women will dare to remove their stockings, and at the same time many mothers will start to frequent café terraces with their husbands in order to prevent them being charmed by so many beauties.[121]

Thus, habits changed: 'The natural ease of the refugees contaminated Portuguese women, who let themselves be seduced by their simplicity and lack of constraint... [They] smoked and talked naturally with men, and this dialogue had no sexual innuendo. The refugees introduced a new form of social behaviour.'[122] The foreign women became 'an example and constant influence on Portuguese women.... They helped transform Portuguese bourgeoisie that integrated, gradually, these new ways of living in society.'[123] The main effect was the changed habits in public space: sitting outside on the *esplanade* and the more independent attitude of the refugee women were the phenomena that had the strongest influence on the Portuguese.[124]

In May 1943, *Mundo Gráfico* presented a double page with photographs entitled *Avenida* (Avenue). It showed women on café terraces with skirts that ended above the knees (see Figure 9.1). Headlines such as 'Skirts are now worn elegantly shorter',[125] stories about legs without stockings or pictures of women sewing on a bench (with the caption stating that Lisbon women do not care anymore about making a bad impression) became a common sight.[126] In a post-war letter, the refugee Ernst Levy wrote: 'One not only got used to this ... but realized that the world did not go under when people wore lighter and brighter clothing in summer, and [Portuguese women] began to do the same.'[127] An inhabitant of Caldas da Rainha who experienced the stay of the refugees when she was young reckons that her place of residence modernized quicker than others thanks to the refugees.[128] A male *Caldense* holds the view that the foreigners had brought with them 'a wind of unconstraint and love for life' and 'freedom of thought'.[129]

The refugees were seen as a symbol of modernity. Rather than being shaped by foreign political activism, it was the refugees' day-to-day behaviours that proved to have a much greater long-term effect on Portuguese habits and national mentalities.[130] The journalist and author Alexandre Babo, a contemporary witness, even discerns a 'before and after the refugees' to indicate the Portuguese standard of living[131] and writes of a 'blow to national provincialism' caused by the foreign women's behaviour.[132] When it comes to women's liberties in Portugal, however, the war years seem to have been just a small half-opened window of opportunity that closed soon afterwards, when most of the female refugees had left. Nonetheless, the change refugee women brought to Portuguese society was a welcome relief for both the host society as well as the refugees themselves during those challenging war years. It may have abated after the end of the Second World War, but it lived on in spirit and would once again gain traction after Portugal embarked on its long-overdue political, economic and social modernization after the overthrow of the *Estado Novo* in 1974.

The example of Portugal before, during and after the Second World War shows that the relationship between refugees and their host society is not a one-way street

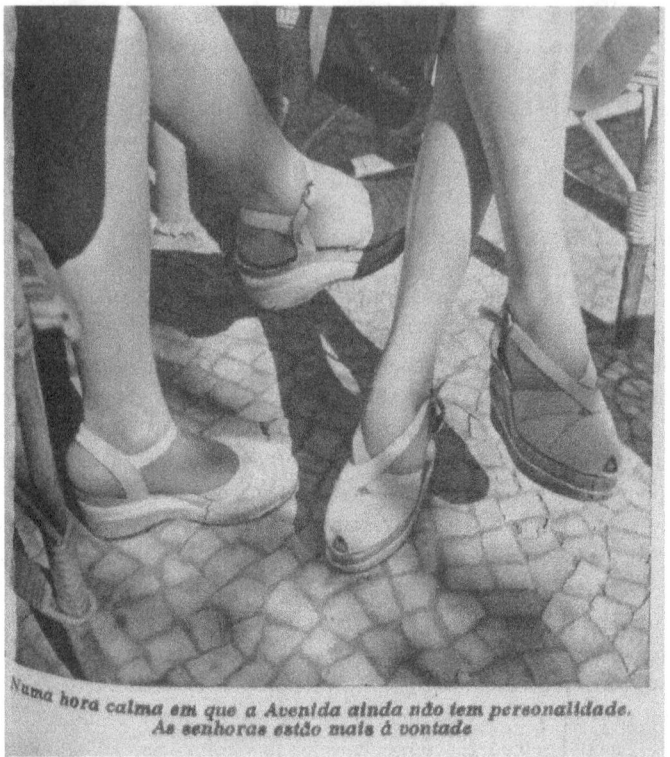

Figure 9.1 Picture in the Portuguese newspaper *Mundo Grafico* showing the legs of women sitting on an esplanada, 1943. © Mundo Gráfico 3, no. 64 (30 May 1943). Hemeroteca Municipal de Lisboa.

to 'assimilation', nor can it be simplified as a binary of 'conflict vs. integration'. On the contrary, refugees in Portugal caused changes in the host society, whereas there is little evidence of influence going in the other direction. However fleeting their wartime presence in Portugal, refugees would leave their mark on the local customs, habits and moralities, as such presenting an image of what modernity and change could be.

Notes

1 This article is based on the results of the research project *Portugal as a country of exile and transit for Austrians 1938–1945*, funded by Austrian National Fund, Zukunftsfonds and David-Herzog-Fonds and supported by the Austrian Society for Exile Studies.
2 The biweekly magazine, richly illustrated as its title indicates, was published in Lisbon between 1940 and 1948.
3 The monthly magazine, official organ of the youth group and intended for its members, was published in Lisbon between 1939 and 1947.

4 Irene Flunser Pimentel, 'Portugal and the Holocaust', in *Portuguese Jews, New Christians, and 'New Jews'. A Tribute to Roberto Bachmann*, ed. Claude B. Stuczynski and Bruno Feitler (Leiden and Boston: Brill, 2018), 441–55, 453.
5 Patrik von zur Mühlen, *Fluchtweg Spanien-Portugal* (Bonn: Dietz, 1992), 115.
6 Interview with Samuel Levy at his home, Lisbon, 23 March 2018.
7 American Joint Distribution Committee (hereafter AJDC) Archives, New York, Item ID 512491, Schwartz to Jointdisco, 7 October 40.
8 José Caré Júnior, *Ericeira, 50 anos depois. Os refugiados estrangeiros da 2a Guerra Mundial* (Ericeira: Mar de Letras, 1998), 62.
9 The contents and addresses can be found, for example, in Central Zionist Archives, Jerusalem, C3 1254–64. The parcels contained, for instance, almonds, dried fruits, sardines, fruit and vegetables in tins, coffee, tea and sweets.
10 See Bundesarchiv, Berlin-Lichterfelde, R 58/6321; Museu Figueira da Foz, lista 2a-2b.
11 Werner Röder, Herbert A. Strauss, Dieter Marc Schneider and Louise Forsyth, *Politik, Wirtschaft, Öffentliches Leben. Biographisches Handbuch der deutschsprachigen Emigration nach 1933–1945*, Vol. 1 (Berlin and Boston: De Gruyter, 2011), 259–60.
12 Michael L. Marrus, *Unwanted. European Refugees in the Twentieth Century* (New York and Oxford: Oxford University Press, 1985), 263.
13 Ansgar Schäfer, 'Hindernisse auf dem Weg in die Freiheit. Der portugiesische Staat und die Deutsche Emigration', *Exil* 1 (1993): 39–47, 39.
14 Irene Flunser Pimentel, *Judeus em Portugal durante a II Guerra Mundial: em fuga de Hitler e do Holocausto* (Lisbon: Esfera dos Livros, 2006), 76.
15 António José Telo, 'Introducção', in Caré Júnior, *Ericeira, 50 anos depois*, 11–21, 12.
16 Maria João Martins, 'Sob céus estranhos. O quotidiano em Lisboa durante a Segunda Guerra Mundial', in *Tempo de guerra. Portugal, Cascais, Estoril e os Refugiados*, ed. Antonio José Telo et al. (Cascais and Vila Real de Sto Antonio: Câmara Municipal, 2004), 52–67, 52.
17 (Hamburg, 1878–1962). She studied at a private arts academy in Hamburg, then in Paris, was a disciple of Matisse, and co-funded, in 1919, the Hamburg Secession. In 1940, she fled to Portugal, where her brother lived, in 1952 she returned to Hamburg.
18 Maria Teresa Oliveira, 'Gretchen Wohlwill', in *Ulyssei@s – Enciclopédia Digital*, ed. Instituto de Literatura Comparada Margarida Losa (2018), 1–4, 3. Available online: https://ulysseias.ilcml.com/en/term/wohlwill-gretchen-2/ (accessed 10 December 2021).
19 Letter to the painter Eduard Bargheer, 1950, quoted in Oliveira, 'Gretchen Wohlwill', 4.
20 née Lieblich (1913 Buer, Germany–Porto 2006). She fled to Portugal in 1934 as a young woman after an interrogation by the Gestapo. She stayed, founded a family, became a Portuguese citizen and worked as a writer and translator.
21 It was first published in Portuguese in 1962, the title *Sob céus estranhos* has been a success and re-used by artists and scholars, such as Daniel Blaufuks for a book (2007) and a documentary (2002) and Maria Teresa Martins for an article (2004).
22 Ilse Losa, *Unter fremden Himmeln* (Freiburg: Beck & Glückler, 1991), 50.
23 Losa, *Unter fremden Himmeln*, 58.
24 Ibid., 108.
25 Ibid., 126.

26 Née Burger (1882 Vienna–Stamford, CN 1971). As her husband, she was a Jewish writer, but less successful. From 1941 on, she lived in the United States.
27 She put up at the hotel *Francfort* on Rossio, in the *Villa Ceres* and the *Chalet Elisa*. Her guest file can be found in the *Arquivo Municipal* (Community Archive) of Cascais: AM Cascais Bol. Al., Casas Particulares do Monte Estoril, CMC, I, 009–0046, 002–1939, 069–S. ind.
28 Friederike Maria Zweig, *Spiegelungen des Lebens* (Vienna, Stuttgart and Zürich: Hans Deutsch, 1964), 230–1.
29 Irene Flunser Pimentel and Helena Pereira de Melo, *Mulheres Portuguesas* (Lisbon: Clube do Autor, 2015), 241, quoted in Marion Kaplan, *Hitler's Jewish Refugees: Hope and Anxiety in Portugal* (New Haven and London: Yale University Press, 2020), 94; Anne Cova and António Costa Pinto, 'Women Under Salazar's Dictatorship', *Portuguese Journal of Social Science* 1, no. 2 (2002): 129–46, 132, 137.
30 Kaplan, *Hitler's Jewish Refugees*, 94.
31 António de Oliveira Salazar, *Comment on relève un état* (Paris: Flammarion, 1937), 39, quoted in Karina Carvalho de Matos Marques, 'Holocausto e exílio. O refugiado no corpo social português e brasileiro', *Abril. Revista do Núcleo de Estudos de Literatura Portuguesa e Africana da UFF* 5, no. 11 (2013): 100–15, 104.
32 Flunser Pimentel and Pereira de Melo, *Mulheres Portuguesas*, 221 and 240 and Ellen W. Sapega, *Consensus and Debate in Salazar's Portugal: Visual and Literary Negotiations of the National Text, 1933–1948* (University Park: Penn State University Press, 2008), 95n13, both quoted in Kaplan, *Hitler's Jewish Refugees*, 94.
33 Darlene J. Sadlier, *The Question of How. Women Writers and New Portuguese Literature* (Westport: Greenwood Press, 1989), 120.
34 Isabel Alves Ferreira, 'Mocidade Portuguesa Feminina: um ideal educativo', *Revista de História das ideias* 16 (1994): 193–233, 193–4.
35 Ibid., 222.
36 Ibid., 208.
37 Ibid., 207.
38 Ibid., 209.
39 Ibid., 222.
40 Ibid., 199–200.
41 Maria Benedita, 'Desportos. Elasticidade, Resistência, Saúde e Beleza do Corpo', *Boletim da M.P.F.* 75–6 (1945): 7.
42 Losa, *Unter fremden Himmeln*, 64.
43 Ibid.
44 Zweig, *Spiegelungen des Lebens*, 232.
45 Peggy Guggenheim, *Out of This Century: The Informal Memoirs of Peggy Guggenheim* (New York: Dial, 1946), 279, quoted in Kaplan, *Hitler's Jewish Refugees*, 95.
46 Margit Meissner, *Margit's Story* (Rockville: Schreiber Publishing, 2003), 122.
47 * Berlin 1922, daughter of a lawyer, came to Lisbon in 1935 with her parents and sister. Ruth stayed in Portugal, studied, married, and became the first elected 'district mayor' of the Lisbon São Mamede district. In 2015, she was still alive.
48 Martins, 'Sob céus estranhos', 59.
49 Kaplan, *Hitler's Jewish Refugees*.
50 (1921 Vienna–Lisbon 2008) stayed in Portugal. She worked as a secretary for the Jewish Community.
51 Marina Pignatelli, 'Os refugiados judeus em Portugal: memórias de exílio', *Arquivo Maaravi. Revista Digital de Estudos Judaicos da UFMG* 11, no. 21 (2017): f. 1–21, f. 16.

52 Her testimony can be found on the website of the Sousa Mendes Foundation: https://sousamendesfoundation.org/family/hahn (accessed 10 December 2021).
53 Losa, *Unter fremden Himmeln*, 54.
54 Telo, 'Introducção', 18–19.
55 Madalena Braz Teixeira, 'The Refugee', in *A Moda do Século. 1900–2000*, ed. Madalena Braz Teixeira, Miguel Fialho de Brito and Museu Nacional do Traje (Lisbon: Museu Nacional do Traje/Instituto Português de Museus, 2000), 117–20, 119. Thanks to Xenia Ribeiro from the Museu Nacional do Traje for sending me this document.
56 Alexandra Weber Ramos Reis Gameiro, 'A Moda e as Modistas em Portugal durante o Estado Novo – As mudanças do pós-guerra 1945–1974' (PhD diss., Universidade de Lisboa, 2017), 375. Thanks to Xenia Ribeiro from the Museu Nacional do Traje for sending me this document.
57 Losa, *Unter fremden Himmeln*, 71.
58 Carvalho de Matos Marques, 'Holocausto e exílio', 104.
59 Kaplan, *Hitler's Jewish Refugees*, 94.
60 Alves Redol, *O Cavalo Espantado* (Sintra: Publicações Europa-América, 1977), 77.
61 Carvalho de Matos Marques, 'Holocausto e exílio', 105.
62 Helena Ferro de Gouveia, 'Lisbon. From Refuge to Home', *Deutsche Welle* (29 November 2012). Available online: https://www.dw.com/en/lisbon-from-refuge-to-home/a-16410819 (accessed 10 December 2021).
63 *Diário de Coimbra* (28 June 1940), quoted in Margarida Magalhães Ramalho, *Vilar Formoso: Frontier of Peace* (Almeida: Almeida Council, 2014), 144.
64 Losa, *Unter fremden Himmeln*, 126.
65 Alves Redol, *O Cavalo Espantado*, 75.
66 The pastry shop and café on the Rossio near the train station had been established in 1922, and, much to the chagrin of locals and visitors, closed permanently in 2018.
67 Flunser Pimentel, *Judeus em Portugal*, 168.
68 Luis Cajão, *Um Secreto Entardecer* (Lisbon: Escritor, 1998), 45, quoted in Magalhães Ramalho, *Vilar Formoso*, 136.
69 Caré Júnior, *Ericeira, 50 anos depois*, 34–5.
70 Fritz Teppich, *Um refugiado na Ericeira* (Ericeira: Mar de Letras, 1999), 28 and 30–1, quoted in Flunser Pimentel, *Judeus em Portugal*, 245.
71 Caré Júnior, *Ericeira, 50 anos depois*, 36–7.
72 Ibid., 43–5.
73 Marion Kaplan, 'Did Gender Matter during the Holocaust?' *Jewish Social Studies* 24, no. 2 (2019): 37–56, 56.
74 Ana Vicente, *Arcádia. Notícia de uma família anglo-portuguesa* (Lisbon: Gótica, 2006), 180. Unfortunately, the mentioned article cannot be found in the *Daily Mirror* archive.
75 Jan Lustig, *Ein Rosenkranz von Glücksfällen. Protokoll einer Flucht* (Bonn: Weidle, 2001), 92–3.
76 Ibid., 104–5.
77 Salamon Dembitzer, *Visum nach Amerika. Geschichte einer Flucht* (Bonn: Weidle 2009), 245.
78 He wrote this on 26 February 1941, see Otto Zoff, *Tagebücher aus der Emigration*, ed. Lieselotte Zoff and Hans-Joachim Pavel (Heidelberg: Lambert Schneider, 1968), 114f.
79 Weber Ramos Reis Gameiro, 'A Moda', 158.
80 Braz Teixeira, *The Refugee*, 119.

81 Ibid.
82 Christa Heinrich, 'Zuflucht Portugal. Exilstation am Rande Europas', *Filmexil* 16 (2002): 4–33, 23; Christina Heine Teixeira, 'Lisboa, símbolo de esperança e de liberdade. Escritores alemães e austríacos em trânsito 1940-41 (algumas observações)', *Arquipélago. História* 2nd series, 2 (2001): 669–80, 675–6.
83 Caré Júnior, *Ericeira, 50 anos depois*, 43–5; Maria João Castro, 'Por entre a bruma dos cais da Europa: Ecos estrangeiros na Lisboa da Segunda Guerra Mundial'. Available online: http://www.fcsh.unl.pt/artravel/pdf/brumadocais.pdf (accessed 10 December 2021).
84 Irene Flunser Pimentel, 'O trânsito e a presença de refugiados em Portugal', in *Tempo de guerra*, 28–40, 36.
85 Weber Ramos Reis Gameiro, 'A Moda', 154.
86 Telo, 'Introducção', 19.
87 Heine Teixeira, 'Lisboa', 676.
88 Interview with Ilda Aleixo, seamstress for *Casa Bobone* at that time, quoted in Weber Ramos Reis Gameiro, 'A Moda', 235.
89 Their registration sheets can be found in the Political Archive of the German Foreign Office, Berlin, LIS 377 MB 1586/38 and 1587/38. They lived in Avenida Duque de Loulé 83 and Calçada do Moinho do Vento 5–1, the first address must have been the Levy's.
90 Interview with Dr Samuel Levy at his home, Lisbon, 23 March 2018.
91 Margit Meissner, *Margit's Story*, 121.
92 'Lisboa a capital da moda', *Mundo Gráfico* 1 (15 October 1940): 7.
93 Ibid.
94 Heinrich, 'Zuflucht Portugal', 23.
95 Decreto-Lei n.°31:247, *Diário do Govèrno*, I série, n.°102, 5 May 1941, 397.
96 Weber Ramos Reis Gameiro, 'A Moda', 74.
97 Margarida Magalhães Ramalho, *Lisbon. A City During Wartime* (Lisbon: Imprensa Nacional Casa da Moeda, 2012), 45.
98 Ministério do Interior (MI), Gabinete do Ministro, M 518 c 76, 'Algumas normas para o uso de fato de banho', 1941.
99 Decreto-Lei n. 31:247, 397.
100 Marta Feuchtwanger, *An Émigré Life: Munich, Berlin, Sanary, Pacifi c Palisades. Interview by Lawrence M. Weschler*, Vol. 3 (Los Angeles: UCLA Oral History Program and the Feuchtwanger Fund of the University of Southern California, 1976). Available online: https://archive.org/details/emigrelifeoralhi04feuc (accessed 10 December 2021).
101 Guggenheim, *Out of This Century*, 280.
102 Susana Lobo, 'O corpo na praia: a cultura balnear em Portugal no século XX', *O Corpo. Revista de História das ideias* 33 (2012): 261–76, 275.
103 Flunser Pimentel, *Judeus em Portugal*, 171.
104 Telo, 'Introducção', 20.
105 Caré Júnior, *Ericeira, 50 anos depois*, 45–6.
106 Telo, 'Introducção', 19.
107 'The White Bears', see Carolina Henriques Pereira, *Refugiados da Segunda Guerra Mundial nas Caldas da Rainha (1940–1946)* (Lisbon: Edições Colibri, 2017), 128.
108 Dulce Soure and Marina Ximenes, 'Dos Refugiados em Caldas', in *Marcas da II Guerra em Caldas da Rainha. Catálogo da exposição 1/10–15/11/98 Osíris Galeria Municipal*, ed. Dulce Soure and Marina Ximenes (Caldas da Rainha: Câmara Municipal, 1998), 13–18, 17–18.

109 Soure and Ximenes, 'Dos Refugiados em Caldas', 17.
110 Henriques Pereira, *Refugiados da Segunda Guerra*, 117.
111 Braz Teixeira, 'The Refugee', 120.
112 Dembitzer, *Visum nach Amerika*, 181.
113 Leon Kane, *Der Fallstrick* (Vienna: Picus, 2006), 116–23.
114 Central Archives for the History of the Jewish People, Jerusalem, Po-Li 507, Baruel, CIL to AJDC, 23 March 1949.
115 Maria Assunção Pinto Correia, 'Glanz im Elend, Elend im Glanz', *Börsenblatt* 81 (10 October 1987): 91–5, 92.
116 Carvalho de Matos Marques, 'Holocausto e exílio', 104.
117 Losa, *Unter fremden Himmeln*, 83.
118 Ibid.
119 Quoted in Vicente, *Arcádia*, 180.
120 Heine Teixeira, 'Lisboa', 676.
121 Magalhães Ramalho, *Lisbon. A City During Wartime*, 44.
122 Braz Teixeira, 'The Refugee', 118–19.
123 Ibid., 119.
124 Flunser Pimentel, 'O trânsito e a presença de refugiados em Portugal', 38; Irene Flunser Pimentel, 'Dificuldades no "paraíso"; os refugiados em Portugal durante a II Guerra Mundial', in *Marcas da II Guerra em Caldas da Rainha*, 7–11, 11.
125 'Avenida 1943', *Mundo Grafico* 64 (30 May 1943): 17.
126 Ibid., 16.
127 Ernst Levy to Irene Shomberg, n.d. [post-war], copy in Marion Kaplan's possession, quoted in Kaplan, *Hitler's Jewish Refugees*, 97.
128 Ducle Soure and Marina Ximenes, 'Das Caldas da Rainha e a II Guerra Mundia', in *Marcas da II Guerra em Caldas da Rainha*, 25–9, 29.
129 Quoted in Henriques Pereira, *Refugiados da Segunda Guerra*, 75–6.
130 Telo, 'Introducção', 18; Braz Teixeira, 'The Refugee', 119.
131 Alexandre Babo, *Recordações de um Caminheiro* (Lisbon: Escritor, 1933), 143, quoted in Flunser Pimentel, *Judeus em Portugal*, 364.
132 Flunser Pimentel, *Judeus em Portugal*, 168.

10

Many journeys of exile

Spanish Republican refugees in France, 1939–46

David A. Messenger

Spaniards began to flee the civil war as soon as it began in 1936 and many, naturally, headed north, to France. Some 15,000 entered in September 1936 as the Basque Country fell to the rebels, the Nationalists led by Francisco Franco; another 12,000 left northern Spain in 1937 as the Republican government lost control of the city of Bilbao; and 25,000 left in 1938 for France.[1] Those numbers radically changed beginning 26 January 1939, the day Barcelona fell. From that evening on through February, hundreds of thousands of Spaniards set off to cross the Pyrenean mountains in winter and escaped to France. Between 26 January and 9 February, some 465,000 Spaniards fled the collapsing Spanish Republic for refuge in France.[2] They consisted of some of the almost 1 million Spaniards who had already fled to Catalonia, fearing life under the Nationalist rebels that had captured their towns and villages during the more than two-year civil war. These Spaniards included some 160,000 Catalans who couldn't imagine living under Franco.[3] The brutality of Franco's troops in attacking and murdering civilians in the towns and villages they took over was well established, even if the greatest number of killings had occurred in the first summer of the war, in 1936. This group of refugees, collectively crossing the border in a movement called the *Retirada*, also included remnants of the Spanish Republican Army, those who had fought to defend the democratically elected government against the Nationalist rebellion and were certain, now that the war was ending, that they would not be treated nicely by the incoming authoritarian regime that looked to fascist Italy and Nazi Germany as models for the new government. In the end, nearly 475,000 set out, then, to find refuge in France for fear they would be targeted for their politics and their actions in the civil war. Some 1,700 would die in France once there.[4]

The fact that many died in their place of refuge tells us that the journeys of these Spanish Republican exiles did not end with the crossing of the Pyrenean border. In fact, multiple journeys had just begun. The first, their entrance into France, was shaped by a surprising reception given to them by the French government and French citizens and included internment and death. The second journey, that of Spanish Republican refugees in the Second World War, was similarly formed by the French and their experience of defeat, occupation and collaboration but gave many Spaniards more freedom in deciding their path in the war, especially for those who joined and participated in the French Resistance against Nazi occupation. By the end of the war, the diaspora attempted to carry on armed resistance into Spain. Once that failed, though, the majority of exiles and the French government itself sought to distance themselves from violence and the possibility of overthrowing Franco's government. Both within the diaspora and within the host country, a way forward was shaped by a desire to recognize the diaspora as unique but one that also settled them into a life of permanent exile that contributed to the reconstruction of France. The multiple journeys that began with Franco's victory in Spain would take Spanish Republican exiles along many paths from 1939 through 1946, although not a path that returned them to Spain as liberators.

The numbers of Spaniards crossing the border in January and February 1939 overwhelmed the French on the other side. Such an influx of people caught the French towns and villages along the border unprepared. In the towns of Cerbère, Le Perthus and Bourg-Madame, some 114,000 refugees entered from 27 to 31 January 1939.[5] France attempted to close the border to all but civilians and injured people from 31 January to 4 February, but it did not last. Another 126,000 people entered the department of Pyrénées-Orientales from 2 to 4 February 1939.[6]

The *Museu Memorial de'Exili* (Memorial Museum of Exile) in La Jonquera, on the border of Catalonia and France, tells the story of this movement. In 2012, the Museum historian Miguel Serrano stated that there is an element of victimhood in the way the Museum presents the story of the exiles, but what is more significant is to recover the memory of these people as not only victims but as part of a historical victimization process of repression of democracy and republicanism that defined not just the civil war but also the Second World War.[7] As such the Museum does not focus all that much on the physical process of exile, on the trauma of crossing the border, although that is contained in the video testimony. The exhibit space stresses the reception of the exiles in France, wherefrom the start they were seen as political exiles, not random people forced to move due to war. Crossing the border was a political choice and a rejection of Franco's Spain that was being established to replace the Spanish Republic.

Many refugees embraced the political label, and most of them admired France for its republicanism and commitment to democracy in the face of rising fascism across Europe. They remembered the role France had played in welcoming leftist supporters of a failed uprising in the Asturias province of Spain, in 1934.[8] They believed they would be welcomed as fellow Republicans. Group identity as Republicans was reinforced since many travelled not just in their family groups but also in politically affiliated groups.[9] However, the France they entered into was quite different from what they had imagined. Compared to many European states, France had a history of assisting refugees and persecuted peoples, and as recently as the 1920s had been a welcoming place for those from Armenia fleeing genocide and from Russia fleeing the Bolshevik Revolution.[10] Although the French in general had supported the Republican side in the civil war and had made efforts to assist refugees, particularly children, creating some 560 refugee centres for Spanish children by December 1937,[11] it was a country that had passed a bill on 12 November 1938 subjecting 'unwanted foreigners' to internment.[12] Xenophobia was growing in France at the same time as the Spaniards sought out exile.[13] The Spanish would be the first significant group to experience this policy, which the French pressed for as soon as towns and villages in the Pyrenean region were overwhelmed by the numbers of those coming from Spain.

As Scott Soo has written, the 'shock and disappointment' that Spaniards felt upon arrival in a country that proved to be less than willing to embrace them 'created a long-standing lens' through which Spanish Republicans viewed the experience of their refugeedom and exile.[14] The most important dimension of the model shaping the Spanish exile, in the beginning, was the reaction of the host country. France was overwhelmed by 'the magnitude and rapidity of events' coming from the border.[15] Despite warnings that went back to 1938, the French government had not planned for a 'flood' of refugees. Local officials often had to make decisions on the ground. As a result, hospitals and clinics were overrun with refugees and quickly constructed barracks were thrown together, and soon enough those barracks were enclosed in barbed wire fence. Although medical treatment was provided, conditions were appalling and many camps opened without permanent housing and without latrines.[16] The French rushed in colonial troops to move the newcomers, and this was met with surprise and anger from the Spaniards.[17] Memoirs of the refugees focus on the sand and the wind that blew it.[18] Families could be separated in the quickly constructed camps that were built in France. Hunger too was a constant theme in the writings when refugees remembered the winter and summer of 1939.[19] Many Spaniards returned to Spain or left France for Latin America, and from the initial exodus, some 150,000–200,000 remained in France by the end of 1939.[20] A recent study confirms that over 1,700 Spaniards died in the camps in France from 1939 to 1940.[21] As they entered the camps, they realized the idealized France in their minds was not here, on the ground.

By spring of 1939 the French government debated using the Spaniards as a military force, in case the approaching war would finally come, or else as workers in a variety of wartime industries.[22] However, in the months leading up to the war, their sentiments changed to suspicions, for the French saw Spanish Republicans as leftists, Marxists, as well as foreigners; all threats in an atmosphere of increasing tension across Europe. By 1940 refugees were invited to return to Spain. In the meantime, the refugees remained in provisional camps, including one on the beach in Argelès, with some 43,000 by April 1939.[23] Women and children spent a limited time in camps before being moved inland to welcome centres. Men remained in the camps, often living in tents, rather than barracks. The camps themselves were constantly under construction. Gurs, which had a capacity for 18,000, became the central camp, began to be built on 15 March 1939 and already by the end of April held some 15,000 refugees.[24] It was one of twelve such camps, the other most notable one being located at Rivesaltes, near Perpignan.[25] Within the camps, in conditions that shocked and appalled them, the Spaniards reorganized along political lines, adhering to the different parties and movements they had been associated with in Spain, including publication of newsletters and militant pamphlets. French intelligence paid close attention to this activity, especially to Communist Party activity that involved not just Spaniards but also German and Italian Communist refugees. German, Italian and other communists ran a newspaper in the Gurs camp in May 1939, bringing multiple diasporas into a relationship with one another, the fourth dimension of the diasporic model employed in this volume.[26] Indeed, concern about 'red vandals' of multiple nationalities was also expressed in the local press.[27] The refugees, disillusioned and feeling ill-treated, lost their enthusiasm for France just as French officials, and civilians, moving with the complex international realities of the pre-war period, came to increasingly distrust them. This situation, the impact of the host country on the refugees, was profound. Their response was to organize first as members of not only their own diaspora but also across diasporas, along political and ideological lines. Once the Second World War began, in September 1939, movement out of the camps commenced. Repatriation was not forced on these Spaniards, and after the Spanish Civil War ended in April 1939, the French Ministry of the Interior, in a 4 May 1939 circular, emphasized to prefects that no repatriation should occur without the consent of the Spaniards themselves.[28] In this sense, the French assisted the refugees more than they had in the challenging and difficult receptions of the winter. Spanish Republican exiles now had some freedom to determine their course of action. Over time, despite the initial shock at not being welcomed, Spanish exiles found that French authorities made a place for them. The response of the host country now allowed the Spanish to shape their own futures to a much greater extent than before. Internment camps emptied out and Spaniards joined the French workforce – about 5,000 Spaniards had jobs in French industry by November 1939 and 40,000 in agriculture. Work groups such as the 'Companies of Foreign Laborers' were now set up by the government.[29] By October 1939, some 55,000 Spaniards served in over 227 individual workers' companies across metropolitan France.[30]

It should be understood that not every Spaniard had full freedom of movement or complete freedom of choice as the Second World War began. Between 1940 and 1944, about 20,000 Spaniards returned to Spain, some against their will, by deportation.[31] These deportations came with a new phase in French policy, France's defeat in the war against Nazi Germany and in the creation of the collaborationist Vichy regime under Marshal Phillippe Pétain, which maintained good relations with Franco's regime. The Nazis occupied northern and coastal France, and on numerous occasions communicated with the Franco government in Madrid, asking for guidance on how to treat Spaniards they now held in their own concentration camps set up to accompany their occupation of France. In September 1940, Spain's foreign minister Ramón Serrano Suñer authorized the Germans to round up Spanish 'reds' as they saw fit.[32] Some 60,000 Spaniards found themselves pushed into forced labour by the Nazis who occupied northern and coastal France.[33] Others were forced into the Nazi camp system, and the majority of Spaniards in Nazi concentration camps ended up in Mauthausen labour camp, in Austria; the first transport of Spaniards to Mauthausen occurred on 6 August 1940.[34]

Cooperation between Franco's new regime in Madrid and the Vichy government in France began when Spanish officials asked the prefect of Paris to pass on information about Spanish exile organizations, on 24 June 1940, just after France surrendered to Nazi Germany.[35] The French sent back to Spain money, goods and documents associated with the former Spanish government. By December 1940, a service to repatriate Spaniards back to Spain was created.[36] Prominent leaders of the former government, such as the former Catalan president Lluís Companys, were arrested in France in 1940 and transferred to Spain, where he was executed in October 1940. The

Spanish ambassador in France Jose Lequerica presented the French government with a list of some 3,000 wanted for deportation back to Spain on 21 December 1940.[37] The Spanish lists prioritized government officials from the Republic and secondarily communists. The Vichy regime created a special service to monitor Spanish exiles and shared information on Spanish 'reds' with the German occupation authorities.[38]

Having said that, for those Spaniards who remained within Vichy territory, in the south of France, there was considerable freedom of movement. By 1941, some 550,000 Spaniards lived in France.[39] Most now were out of camps, living and working in communities across the country. Most did not face deportation. There was opportunity, maybe more than before, to shape one's own path of refugeedom. This was a time of real terror, with the threat of deportation to Mauthausen and other Nazi camps, an inability to really unify into organizations for support and so on.[40] About 26,000 Spaniards ended up in the forced labour Todt Organization run by the German occupiers from 1942 to 1944.[41] Work conditions were rarely decent and the pay suffered in comparison to work done at other businesses.[42] By February 1942, one work site indicated that 982 Spaniards had abandoned the forced labour situation and by April only 81 were found and apprehended for this.[43] This experience was one the Spanish exiles shared with the French in the Todt Organization, where by 1943 45 per cent of those called up for forced labour simply did not show up.[44]

Spanish and French youth increasingly rejected forced labour and fled to the hills of France, many joining the growing French Resistance in the process. By 1943 the Spanish Communist party emerged as the leading group of the Resistance, working alongside Spanish transit networks across the Pyrenees that assisted downed Allied airmen and Jewish refugees in their escape from German-occupied lands. The communists created the Unión Nacional Española (UNE) as a 'popular front', uniting communists, socialists, anarchists and other Republicans to join their French compatriots in resistance activity against the Nazis.[45] The period of war, despite its threat to Spanish exiles, also created opportunities for the diaspora to become active within their own community, and to take leadership in multiple ways. In some respects, then, the war presented opportunities as well as threats and shifted focus from how the host country shaped the Spanish exile to how those within the diaspora shaped it themselves. The armed resistance was most active in the south, in the mountains, as was the French Resistance at the time. In the summer of 1944, as the Nazis began their retreat from southern France following the D-Day landings, Spaniards joined their French compatriots in liberating towns and villages across the south. In the city of Foix, the Spaniards were the first resistance fighters to enter the community.[46]

The participation of Spaniards, particularly leftist Republicans, in the French Resistance was no surprise. It was a continuation of their fight in Spain, delayed by a few years of labour and exile, but picked up again when the opportunity arose, in 1943 and 1944. They saw the struggle against Hitler as a necessary precursor to the renewed battle against Franco within Spain itself. Indeed, even in France their focus never left Spain. In June 1944, the UNE newspaper *Reconquista de España* stated that Spanish Republicans must work with the Allies and the FFI first and foremost, but that such Resistance was ultimately only a precursor to the goal of removing Franco from power in Spain.[47] A member of the British Special Forces who parachuted into the region of Perpignan on 17 August 1944 reported back to the British military attaché in Madrid that 'the expulsion of the Germans and the liberation of this section of France constituted only a beginning for them [Spanish maquis], and that their main object was to make trouble for the present Spanish regime'.[48] The refugee experience, then, was about acting to end refugee status and bring permanent change to Spain. The end of a world war against fascism created opportunities to right the perceived wrongs of 1939 and end fascism in Spain as well.

As most of southwest France became liberated over the course of August 1944, Spanish guerrillas in the region turned their thoughts towards the 'reconquest' of Spain. Their campaign for Republican Spain took shape initially through the occupation of Francoist consulates-general located in the major towns and cities of the southwest. By the end of August 1944, the Spanish government reported that the Consul at Pau had been arrested and the consulate occupied; the Consul at Toulouse had been assassinated and the consulate occupied; similarly, the Republican flag was flown over the Spanish consulate in Perpignan.[49] Throughout August and September, Republican exiles would occupy many other properties owned or operated by the Spanish government. In December 1944, the Quai d'Orsay was able to conclude that of fifteen Spanish consulates in France, five were open but only four of these had been untouched.[50] Meanwhile, arms that Spanish guerrillas had used and stored in the fight for France's liberation began to move closer to the Spanish border in the Pyrenees. In late September, it was reported that a group of Spanish guerrillas had crossed the border into Spain near Puigcerda and stolen arms from the Spanish border patrol there.[51] In the eastern area of the Pyrenees, there were reports that twenty to forty armed men per day were crossing the border near Auzat and laying the groundwork for a revolt on the Spanish side. Numerous other incidents involving border crossings and skirmishes with Spanish troops were reported throughout September, October and November 1944.[52]

The fact that the Spanish guerrillas were able to advance at all was due to the chaotic situation on the ground in liberated southwestern France. The Provisional government did not have complete control. As France gradually became liberated over the course of August 1944, the various troops of the FFI were transformed on the spot into units of the army and the border patrol; the majority of the regular French Army, itself composed mainly of Resistance fighters and the remnants of de Gaulle's North African army, was still fighting the Germans in eastern France and the Low Countries. A French officer responsible for border security admitted in early October that, in many regions, France's ability to control its own side of the Pyrenean border was 'extremely weak', and that the government could not expect to impose its decisions on the Spanish *maquis*.[53] In the eastern Pyrenees especially, Spanish guerillas generally outnumbered the French FFI soldiers: in the department of Pyrénées-Orientales, there were 1,500 Spaniards and only 500–600 French among the FFI contingent, as of 1 October 1944.[54] The prefect of Pyrénées-Orientales acknowledged that the situation was potentially explosive, with possible international repercussions, but that as much as he found the situation 'distasteful', he was 'powerless' to change it until regular army troops arrived.[55] In autumn 1944, despite objections from the minister of war, André Diethelm, the regional military commander in the southwest, General Collet, had agreed with

General Luis Fernandez of the UNE that the roughly 7,500 UNE troops should remain armed and part of the FFI in the short term.[56]

This was thought to be just one part of a potential guerilla movement. French intelligence reports called the total number of armed Republican exiles, 'a veritable Spanish Republican army', consisting of anywhere from 20,000 to 30,000 men. The Spanish *maquis* had trucks, armoured vehicles, rifles, handguns, mortars and canons as well.[57] A document by a *guerrillero* member put the actual number of Spanish *maquis* organized into 11 battalions throughout the southwest at 12,000.[58] They faced an estimated sixteen Spanish divisions, or 230,000 troops, based between the River Ebro and the border.[59]

It was clear that the leadership of the UNE, as well as of many other Spanish Republican groups, viewed the armed invasion of Spain as the next step, after French liberation, in the war against fascism.[60] The most significant attempt to instigate a new phase in the political history of Spain came when Spanish guerrillas invaded the Val d'Aran on 19 October 1944. This Spanish valley extends northward into France west of Andorra and was separated from Spain by mountains that remained impassable in winter. The decision to invade, in the hopes of provoking a general uprising against Franco, was made by the leadership of the Spanish Communist Party in exile.[61] The night of 18–19 October 1944, some 3,500–4,000 members of 7 UNE divisions crossed into the valley and, between 19 October and 28 October, some 7,000 Spanish Republicans were in the Aran at various times fighting with forces from the Spanish Army. They retreated only when it was clear that the national revolution they hoped to provoke was not forthcoming.[62] This retreat marked the end of any effort to use force to change the regime in Spain. As a result, it shifted the experience of the diaspora from one of being active in shaping their own destiny back to one based on what opportunities or actions their host country, France, could take with regards to the future of the Franco regime in Madrid.

In dealing with Republican exiles, resolving the crisis caused by the presence of armed *guerilleros* was the most pressing matter facing the French government in the immediate aftermath of liberation. However, within the Spanish diaspora, many agreed that the tactics of armed resistance were not the way forward. As a result, many of the exiles came to accept that life in France would be more or less permanent. By the end of 1944, all agreed that there was little chance of foreign military intervention against Franco or foreign support for the *guerrilleros*. Moreover, those who continued to cross into Spain posed less and less of a serious threat. Many, indeed, questioned the utility of the guerrilla warfare strategy in the weeks after the failure of the Val d'Aran invasion, which had indicated that the prospects for launching a revolt inside Spain were virtually nil. As David Wingeate Pike has observed, 'it was a mistake to imagine that the Resistance in France could serve as a model for the Resistance in Spain, and that the Spanish people burned with a desire to rise against their oppressors'.[63] After Val d'Aran, the majority of the Spanish Resistance in France chose to abandon the UNE and its emphasis on guerrilla tactics. On 23 October 1944, less than two months after the Liberation of Toulouse, the socialists (and their trade union, the UGT), anarcho-syndicalists (and their trade union, the CNT) and the smaller left-of-centre Republican parties had left the UNE and formed the rival *Junta Española de Liberación* (JEL), also known in various places as the *Agrupación Democrática Española*. This group was quick to announce that it had no intention of becoming involved in French politics and that it opposed the preparation of any 'reconquest' of Spain from French territory.[64] Local French officials found it easier to deal with the non-violent approach of the JEL/*Agrupación*, and expressed relief that the UNE militants were not the only Spanish exiles with whom they had to deal.[65] Division over the UNE and its guerilla activities contributed greatly to the dissipation of the crisis atmosphere along the Pyrenees. Inter-Republican debates had weakened the Spanish government in the civil war against Franco, but had been somewhat patched over in the French Resistance, for initially the UNE included all Spanish Republican groups except for the anarchists. Now they returned, albeit in relation to a very different debate about tactics and approaches, with the vast majority rejecting any future for armed invasion.

As Geneviève Dreyfus-Armand has emphasized, many exiles simply wanted steady employment and an end to relying on social assistance provided by aid organizations like the American Unitarian Service Committee that had been working with Spanish exiles in France since 1938.[66] As one prefect reported, the demobilization of *guerillero* groups from the end of 1944 greatly assisted in the reduction of local tensions and the movement of Spanish exiles into local economies and local community life.[67] The Spanish exile community played a major role in this process. Similarly, the new democratic French government looked at the refugees as a problem that needed to be solved. Subsequently, the response of the host country to the new challenges of the exile community after the European war would dovetail with the demobilization of the guerrilla movement itself. However, they could not simply ignore the refugee movement, which still was organized into multiple groups, political associations and organizations.

Therefore, one of the first policies pursued by the French government in relation to the Republican exile community after liberation was its pursuit of international protection and aid for Spanish refugees in France. Such a policy sought to provide economic security for the majority of refugees who simply wanted some form of normality. It also, however, would hopefully satisfy the activist exiles and their French supporters by showing that the French government of the emerging Fourth Republic was indeed a supporter of Spanish Republicanism. Foreign Minister Georges Bidault made the proposal for refugee protection in the midst of the border crisis in October 1944, at the time of the Val d'Aran invasion. Bidault wrote to Interior Minister Adrien Tixier with the idea that the French government could grant Spanish Republican refugees a statute of protection that would provide them with work status and aid but do so in a manner that would avoid raising protests from the Spanish government.[68] Bidault's plan centred on international, rather than French-mandated, protection; with international support, the cost to the French government would be minimal and the Spanish government would have fewer grounds upon which to protest.

The precedent for such assistance to refugees came through the League of Nations. The 1920 and 1928 Geneva Accords on refugees had placed Russian and Armenian refugees under the protection of the League instead of their respective national consulates, due to the fact that their governments had refused, for political reasons, to recognize them as citizens. In the case of White Russians and Armenians, the national governments of the Soviet Union and Turkey, respectively, had no interest in representing individuals from groups they considered political and/or ethnic enemies of the state. These refugees were commonly known as Nansen refugees, after Fridtjof Nansen, the Norwegian scientist, explorer and diplomat who introduced identity certificates for stateless refugees as the League of Nations High Commissioner for Refugees. The Nansen scheme began with legal protection, but by the time of the 1933 Convention on Refugees, it had extended to include the distribution of benefits to refugees as well.[69]

Within France, offices that provided aid and identity papers to Russian and Armenian exiles were established and run by the League with some French government input. In 1936, the system was extended to refugees from the Saar, although in this case France bore the brunt of the costs associated with assistance.[70] A similar model was proposed by Bidault in the case of Spanish refugees, who, it was argued, should not be forced to seek representation from consulates occupied by Franco's appointees. As with the earlier programmes, he too looked to the League of Nations to step in, for the League was still, barely, alive in the days before the creation of the United Nations in 1945. The programme would be run by the League's High Commission for Refugees, with a committee composed of French government representatives and representatives from various Spanish Republican groups established in France since the end of the civil war in 1939, including the UNE, UGT, CNT, Catalan and Basque Nationalist groups.[71] The League of Nations High Commission for Refugees representative in France, Lester, was brought into the French planning by mid-October 1944.[72] The former president of the Spanish Republic, Juan Negrín, also welcomed the French policy initiative.[73]

The effort to appease the majority of exiles, and encourage their settlement into everyday life, combined with an action meant to underline the special status of Republican refugees, seemed on course. However, even though the French goal was not to demonstrate open support for the Republican goal of removing the Franco regime, a number of problems existed in getting an agreement for international support. The weakness of the League of Nations was perhaps the greatest challenge. The League was by 1944 a skeleton body being run out of the British Foreign Office. Rene Massigli, the French ambassador in London, would thus be in charge of getting the League – and thus the British – to agree to such a programme. Second, in contrast to the White Russian and Armenian cases where the respective governments had publicly stated their desire not to represent political refugees, the Spanish government had said no such thing concerning exiles in France, and this raised concerns for many, especially within the British government. Third, rather than introduce an entirely new regime of protection based on the Republican nature of the exiles, and thus explicitly support the goal of returning Republican government to Spain, the actual legislation proposed and enacted by France was seen in large part as a gesture meant to calm down refugees rather than press for a particular cause.

Eventually, seeing that the League of Nations would soon be dead, the League's secretary-general, Kuhlmann, suggested that the French abandon the League of Nations but instead approach the Intergovernmental Committee on Refugees (IGC) with a Nansen-like proposal. The IGC was a body of Allied states created in 1938 to negotiate with Nazi Germany and possible receiving states in order to move Jewish and other refugees out of Germany. In this it largely failed but was revived in 1943 to open talks with neutral states in order to find safe receptions for wartime refugees.[74] The practical aspect of working through the IGC also appealed to the British, for under all IGC programmes, money was distributed to refugees not through international or national bodies, but rather through private charitable organizations. In the case of France, many of these groups were already working with Spanish refugees (as they had been since the civil war era) and simply would use IGC and French government funds to supplement existing programmes. The implication was that relief, not international recognition of the Republican cause, was the main motivation behind the effort to internationalize assistance. Members of the IGC on the ground in France, led by the IGC chief representative Valentin-Smith, supported such a proposal with the argument that the creation of 'reception centers' for Spanish refugees would more easily move them away from the activity of guerilla warfare and consulate occupations.[75] The idea of appeasing and calming down refugees was equally a goal of the French, especially in light of the ferment that occurred along the border in the last part of 1944. Indeed, by using the League of Nations model of consulting with exiled groups, Georges Bidault expressed the hope that what would result was not only refugee assistance but also the ability of the French government 'to exercise an influence over the Spanish colony that we lack at the present'.[76]

The French statute for protection of Spanish refugees was issued in March 1945 and was subsequently given international status through the IGC in June. The Office Central des Refugies Espagnols was created under IGC authority and was advised by both the French government and the exile community in France. From March 1945 through November 1946, over 40,000 work-related documents were issued by the Office.[77] Recently arrived refugees who crossed the Pyrenees clandestinely were welcomed alongside those who had been in France since the civil war. Only in 1950 was a more restrictive policy enforced that limited assistance to 'established' exiles.[78]

The Spanish exiles discussed in this chapter went through many journeys beyond simply crossing the Pyrenees in 1939. They were subject to suspicion and internment from the moment they entered France, an action by the host country that was in contradiction to how they thought they would be welcomed. As France fell and many Spaniards came under the policies of Nazi occupation and internment, others found themselves freer to be politically active, away from French internment camps, and with opportunity to shape their own story by involving themselves in the French Resistance against Nazism and the actions and activities of the Second World War. By the end of that conflict, many wanted to continue the fight in Spain, but the actions of France and other nations in accepting the Franco regime put an end to that. Many Spaniards made their own choice to settle into a life of permanent exile in France. The French government sought a solution that allowed for this while also recognizing the political nature of their exile. The actions of France, the host country, and the opportunities taken by the diaspora itself, especially in war and resistance, were the most notable factors that shaped the exile experience and contributed to the many journeys Spanish Republican refugees found themselves on from 1939 through 1946.

Notes

1. Scott Soo, *The Routes to Exile: France and the Spanish Civil War refugees, 1939–2009* (Manchester: Manchester University Press, 2013), 33.
2. Ibid., 38.
3. Museu Memorial d'Exili, La Jonquera, permanent exhibit.
4. 'El Memorial Democràtic publica una llista amb prop de 1.700 exiliats morts als camps d'internament de França', 4 February 2021. Available online: https://govern.cat/salapremsa/notes-premsa/395825/memorial-democratic-publica-llista-prop-1700-exiliats-morts-als-camps-dinternament-franca (accessed 14 July 2021).
5. Emmanuelle Salgas, 'L'Opinion Publique et les Représentations des RéfugiésEspagnols dans les Pyrénées-Orientales (janvier-setempbre 1939)', in *Les Françias et la Guerre d'Espagne: Actes du Colloque de Perpignan*, ed. Jean Sagnes and Sylvie Caucanas (Perpiganna: Presses Universitaires de Perpignan, 1990), 186.
6. Ibid., 187.
7. Author Interview with Miguel Serrano, Museu Memorial de l'Exili, November 2012.
8. Sharif Gemie, Fiona Reid, Laure Humbert, with Louise Ingram, *Outcast Europe: Refugees and Relief Workers in an Era of Total War 1936–48* (London: Continuum, 2012), 31.
9. Sharif Gemie, 'The Ballad of Bourg-Madame: Memory, exile and the Spanish Republican Refugees of the Retirada of 1939', *International Review of Social History* 51, no. 1 (2006): 29.
10. See, for example, Michael Boyajian, *The Armenians in Paris: The Joy after the Sorrow* (New York: Jera Studios, 2018); Maud S. Mandel, *In the Aftermath of Genocide: Armenians and Jews in Twentieth-Century France* (Durham: Duke University Press, 2003); and Héléne Menegaldo, *Les Russes à Paris: 1919–1939* (Paris: Autrement, 1998).
11. Gemie et al., *Outcast Europe*, 29.
12. Geneviève Dreyfus-Armand, 'Spanish Republicans Exiled in France during the Second World War: War and Resistance', in *Spain, the Second World War and the Holocaust: History and Representation*, ed. Sara J. Brenneis and Gina Herrmann (Toronto: University of Toronto Press, 2020), 186.
13. Gemie, 'The Ballad of Bourg-Madame', 31.
14. Soo, *The Routes to Exile*, 12.
15. Ibid., 43.
16. Martyn Lyons, *The Pyrenees in the Modern Era: Reinventions of a Landscape, 1775–2012* (London: Bloomsbury Academic, 2018), 148.
17. Soo, *The Routes to Exile*, 48.
18. Lyons, *The Pyrenees in the Modern Era*, 148.
19. Josep Clara, 'Camps de Reclusió, Camps de Concentració', in *L'Exili Republicà als Països Catalans: Una diaspora històrica*, ed. Pelai Pagès i Blanch (Barcelona: Editorial Base, 2014), 123.
20. Dreyfus-Armand, 'Spanish Republicans Exiled in France', 186.
21. 'El Memorial Democràtic'.
22. Denis Peschanski, *La France des Camps: L'internement, 1938–1946* (Paris Gallimard, 2002), 38.
23. Ibid., 42.
24. Ibid., 43.
25. Clara, 'Camps de Reclusió', 116–19.

26 Peschanski, *La France des Camps*, 60–1.
27 Clara, 'Camps de Reclusió', 111.
28 Ibid., 130.
29 Ibid., 131.
30 Robert S. Coale, 'From Internees to Liberators: Spanish Republican Exiles in France, 1939–1945', in *Spain, the Second World War and the Holocaust*, 202.
31 Clara, 'Camps de Reclusió', 132.
32 Sara J. Brenneis, 'Spain's Mauthausen: Narratives of the Nazi Deportation of Spanish Republicans, 1946–2018', in *Spain, the Second World War and the Holocaust*, 273.
33 Juan M. Calvo Gascón, 'The Stateless Monument: Memory of the Spanish Republicans who Died in Mauthausen', in *Spain, the Second World War and the Holocaust*, 216.
34 Brenneis, 'Spain's Mauthausen', 273.
35 Jordi Guixé Coromines, *La República Perseguida: Exilio y repression en la Francia de Franco, 1937–1951* (Valencia: Presses Universitat de Valencia, 2012), 224.
36 Ibid., 239.
37 Ibid., 273.
38 Dreyfus-Armand, 'Spanish Republicans Exiled in France', 189.
39 Guixé Coromines, *La República Perseguida*, 285.
40 Gemie, 'The Ballad of Bourg-Madame', 14.
41 Scott Soo, 'Ambiguities at Work: Spanish Republican Exiles and the Organisation Todt in Occupied Bordeaux', *Modern & Contemporary France* 15, no. 4 (2007): 462.
42 Ibid., 469.
43 Ibid.
44 W. D. Halls, 'Young People in Vichy France and Forced Labour in Germany', *Oxford Review of Education* 4, no. 3 (1978): 297.
45 Dreyfus-Armand, 'Spanish Republicans Exiled in France', 191.
46 Ibid., 193.
47 Marie-Claude Rafaneau-Boj, *Odyssée pour la Liberté: Les Camps de prissoniers espagnols, 1939–1945* (Paris: Denoël, 1993), 271.
48 Quoted in United States National Archives and Record Administration II, College Park, MD (hereafter NARA), RG 59, 740.0011EW1939/9–144, Hayes to Hull, 1 September 1944.
49 Archives of the Ministry of Foreign Affairs, Paris [now found at Centre des Archives diplomatiques de La Courneuve] (hereafter MAE), Series Z/Espagne, 34, Embassy at London to Ministry of Foreign Affairs, Paris, 2 September 1944.
50 Ibid., Z/Espagne, 5, Note General, MAE Direction d'Europe, 28 December 1944.
51 Ibid., Z/Espagne, 34, Coiffard (Barcelona) to Truelle, 27 September 1944.
52 Ibid., October and November 1944 reports.
53 Ibid., Lt Col Richard to MAE Europe, 1 October 1944.
54 Ibid.
55 NARA, RG 59, 740.0011EW1939/8-3144, Hayes to Hull, 31 August 1944, Report of US Consul-General in Barcelona, Key, on his visit to Perpignan.
56 French National Archives, Paris (hereafter AN), F1A/ 3346, Serreulles, Republican Commissioner Bayonne to Tixier, Minister of Interior, 20 November 1944. Collet believed that demobilization of Spanish FFI forces would be easier in the future, and too difficult, at the time, given the large number of tasks which the FFI was expected to accomplish in the southwest over the autumn of 1944.
57 MAE, Z/Espagne, 34, Lt. Col. Richard to MAE Europe, 1 October 1944.

58 Sixto Agudo, 'Participation des Espagnols à la Résistance dans le 4e région', 15 April 1976, reproduced in Daniel Latapie, *L'Affaire du Val d'Aran: Témoignages et Documents* (Toulouse, 1984), no page.
59 NARA, RG 59, 740.0011EW1939/10-1644, Coordinated Military Intelligence Report on Iberia, 13 October 1944, copied in Hayes to Hull, 16 October 1944. The American Military Attaché, Colonel Frederick Sharp, received these figures directly from the assistant chief of the Spanish general staff.
60 Agudo, 'Participation des Espagnols'.
61 Ibid. Agudo claims it was a Central Committee decision against the wishes of UNE military commanders; David Wingeate Pike, *Jours de Gloire, Jours de Honte: Le parti communiste d'Espagne en France depuis son arrivée en 1939 jusqu'à sone départ en 1950* (Paris: CDU-SEDES, 1984), 119–20 agrees. It is quite clear that the decision to invade was made without Moscow's approval and against the express wishes of French Communists involved with the Spanish guerrilleros, most notably André Marty. See Geoffrey Swain. 'Stalin and Spain, 1944–1948', in *Spain in an International Context, 1939–1959*, ed. Christian Leitz and David J. Dunthorn (New York: Berghahn Books, 1999), 246–7.
62 For a detailed account of the Val d'Aran invasion and its political motivations, see Jean-Louis Dufour and Rolande Trempe, 'La France, Base Arrière d'une Reconquete Républicaine de l'Espagne: L'Affaire du Val d'Aran', in *Les Français et la Guerre d'Espagne*, ed. Jacques Sagnes and Sylvie Caucanas (Perpignan: Presses Universitaires de Perpignana, 1990), 261–84; see also Pike, *Jours de Gloire, Jours de Honte*, 119–32 and Daniel Arasa, *Años 40: Los maquis y el PCE* (Barcelona: Argos Vergara, 1984), 121–241.
63 David Wingeate Pike, *In the Service of Stalin: The Spanish Communists in Exile, 1939–1945* (Oxford: Clarendon Press, 1993), 282.
64 MAE, Z/Espagne, 34, Interior Ministry to MAE Europe, 23 October 1944. The JEL was linked to a similar organization in Mexico which ultimately helped form a Republican Government-in-exile.
65 MAE, Z/Espagne, 34, Prefect of l'Aude to Bidault, 1 December 1944.
66 Dreyfus-Armand, *L'Exil*, 188.
67 Ibid.
68 MAE, Series Z/Espagne, 34, Bidault to Tixier, 16 October 1944.
69 Claudena Skran, *Refugees in Inter-War Europe: The Emergence of a Regime* (Oxford: Clarendon Press, 1995), 102–30.
70 Vicki Caron, *Uneasy Asylum: France and the Jewish Refugee Crisis, 1933–1942* (Stanford: Stanford University Press, 1999), 52.
71 AN, 457 AP (Bidault) 100, Ministry of Foreign Affairs to League of Nations High Commission for Refugees Representative in France, 31 October 1944.
72 Lester was informed on 6 October 1944, see AN, 457 AP 100, Direction des Etrangers et Conventions Administratives, MAE to Massigli, 22 February 1945.
73 MAE, Z/Espagne, 34, Massigli to Bidault, 12 December 1944.
74 Michael Marrus, *The Unwanted: European Refugees in the Twentieth Century* (Oxford: Oxfrod University Press, 1985), 171, 216–18 and 285–6.
75 AN, AJ(43) 584-136-1 no. 4, Valentin-Smith to IGC HQ, 10 January 1945.
76 MAE, Z/Espagne, 34, Bidault to Tixier, 16 October 1944.
77 AN, AJ(43) 584-136-2 no. 27, Valentin-Smith to Kuhlman, 25 February 1947.
78 Dreyfus-Armand, *L'Exil*, 204.

11

Reclaimed for the *Volk*

Forced migration and assimilation in the wartime Third Reich

Bradley J. Nichols

Among the millions of Europeans displaced by war and ethnic conflict during the first half of the twentieth century, the vast majority of those removed from their lands of origin were targeted for expulsion as a harmful, alien presence. Throughout the course of what Donald Bloxham has dubbed the 'great unweaving', aggressive drives for national homogeneity and internal security incited a multitude of governments to purge undesired groups from territories over which they asserted sovereignty.[1] The list of peoples who fell victim to the trauma of forced migration is long and diverse, as is the list of countries they once called home, and the prevailing scholarly consensus rightly attributes their woes to the tendency of modern nation states to obliterate that which they deem foreign and seditious.[2] It is thus easy to forget that many expellees during this era were pushed inward to core areas instead of outward beyond a periphery, that the impetus for uprooting them derived from notions of affinity as well as regimes of difference and that such measures aimed to bind them to the dominant body politic rather than excluding them from it. Forced migration often operates in a centripetal fashion; by the same token, it can serve the goal of consolidating an imagined diaspora and converting 'Others' into members of the in-group.

Although hardly the only relevant context, the wartime Third Reich provides a highly illustrative setting in which to explore population transfers in this lesser-known mould. To that end, the most salient object of inquiry is what was known as the Re-Germanization Procedure (*Wiedereindeutschungsverfahren*, WED). Established in the spring of 1940 to 'recover' a select pool of foreign subjects on the basis of alleged Germanic ancestry, the WED epitomized the Nazis' obsession with biological rejuvenation. In the interest of promoting 'rapid demographic growth', the programme's organizers sent some 60,000 civilians from across the continent to live with private households in Germany itself.[3] In contrast to Europe's self-identifying ethnic German minorities, these individuals almost always stemmed from non-German cultural backgrounds – and therein lay the problem. According to SS and Police Chief Heinrich Himmler, the architect of the WED, their 'Nordic blood' had endowed hostile nations with 'leaders who fought bitterly against their own German people ... due to a wilful or unconscious misunderstanding of their racial kinship'.[4] To reap their 'value' and prevent them from continuing to fortify the enemy, it was imperative that all 'persons of German blood' be brought back into the fold, 'extracted' from their native habitat and 'immersed in the German way of life'. This was the essence of what the Nazis referred to as ethnic reclamation.[5]

Such an endeavour could only succeed if inductees abandoned their nationality; it demanded not just a change of scenery but a change in behaviour. Ethnic reclamation, in other words, entailed forced assimilation, and this feature ties the WED to a range of nation-making projects that have sought to 'improve' non-normative populations by erasing the characteristics that set them apart. From the mountains of the Caucasus to the plains of the American Midwest, from the tundra of the Arctic to the deserts of the Outback, the history of the modern world is littered with episodes of cultural genocide orchestrated with or without the baleful enhancement of geographical dispersion.[6] Although motivated by a variety of ideologies and implemented with a plethora of disciplinary techniques, the key element in each case is the coerced integration of marginal groups considered backward or inimical, typically on the pretext and under the cover of war. While often disdained as outsiders, these people are not altogether unwanted, else there would be no desire to 'salvage' them. Forced assimilation constitutes an alternative modality for annihilating difference that hinges on the manufacturing of sameness; while no less predicated on bigotry, it sublimates the urge to destroy or banish with a more constructive purpose. Indeed, in many instances, it is envisioned as essential for the welfare of the polity as a whole.

The WED offers a textbook example of an enterprise conducted along these lines, and therefore opens up a window into the broader experiences of expellees who are 'returned' to a homeland they never knew. It also illuminates the complexity of the responses that emerge in the host societies charged with incorporating them. Candidates for re-Germanization, or 're-Germanizables', occupied a liminal position within the hierarchies of the Nazi empire, neither truly 'us' nor fully 'them'. It was a status postcolonial theorists would instantly recognize as a manifestation of hybridity – the condition of embodying two separate cultures – though Balkan historian Edin Hajdarpasic's concept of the '(br)other' is equally apropos. A paradoxical figure, the (br)other exposes the volatility of national boundaries by at once signifying an ideal of absolute cohesion and the inescapable reality of pluralism.[7] Quite in keeping with this ambiguity, the 'deployment' of WED candidates triggered popular unease on the home front because their racialized classification muddled, transgressed and subverted the traditional dichotomies that distinguished German from non-German. The result was a reluctance to extend them even the slightest bit of hospitality, let alone accept them as 'ethnic comrades'.

Yet despite the challenges they faced, many re-Germanizables did manage to adjust to their new surroundings and stake a claim to civil rights as naturalized citizens. In conjunction with the backing of sympathetic benefactors, the emotional appeal of conformity exerted a potent incentive to defect, even if some refused to forsake their nationality no matter what. All of this indicates that the consequences of forced migration could be empowering as well as oppressive, that expellees could reify as well as undercut the categories that prompted their relocation. More than a few WED candidates chose to join the German *Volk*, and some persisted in venerating it even after the collapse of the Third Reich. What follows is an overview of how this process transpired at the grassroots level, a survey framed to shed light on the nature of ethnic reclamation as a transnational phenomenon.

Purging the borderlands

Regardless of where inductees hailed from, the Re-Germanization Procedure began with ethnic cleansing. In an arc of annexed territory adjacent to the pre-war frontiers of the Third Reich, the onset of Nazi administration inaugurated a reign of terror with the intent of driving out all non-Germans.[8] In western Poland, SS security units evicted no fewer than 535,384 people between December 1939 and January 1944, dumping most of them in the 'General Government' (the central portion of the country that was not subsumed into Germany).[9] On the opposite edge of Hitler's empire, in the contested provinces of Alsace and Lorraine, a total of 70,977 residents were deported to the unoccupied zone of France during 1940 alone.[10] In the old Habsburg domains of Upper Carniola and Lower Styria (present-day Slovenia), the number of expellees reached upwards of 54,000.[11] What tied these 'evacuations' together was the fear that living alongside foreigners compromised the integrity of the local German population, which in turn jeopardized the biopolitical structure of Nazi hegemony. With respect to western Poland, one advisor argued that '[t]he burden of ethnically alien and racially inferior inhabitants would inevitably cause bastardization . . . Mixing between Germans and Slavs must be avoided at all costs; that can only be assured by getting rid of the Poles'.[12]

There was one major complication that hindered such a straightforward approach: the long history of cultural syncretism in these regions, not to mention the frequency with which they had changed hands, made it incredibly difficult to figure out who was who.[13] SS functionaries in Poland and elsewhere repeatedly complained about opportunistic 'side-switchers' and bilingual 'amphibians' who straddled nationality benchmarks or flouted them altogether.[14] For the head of the Gestapo, the same confusion gave rise to a concern 'that German descent is not always being taken into account at the time of resettlement'.[15] Soon enough, German officials began contemplating an even more disturbing probability: that a significant number of people in the area had lost touch with their 'Germanic heritage'.[16] This was certainly what one Nazi activist thought had happened to a group of 'Polonized' villagers she encountered in rural Galicia; while insisting that they had 'kept their bloodlines pure', she also noted that they had 'forgotten their native tongue', revealing the need for a programme 'to teach [them] the German language, and gradually introduce them to German culture'.[17] Himmler created the WED with this exact prescription in mind, and he delegated responsibility for selecting 'suitable' prospects to the so-called race examiners of the SS, who scrutinized the physical appearance of outgoing deportees to determine their genealogy.[18] Applying supposed racial criteria enabled these men to circumvent the limits of an ethnic taxonomy that, as Himmler saw it, had 'proven to be historically incorrect' over the course of a century in which 'everyone was German when the Germans were in charge and Polish when the Poles were in charge'.[19]

Still, a positive evaluation did not put subjects above suspicion, for many Nazis believed that the 'best blood' flowed in the veins of those individuals who posed the gravest threat to German authority in the borderlands.[20] This bizarre postulate explains the paranoid sense of exigency that suffused ethnic reclamation. From the outset, the WED was conceived of as a security measure, an instrument for neutralizing reputed agents of unrest in newly acquired districts by shipping them to the Reich, where their propensity to 'stir up trouble' would ostensibly be diminished. In Alsace and Lorraine, Nazi governors concurred with the SS that re-Germanization was the soundest policy for dealing with 'suspect Francophiles'. On account of their 'racial fitness', deporting them to France would only 'enrich the French with a new leadership class', and one could not 'win them back for Germandom' anyhow unless they were 'removed from their current negative influences'.[21] The same cluster of priorities dictated the 'extraction' of eligible subjects from Slovenia; here too the Nazis presumed that the native intelligentsia had 'retained' sizeable quantities of 'Nordic stock' and could not be deposited in the interior of Yugoslavia 'since that would relinquish blood which the Serbs will benefit from'.[22] A subsequent memorandum elaborated on the logic behind resettling them in Germany: 'Racially valuable individuals who are politically unreliable were transferred to the Reich in order to be re-Germanized . . . their presence in this ethnically endangered environment was unacceptable'.[23] Apparently the anticipated biological dividends of their 'recovery' outweighed the attendant risk to political security on the home front.

A new homeland

If terror was the overarching theme of the Re-Germanization Procedure in its initial stage, for many inductees the tone quickly shifted to one of optimism during their transport to Germany. Buoyed by promises that their worries lay behind them, they conveyed feelings of relief, even excitement. 'The journey was pleasant', Józef Szykowski recalled, filled with beautiful views of the countryside and the sight of German farmers preparing for the harvest. Also encouraging was the welcome his family received at each stop en route to their assigned household; in Breslau, Dresden and Leipzig, nurses from the German Red Cross served hot meals and played with the children, and in Stuttgart the Szykowskis spent the night in a fine hotel 'with clean sheets too'.[24] The Third Reich seemed like a nice place to live, and the SS went to great lengths to lionize these people. From the chaperons who escorted them to the pomp that greeted their arrival, every aspect of the trip was choreographed to present a hospitable atmosphere.[25] Hence the speech delivered to newcomers at the resettlement camp in Schelklingen, in which the commandant predicted that, whether Polish, French or Slovenian, each of them would 'swiftly return to the German ethnic community' (Figure 11.1).[26]

Yet for all the hope invested in this expectation, it soon became clear that many hosts blatantly ignored guidelines stipulating equitable treatment and deprived WED candidates of even the barest amenities. Nazi bureaucrats in the provinces were not very cooperative either; they cited inadequate funds or depleted stockpiles as a pretext

Figure 11.1 A Polish family selected for re-Germanization, c. 1941. © United States Holocaust Memorial Museum Photo Archives #77867, courtesy of Instytut Pamięci Narodowej.

to withhold subsidies and vouchers for food and clothing.[27] When SS officers tried to intercede, they found themselves hamstrung by curt replies like 'I do not see why I should make an exception for these people'.[28] Stymied at nearly every turn, there was little they could do to combat malfeasance, as one of Himmler's minions conceded: 'I have instructed the employers on numerous occasions that re-Germanizables must be placed on an equal footing with German citizens regardless of their as-yet incomplete naturalization. My efforts have been consistently undermined by third parties and, to be sure, by the state itself.'[29] Of course, it was not out of the ordinary for *German* farmhands to sleep in barns or shacks with no electricity or indoor plumbing, as WED candidates did. Nor was it unusual for them to toil from dawn to dusk for meagre wages and cheap meals. These conditions reflected disparities of class, not ethnicity or 'race'. But it is hard to imagine even the lowliest German seasonal labourer being denied blankets, stoves, soap, and kitchen utensils, or being compelled to work eighteen hours a day without pay on a diet of rotten potatoes and spoiled milk.[30] However authoritarian the routine in the resettlement camps may have been, people interned there could at least count on a guarantee of subsistence. For re-Germanizables allocated to the private sector, on the other hand, the tenor of daily life often resembled the plight of those Eastern Europeans whom the Nazis enslaved and imported into the Reich in massive numbers from 1942 onward (the *Ostarbeiter*). One candidate captured their understandable disappointment with this state of affairs when he wrote to his SS handlers, 'You said we would have the same rights as Germans, but here it is not so'.[31]

Even if we allow for the idiosyncrasies that shaded individual motives, it is obvious that discrimination emanated from the animosity towards foreigners that pervaded

German society. Poles bore the brunt of this sentiment, though Slovenes in the resettlement camps were also the focus of wild rumours depicting them as thieves, rapists and murderers.[32] All the same, the evidence suggests a more nuanced set of causes. The unprecedented influx of immigrants that accompanied the Second World War in Germany unleashed widespread nativism and xenophobia on the home front, though WED candidates became a lightning rod for resentment precisely because they were entitled to 'the same rights as Germans'. A civil servant in Frankfurt am Main observed in February 1941 that '[t]o a general populace unfamiliar with the inner logic of the Re-Germanization Procedure, the extensive concessions granted to these families are totally incomprehensible'.[33] That most Germans interpreted nationality in terms of language and culture rather than 'race' predisposed them to look upon inductees as uppity interlopers. Indeed, WED candidates lodged numerous protests accusing overseers of singling them out for gruelling tasks, 'dirty jobs', and corporeal punishment.[34] Physical abuse was not merely an occupational hazard either; those who ventured out in public courted danger as well. In one particularly vicious incident in the autumn of 1941, a gang of German teenagers in Mönchberg assaulted Grzegorz Rynkowski and warned him not to go walking in town ever again.[35] What impeded the programme above all was not just scepticism about 'whether these people are actually German' – an issue several hosts raised explicitly – but the inability to answer that question.[36] Time and again, members of participating households expressed a vague yet profound distaste for the cultural duality that WED candidates seemed to represent, a quality they perceived as detrimental to communal mores. We see this in the story of young Barbara Ciepłuch, for instance, whose mistress forbade her from mingling with local boys because she was 'not a Pole anymore, but not a German either'.[37] The same mentality imbued the trend of denigrating inductees like Barbara as 'shitty Polish-Germans'.[38] The chief obstacle to integration had more to do with their hyphenated identities than with their foreignness per se.

How did WED candidates react to all of this? By fighting back any way they could. Many absconded, refused to work or committed minor acts of sabotage, such as senselessly killing livestock, while others reckoned they had nothing left to lose and retaliated in kind against bosses who beat them.[39] By early 1942, there were reports from across the country condemning the re-Germanizables as 'obstinate', 'obstreperous', 'insolent' and 'rebellious'.[40] Morale in the resettlement camps had also deteriorated markedly, as inmates grew increasingly restive and fed up with the overbearing demeanour of SS personnel.[41] Escapes multiplied, and a few Slovenes even made it all the way back to their homeland.[42] From Himmler's perspective, however, the most vexing dilemma was the mounting number of candidates who flaunted their indigenous nationality and rejected the very idea of 'assimilating into Germandom'. One of his underlings opined that the Alsatians and Lorrainers had demonstrated through 'gross insubordination' that 'they consider themselves French and wish to remain as such'.[43] Another commented that most of the Slovenes likewise 'displayed an anti-German attitude'.[44] As for the Poles, we know from their own letters that many vented a fiercely defiant anger, as Józef Świątek did when he declared, '[t]hey can beat me to death if they want, but I will always be a Pole'.[45] Despite such provocations, SS leaders ultimately decided that 'subversive conduct does not warrant dismissal from the Re-Germanization Procedure'. Instead, these 'bad apples' were to be sent to a concentration camp for 'punitive educational measures'.[46] Some of them did not survive, though a brief spell usually sufficed to break those who did.[47]

The threat of imprisonment or worse undoubtedly deterred many re-Germanizables from engaging in outright resistance. But that was neither the only option available to them nor the most common means by which they aired their grievances. Long before the SS resorted to overt coercion, some inductees hit upon a much safer strategy for gaining redress: they invoked ethnic solidarity by loudly avowing their Germanness. The letters of Polish candidates articulated a certain moral economy steeped in the Nazis' own ideological value system, a racialized code of decorum couched as indignation to shame the authorities into helping them. This kind of lobbying almost always zeroed in on specific material hardships as grounds for government officials to reprimand negligent hosts or arrange for a transfer elsewhere. So, for example, Stefan Kulawczyk complained about the favouritism shown to his German counterparts with respect to wages and leave: 'We belong to the German nation just as much as they do. Why should they earn more and work less than us?'[48] Banking on a different tack, Elżbieta Rolnik appropriated the Nazi worldview by leveraging her role as a mother and angling to profit from the dispossession of 'undesirables': 'There are still so many Jewish flats that are vacant', she wrote in a letter to the SS, 'and one could surely let me have one of these apartments. . . . I would then have more time to devote to educating my children properly.'[49] Some re-Germanizables went further and openly vilified 'racial aliens', aping the superiority complex of their overlords by casting the menial chores they performed as a grind fit for 'inferior' *Ostarbeiter*, for 'slovenly Poles' and 'the Russian horde'.[50] This rhetoric signalled their awareness that recognition as a German would require all the trappings of social and cultural capital one could muster.

It is therefore quite apposite that the most direct and tangible support came from those ordinary citizens who did seek to integrate the re-Germanizables or at least ease their transition. For every supervisor who held them in contempt, there were just as many who strove to ensure their well-being – either out of compassion, a sense of patriotic duty, or some synthesis of the two. Despite wartime shortages and rationing, a number of hosts set aside livestock and plots of land for WED candidates, built and furnished new domiciles to accommodate them, supplied them with clothing and shoes, and indulged them with an array of choice foods.[51] Just as important as the provision of creature comforts, many host families formed genuine bonds of affection with the people entrusted to their 'tutelage'. They ate their meals at the same table, exchanged gifts at Christmas and went to the movies or on vacation together, all of which explains how inductees learned the German language – the first step towards assimilation – so quickly.[52] For victims of ethnic cleansing and strangers in a strange land, the solace imparted by such camaraderie had a validating psychological impact that can hardly be exaggerated, all the more so for those who had been separated from loved ones. This was certainly the case with Stanisława Kowalska; lonely and depressed following her dispatch to Württemberg in the fall of 1940, her mood rapidly improved because 'the woman to whom I was assigned is very kind and we get along famously'.[53]

The generosity of participating households paved the way for a warm reception by the general populace. Among other things, WED candidates were invited to attend festivals and enrol in local branches of the Nazi Party.[54] The SS even permitted them to join church congregations, albeit reluctantly and with a wary eye.[55] What bolstered the spirits of those blessed with a favourable situation more than anything else was the chance to insert themselves into new social milieux. Nestled in the hamlet of Rosengarten outside Hamburg, Stefan Wejmann informed the SS that '[r]elations with my comrades at work and my neighbours have blossomed to complete satisfaction'.[56] Jan Ratajski and his family were 'well-respected by the inhabitants' of the Dortmund borough where they resided too.[57] Much to their surprise, inductees also discovered that some Germans took civic slogans of mutual aid very seriously. When his six small children fell ill and lay bedridden in the winter of 1940–1, Józef Papier was deeply grateful for the attentiveness of the doctor and nurses who visited regularly to care for them.[58]

None of these anecdotes should be construed to imply that Germans by and large embraced WED candidates as fellow compatriots. Many plainly did not. One pattern we can discern, however, is the link between conviviality and a type of ethnogenesis – the engine of what anthropologists refer to as fictive kinship. Simply put, personal connections with individual Germans inspired inductees to associate with the German *Volk* as a whole. It goes without saying that this facilitated their 'acclimation' in the Reich, a point to which Józef Frąckowiak attested by crediting his wish to 'stay in Germany forever' to the 'courteous' behaviour of his overseers.[59] The perks of a decent standard of living strengthened that correlation, and Władysław Mazurek gave voice to both its material and emotional components when he proclaimed, 'I have everything I've ever wanted, and can now truly announce with pride that I am a son of Germany'.[60] The longer sweep of a history shaped by ethnic rivalries adds a further layer of meaning to these 'conversions'; having come of age in regions where alternating campaigns of nationalization had primed inhabitants to side with the winners, it was only natural that WED candidates would do so too. In any case, the weight of emphasis leans towards the same conclusion: whether or not people actually bought into its underlying ideology, the cumulative effect of re-Germanization was powerful enough to convince subjects to renounce their nationality. By extension, the grand irony of the WED is that Germans who acknowledged the dignity of these downtrodden immigrants endorsed and contributed to Himmler's goal of ethnic reclamation, while those who demeaned and mistreated them obstructed it.

We cannot verify the sincerity of the statements made by the re-Germanizables any more than we can confirm that they amounted to nothing beyond mere lip service. Yet even if purely a ruse, they communicated an impression of success because their accounts of 'progress' tallied with what agents of the Nazi security apparatus gleaned from their intelligence and monitoring operations. According to one SS officer, the Slovenes in particular had acquitted themselves well, both in and outside the camps; although it would take years to dispel the apathy of many, others were 'eager to remain in the Reich' thanks to their 'almost complete assimilation'.[61] A gendarme stationed in Lower Franconia inferred that residents there were reciprocating this 'good faith': 'The villagers . . . speak highly of them; they judge the pro-German attitude of these persons to be authentic, not camouflage, and mostly agree that they can be absorbed into Germandom through the cultural influence of their surroundings'.[62] Superiors in

Berlin painted a similarly rosy picture, reporting to Himmler in December 1942 that the WED had 'backfired' in only 'a tiny number of hopeless cases', whereas most inductees had 'adapted and settled in', and some had 'reached their full potential'. To substantiate these assessments, one needed to look no further than their 'stellar reputation' among and 'close rapport with German comrades'. There was also the fact that even those who suffered under the yoke of 'ignorant' custodians nevertheless 'affirm in their letters that they belong to the German Volk'.[63] In short, the Nazis had more than enough evidence to justify their conviction that the time had come to move forward with naturalization. And so it was that in early 1943, re-Germanizables from Alsace-Lorraine and Slovenia were the first to be awarded 'conditional state subjecthood'.[64] In April of that year, the Interior Ministry unveiled legislation that conferred the same 'honour' upon WED candidates from western Poland.[65] In the words of one of the programme's managers, it was the least the regime could do for those who had 'already merged into Germandom and are now understandably yearning to be recognized as German citizens'.[66]

A peculiar diaspora?

The story of the Re-Germanization Procedure did not end with the Second World War. On the contrary, for nearly every candidate, the onset of peace in 1945 brought a whole new set of challenges. The vast majority registered as Displaced Persons (DPs) and entered the huge network of refugee camps erected under the auspices of the United Nations Relief and Rehabilitation Administration (UNRRA). Afterwards, however, their biographical trajectories varied dramatically. Those who endured exploitation and persecution in the Third Reich were usually itching to return to their native soil and pick up where they had left off. While some languished in the DP camps for years, others were repatriated within months – that is, if they had not already gone home on their own.[67] Yet there were also many erstwhile re-Germanizables who dreaded what might await them in their lands of origin. Regardless of whether those now lay behind the Iron Curtain, and beyond the spectre of communist rule (namely in Poland and Yugoslavia), the most pressing concern was the likelihood of being branded as a traitor and punished accordingly. There was ample reason to worry too, for expellees who had just escaped a nightmarish ordeal under the heading of re-Germanization found themselves compelled to undergo analogous measures of 're-Polonization', 're-Frenchification' and so forth.[68]

In light of said circumstances, it is little wonder that many of these people opted for permanent exile and emigrated overseas – mainly to the United States, Canada and Australia – or chose to remain in Germany.[69] For the latter, preserving intimate relationships cemented during the war assumed paramount importance. Despite having re-established contact with relatives in Poland, Zygmunt Rząźewski decided to stay in the village where the SS had 'deployed' him because he could not bear to desert the farmers who had taken him in. He subsequently married a local *Fräulein*, cultivated a business from scratch, and relished in the standing bestowed upon a pillar of the community. For sixty years, he never shied away from telling friends and acquaintances how he had come to live in their midst, and they never held it against him. Nor did he have any qualms about admitting that his memories of Poland quickly faded into the murky image of a 'totally alien country'.[70]

Zygmunt's openness proved to be exceptional, as neither fitting in nor severing ties was always so easy. Roman Sobkowiak started a family with his German fiancée and worked for four decades as a radio technician at the AEG-Telefunken in Ulm. Yet while he never regretted breaking with his past, Roman struggled to reconcile his contradictory experiences as a transplant. The affinity he shared with some Germans did not shield him from casual racism and institutional discrimination at the hands of others. Although he styled himself neutrally as a 'European' when queried about his nationality, his accent left him vulnerable to prejudice, and he did not obtain full citizenship from the West German government until December 1960. He also had to deal with the generational cleavages and divided loyalties that émigrés of every stripe are frequently obliged to navigate, which for him revolved around the disapproval of his father: 'He saw Poland as his homeland; I saw Germany as mine.' Even so, Roman hardly ever felt truly estranged from his native heritage. He grappled with the tension of being an heir to 'two homelands' with a facility that younger expellees whom the Nazis sought to re-Germanize often could not replicate.[71] Among the most odious legacies of this entire endeavour was the extent to which minors were 'completely poisoned against their countries' and would 'not countenance a return to the land of their birth'. In 1946, one UNRRA volunteer interviewed scores of adolescents from Poland and Yugoslavia who 'disavowed their language and culture and vehemently insisted they were Germans'.[72] The damage inflicted by such repression was symptomatic of an initiative that ripped families apart, and it mirrored a conspicuous mental habit among the adults involved too: forgetting.

Whether they benefitted from the programme or not, virtually everyone who participated in the WED avoided or concealed that fact in the aftermath of the war – either to preclude accusations of complicity or simply to put it behind them. Roman Sobkowiak tried to draw attention to what was being 'hushed up', but his attempts to elicit the truth via everyday conversations foundered on a collective recourse to deliberate amnesia: 'Nobody in our town was interested. . . . Nobody remembered anything.' Exasperated by the indifference incurred whenever he broached the topic, Roman soon stopped dwelling on it himself. It was only upon retiring in 1984 that he began composing the manuscript that would eventually be published as his autobiography a quarter-century later. Even then he could not quite square his victimhood with the path he had charted as a result of it, maintaining that '[t]he Nazis did their best to assimilate us forcibly . . . but I became a German of my own accord'.[73] In any event, he was not alone in staying silent for such a protracted stretch of time. Like Roman, the renowned Alsatian literary scholar Marie-Louise Roth-Zimmermann had been deported to Germany as a teenager. Like Roman, she spent the autumn of 1942 in the resettlement camp for WED candidates at Schelklingen. Like Roman, she rarely talked about any of this until passing into old age, when she too wrote a book about it.[74] By that point, halfway around the world, another former re-Germanizable had carried his secrets to the grave. Feliks Grzelka was one of those 'bad apples' whom the SS detained for the 'crime' of 'subversive conduct'. He survived internment at Dachau as well as the fraught limbo of DP status and finally received asylum in Argentina in 1951. There he enjoyed a pleasant middle-class life as a grocer in Buenos Aires – all the while keeping his wife and sons in the dark about why he had fled Europe. They knew nothing of Feliks' troubled personal odyssey until shortly after his death in 1997, when they stumbled across a file hidden among his papers which contained a correspondence with the International Red Cross detailing what had happened to him. Although reticent to confide his trauma to those closest to him, Feliks did not retreat from confronting it; at the very least, he thought he was entitled to some form of restitution or catharsis.[75]

Can a diaspora be actualized and consolidated by the society that claims to be its source? Can a diaspora dissolve when the categories animating its existence are rendered untenable? The fallout from Nazi resettlement policies suggests more than one right answer to these questions. Among those selected for inclusion, the WED did alter and sometimes invert previous affiliations; it created an environment where modes of belonging to a new community could develop organically in the metropole through sustained interaction with its members. The identities fashioned therefrom were deeply ambivalent and unstable nonetheless, as underscored by their post-war flexibility, and there was no guarantee that any real acceptance by the in-group or change in ethnic alignment would occur in the first place. What began as a state-sponsored process of racial ascription acquired a grassroots dynamic that made integration a matter of personal preference on both sides. The likelihood that someone would adopt the mantle of Germanness depended just as much on how they responded to the conditions of their displacement as it did on the temperament of their hosts. In each respect, the unifying factors are difficult to grasp from the vantage of any one discrete national history, not least because inductees derived from multiple countries and wound up scattered across multiple continents. And yet, while distinctive in its ideological premise, the Re-Germanization Procedure was not wholly unique. The coping mechanisms summoned by those who had to submit to it, along with the reactions of those enjoined to watch over them, offer useful insights into other episodes of centripetal forced migration. That WED candidates had to stomach compulsory 're-nationalization' in their lands of origin after the war gestures towards the merit of transnational comparisons – as do several of the case studies in this volume. No less evocative are the parallel quandaries faced by Muslim and Orthodox Christian populations whom the Greek and Turkish governments 'exchanged' after the First World War, or the fate of various nationalities shuffled from the periphery to the interior of the Russian Empire and the Soviet Union throughout the first half of the twentieth century. While it may be true, as Roman Sobkowiak liked to assert, that '[y]our homeland is where you earn your bread', the bitter fruits of expulsion and cultural genocide have certainly been dispensed far and wide.[76]

Notes

1 Donald Bloxham, *Genocide, the World Wars, and the Unweaving of Europe* (Portland: Valentine-Mitchell, 2008), 1–15.
2 See the introduction in Richard Bessel and Claudia B. Haake (eds), *Removing Peoples: Forced Removal in the Modern World* (New York: Oxford University Press, 2009).

3 Bradley J. Nichols, *The Hunt for Lost Blood: Nazi Germanization Policy in Occupied Europe* (New York: Cambridge University Press, forthcoming).
4 Bundesarchiv, Berlin-Lichterfelde (hereafter BArch), R 49/73/1-2: Himmler, Anordnung 17/II, 9 May 1940. This and all subsequent translations from German are the author's.
5 Ulrich Greifelt, 'Die Festigung deutschen Volkstums als zentrale Ostaufgabe', *Reichsverwaltungsblatt* 62 (1941): 509–14.
6 See the essays in Andrea Fischer-Tahir and Sophie Wagenhofer (eds), *Disciplinary Space: Spatial Control, Forced Assimilation, and Narratives of Progress since the 19th Century* (New York: Columbia University Press, 2017).
7 Edin Hajdarpasic, *Whose Bosnia?: Nationalism and Political Imagination in the Balkans, 1840–1914* (Ithaca: Cornell University Press, 2015), 16–17 and 202; Homi Bhabha, *The Location of Culture* (New York: Routledge, 1994), 121–31.
8 Alexa Stiller, 'Grenzen des "Deutschen". Nationalsozialistische Volkstumspolitik in Polen, Frankreich und Slowenien', in *Deutschsein als Grenzerfahrung. Minderheitenpolitik in Europa zwischen 1914 und 1950*, ed. Matthias Beer, Deitrich Beyrau and Cornelia Rauh (Essen: Klartext, 2009), 61–84.
9 Arolsen Archives – International Center on Nazi Persecution [formerly the International Tracing Service], Bad Arolsen (hereafter ITS), 1.2.7.9.1/82189531: Krumey, 'Abschlussbericht über die Arbeit der UWZ im Reichsgau Wartheland', Anlage 1, 31 December 1943. This tally does not encompass Polish Jews.
10 Christopher Browning, *The Origins of the Final Solution: The Evolution of Nazi Jewish Policy, September 1939–March 1942* (Lincoln: University of Nebraska Press, 2004), 90.
11 Tone Ferenc, '"Absiedler". Slowenen zwischen "Eindeutschung" und Arbeitseinsatz', in *Europa und der 'Reichseinsatz'. Ausländische Zivilarbeiter, Kriegsgefangene und KZ-Häftlinge in Deutschland 1938–1945*, ed. Ulrich Herbert (Essen: Klartext, 1991), 201.
12 Otto Reche, 'Leitsätze zur bevölkerungspolitischen Sicherung des deutschen Ostens', 24 September 1939, in *Der 'Generalplan Ost'. Hauptlinien der nationalsozialistische Planungs und Vernichtungspolitik*, ed. Mechthild Rössler, Sabine Schleiermacher and Cordula Tollmien (Berlin: Akademie, 1993), 351–5.
13 Tara Zahra, 'Imagined Noncommunities: National Indifference as a Category of Analysis', *Slavic Review* 69, no. 1 (2010): 93–119.
14 United States Holocaust Memorial Museum Archives, Washington, DC (hereafter USHMMA), 15.015M/3/164/1: SD Neutomischel to SD Posen, 8 April 1940.
15 Ibid., 15.015M/3/159/6-7: Müller to Rapp, 29 December 1939.
16 Michael Burleigh, *Germany Turns Eastwards: A Study of Ostforschung in the Third Reich* (New York: Cambridge University Press, 1991), 111 and 127.
17 Nancy R. Reagin, *Sweeping the German Nation: Domesticity and National Identity in Germany, 1870–1945* (New York: Cambridge University Press, 2006), 203.
18 Isabel Heinemann, *Rasse, Siedlung, deutsches Blut. Das Rasse und Siedlungshauptamt der SS und die rassenpolitische Neuordnung Europas* (Göttingen: Wallstein, 2003), 252–3.
19 BArch, NS 2/61/30-31: Himmler to Bormann, 20 May 1940.
20 Ibid., NS 19/2875/3: Künzel to Schulte-Schomberg, February 1942.
21 Library of Congress, *Trials of War Criminals before the Nuremberg Military Tribunal: Green Series*, Vol. IV (hereafter LOC/NMT), 912–16, Doc. 1470-PS: Guidelines for the Treatment of Expelled Alsatians (English transcript), unsigned, 7 August 1942; LOC/NMT, 918–919, Doc. NO-247: Berndt to Wolff, 20 May 1942.

22 Starzacher, 'Denkschrift über die Wege, die besetzten Gebiete Kärntens kulturell und völkisch in den Altgau Kärnten und das Reich einzugliedern', 22 May 1941, in *Quellen zur nationalsozialistischen Entnationalisierungspolitik in Slowenien 1941–1945*, ed. Tone Ferenc (Maribor: Obzorja, 1980), Doc. 67.
23 National Archives and Records Administration, College Park, MD (hereafter NARA), T-81/307/2435225-227: Abschlussbericht der EWZ über die Erfassung der im Altreich untergebrachten Slowenenabsiedler, unsigned, 3 October 1943.
24 USHMMA, 15.021M/2/20/129: Szykowski to RuSHA Aussenstelle, 4 August 1940. Because these letters were always addressed to the same location, I will henceforth use the author's last name only when citing them.
25 USHMMA, 15.021M/1/1/26-27: Aktenaufzeichnung über die Mitteilungen des SS-Stf. Dr Seitz, unsigned, 21 June 1940.
26 Marie-Louise Roth-Zimmermann, *Denk' ich an Schelklingen. Erinnerungen einer Elsässerin an die Zeit im SS-Umsiedlungslager Schelklingen 1942–1945* (Sankt Ingbert: Röhrig Universitätsverlag, 2001), 57–8.
27 BArch, R 36/1052/19: Fürsorgeamt Frankfurt am Main to Preiser, 20 January 1941.
28 Hessisches Staatsarchiv, Darmstadt (hereafter HStD), G 15 Lauterbach, Nr. 5279: Landrat Lauterbach to Arbeitsamt Giessen, 24 December 1942.
29 BArch, R 59/46/6: Adam to Fähndrich, 14 December 1942.
30 USHMMA, 15.021M/2/20/72: Żelazek, 1 July 1940; USHMMA, 15.021M/3/20a/67: Grześkowiak, 21 May 1941; USHMMA, 15.021M/5/32/60: Kwaśniewska, 20 April 1941; USHMMA, 15.021M/5/32/123: Syguła, 12 July 1941; USHMMA, 15.021M/5/35/4: Lesiński, 10 May 1942; USHMMA, 15.021M/2/20/123: Słowiński, August 1940; USHMMA, 15.021M/2/20/26: Stańczak, 10 November 1940; BArch R 36/1052/45: Landrat Zempelburg to Deutsche Gemeindetag Berlin, 9 November 1942. Also see Jill Stephenson, *Hitler's Home Front: Württemberg under the Nazis* (New York: Humbledon Continuum, 2006), 17.
31 USHMMA, 15.021M/5/31/25-26: Stańczak, 7 August 1940.
32 Brigitte Entner, 'Deportation', in *Pregon koroških Slovencev – Die Vertreibung der Kärntner Slowenen, 1942–2002*, ed. Augustin Malle (Klagenfurt: Drava, 2002), 176.
33 BArch, R 36/1052: Preiser to Oberbürgermeister Frankfurt am Main, February 1941.
34 USHMMA, 15.021M/5/35/116: Seweryn, 4 November 1942; USHMMA, 15.021M/5/35/155: Karlikowski, 16 May 1943.
35 USHMMA, 15.021M/5/33/34: Rynkowski, 9 September 1941.
36 Hessisches Hauptstaatsarchiv, Wiesbaden (hereafter HStW), Abt. 411, Nr. 1008, Bd. 1138: Wagner to Landrat Limburg-Lahn, 14 December 1944.
37 USHMMA, 15.021M/5/32/113: Ciepłuch, 1 July 1941.
38 USHMMA, 15.021M/5/33/34: Rynkowski, 9 September 1941.
39 USHMMA, 15.021M/5/34/68-70: Kółeczko, 3 March 1942; USHMMA, 15.021M/5/35/85-86; Urbański, March 1942; USHMMA, 15.021M/5/35/159: Kaczorowska, 30 July 1943; BArch, R 49/3562/18: Eberstein to Gestapo Munich, 28 January 1943.
40 LOC/NMT, 787–789, Doc. NO-2267: Creutz to Himmler, 20 February 1942; BArch, NS 2/82/171-2: Hofmann to Heissmeyer, 25 September 1942.
41 NARA, T-81/307/2435225–227: Abschlussbericht der EWZ über die Erfassung der im Altreich untergebrachten Slowenenabsiedler, unsigned, 3 October 1943.
42 LOC/NMT, 899–900, Doc. NO-3220: Brandt to Lorenz, Schmauser, and Rösener, 22 September 1942.
43 BArch, R 49/73/85-6: Greifelt, Behandlung und Arbeitseinsatz der abgesiedelten Personen aus Elsass, Lothringen und Luxemburg, 3 October 1942.

44 BArch R 59/57/15: Brückner to Altena, 2 February 1943.
45 USHMMA, 15.021M/5/34/57: Świątek, 24 February 1942.
46 BArch, R 59/46/35-7: Greifelt, Strafmassnahmen und Herausnahme aus dem Wiedereindeutschungs-verfahren, 22 June 1942; BArch R 59/46/46: Ehlich to SD- and Stapostellen, undated.
47 See the death certificate for Zdzisław Lorek in ITS, 0.1/39189472. Also see HStW, Abt. 483, Nr. 11375: SD Frankfurt am Main to Waldeck and Stroop, 1 July 1944.
48 USHMMA, 15.021M/5/33/72: Kulawczyk, 26 October 1940.
49 USHMMA, 15.021M/5/35/120-121: Rolnik, 8 December 1942.
50 USHMMA, 15.021M/5/35/84: Spychalski, undated; USHMMA, 15.021M/5/35/51: Fornalczyk, 28 June 1942.
51 See the correspondence from the autumn of 1941 between Günther Pancke and Wilhelm Dörhöfer in Niedersächsisches Landesarchiv - Hauptstaatsarchiv, Hannover (hereafter NLH), Hann. 310 I, Nr. 358; USHMMA, 15.021M/2/20/121: Zbyrski, 4 August 1940; USHMMA, 15.021M/5/36/41: Pudelska, 27 May 1941.
52 NARA, M-894/15/5269: Testimony of Zofia Pieskarska, undated; NLH, Hann. 310 I, Nr. 358, Bd. 73: Dörhöfer to Pancke, 11 September 1941.
53 USHMMA, 15.021M/2/20/10: Kowalska, 19 October 1940.
54 Heinemann, *Rasse, Siedlung, deutsches Blut*, 296-7; USHMMA, 15.021M/5/33/50: Konrad, 5 October 1941.
55 USHMMA, 15.021M/5/36/40: Brandt to Heydrich and Greifelt, 7 July 1941.
56 USHMMA, 15.021M/3/20a/47: Wejmann, 23 March 1941.
57 USHMMA, 15.021M/2/20/181: Ratajski, 13 October 1940.
58 USHMMA, 15.021M/5/32/39a: Papier, 9 March 1941.
59 USHMMA, 15.021M/5/32/32: Frąckowiak, 23 February 1941.
60 USHMMA, 15.021M/5/35/148: Mazurek, 26 April 1943.
61 NARA, T-81/307/2435225-227: Abschlussbericht der EWZ über die Erfassung der im Altreich untergebrachten Slowenenabsiedler, unsigned, 3 October 1943.
62 HStW, Abt. 483, Nr. 11374: Gendarmerie Mömbris to Landrat Alzenau, 23 September 1944.
63 BArch, NS 2/82/167: Heissmeyer to Hofmann, 30 September 1942; USHMMA, 15.021M/6/38/11-21: Ehlich, Bericht über den Verlauf der Eindeutschung von rassisch wertvollen Fremdstämmigen, 19 December 1942.
64 BArch, NS 2/152/128-130: Hildebrandt, Anordnung über die Verleihung der deutschen Staatsangehörigkeit auf Widerruf an Elsässer, Lothringer und Luxemburger, 5 August 1943; BArch, R 59/57/3-4: Vermerk über die Sitzung im Stabshauptamt betr. Einbürgerung und Durchschleusung der abgesiedelten eindeutschungsfähigen Slowenen, unsigned, 12 January 1943.
65 Diemut Majer, *Fremdvölkische im Dritten Reich. Ein Beitrag zur nationalsozialistischen Rechtssetzung und Rechtspraxis in Verwaltung und Justiz unter besonderer Berücksichtigung der eingegliederten Ostgebiete und des Generalgouvernements* (Munich: Oldenbuurg, 1993), 122-3.
66 BArch, R 186/11: Künzel, Allgemeine Bemerkungen zum Wiedereindeutschungsverfahren, 18 May 1944.
67 See the ITS index cards on Eugenia Wójcik and Jan Nowakowski in ITS 0.1/50026387 and 3.1.1.1/44353657, respectively.
68 Michael G. Esch, *Gesunde Verhältnisse. Deutsche und polnische Bevölkerungspolitik in Ostmitteleuropa 1939-1950* (Marburg: Herder-Institut, 1998), 297-8 and 319; Elizabeth Vlossak, *Marianne or Germania? Nationalizing Women in Alsace,*

1870-1946 (New York: Oxford University Press, 2010), 288; Karl Stuhlpfarrer, 'Umsiedlungen und Deportationen während des zweiten Weltkriegs', in *Pregon koroškik Slovencev*, 131.
69 ITS, 0.1/29170607: Index Card on Alfons Królikowski; ITS, 0.1/21502968: Index Card on Stanislaw Furmanek; ITS, 0.1/15999039: A.E.F. Assembly Center Registration Card for Henryk Borowski.
70 Ines Hopfer, *Geraubte Identität. Die gewaltsame 'Eindeutschung' von polnischen Kindern in der NS-Zeit* (Vienna: Böhlau, 2010), 188 and 251–2.
71 Roman Sobkowiak, *Eindeutschungsfähig?! Eine polnisch-deutsche Biografie im NS-Staat und in der jungen Bundesrepublik* (Ulm: Klemm & Oelschläger, 2009), 8–9, 83, 91, 94–102 and 107.
72 Lynn H. Nicholas, *Cruel World: The Children of Europe in the Nazi Web* (New York: Knopf, 2005), 479.
73 Sobkowiak, *Eindeutschungsfähig*, 9 and 102.
74 Roth-Zimmermann, *Denk' ich an Schelklingen*, 21, 53, 57–8, 114–16, 163–6.
75 ITS, 3.2.1.1/90040730–731: Grzelka to ITS Arolsen, 11 January 1990; ITS, 3.2.1.1/90040773–774: ITS Arolsen to Grzelka (Alejandro), 27 September 2010.
76 Sobkowiak, *Eindeutschungsfähig*, 83.

Part IV

Refugees and displaced persons and the Second World War

12

The surviving remnant

Subjectification and self-organization in the Jewish DP camp Bergen-Belsen, 1945–8

Lennart Onken

When British troops liberated the Bergen-Belsen concentration camp on 15 April 1945, they faced an 'inferno':[1] an estimated 10,000 unburied corpses lay scattered around the camp grounds, piled up in small hills, with survivors wandering between them in search of leftover food, soup bowls, shoes, jackets and caps. Between January and April 1945, more than 35,000 people died in the camp, which had become the destination for death marches and deportation trains carrying inmates from concentration camps near the front line which were evacuated during the last months of the war. Sixty thousand people rescued by the British suffered from typhus and were severely emaciated, deserted and traumatized.

Liberation by no means meant an end to their suffering. The British military immediately launched rescue operations, installed a water pipe from the local river to the camp and set up an emergency hospital on the military training ground less than 2 kilometres away. Though they did everything in their power to save the survivors, they could not prevent another 14,000 people from dying of the direct consequences of their concentration camp imprisonments.

As the year progressed, the military training area was gradually converted into a displaced persons camp. According to Memorandum No. 39 of the Supreme Headquarters, Allied Expeditionary Forces, all 'civilians outside the national boundaries of their country by reasons of war', who were 'desirous but unable to return home or find homes without assistance' were considered so called displaced persons (DP).[2] At the time of liberation, this definition applied to about 7 million people living in what later became the territory of the three western occupation zones of Germany. We are thus faced with a historical paradox:

> Instead of creating a solely 'Aryan' empire, a genocidal war aimed at the enslavement and extermination of 'racial others' had transformed postwar Germany into a remarkably multi-ethnic territory.[3]

The Allies took care of the registration, administration and support of these DP. For accommodation, they often used the barracks of former concentration and forced labour camps. The main objective was the rapid repatriation of the DPs. This proved to be a particular problem for the small group of about 50,000–75,000 Jewish DP. Their situation was desperate: they were in a terrible state of health and had often lost their entire family, possessions and home. In Poland, Jews returning home from the ghettos, concentration and extermination camps as well as those Polish Jews who survived the war in the Soviet Union fell victim to antisemitic pogroms, which made returning all the more futile. At the latest after the pogrom in Kielce in 1946, tens of thousands of Jewish *infiltrees* began emigrating westwards – and landed in the DP camps, because legal emigration to the United States, Canada, Australia and Western Europe remained strictly quota-based. Until the founding of the State of Israel in 1948, even the route to Eretz Israel[4] remained closed due to the restrictive immigration policy of the British Mandate power in Palestine. Germany, the land of the perpetrators, thus involuntarily became a long-term place of residence for these Jewish DPs.

Inevitably, the Jewish survivors began to search for ways to return to a normal life. However, throughout this time, they considered their presence in Germany to be transitory. It can therefore be stated that the DP camp Bergen-Belsen

> was the place and framework for individual and collective rehabilitation in physical, psychological and social terms, the regaining of independence and self-reliance with the aim of a new beginning, which the Jewish DPs could only imagine outside Germany and, for the majority, only within a Jewish state in Palestine.[5]

Of particular importance for this process of individual and collective rehabilitation of the Jewish survivors was their self-organization in the Central Committee of Liberated Jews in the British Zone. The committee did not limit itself to the administrative management of the camp but claimed to represent and advocate for all Jews living in the British zone. From the very beginning, it thus fulfilled a political mission: to fight for the individual and collective rights of the Jews.[6]

It was Dan Diner who perceived the history of the Jewish DPs as a '[p]rism for understanding the central developments in Jewish history per se':[7] the fate and history of the Jewish DPs reflected their 'subjectification as a nation'.[8] Yet in reality, the self-organization of the Jewish DPs in particular reflected a dual process of subjectification: both as individuals and as a nation. Self-organization offered the liberated Jews a possibility to overcome the persistent object status and to newly constitute themselves as subjects – as individuals, as well as a people. Without a collective recognition as Jews and the end of homelessness and statelessness, all cultural or educational measures aimed at individual rehabilitation remained inevitably precarious.

Further developing the thesis of double subjectification, this chapter will analyse the relationship between subjectification and self-organization as exemplified by the Central Committee of Liberated Jews in the British Zone and examine the form(s) and function(s) of self-organization of the liberated Jews in more detail. The 'She'erit Hapletah', 'the surviving remnant', as the Jewish DPs named themselves, formed a very special group, which had no historical antecedents and no affirmative benchmarks. Rather, this community of destiny was constituted solely *ex negativo*: their only commonality was the experience of persecution, disenfranchisement, expulsion and extermination. Due to this specific constellation, the Jewish DPs are challenging the four-dimensional model of diaspora as presented by Willems and Palacz in the introduction to this volume. Its categories begin to blur against the backdrop of the British DP-policy. As will be shown, it was precisely the self-organization of the Jewish DPs that enabled them to create their very own 'host society' in the midst of a hostile environment.

Already in 1985, Wolfgang Jacobmeyer stated in his fundamental work on DP research: 'The DP problem is ... first and foremost the problem of the heteronomy of a group of people.'[9] This is particularly true for Jewish survivors. The thesis of this chapter assumes that life in the DP camp was highly politicized: since the DPs had gone from being an object of National Socialist violence and brutality to becoming an object of world politics, particularly the British policy on Palestine, self-organization and their self-definition as Jews were familiar means of asserting themselves both individually and collectively. Therefore, the self-organization of the Jewish DPs took on a mediating role between individual and collective subjectification, which in this sense is to be understood as the attempt to (re)gain personal responsibility and sovereignty, as well as a self-determined future.

British DP policy

At the end of May 1945, around 27,000 people of various nationalities were registered at the DP camp in Bergen-Belsen. Though the British were able to quickly repatriate a large proportion of the Western and Northern European DPs, there were still some 16,000 DPs left in November 1945, of which around 11,000 were Jews, mainly from Poland, Hungary and Romania. In order to facilitate their repatriation, the DPs were housed separately, according to nationality. However, the Jews were not regarded as an independent group, but were categorized according to their country of origin. In many cases, this even led to Jewish survivors of National Socialist persecution being housed as Poles, Balts or Ukrainians in one barrack together with former collaborators.

While in the aftermath of the Harrison Report, published in August 1945, separate Jewish DP camps were established in the American zone, the British continued to refuse to take this step. Superficially, they argued that recognizing Jews as Jews reproduced the National Socialist racial categories, something that liberal Britain could by no means accept. However, in reality, concrete political interests also had an impact: after decades of resolutely anti-Zionist policy for fear of conflict with the Arab population, the British now feared that recognition of the Jews as a separate group of persecuted people would lead to a greater claim to the founding of a Jewish state, and they sought to prevent this. Particularly risqué: due to the refusal of the British military government to recognize the Jews as an independent group, the absurd situation arose that Jews of German and Austrian origin were not recognized as DPs but rather fell within the jurisdiction of German or Austrian authorities. They were thus excluded from any gratuity that the DP status entailed.

British DP policy thus also outlined the framework for the self-organization of Jewish survivors, for whom insisting on the Jewish collectivity was an equally effective means of resisting repatriation. This basic constellation led to a 'paradoxical relationship'[10] between the liberated Jews and their liberators in the British zone. Josef Rosensaft, the chairman of the Central Jewish Committee, phrased it later this way: 'We could not avoid this struggle, although it had never occurred to us that we would have to fight our liberators.'[11] With its DP policy, the British government had provoked massive resistance among the Jewish DPs. Unintentionally, its unyielding stance created enormous cohesion among the Jewish survivors, who were united in the goal of fighting for the recognition of the Jews as a people and as a nation alike.

It was only when reports of antisemitic attacks on Jews began to emerge that the British liberators began to rethink their position. The camp newspaper, *Unzer Sztyme* (Our Voice), for example, reported on 'Polish hooliganism' against Jews and their institutions throughout the British zone.[12] In the wake of these acts of violence, the British decided to separate the Polish and Jewish DP camps in Bergen-Belsen. With the relocation of the last Polish DPs to other camps in the spring of 1946, the Bergen-Belsen DP camp became a solely Jewish DP camp, with up to 10,000 inhabitants at times. This led to the second paradox: in spring of 1946, less than 2 kilometres from the site of the former concentration camp, which in the last weeks of the war became the destination for clearance and evacuation transports from various concentration camps in Germany, 'the largest Jewish community ever to have existed in Lower Saxony was being created: the Jewish DP camp Bergen-Belsen'.[13]

Life in the Jewish DP camp Bergen-Belsen

The establishment of the purely Jewish DP camp had been one of the demands of the Central Jewish Committee, which organized everyday life and was responsible for all matters concerning Jewish DPs in the camp. In a sense, it steered the camp's fortunes in a quasi-state manner. German authorities had no authority whatsoever in the DP camp. Josef Rosensaft even spoke in this context of an 'extra-territorial unit inside Germany to its last day'.[14] By setting up their own camp police and jurisdiction, establishing schools and training centres, as well as cultural and religious institutions, the Jewish survivors 'executed the process of becoming a Jewish state in their own living environment'.[15]

In demographic terms, the Bergen-Belsen DP camp was an anomaly: the Nazis' counter-rational extermination policy had almost completely wiped out the young and old in particular among the prisoners; the overwhelming majority of Jewish DPs were between fifteen and thirty-five years old and had lost most or even all of their relatives. The survivors were completely deserted. Their longing for security and family support is an important explanation for the high rate of relationships and marriages immediately after or, in some cases, still in the midst of the survivors' convalescence.[16]

The shared experience of persecution bonded the Jewish survivors together and created a feeling of familiarity. The fact that Rosensaft's advice to marry out of love and not out of necessity[17] was largely ignored is certainly an indication of the longing for a return to normality, no matter how fragile that normality would remain. Marriage and starting a family became one of the most important social events in the DP camp.[18] In turn, the high number of families founded made an extremely strange impression on outsiders. For example, Roy Beaumont wrote in the British *Daily Express* on 22 August 1945 about his visit to the Bergen-Belsen DP camp:

> I have just spent two days in Germany's happiest and most cheerful city, where laughing men and girls walk the streets, swim, fish, go by boat, ride, dance, go to the theater, hold lavish wedding celebrations and open-air concerts, and play every kind of game imaginable. . . . Not a day goes by without four or five weddings. . . . I have attended one of these weddings. It could have been an elegant event in London: the bride in white, beautifully dressed bridesmaids and countless flowers and bouquets. . . . The wedding couple did not need to go anywhere for the honeymoon. They stayed in this happy and pleasant city. Its name? Belsen.[19]

Certainly, the reporter's gaze only glanced at the surface. Beneath it were deeply drawn and broken biographies of grief, anger and pain. Official DP authorities repeatedly criticized the brutalization of the camp youth in particular. In July 1945, *Unzer Sztyme* wrote: 'The youth testifies of an atmosphere of moral decay, and the demoralization by the camps has made us forget the "Halakhah tradition" of the "People of the Book".'[20] Not without reason, therefore, the Cultural Department of the Central Jewish Committee stated in June 1946 that it was very much interested in 'improving the spiritual and cultural situation of the neglected Jewish youth'.[21]

Therefore, the first Jewish primary school, named after the Czech Zionist and Elder of the Theresienstadt ghetto, Dr Jacob Edelstein, was opened in July 1945. Although there was a lack of suitable teaching materials, such as books, maps and the like, by September of the same year, the primary school already had ninety-two pupils who, in addition to general cultural techniques such as reading, arithmetic and writing, were also taught drawing, biology, Palestine studies, Hebrew and Jewish and general history.[22] The number of pupils reached its peak in March 1948 with around 340 children. In addition to the primary school, a secondary school was also founded, which accepted the graduates of the primary school. The Jewish Brigade Hebrew Secondary School, as it was officially called, had a proud 198 pupils in March 1948.[23] There were also various religious schools, Yeshivot and kindergartens.

In December 1945, the Organization for Rehabilitation through Training (ORT) opened a vocational school in Bergen-Belsen. Courses for men's and women's tailors, knitters, carpenters, locksmiths, shoemakers, prosthesis makers, radio engineers, electrical engineers, mechanics and watchmakers were intended to prepare the youth for emigration, primarily to Palestine. In particular the course for dental technicians, which was set up in July 1946, enjoyed a high reputation, especially among the Jewish DPs. By mid-July 1947, more than 700 course participants were to hold their diplomas in their hands,[24] which is one of the reasons why the ORT school in Bergen-Belsen became 'a symbol of newly won Jewish self-esteem'.[25]

However, the cultural department also became active in adult education. It built up a library, organized social gatherings such as lecture evenings and concerts (violinist

Yehudi Menuhin and pianist Benjamin Britten, for instance, performed in the Roundhouse in the DP camp Bergen-Belsen as early as July 1945), published the camp newspaper *Unzer Sztyme* and founded a Yiddish theatre.

The 'Kazet Theatre' was of great importance in terms of the individual and collective rehabilitation of the survivors. Even the name of the theatre group contained a direct reference to the experience of the concentration camps. Besides classical Yiddish plays, it also integrated the experience of persecution and extermination into its performances. Often, it chose a drastically realistic staging, which was particularly disturbing for foreign observers and visitors, precisely because it corresponded very specifically to the experiences and the reality of life of the survivors. American Jewish Joint Distribution Committee (AJDC) staff member Joseph Wollander described the reactions in the audience in a report published in the *New York Times*:

> At the finale there never is applause, just significant and painful silence that hangs heavily over the theatre. It is not uncommon to see an audience of over 3,000 persons burst into tears and hysterical sobbing throughout the production. In seeing their former miseries acted out, their lives projected onto a stage, so to speak, the displaced persons have come to regard their theatre as something a great deal more than 'entertainment'. The theatre symbolizes their will to live.[26]

It was precisely the connection between the staging of the concentration camp reality and plays of the classical Yiddish theatre, which made the 'Kazet Theatre' so fascinating. For both the performers and the audience it was a form of individual and collective self-therapy. The reference to the destroyed world of Yiddish culture gave the older audience a feeling of security and familiarity, while for the younger audience it usually meant the first contact with a culture that could no longer be experienced.[27]

The demise of the theatre group in turn is emblematic of the Jewish DPs' desperate situation after their liberation. Having performed in Belgium and France, the group disbanded in Paris in July 1947, as plans for further shows in London, New York and Palestine could not be realized. Sami Feder, the director of the theatre group, wrote in his diary:

> Due to political reasons we would have had to wait a long time for our onward journey to London, New York or Palestine. . . . We had no possibility to stay in Paris any longer. . . . Our members had no desire to return to Germany to the camps from where we had just come. We could not go any further.[28]

The self-perception of the She'erit Hapletah

Already the self-designation of the Jewish DPs as 'She'erit Hapletah', 'the surviving remnant' indicates their self-perception as a community of destiny with hardly any positive points of reference. What they had in common was the experience of the

Shoah. Out of this, however, arose the will to no longer be the object but the subject of one's own actions:

> 'This experience of Auschwitz then brought us together as a coercive community, in an effort to do something together after everything was destroyed, to do something together, precisely out of the conviction that as Jews we had experienced all this, that as Jews we had been exposed, that as Jews we wanted to redesign our new life.'[29]

Inherent to the identity of the 'She'erit Hapletah' was an understanding of past, present and future as a meaningful unity. This was already evident in the discussion about the name to be chosen for the DP camp. While the British preferred a neutral formulation with the name 'Bergen-Belsen D.P. Hohne-Camp' in order to create a semantic distance to the former concentration camp, the Jewish survivors quite deliberately insisted on the name Bergen-Belsen. Not only did the experience of persecution, disenfranchisement and extermination in the past connect inseparably with this place, rather, it also revealed the problem of foreign domination that continued into the present. *Unzer Sztyme* commented:

> Belsen is forever a disgrace to the Jewish people. . . . By changing the name Belsen to Hohne, the stain is blotted out, the murderers who are in prison are given full rehabilitation. Hohne is an approval of the National Socialist atrocities, a humiliation of all who fell in the fight against National Socialism. If Belsen is an indictment of the German people, Hohne will not be a minor indictment of our English liberators. For us, Hohne will be a greater pain than Belsen. Belsen was created by our worst enemies, Hohne by our greatest friends, whom we dreamed of in our sleepless nights in the concentration camps. . . . Let them do what they think. The place where tens of thousands died, . . . will for us and generations to come remain Bergen-Belsen.[30]

The very fact that they had been degraded by the National Socialists into completely disenfranchised and dehumanized objects made the disappointment about their perpetual homelessness and continued presence in the camp even after liberation all the greater. The vice-president of the Central Jewish Committee, Norbert Wollheim, expressed this disappointment in August 1945 in a letter to his friend, US Sergeant Hermann E. Simon: 'We are saved, but not liberated.'[31]

Bergen-Belsen was not only 'a place of mourning for the Jewish survivors, but as a symbol was also linked to current political aims',[32] as became particularly apparent on the first anniversary of the liberation of the concentration camp, on 15 April 1946. In a certain sense, the function of remembrance was to 'give meaning to and rehabilitate the dead'.[33] Accordingly, the memory of the deceased was linked to the longing for a Jewish state.

The first anniversary celebrations were organized by the Central Jewish Committee. *Unzer Sztyme* published an extra issue, the title page of which illustrated the liberation of the concentration camp. Additionally, a temporary wooden memorial, which had been opened on the site of the former concentration camp on the occasion of the first congress of the She'erit Hapletah in September 1945, was replaced by a stone one. The first anniversary in particular provided an opportunity to look back and reflect on the situation: Where did the Jewish survivors stand one year after liberation? The answer was sobering. The atmosphere in the DP camp was carried by an ambivalent tension between joy over the rescue and disappointment over the failure to achieve final liberation. In the ninth issue of *Unzer Sztyme* the following was published just before the anniversary:

> The day of April 15 will go down in the history of the Jewish people as the happy date on which the remnants of European Jewry were saved. But the year from April 15, 1945, to April 15, 1946, will remain a blemish in the history of world democracies who have no understanding of our tragedy, and who carry out all sorts of political intrigues at the expense of the Jews and disrupt the construction of Eretz Israel. Twelve months after liberation, the Jewish kibbutz in Germany stands firm and determined, driven by the only sacred aspiration to build life in the longed-for country.[34]

Although they continued to see themselves as objects of international power politics, they were determined to break with this status,

> for there is not such a force in the world that could break the strong, uniform will of a whole people. We will break through the gates of Eretz Israel with our tenacity, whether the other nations like it or not![35]

These words testify to a will to fight, which also impressed the British. After all, the Jewish survivors appeared increasingly self-confident. At the inauguration of the stone memorial on the grounds of the former concentration camp, the speaker Norbert Wollheim did not hesitate to accuse the British of tolerating the National Socialists for too long. Unfortunately, the speech itself was not preserved, but there remains a telegram from the commander of the DP camp, Major D. H. Murphy, dated 15 April 1946, in which he reported on the commemoration ceremonies. Murphy wrote of some 7,000 Jewish guests who travelled 2 kilometres from the DP camp to the former concentration camp for the well-organized commemoration ceremony. However, he was offended by Wollheim's speech, which he found to be 'quite scurrilous in its denunciation of the British for the lack of assistance and defence afforded to the Jews in their desperate struggle against extermination'.[36] Murphy further wrote that Wollheim even accused the British of being partly responsible for the Nazi crimes:

> [It] was alleged that the British like other nations allowed their minds to be poisoned by Hitler propaganda with the consequence that 6,000,000 Jews were exterminated, a crime for which the BRITISH should hang their heads in shame.[37]

Wollheim was already taken aside and reprimanded by the 'Jewish Adviser' of the British military government, Colonel Robert Solomon, following the speech. Even though correspondence between the military governor, Sir Brian Robertson, and subordinate authorities revealed great displeasure with the words chosen, the self-confidence of the Jewish survivors made an impression. In a letter to Robertson, the following was written:

> I know that the whole of this Jewish question is very difficult and that the political implications of the Jewish situation in our Zone are very considerable, and also that the members of this Jewish Committee have very strong backing both in England and America, and elsewhere. The Jewish Committee itself in Hohne is becoming a very powerful organisation.[38]

The struggle for self-determination

Some Jewish survivors had already formed a provisional committee shortly after liberation, as did survivors from other nations. But it became apparent at an early stage that many of the problems the Jewish survivors faced could not be solved on a local level but required a more centralized organization.[39] The Central Jewish Committee was then elected at the first Prisoners' Congress, which took place between 25 and 27 September 1945 in the Bergen-Belsen DP camp. Josef Rosensaft, a Polish Jew, was elected chairman, and Norbert Wollheim, a German Jew, was elected vice-chairman. Apart from him, only Eastern European Jews were part of the first elected Central Jewish Committee; with Hadassah Bimko, the future wife of Josef Rosensaft, there was only one woman among the seventeen members. The Central Committee established various sub-departments to take over the material, health, cultural, educational, religious and legal care and rehabilitation of the survivors. For this purpose, it coordinated the activities of the international Jewish aid organizations. In a letter sent to UNRRA, the Central Jewish Committee described its own tasks as follows:

> The Committee co-operate[s] with the [international Jewish Voluntary Societies] and has, we know, their complete confidence. Meetings are constantly held between our various sub-committees and the Jewish Voluntary Societies, and as a result, a flow of communal life is apparent which is comparable to the running of a small township.[40]

Although the Central Jewish Committee never received de jure official recognition from the British authorities, they were able to achieve de facto recognition through their resolute conduct and their quickly established and well-maintained contacts with various influential individuals and aid organizations abroad. Within a very short time, the Central Jewish Committee developed into a well-organized and powerful organization that took over the leadership of all Jews in the British zone of Germany.

The first Prisoners' Congress was of central importance for the self-organization of the liberated Jews. Backdropping the assembly was the disappointment of having been left on their own and abandoned by the international community only several months after liberation. Consequently, there was a growing desire for central organization in order to confront the international community with their desperate situation. For this purpose, representatives of the Jewish Committee from Bergen-Belsen met with representatives from the American zone, as well as staff members of the AJDC, the Jewish Relief Unit and the London Chief Rabbinate on 8 July 1945 to agree on the agenda and topics for the congress. A few weeks later, on 25 July 1945, the Jewish Brigade called for a general conference in St. Ottilien (in the American zone) to sound out possibilities for all-German networking and cooperation. But this did not happen; the reasons for the failed inter-zonal cooperation remain largely unclear. It is possible, however, that the Jewish Committee in Bergen-Belsen and above all Josef Rosensaft feared a massive loss of significance as there were much larger numbers of Jewish DPs in the American zone than in the British.[41] Nevertheless, the DP camp Bergen-Belsen had great expectations of the congress and was proud to be able to host it:

> Bergen-Belsen is now a place of Jewish liberty work, because the teaching of national pride and dignity emanates from Bergen-Belsen. The Prisoners' Congress will be a historic event in our lives.[42]

It is already striking here that the concepts of freedom, nation and dignity are placed in a direct semantic context. Under the motto 'Open the Gates of Eretz Israel!' the congress commenced on 25 September 1945 in the cinema hall of the DP camp – without the permission of the British military government. Although no representatives from the American zone had officially arrived, a proud 210 delegates were present, representing a total of about 40,000 Jews from 42 camps and communities. Josef Rosensaft, who, as usual, delivered his speech in Yiddish, welcomed them:

> Comrades, this is not the time to despair, this is the time to hope. . . . You must not fall into apathy and hopelessness while you are here. You must make your hands and brains fit for the new life ahead; you must make full preparations for that end. We have been saved from death; we are saved for life.[43]

Apart from questions of internal organization, the congress addressed the world public 'in the name of the six million Jews who fell victim to the Nazi terror and also in the name of the survivors' with a resolution comprising of eleven points. The most important demand was to put an end to 'the homelessness and statelessness of the Jewish people' and to allow an unhindered aliyah.[44] The catalogue of demands therefore begins with the following points:

> I) We swear that we will not be deterred by any disturbance or political machinations from emigrating to Eretz Israel.
> II) We warn all those responsible, and especially the British government, of the consequences of a policy that is contrary to the vital interests of the Jewish people and the foundations of justice and national freedom on which peace is based.[45]

Furthermore, the Prisoners' Congress demanded the recognition of Jews as an independent group and the Central Jewish Committee as their representation. The congress also called for the establishment of schools and training centres as well as for the provision of opportunities to correspond with relatives and friends. It is conspicuous – as Juliane Wetzel has quite rightly pointed out[46] – that the catalogue of demands only addressed the outside world, thus making it aware of its obligations. The fact that the first Bergen-Belsen trial took place in nearby Lüneburg parallel to the congress also ensured massive media coverage. Josef Rosensaft later spoke of some seventy journalists present. Thus the Central Jewish Committee had succeeded in making its own demands accessible to a broad international public. The reporting British military officer, Major Rickford, was once again impressed by the excellent organization of the congress and suspected that the presence of Selig Brodetsky, the president of the Board of Deputies of British Jews, as well as of the British member of parliament Sydney Silverman, would help to spread the demands of the Jewish DPs.[47] Rickford's conclusion reads almost like a prediction of what would happen in the coming years: 'Pending a statement of policy on the Palestine question, it is quite certain that a good deal of agitation may be expected regarding the conditions and treatment of Jewish DPs.'[48]

The 'paradoxical relationship' to the liberators

The extent to which Rickford was right in this assertion was demonstrated by the Central Jewish Committee at regular intervals. As early as June 1945, when the British wanted to transfer a number of Jewish DPs to Lingen in Emsland due to the hopeless overcrowding of the camp, the Jewish Committee had not only protested vehemently but had also taken it upon itself to bring the transports already sent out back to Belsen, as it feared that the separation of the Jewish DPs could lead to their repatriation. During a press conference in November 1945, British foreign secretary Ernest Bevin announced his intention to place the Mandate of Palestine under international trusteeship. Furthermore, he declared, 'that the Jews were not the only victims of fascism, and that they should not put themselves too much in the limelight, as this could lead to new antisemitic reactions'.[49] The Jewish DPs came together for a protest rally. Among others, Josef Rosensaft spoke at this rally:

> We declare to the world that for us there is no law that weakens the legacy of the oppressed. And the legacy was: Avoid in your life the paths that led to the crematoria. We want to go to Eretz Israel at all costs and build our future there, which guarantees us free and human life. We do not want to wait any longer![50]

However, the wait was far from over. The Grand National programme started only in 1947, which for the first time allowed a certain – albeit very small – monthly contingent of Jewish emigrants to leave legally. Yet, this remained strictly quota-based, which is why the Bricha[51] continued to organize illegal emigration in parallel. Between April 1945 and January 1948, some sixty-three ships sailed illegally towards Palestine, of which only five reached their destination. All other ships were intercepted en route, and the Mapilim, as the illegal immigrants were called, were mostly interned in Cyprus.

The best known of these ships was undoubtedly the *Exodus*. The ship set sail for Palestine on the morning of 11 July 1947 with over 4,500 Mapilim on board, including many Holocaust survivors. But while still in international waters, the ship was intercepted and damaged by British destroyers. Instead of taking the Mapilim to Cyprus as usual, they were sent back to the port of Hamburg, where they were violently driven off board, loaded onto trains and taken to the camps at Pöppendorf and Am Stau, where they lived behind barbed wire surrounded by watchtowers and searchlights before being taken to other camps.

The Central Jewish Committee reacted to the actions of the British in a variety of ways. A general strike was called on 25 August, even before the Mapilim reached Hamburg. A week later, on 4 September, the Central Jewish Committee held a press conference in Hamburg, criticizing the British actions and reporting on the situation of DPs in the camps. In addition to the monthly issue of *Unzer Sztyme*, there was an eight-page extra supplement devoted exclusively to the *Exodus* affair. On 7 September, some 4,000 Jewish DPs demonstrated on the Freedom Square in the Bergen-Belsen DP camp. They carried signs with inscriptions such as 'Down with Bevin', 'Exodus is a disgrace for England' and 'Mapilim on the Exodus, we are with you!'[52] The participants waved white-blue flags; a Bevin effigy was also burned. In addition to these forms of protest, however, there was also a desire to show practical solidarity. For example, Rabbi and Central Jewish Committee member Zvi Asaria visited Mapilim for the Jewish New Year Rosh Hashana. Aid supplies and goods were donated and Palestine certificates issued to DPs in Belsen were also given to the Mapilim.[53]

The Exodus affair provoked worldwide criticism of the British, who subsequently felt compelled to surrender the Palestinian mandate and agree to the UN partition plan of November 1947. Finally, on 14 May 1948, Ben-Gurion proclaimed the State of Israel. For Norbert Wollheim, this day marked the beginning of the actual liberation, as it made independent Jewish life possible: 'This day brought us closer to the realisation of the ultimate goal, which the She'erit Hapletah had set for itself: the final liberation.'[54] The founding of the State of Israel was celebrated extensively in Bergen-Belsen: the Jews sang and danced 'as if electrified' in the streets, while prayers were said in the Yeshivot[55] and the young people demonstrated in the colours of the newly founded State of Israel.[56]

In the cinema hall, the Central Jewish Committee organized a solemn ceremony opened by Josef Rosensaft. The first group of young volunteers under the leadership of Zvi Asaria then entered the room and was greeted with 'thunderous applause'[57] – a scene that impressively demonstrated the newly won sovereignty. The Central Jewish Committee also launched a collection for the Haganah in close cooperation with the local Jewish communities.[58]

With the proclamation of the State of Israel, Jewish subjectification as a nation was accomplished. Thus, the last hurdle on the road to self-determination was overcome by the Jewish survivors: their homelessness and statelessness were brought to an end.

Conclusion

As a direct product of the National Socialist extermination policies, the Jewish DP group was constituted entirely *ex negativo*. Under the self-denomination 'She'erit Hapletah', Jews of all origins and different cultural, political and religious convictions came together. Their only commonality was the experience of disenfranchisement, expulsion and extermination – and their will to constitute themselves anew as self-determined Jewish subjects. After the Shoah, most of the Jewish survivors did not identify anymore as citizens of their pre-war countries of origin, but as homeless Jews, yearning for a Jewish homeland. It was precisely this lack of a real homeland that allowed Zionism to have such a massive integrative effect on Jewish survivors.

This community of destiny was confirmed and perpetuated by persistent spatial concentration in DP camps. Essentially, the Jewish DP camp Bergen-Belsen needs to be regarded as an exclave. Even though it was located on German territory, it functioned as an 'extra-territorial unit inside Germany to its last day'.[59] By founding their own families, schools, educational centres, religious and cultural institutions, jurisdictions and police forces – in short, everything that constitutes a modern state – the Jewish survivors, organized in the Central Jewish Committee, created, in a sense, their very own 'host society'. However, this process of individual subjectification of the once disenfranchised and powerless prisoners had to remain precarious as long as their Jewish homeland remained merely a pipe dream.

Self-organization thus fulfilled the function of a mediator between individual and collective rehabilitation. Only in the struggle for collective recognition, national independence and an end to homelessness and statelessness did the Jewish survivors see an opportunity to break with their persistent object status and to newly constitute themselves as subjects. Thus, the individual and collective subjectification of Jewish survivors stood in a dialectical relationship: subjectification as a nation was for them not only the sole legitimate historical answer to the Shoah but also the basic condition for their subjectification as individuals, indeed for their very existence in general. This connection becomes particularly clear in a speech given by Norbert Wollheim to the Jewish Community of Hamburg on the occasion of the tenth anniversary of the November pogrom on 9 November 1948:

> Let us allow ourselves to be flooded with the feeling of happiness that on the darkest night in the history of the world a new light was kindled for the Jews, the bright light of which gives us hope and confidence, and which we want to warm ourselves in the cold and loneliness of our own lives and help to cultivate, so that it never extinguishes again.... We want nothing more than for the years that are left to us: living a life that is our own.[60]

Notes

1 Derrick Sington, one of the first British soldiers to enter the Bergen-Belsen concentration camp, described his first impression as 'Dante's inferno', quoted in

Niedersächsische Landeszentrale für politische Bildung (ed.), *Konzentrationslager Bergen-Belsen. Berichte und Dokumente* (Göttingen, 1996), 183.

2   See Arolsen Archives – International Center on Nazi Persecution [formerly the International Tracing Service], Bad Arolsen (hereafter ITS), 6.1.1/82495539, SHAEF Memorandum No. 39, Revised Version of 16 April 1945.

3   Atina Grossmann and Tamar Lewinsky, 'Zwischenstation', in *Geschichte der Juden in Deutschland von 1945 bis zur Gegenwart*, ed. Michael Brenner (Munich: Beck, 2012), 68. All German quotes in this article were translated by the author.

4   *Eretz Israel* is a biblical term used for the ancient land of Kanaan. With the emergence of political Zionism in the nineteenth century, the term underwent a renaissance. During the period of the League of Nations mandate, it denoted the official name 'Palestine' in Hebrew.

5   Thomas Rahe, 'Bergen-Belsen. Das Jüdische Displaced-Persons-Camp', in *Historisches Handbuch der jüdischen Gemeinden in Niedersachsen und Bremen*, ed. Herbert Obenaus (Göttingen: Wallstein, 2005), 198–211.

6   Josef Rosensaft, 'Our Belsen', in *Belsen*, ed. Irgun Sheerit Hapleita Me'Haezor Habriti (Tel Aviv: 1957), 27.

7   Dan Diner, 'Elemente der Subjektwerdung. Jüdische DPs in historischem Kontext', in *Überlebt und unterwegs. Jüdische Displaced Persons im Nachkriegsdeutschland*, ed. Fritz Bauer Institut (Frankfurt am Main and New York: Campus, 1997), 229.

8   Ibid., 230.

9   Wolfgang Jacobmeyer, *Vom Zwangsarbeiter zum Heimatlosen Ausländer* (Göttingen: Vandenhoeck & Ruprecht, 1985), 20.

10 Nicola Schlichting, *'Öffnet die Tore von Erez Israel'. Das jüdische DP-Camp Bergen-Belsen 1945–1948* (Nuremberg: Antogo, 2005), 26.

11 Rosensaft, 'Our Belsen', 35.

12 Rafael Olewski, 'Polnischer Hooliganismus', *Unzer Sztyme* 6 (1 January 1945): 14, quoted in Hildegard Harck, *Unzer Sztyme. Jiddische Quellen zur Geschichte der jüdischen Gemeinden in der Britischen Zone 1945–1947* (Kiel: Landeszentrale für Politische Bildung Schleswig-Holstein, 2004), 28.

13 Rahe, 'Bergen-Belsen', 198.

14 Rosensaft, 'Our Belsen', 47.

15 Rahe, 'Bergen-Belsen', 199f.

16 See for example Katja Seybold, 'Gruppenbildung innerhalb einer Schicksalsgemeinschaft. Das jüdische DP-Camp Bergen-Belsen 1945–1951', in *Bergen-Belsen. Neuere Forschungen*, ed. Habbo Knoch and Thomas Rahe (Göttingen: Wallstein, 2014), 177–205.

17 See Hadassah Rosensaft, *Yesterday. My story* (Washington: United States Holocaust Memorial Museum and the Holocaust Survivors' Memoirs Project 2004), 109.

18 Thomas Rahe, 'Polnische und Jüdische Displaced Persons im DP-Camp Bergen-Belsen', in *Displaced Persons. Leben im Transit: Überlebende zwischen Repatriierung, Rehabilitation und Neuanfang*, ed. Rebecca Boehling, Susanne Urban and René Bienert (Göttingen: Wallstein, 2014), 68.

19 Quoted in Rainer Schulze, '"Germany's gayest and happiest town?" Bergen-Belsen 1945–1950', in *Dachauer Hefte* 19 (2003): 216.

20 *Unzer Sztyme* 1 (12 July 1945), quoted in Schlichting, 'Öffnet die Tore von Erez Israel', 18.

21 Quoted in Sophie Fetthauer, *Musik und Theater im DP-Camp Bergen-Belsen. Zum Kulturleben der jüdischen Displaced Persons 1945–1950* (Neumünster: Von Bockel, 2012), 69.

22 Angelika Königseder and Juliane Wetzel, *Lebensmut im Wartesaal. Die jüdischen Displaced Persons im Nachkriegsdeutschland* (Frankfurt am Main: Fischer Taschenbuch, 2004), 188.
23 Ibid., 189.
24 See Zentralarchiv zur Erforschung der Geschichte der Juden in Deutschland, Heidelberg, B 1/28-12, Bericht der Kulturabteilung des Zentralkomitees der befreiten Juden in der Britischen Zone, 4.
25 Königseder and Wetzel, *Lebensmut im Wartesaal*, 193.
26 Quoted in Thomas Rahe, 'Kultur im jüdischen DP-Camp Bergen-Belsen. Bedingungen und Strukturen', in *Bergen-Belsen. Neue Forschungen*, 214.
27 See Nicolas Yantian: '"Aus der Versteinerung heraustreten". Das "Kazet-Theater" im jüdischen Displaced Persons Lager Bergen-Belsen 1945–1947', in *Im Schatten des Holocaust. Jüdisches Leben in Niedersachsen nach 1945*, ed. Herbert Obenaus (Hannover: Hahn, 1997), 144.
28 Quoted in ibid., 139.
29 Archive of the Bergen-Belsen Memorial, Lohheide (hereafter ABB), BT 735, transcription of an interview with Norbert Wollheim, 12 May 1993, 18.
30 *Unzer Sztyme* 5 (29 November 1945): 7f., quoted in Schlichting, 'Öffnet die Tore von Erez Israel', 16.
31 United States Holocaust Memorial Museum Archive, Washington, DC, Wollheim estate, Box 9, Correspondence File, Simon Letters, 2.
32 Martina Staats, 'Erste Schritte zur Gestaltung der Gedenkstätte Bergen-Belsen', in *Bergen-Belsen. Neue Forschungen*, 339.
33 Ibid., 340.
34 *Unzer Sztyme* 9 (15 April 1945): 23, quoted in Schlichting, 'Öffnet die Tore von Erez Israel', 49.
35 Ibid.
36 The National Archives, Kew (hereafter TNA), FO 1030/307, telegram 'Unveiling of Memorial Camp I Belsen', 15 April 1946.
37 Ibid., highlights in the original.
38 TNA, FO 1030/307, letter from Lit. Gen. A. Galloway to Lit. Gen. Sir Brian H. Robertson, 21 April 1946.
39 ABB, BO 4327, Barict vom 1. Häftlingskongress, Jidischer Central Komitet Bergen-Belsen, 25 September 1945.
40 Yad Vashem Archive, Jerusalem, O.70-6, Report submitted by Central Jewish Committee, British zone, Germany, 23 August 1946, 1.
41 Juliane Wetzel, 'Die Selbstverwaltung der She'erit Hapletah. Die Selbstverwaltung der befreiten Juden in der britischen Zone 1945–1951', in *Im Schatten des Holocaust*, 47.
42 *Unzer Sztyme* 1 (12 July 1945):12, quoted in Schlichting, 'Öffnet die Tore von Erez Israel', 36.
43 Quoted in Leslie Hardman, *The Survivors. Story of the Belsen Remnant* (London: Vallentine Mitchell, 1958), 102f.
44 *Aliyah* (Hebrew for 'ascent') is the Hebrew term for the immigration of Jews from the diaspora to the Land of Israel.
45 See resolutions of the first Prisoner's Congress, *Unzer Sztyme* 4 (15 October 194): 64f.
46 Wetzel, 'Die Selbstverwaltung der She'erit Hapletah', 45.
47 TNA, FO 1049/81, 'Report on "Jewish Congress" at Hohne Camp 25/27th September by Major C.C.K. Rickford'.
48 Ibid.

49 Quoted in Schlichting, 'Öffnet die Tore von Erez Israel', 47.
50 'Das Echo der She'erit Hapletah auf die Erklärung von Außenminister Bevin', *Unzer Sztyme* 6 (1 January 1946): 9.
51 The *Bricha* (Hebrew for 'escape') was an underground Jewish organization that helped Jews enter Palestine illegally from 1944 to 1948.
52 Schlichting, 'Öffnet die Tore von Erez Israel', 70.
53 See Josef Rosensaft, 'Bergen-Belsen 1945–1965', in *Holocaust and Rebirth*, ed. Sam E. Bloch (New York: Bergen-Belsen Memorial Press, 1965), livf.
54 Norbert Wollheim, 'Belsen's place in the Process of "Death-and-Rebirth" of the Jewish People', in *Belsen*, 66.
55 Rafael Olewski, *Tor der Tränen. Jüdisches Leben im Schtetl Osieciny in Polen, Leiden unter NS-Terror und in Auschwitz, Überleben im KZ Bergen-Belsen, dort im DP-Camp und in Celle 1914–1981* (Constance: Hartung-Gorre, 2014), 321f.
56 Zvi Asaria, *Wir sind Zeugen* (Hannover: Niedersächsische Landeszentrale für politische Bildung, 1975), 169.
57 Ibid.
58 Staatsarchiv Hamburg, 522-2-1665, Letter to the Jewish Community of Hamburg, 4 June 1948.
59 Rosensaft, 'Our Belsen', 47.
60 ABB, BO 2428, Norbert Wollheim, 'Zum 9. November 1948 – Rede an die Jüdische Gemeinde Hamburg auf der Gedenkstunde zum zehnten Jahrestag des Beginns der Pogrome in Deutschland', 14f.

13

Resettling, repatriating and 'rehabilitating' Polish displaced persons in British-occupied Germany, 1945–51

Samantha K. Knapton

Introduction

Towards the end of the Second World War, in April 1945, the Western Allied armies encountered millions of displaced persons (DPs) throughout Germany as they fought their way to Berlin. The sheer volume of DPs necessitated the speedy construction of transit and assembly centres to hold these people until the newly created United Nations Relief and Rehabilitation Administration (UNRRA) could take over. Although throughout the war, observers in Britain and the United States had speculated over the scale of displacement, nothing could have prepared them for what they encountered in Germany. Repatriation quickly became the word of the day as the Allied armies and UNRRA worked tirelessly to help people return to their homes, whether they were recently liberated French Resistance fighters or former forced labourers (*Zwangsarbeiter*). In the three western zones of occupation (British, French and US zones), Poles were the most numerous DPs as the majority were *Zwangsarbeiter* working in agriculture and industry throughout the Reich.[1] Many were ready and willing to repatriate to Poland when the war ended in May 1945; however, the Allies had agreed to give Western DPs and Soviet 'DPs' priority for repatriation.[2] Once the dust had settled, it was late summer before the Poles could be transported. Unfortunately, by this time many were reluctant to return to Poland for two reasons. First, the London-based government-in-exile had been ousted from its position of authority and the new Soviet-backed Polish Provisional Government of National Unity had been installed in Warsaw.[3] To many in the DP camps, this change of regime made them fearful of reprisals upon return to Poland. Second, at the Potsdam conference between July and August 1945 the Allies had agreed to Stalin's demands to re-draw Poland's borders, thus displacing those originally living east of the River Bug. The 'brothers-in-arms' became the 'betrayed ally', as General Władysław Anders recounted in his memoirs:

> Each had trusted that at the end of his struggles, toil and suffering, he would be able to return to his own country, his family, his cottage, his trade or his piece

of land; now he knew that the reward for his efforts and his comrades' sacrifices was to be either further wandering in alien lands, or a return to a country under foreign rule.[4]

At the same time, Poland was given an equitable portion of land to the west taken from Germany, referred to as 'the Recovered Territories' by the new Polish government. In effect these events meant that Poland's borders had been shifted 150 miles westwards as the eastern lands were absorbed into the Soviet Union's satellite states and former eastern Germany became modern-day Poland. Margaret McNeill (a Quaker welfare worker in the camps) recounted in her memoirs that 'no matter how wretched their present lives, the uncertainty of the future in Poland seemed to produce a kind of mental paralysis'.[5] The combination of the shift in territory and the Allied recognition of a Soviet-backed government in the summer of 1945 caused a halt to Polish DP repatriation and an odd form of stalemate ensued.

The Polish DPs found themselves in a difficult position. Having already undergone displacement at the hands of the Nazis during wartime or while fleeing from the encroaching Red Army, they were now at the mercy of the occupying Allied armies. In the British zone of occupation, however, tensions were higher than elsewhere as the Polish DPs expected to be treated like equals once the war ended. As Michał Palacz asserts when discussing Polish refugees in Britain, Poles were expecting a 'brothers-in-arms' welcome, but this was almost exclusively reserved for Poles who had actively fought alongside the British and was based on the assumption that those in Britain and in the British zone would quickly and efficiently return to Poland. The majority of Polish DPs in the camps were not ex-military; many were former forced labourers. The rhetoric perpetuated by the London-based Polish government-in-exile, however, grouped all Poles under the 'brothers-in-arms' banner. In reality, many Polish DPs experienced disappointment once they were in the British zone's DP camps. Their unwilling displacement was only further exacerbated in the DP camps under British military and international welfare organizations' care as it soon became obvious their presence was unwelcome.

The existence of Poles in the north-west corner of Germany, later the British zone of occupation, was no new thing. Seasonal and temporary migrants from Poland had become permanent communities and settled in the industrialized Ruhr area in the late nineteenth century.[6] In 1945, the newcomers did not receive a warm welcome as their mere presence highlighted the existing community's 'otherness', something they had spent half a century trying to repress. At the same time, Poles in Britain were very different to the rural *chłop* (peasant) Poles in the DP camps of Germany. Many in Britain had close ties to the London government-in-exile and were often polyglot urban intellectuals that fled Poland through France at the beginning of war. Their highly politicized agendas set them apart from the ordinary Poles in the camps, yet the loss of a perceived homeland also bound them together. As Willems and Palacz note in the introduction to this volume, diasporas are often in conflict with one another, particularly those who hail from the same areas but with different social and cultural backgrounds. In British-occupied Germany, the Polish DPs found themselves in a difficult position. Ignored by the existing community that seemingly preferred to adopt the attitudes of the hostile host society, they were also used as political fodder by the cosmopolitan Poles in London attempting to secure a free Poland while finding their status as 'brothers-in-arms' rescinded by a weary and financially crippled Britain.

The combination of these events had a lasting and indelible effect on Anglo-Polish-German post-war relationships. Britain's attempts to cultivate beneficial post-war relationships with Germany, the United States and the Soviet Union over their Polish 'brothers-in-arms' prolonged and exacerbated a forced transnational migration that was rooted in racially motivated expulsions, forced labour and imprisonment during wartime. Indeed, the Anglo-Polish 'brothers-in-arms' rhetoric shifted to 'betrayed ally' as relationships changed in 1945.[7] The prolonged stay of some Polish DPs in Germany due to lack of opportunity to resettle elsewhere put the new community in conflict with the pre-existing (yet integrated) Polish community, as well as the host society that was the cause of their original displacement. Although attempts have been made to analyse and examine the experiences of Poles in Germany pre- and post-1945, as well as Poles in post-war Britain, a comparison of these competing diasporas set within the framework of forced displacement is lacking.[8] Following the four-dimensional model of diaspora set out by Willems and Palacz in the introduction, this chapter analyses the influence of the host society, the draw of the homeland and the impact of other diasporas, as well as British officials, on the two competing Polish diasporas through three sections. The first section looks at the formation of the *Ruhrpolen* community and the start of the post-war Polish DP diaspora in north-west Germany. The second section addresses Polish DP experiences in the camps focusing on issues of repatriation, resettlement and notions of 'rehabilitation', as well as conflicts with the German host society. The last section examines the competing diasporas within the context of post-war Britain and British-occupied Germany as different diasporas took priority over Polish DPs in the post-war world. Consequently, this chapter addresses the often-indirect consequences of piecemeal and ad hoc policies implemented in the British zone, alongside concerted efforts to avoid 'ghettoization' of Poles in Britain, to underscore the effects of forced migration on transnational relationships.

From *Ruhrpolen* to displaced persons

As previously mentioned, the migration of Polish peoples to Germany was not something unique to the twentieth century. A sizeable Polish and Masurian population had resided in the north-west Ruhr area of Germany since the late nineteenth century.[9] These Poles came to Germany as seasonal and temporary labourers, mostly working in the Hellweg area (Duisburg, Mülheim, Essen, Bochum and Dortmund) within mines and new industries, although some were also working the land. Similar to many other stories of migration before and since, the seasonal and temporary labourers turned into permanent residents. The community had been growing since the mid-eighteenth century, but it was only with the expansion of mines and industry that a sizeable community formed. Those who came to the Ruhr, and were collectively referred to as *Ruhrpolen*, were from Germany's eastern lands (the provinces of Posen and Silesia, as well as East and West Prussia). Although lumped together by local Germans in the

Ruhr as *Ausländer* (foreigners) and sometimes referred to by the derogatory 'Polack', numerous distinctions based on land, language and religion were evident. They were by no means an ethnically homogenous group. For instance, during the great move westwards (*Ostflucht*) at the end of the nineteenth century, up to 20 per cent of migrants were Poles who had lived in the Province of Posen whose mother tongue and national affiliation was Polish but whose citizenship was Prussian-German.[10] As noted in Willems's case study of East Prussian expellees, the use of derogatory names such as 'Polack' was continued in the post-1945 era and emphasized the existence of a newer migration.

Before the First World War, the presence of *Ruhrpolen* was accepted as necessary, although there were often long and protracted debates about securing rights for workers born in the Ruhr (believed to be the true Germans) and the fear of a subculture forming. Yet, with the outbreak of the war in 1914, the *Ruhrpolen* changed from *Saisonarbeiter* (seasonal labourers) to *Zwangsarbeiter* (forced labourers). The Prussian War Ministry wanted to prevent those deemed 'Russian-Polish' workers returning to their homes, now viewed as enemy lands. The solution was to keep them in Germany against their will. Their displacement, although initially voluntary and under dubious contractual arrangements, was now forced for the benefit of the German war effort.[11]

Those who remained in the Ruhr area in 1918 faced two choices: remain in Germany and become a German citizen by default, or return to Poland. The approximations of how many chose to return to Poland are dubious but estimates lie at around 75,000.[12] During the interwar years, although Polish associations continued to attract a strong membership, it was much more common for *Ruhrpolen* descendants to limit Polish language to religious services rather than everyday activities, as assimilation was strongly encouraged over integration. In 1922, the Union of Poles in Germany (*Bund der Polen in Deutschland / Związek Polaków w Niemczech*) was formed in Bochum, and became the cornerstone of Polish activity for the Ruhr. By the time Adolf Hitler became Chancellor in Germany in 1933, the majority of the *Ruhrpolen* had assimilated, rather than integrated. When the German People's List (*Volksliste*) was introduced by Heinrich Himmler, *Ruhrpolen* had to forefront their Germanness in an effort to remain under the radar of Nazi authorities.[13] Consequently, as new Poles arrived through forced labour schemes, they were not greeted with open arms as their presence brought unwanted attention to the pre-existing community. Many *Ruhrpolen* had forcibly suppressed their 'Polishness' (*polskość*), in order to be classed as one of the lower two categories on the *Volksliste*.[14] In post-war Germany, however, this caused friction between seemingly similar but realistically opposing diasporas within an already hostile host community. Additionally, the Ruhr was firmly within British-occupied Germany. Under British military and UNRRA control, the officials and welfare workers struggled to understand what separated *Ruhrpolen* and Polish DPs. This widespread confusion in the immediate post-war period caused the two distinctly separate diasporas to be viewed as equally troublesome by the occupying forces.

The Polish DP group was made up largely of former forced labourers, although estimates of how many were brought to work throughout the Reich varied. Initially many were coerced into signing up for 'voluntary' positions throughout Germany; however, once their contracts expired, they were often kept involuntarily for an extended period of time. As the war years continued, the method of displacement became more brutal until *łapanki* (street round-ups) became the common way of forcing Poles to work for the benefit of the German Reich. According to Ulrich Herbert, by August 1944, Poles accounted for 1,688,080 of the foreign civilian workers and prisoners of war (POWs) working in the Reich, the majority (66.7 per cent) in agriculture.[15] Yet the Institute for Occupation Issues estimates the overall number brought to Germany from Poland throughout the war was closer to 3.5 million (with 700,000 POWs).[16] By the end of the war, according to Malcolm J. Proudfoot, over 1.5 million Poles had been displaced, with 910,000 recorded in the SHAEF (Supreme Headquarters Allied Expeditionary Forces) areas of Germany, Austria and Czechoslovakia. Due to the prioritization of Western and Soviet DPs for repatriation, 816,012 Poles remained in the 3 western zones alone by 30 September 1945. The largest proportion were in the British zone of occupation, accounting for 510,238, or 79 per cent, of its total DP population.[17]

Those in the camps were largely former forced labourers; however, many had been members of the *Armia Krajowa* (Home Army or AK) and had been captured and interned after the Warsaw uprising in 1944.[18] Initially the Soviets pressed for Poles originally east of the River Bug to be incorporated into Soviet statistics; however, as the screening process in the camps was haphazard at best, Polish DPs with an assortment of wartime experiences were included in Soviet demands. From former forced labourers to members of the AK, the immediate danger of handing any Polish DPs over to Soviet officials was realized. The Poles presented a curious problem in US and British zones: they were numerically strong and fiercely nationalist but almost entirely dependent on the Allies. The British had pledged allegiance to the Poles and joined the war in retaliation for the German invasion in 1939. Now, six years later, confronted with a mass of Polish DPs in a zone utterly devastated by war, low on supplies and staffed by physically and mentally exhausted military personnel, the Poles' immediate fate was once again in British hands.

Into the camps: Polish DPs in British-occupied Germany

Once the Soviet and Western 'DPs' had been repatriated, the Allies turned their attention to the Polish DPs and focused on getting them back 'home' as quickly as possible. It was a sizeable and visible group, which in the Allies' view had little reason not to return to Poland. For many military officials, 'Rehabilitation', UNRRA's second R, had become synonymous with repatriation and therefore what they perceived to be the return of the 'status quo'. The British zone contained 63 per cent of all Polish DPs across the three western zones of occupation by September 1945, with the US zone containing 31 per cent and the French zone just 6 per cent. Therefore, when problems with repatriation emerged, the British zone was the most affected. Many running the camps were hoping for swift and efficient repatriation. As chief of operations for the UNRRA mission in Germany Lt. Gen. Sir Frederick Morgan stated, 'almost everything depends on the solution of the Polish problem. If the Poles agree to go home, and there is every likelihood that the vast majority of them will, the whole thing is comparatively simple'.[19] Unfortunately for Morgan, due to the shift in borders, the change of government in Poland and the initial halt on repatriation, many Poles refused repatriation as winter approached in 1945. These unwilling nomads became stalwart 'unrepatriables' in the western DP camps.

The Polish DPs in the British zone's camps soon became viewed as 'troublesome' and a 'nuisance', as the British believed the Poles' steadfast refusal to repatriate was driven by greed rather than necessity. For many Polish DPs, returning to the new Poland was not a welcome idea and for some it was impossible. In her memoirs, Leokadia Rowinski, a former AK member and POW in Oberlangen camp, realized soon after liberation that 'there was no place in the world for the likes of us' as Poland 'whose freedom we had sacrificed our youth, had another occupant, as eager to destroy the patriotic element as the Germans had been'. She lamented that 'no triumphant return awaited us – just arrests, even torture, and Russian forced labor camps in Siberia'.[20] Simultaneously, the now 'Recovered Territories' of formerly eastern Germany were being referred to by some Poles as 'The Wild West' – a place of lawlessness and chaos.[21] As a consequence of the expulsions in the east, this change of borders displaced an estimated 12–14 million ethnic German peoples predominantly from Poland and Czechoslovakia, many of whom slowly made their way westward to one of the three Allied occupation zones.[22]

The multiple diasporas in distress present in the British zone of Germany impaired the military authorities and international organizations' ability to simultaneously 'clear the camps' and aid the reconstruction of supply and transport chains. The relationship between those viewed as 'carers' (UNRRA and other welfare organizations) and 'protectors' (the Allied forces) were also strained as duties were meticulously divided and assigned on paper, yet in practice this scheme became impossible to implement. In the midst of this bureaucratic entanglement, Polish DPs who had unwillingly left their homes in the first instance were now being treated like a burden, even though their continued displacement was largely due to Allied sanctioned policies. Indeed, the initial 'brothers-in-arms' attitude was often invoked by the actively serving members of the Polish army as well as the exiled elites in London, and it soon cascaded down to the ordinary Polish DPs in the camps until the rhetoric was common among all. These elites were looked up to by Polish DPs in the camps and quickly a new form of social hierarchy developed based on wartime experiences and suffering. Political prisoners were at the top of this new hierarchy, often continuing to display the purple 'P' symbol on their clothing as a badge of honour, whereas former forced labourers were at the bottom. Amid these new hierarchies, the belief in Poland and Britain's 'brothers-in-arms' status was fervently repeated. Yet, when the British did not show the same attitude towards their Polish allies in the camps, the 'brothers-in-arms' quickly transformed into the 'betrayed ally'.

From the British point of view, Poles had misconstrued the British declaration of war on Germany as an act of loyalty rather than practicality. In reality, Britain was more concerned with territorial integrity and the repercussions of another possible partitioning than defending their ally against tyranny. Britain's weakened status throughout the war had reduced Churchill's ability to influence Stalin and Roosevelt at Yalta; giving in to territorial changes to stem the tide of communism became paramount for Britain. Unlike the Poles in Britain that Willems and Palacz detail in the conclusion to this volume, the Polish DPs in the camps of Germany were not viewed in the same way. They were a different kind of Pole, one that the British were unwilling to accept needed a place to resettle elsewhere.

By the end of the summer in 1946, British military perceptions of Poles were unfavourable. A Foreign Office telegram to Berlin on 4 July 1946 describes the situation in the British zone as unsatisfactory. It accused Poles of a tendency to cause disturbances and requested a more thorough screening procedure so that only those who would otherwise be in personal danger are allowed to remain in the camps. Point five of the telegram states what the British expected of the Polish DPs:

> The rest of the D.P.'s would be informed that they must now choose between going home, settling in Germany on German rations or finding themselves other emigration possibilities (if they can). We cannot help with the latter. We have our hands full with Polish armed forces. We should add that the exact date at which D.P. camps will be terminated cannot be stated now, but the present state of affairs cannot continue indefinitely. D.P.'s would be well advised to return before the hardships of next winter. We should explain frankly that we cannot afford to keep them much longer at expense of taxpayer, that we are under no special obligation as we did not take them to Germany, that there is no work for so many in Germany in its present condition and that they should return home where there is a shortage of manpower.[23]

The reply received from the Allied Control Council in Berlin, dated 10 July 1946, agreed with point five and the need to close camps to encourage repatriation, stating that 'after a suitable interval to allow our announcement to the Poles to become known, we should begin to empty and close the camps'.[24] It appeared the British no longer regarded the Poles' unique plight as their concern. They increasingly felt burdened, particularly in a financial sense, and a solution was needed immediately. UNRRA devised a plan to encourage Polish repatriation to ensure the maximum number of Poles returned to Poland before the end of the year. Fiorello LaGuardia, then director of UNRRA, instigated 'Operation Carrot', wherein sixty days' worth of food rations were to be given to any Pole wishing to repatriate. The parcels were perceived by many UNRRA staff as nothing short of a bribe, although some thought it was a 'bright idea'.[25] The ever-dangling carrot of British assistance was suddenly given a new connotation. Alongside 'Operation Carrot', LaGuardia commissioned newsreels and a veritable bombardment of pro-Warsaw literature to ensure high uptake.[26] 'Operation Carrot' caused a spike in repatriation numbers across the summer of 1946, but these quickly dwindled as stories of food parcels not arriving in Poland filtered back to the camps. Any loyalty Britain had felt towards Poland in 1939 was waning. The British were tired of their responsibilities and, although they had helped to create the very conditions that led to the Poles' steadfast refusal to repatriate, they had effectively disowned their 'plucky little ally'.

UNRRA and other welfare workers worked alongside the Allied military and liaison officers to support DPs in the camps. The liaison officers were appointed by the respective governments they were representing and served as emissaries to the DPs' former country of residence as they liaised between those governing the camps, the DPs and their government's representatives. In theory, this communication allowed Poles to gain knowledge of the situation in Poland in order to dispel any lingering apprehension. In reality, however, the liaison officers were a hindrance to Polish repatriation as the majority had been appointed to DP camps prior to the change in government and were therefore loyal to the London-based government-in-exile; most would do anything but promote a return to Poland under the new regime. Alongside giving advice, these officers disseminated literature among the DPs. Although restrictions were imposed by both British and Warsaw authorities on literature being brought into the camps, pro-repatriation newspapers such as *Repatriant* enjoyed a wide circulation.[27] Whether the newspaper's high circulation was due to genuine interest or reading through boredom, however, is harder to discern.[28] Repatriation, however, continued to remain unpopular and by February 1946 there were 176 Polish liaison officers working in British-occupied Germany, only nineteen of whom were appointed by Warsaw.[29] As the numbers coming forward for repatriation were still low, questions were posed by Britain's MPs within the House of Commons as to whether the liaison officers' 'bitterly anti-Soviet views' might be considered a hindrance to the goal of repatriation; the questions were ignored.[30] Reluctantly, to counter the anti-Soviet views, Warsaw sent some new representatives into the camps, although only amounting to forty-one by March 1946. The situation with the liaison officers reached a stalemate as Warsaw acknowledged they could not supply the numbers needed to help the Polish DPs in the camps and instead had to rely on the already-existing officers.

The presence of liaison officers in the camps supporting the London government-in-exile created a twisted and oddly supportive infrastructure for the Poles refusing to repatriate. Due to the restrictive measures put into place on Polish DPs, which discouraged recreational activities and anything else that would anchor them to the camps and Germany, the host society had become the camp itself for many.[31] Run by military officials and welfare workers with liaison officers as interlocutors, this new space became a microcosm of pre-1939 Poland as the DPs actively rejected agents and structures of the newly constructed homeland in favour of *their* homeland: a homeland that no longer existed.

By the end of 1946, it was clear that those who remained in the British zone were unwilling to repatriate to Poland. UNRRA closed its European operation in July 1947 and DPs came under the supervision of the newly created International Refugee Organisation (IRO). Soon after taking over the DP camps, the IRO's primary objective became resettlement over repatriation. Britain, along with other countries, agreed to take in large numbers of DPs on foreign worker schemes, and, as UNRRA worker Marvin Klemmé stated, 'once the many emigration rumours got going, most of the people lost interest in employment, going home or anything else. They became interested only in getting to a new country'.[32] The main scheme in Britain, known as 'Westward Ho!', was to allow between 60,000 and 100,000 foreign workers to move to Britain with the possibility of their dependants joining them later. Balts and Ukrainians were favoured as they were accepted in Britain as being 'of good human stock' and consequently were highly sought after for work in care homes, factories and fields.[33] Eventually, as the British realized that the quota could not be filled with only Balts and Ukrainians, Poles were also accepted.[34]

The language used by the British in governmental, military and personal memoranda to describe Poles often contributed to the 'betrayed ally' rhetoric that formed between the elites in the camps and London government-in-exile. Polish DPs in the camps in particular saw UNRRA, IRO and British military workers strike up relationships with Germans shortly after the war's end.[35] The commander-in-chief of the British Army of the Rhine, Field-Marshal Montgomery, declared in March 1945 that interaction between British soldiers and Germans was strictly prohibited. Between March and September 1945, however, through four separate proclamations, the non-fraternization orders were gradually rescinded until only prohibition of marriage between British soldiers and German women remained.[36] At the same time, Poles were treated with disdain as their opposition to repatriation continued to be misconstrued as an act of economic greed rather than personal security. Although there is no doubt that some will have viewed their suspension in the DP camps of Germany as an opportunity to pursue a life abroad, there was little recognition by those in charge that this was also motivated by fear of political persecution and the uncertainty of what awaited them in post-war Poland. From the British military's perspective, and certainly some welfare workers' too, the Poles presented a problem with an easy solution: repatriation. Once it became clear that many were unwilling to repatriate, their presence not only caused friction between the 'brothers-in-arms' in the camps but domestic disturbance in Britain as bread rationing was introduced in 1946 to help alleviate supply issues to British-occupied Germany. Although this was mainly in order to feed the native German population, the large and visible group of Polish DPs in the camps were a constant reminder that they were now extra mouths to feed. Consequently, the Polish allies were continually treated as a 'troublesome nuisance' in the camps – a problem that just needed to be solved.[37]

Competing diasporas in Germany

The shift in emphasis from repatriation to resettlement was certainly greeted with a sigh of relief by the Polish DPs in the camps. The reluctant creation of foreign worker schemes that would eventually accept Poles – in some cases accompanied by their dependants – was, nevertheless, no easy feat. For most DPs, the workers' schemes were not meant to be a long-term solution. Britain was different to some countries in this regard as those DPs accepted as part of 'Operation Westward Ho!' were seen as permanent migrants, 'working their passage to British citizenship'.[38] For Polish DPs to get on the scheme, however, was quite a challenge at first. Alongside those who had sought refuge in Britain throughout the war, the Polish Resettlement Corps was created in 1946 with the aim of easing soldiers into civilian life before repatriating.[39] The majority of those who became part of the Corps ended up in Britain, as Willems and Palacz emphasize in the conclusion to this volume, under the Polish Resettlement Act of 1947 alongside many from the Polish enclave of Maczków in British-occupied Germany.[40] Due to these migrations, the number of Poles in Britain was already considered high at the time 'Westward Ho!' was implemented. The reluctance to accept Polish DPs as migrant workers (and potentially permanent migrants) was also due to fears among government officials of ghettoization, another reason for preferring Balts and Ukrainians over Poles.⁴¹ For those who were neither soldiers nor their dependents, and unable to attach themselves to a worker scheme, passage to any country proved difficult. For many in the camps this situation led to the character traits Edward Bakis associated with DP apathy.⁴² Bakis, an Estonian DP and psychology lecturer, realized that many had entered into an apathetic state by mid to late 1946 as their own skillsets, personal background, family situation or health pronounced them ineligible for recruitment or resettlement schemes abroad. Peter Gatrell succinctly summarizes DPs' frustration as they 'could not get it right: too much determination, and they were deemed unruly or ungrateful; too little, and they were regarded as helpless or even "norm-less" people with a "low predisposition to change".⁴³

There were some mild successes in resettling Polish DPs, some on to the labouring schemes in Britain, others to the Belgian mines under 'Operation Black Diamond', but many were left in Germany in the camps awaiting other opportunities. The IRO's official mandate was to wind up its European operations by the end of 1951. In an official letter to Konrad Adenauer, the Chancellor of the newly created Federal Republic of Germany (FRG), the IRO stated that as of 30 June 1950, 'all refugees and displaced persons other than those in the process of repatriation or resettlement would become the responsibility of the Federal Government, both financially and administratively'.⁴⁴ The FRG guaranteed the rights of the refugees referred to in Articles 1–19 of the Basic Law of the Federal Republic, including an assurance that they would be given all necessary provisions for their integration into German society. These assurances laid the foundations for the principles by which the Homeless Foreigners Law (*heimtlose Ausländer Gesetz*) was created on 25 April 1951. As the IRO wound up its operations in Germany the continuous questions from welfare workers and military officials alike regarding who, how, when, and why were left largely unanswered as the FRG took over all control of the remaining 'hard core' of DPs. The once-regular attention bestowed on DPs by newspapers and other media, albeit largely negative and particularly anti-Slavic, abruptly came to an end, and as Anna Holian remarks, the 'negative interest was replaced by almost total silence'.⁴⁵ The focus on DPs in Germany after the closure of the IRO and the introduction of the Homeless Foreigners Law in 1951 certainly concentrated on ethnic German refugees (*Vertriebene*) and not the 'others'.

After the official handover of authority, the British attitude turned to one of almost total indifference as the lingering reminder of the war's end threatened to destabilize the teetering political balance in the new Cold War world. At the same time, the IRO and FRG's self-professed achievable aims of resettlement were framed within the loosely defined policy of *Eingliederung* (integration) over *Einschmelzung* (assimilation). Integration is a notoriously tricky concept to define and its shortcomings do not need to be repeated here.⁴⁶ Yet when attempting to resettle Polish DPs in a society that was likely to reject 'newcomers', especially as they had already spent a considerable amount of time in Germany being treated as inferior, the FRG's definition of integration proved problematic. Additionally, Germany's attention had been fully diverted to issues with eastern expellees, another forced migratory movement brought by the hands of the Allies to placate Stalin.

By October 1951, the statistical yearbook for West Germany records 38,808 remaining Poles classed as 'foreigners' across the British zone who were now living within the German economy.⁴⁷ By October 1952, this number had dropped to 31,836, although this reduction of 6,972 is thought to have been largely a by-product of the high concentration of elderly and/or infirm, rather than a consequence of further repatriation or resettlement. It is questionable, however, whether these statistics included those not covered by the Homeless Foreigners Law and therefore not deemed *Ausländer*. These were often excluded (sometimes willingly) from the earlier IRO statistics or had arrived in earlier migrations to the north-west corner of Germany. As we have seen in the case of the *Ruhrpolen*, due to the brief time classified as Germans through their place on the Nazi *Volksliste*, they were then unable to register as Poles after the war and constituted a significant contingent of Poles in the British zone of Germany that is unaccounted for in the above statistics. Although there remained a visible Polish community in the British zone of Germany, it was a community that was split by its own internalized sense of national identity, which would have a lasting effect on the make-up of diasporic Polish communities thereafter.

Conclusion

The forced migratory movements of numerous diasporas culminated in a fractured, confused and often competing set of communities in the post-war years. *Ruhrpolen*, hoping to go unnoticed, attempted to assimilate into German society in the interwar years to avoid discrimination. In the post-war years their status as both German and Pole confused the Allied authorities occupying the area. Simultaneously the presence of a new Polish community in the north-west corner of Germany highlighted their 'otherness' and caused renewed friction with the reluctant host society. Those born to *Ruhrpolen* in the Ruhr at the start of the twentieth century were almost fully assimilated into German society, as Polish parents gleefully celebrated their child speaking only German. Despite downplaying their Polish heritage, however, the second generation of *Ruhrpolen* was not accepted within Nazi society. Not quite German, but also not Pole, they feared rejection from the *Volksliste* and a fate of forced labour. Rejecting association with wartime Polish forced labourers was just one way they were able to ensure their safety in Nazi Germany. The separation of diasporas was created in the war years but cemented in the post-war period as *Ruhrpolen* actively continued to disassociate themselves from DPs.

The Polish DPs in the camps were the victims of Nazi and Soviet aggression throughout the war years who came to rely on their 'brothers-in-arms' to help rebuild a stable and secure Poland. The British, however, had other priorities. Their reluctance to help their former allies was motivated by concern over their global status and restricted by their financial situation, causing a heavy reliance on the United States and a need to placate the Soviet Union. This culminated in a prolonged 'betrayed ally' rhetoric in Poland and among Poles in diaspora as many asked, 'How could our British allies and friends betray us so shamefully?'[48] Their forced displacement was ongoing in Germany after the British relinquished administrative control to the FRG, and Polish DPs became all but forgotten as ethnic German *Vertriebene* took priority. The longer arc of Polish (forced) migratory history in Britain and Germany has caused a divided and competing set of diasporas and strained post-war Anglo-German-Polish relations.

Notes

1. Although there were more displaced Russians in Germany than any other group, the Soviet authorities refused to recognize Soviet citizens as being 'displaced', and they were therefore not deemed to come under UNRRA's remit. See Malcolm J Proudfoot, *European Refugees, 1939-1952. A Study in Forced Population Movement* (Evanston: Northwest University Press, 1956), 230; George Woodbridge (ed.), *UNRRA: The History of the United Nations Relief and Rehabilitation Administration*, Vol. 2 (New York: Columbia University Press, 1950), 257-320; William Arnold-Forster, 'U.N.R.R.A's Work for Displaced Persons in Germany', *International Affairs (Royal Institute of International Affairs 1944-)* 22 (1946): 1-13.
2. See above. Soviet peoples/DPs also included states newly absorbed into the Soviet sphere of influence. Classifying who was Soviet was complicated and many UNRRA workers and Military officials allowed anyone who was not clearly Russian to stay in the DP camps. Western DPs included, but were not limited to, Dutch, French, Belgians, Luxembourgers, Danes, Norwegians and Italians. See Proudfoot, *European Refugees*, 189-205.
3. *Tymczasowy Rząd Jedności Narodowej* – The Polish Provisional Government of National Unity.
4. Władysław Anders, *An Army in Exile: The Story of the Second Polish Corps* (Nashville: Battery Press, 1981), 250-1.
5. Margaret McNeill, *By the Rivers of Babylon* (London: Bannisdale Press, 1950), 161. For more on the 'mental paralysis' and its ensuing consequences see Samantha K. Knapton, '"There Is No Such Thing as an Unrepatriable Pole": Polish Displaced Persons in the British Zone of Occupation in Germany', *European History Quarterly* 50, no. 4 (2020): 689-710.
6. See Ulrich Herbert, *Geschichte der Ausländer beschäftigung in Deutschland 1880 bis 1980* (Bonn: J. H. W. Dietz, 1986).
7. Halik Kochanski, *The Eagle Unbowed: Poland and the Poles in the Second World War* (Cambridge, MA: Harvard University Press, 2012), xxv and 579.
8. A selection of works is listed here, but this is by no means an exhaustive list. For further works on Polish migrants in post-war Britain, see Keith Sword, Norman Davies and Jan Ciechanowski, *The Formation of Polish Community in Great Britain 1939-1950* (London: The University of London School of Slavonic and East European Studies, 1989); Diana Kay and Robert Miles, 'Refugees or Migrant Workers? The Case of the European Volunteer Workers in Britain (1946-1951)', *Journal of Refugee Studies* 1, no. 3/4 (1998): 214-36; Peter D. Stachura (ed.), *The Poles in Britain 1940-2000: From Betrayal to Assimilation* (London: Frank Cass 2004). For works on *Ruhrpolen* in the nineteenth and twentieth centuries, see Christoph Kleßmann, 'Integration und Subkultur nationaler Minderheiten. Das Beispiel der "Ruhrpolen" 1870-1939', in *Auswanderer. Wanderarbeiter. Gastarbeiter. Bevölkerung, Arbeitsmarkt und Wanderung in Deutschland seit der Mitte des 19. Jahrhunderts*, ed. Klaus J. Bade (Ostfildern: Scripta Mercaturae, 1984); Michaela Bachem-Rehm, 'A Forgotten Chapter of Regional Social History: The Polish Immigrants to the Ruhr: 1870 - 1939', in *The Economies of Urban Diversity: Ruhr Area and Istanbul*, ed. D. Reuschke, M. Salzbrunn and K. Schönhärl (New York: Palgrave Macmillan, 2013), 93-113; Elke Hauschildt and Brian D. Urquhart, 'Polish Migrant Culture in Imperial Germany', *New German Critique* 46 (1989): 155-71. For works on Polish DPs in

British-occupied Germany, see Czesław Łuczak, *Polacy w Okupowanych Niemczech 1945-1949* (Poznań: Pracownia Serwisu Oprogramowania, 1993); Wolfgang Jacobmeyer, *Vom Zwangsarbeiter zum Heimatlosen Ausländer. Die Displaced Persons in Westdeutschland, 1945-1951* (Göttingen: Vandenhoeck & Ruprecht, 1985); Stefan Schröder, *Displaced Persons im Landkreis und in der Stadt Münster 1945-1951* (Münster: Aschendorff, 2005).
9   See Andreas Schlieper, *150 Jahre Ruhrgebiet: ein Kapital deutscher Wirtschaftsgeschichte* (Düsseldorf: Schwann, 1986); Bachem-Rehm, 'A Forgotten Chapter', 93-113.
10 Kleßmann, 'Integration und Subkultur nationaler Minderheiten', 491; Herbert, *Geschichte der Ausländer beschäftigung*, 71.
11 Herbert, *Geschichte der Ausländer beschäftigung*, 82-3.
12 Mirosław Piotrowski, *Reemigracja Polaków z Niemiec 1918-1939* (Lublin: Redakcja Wydawnictw Katolickiego Uniwersytetu Lubelskiego, 2000), 293.
13 The first two categories of the *Volksliste* were classed as suitably German, whether actively or passively embracing their Germanic roots. The third category was seen as a diluted type of German who more closely identified with being Polish, yet to whom conditional German citizenship could be granted. The fourth group were classified as non-Germans, rebels with no ties to their German ancestry. For more on the *Volksliste*, see Peter Longerich, *Heinrich Himmler: A Life* (Oxford: Oxford University Press, 2012), 450-5; Kochanski, *The Eagle Unbowed*, 540.
14 *Eingedeutschte* – Voluntarily Germanized, or *Rückgesdeutschte* – Forcibly Germanized. For more on Poles being added to the Volksliste, see Tadeusz Piotrowski, *Poland's Holocaust: Ethnic Strife, Collaboration with Occupying Forces and Genocide in the Second Republic, 1918-1947* (London: McFarland & Co., 1998).
15 Ulrich Herbert, *A History of Foreign Labour in Germany, 1880-1980. Seasonal Workers/Forced Laborers/Guest Workers* (Ann Arbor: University of Michigan Press, 1990), 156.
16 Institut für Besatzungsfragen, *Das DP-Problem: Eine Studie über die ausländischen Flüchtlinge in Deutschland* (Tübingen: J. C. B. Mohr, 1950), 15-16.
17 Proudfoot, *European Refugees*, 238-9; Anna D. Jarosyńska-Kirchmann, *The Exile Mission: The Polish Political Diaspora and Polish Americans, 1939-1956* (Athens: Ohio University Press, 2004), 60.
18 For more on the Warsaw Uprising and Home Army, see Norman Davies, *Rising '44: The Battle for Warsaw* (London: Penguin Books, 2004); Kochanski, *The Eagle Unbowed*.
19 Imperial War Museum, London (hereafter IWM), 02/49/01, Lt. Gen. Sir F. Morgan, 'Diary as Director of Operations for UNRRA mission in Germany 01.09.1945 - 27.08.1946'. Wed. 10 September 1945 (7).
20 Leokadia Rowinski, *That the Nightingale Return: Memoir of the Polish Resistance, the Warsaw Uprising and German P.O.W. Camps* (North Carolina: McFarland & Co., 1999), 137.
21 Beata Halicka, *Polens Wilder Westen: Erzwungene Migration und die kultrelle Aneignung des Oderraums 1945-1948* (Paderborn: Ferdinand Schöningh, 2016).
22 For more see Bastiaan Willems and Michał Adam Palacz, 'Polish refugees and East Prussian expellees: Applying the four-dimensional model' in this volume.
23 The National Archives, Kew (hereafter TNA), Foreign Office (FO) 1049/622, 'Repatriation of Poles, 1946-1947' – Foreign Office to Berlin, Telegram No. 1009 of 4 July 1946.

24 TNA, FO 1049/622, 'Repatriation of Poles, 1946–1947' – Steel (Berlin) to Foreign Office, Telegram No. 832 of 10 July 1946.
25 Marvin Klemmé, *The Inside Story of UNRRA: An Experience in Internationalism; A Firsthand Report on the Displaced People of Europe* (New York: Lifetime Editions, 1949), 143.
26 For more on Operation Carrot, see Knapton, 'There Is No Such Thing as an Unrepatriable Pole'.
27 When concerning Liaison Officers, the 'Warsaw' authorities refer to those appointed by the new Polish Provisional Government of National Unity based in Warsaw and the 'British' ones to those appointed by the London-based government-in-exile (Poland's pre-war government).
28 A list of all Polish newspapers and the times/areas of their circulation can be found here: French National Archives, Paris (hereafter AN), AJ-43–608, 'Polish Repatriation, 1947–1948', Informational Material Bulletin, No. 4 – Polish News Publications.
29 TNA, FO 1049/622 'Repatriation of Poles, 1946–1947' – Original letter from Troopers to Bercomb regarding Polish LOs in BZ, 11 March 1946 – reply from Bercomb to Troopers, point 2.C., 20 March 1946.
30 United Kingdom, *House of Commons Sitting*, 19 February 1946, Vol. 419, c940 – 'Polish Liaison Officers, Germany', Mr Zilliacus to Mr Lawson.
31 Resolution 92 was implemented by UNRRA to 'remove any handicaps' and 'prompt repatriation', see Resolution 92 in Woodbridge, *U.N.R.R.A.*, Vol. 3, 155–6.
32 Klemmé, *The Inside Story*, 275–9.
33 Royal Commission on Population, *Report* (London: His Majesty's Stationery Office, 1949), 124.
34 Louise Holborn, *The International Refugee Organization: A Specialized Agency of the United Nations: Its History and Work, 1946–1952* (Oxford: Oxford University Press, 1952), 391.
35 Sherif Gemie et al., *Outcast Europe: Refugees and Relief Workers in an Era of Total War, 1936–48* (London: Continuum International Publishing, 2012), 210–11.
36 IWM, Doc. 1851, Field-Marshal Montgomery Commander-in-Chief 21 Army Group BOAR, 'Montgomery's 4 Letters on Non-Fraternisation and Personal Message to the German Populace, 1945, and 1950s Ration Books', March–September 1945.
37 For more on the British treatment of Poles and a discussion on this rhetoric, see S. K. Knapton, '"A Troublesome Nuisance": Polish Displaced Persons in the British Zone of Occupation in Germany, 1945–1951' (PhD Diss., Newcastle University, 2019).
38 United Kingdom, *House of Commons Debate*, 11 November 1948, Vol. 457, cc1721–2 – 'Foreign Workers', Mr Joyson-Hicks to Mr Isaacs (Minister of Labour).
39 Sword, Davies and Ciechanowski, *The Formation of Polish Community*, 245–56 and 320–31.
40 For more on Maczków, see Łuczak, *Polacy w Okupowanych Niemczech*; Jan Rydel, *'Polska okupacja' w północo-zachodnich Niemczech 1945–1948: Nieznany rozdział stosunków polsko-niemieckich* (Cracow: Fundacja Centrum Dokumentacji Czynu Niepodległościowego / Księgarnia Akademicka, 2000).
41 Sword, Davies and Ciechanowski, *The Formation of the Polish Community*, 338.
42 Edward Bakis, 'The So-Called DP-Apathy in Germany's DP Camps', *Transactions of the Kansas Academy of Science* 55, no. 1 (1952): 62–86.
43 Peter Gatrell, *The Making of a Modern Refugee* (New York: Oxford University Press, 2013), 116.

44 Holborn, *The International Refugee Organization*, 476.
45 Anna Holian, 'A Missing Narrative: Displaced Persons in the History of Postwar West Germany', in *Migration, Memory, and Diversity: Germany from 1945 to Present*, ed. Cornelia Wilhelm (Oxford: Berghahn, 2017), 33.
46 For more on the contested meaning of 'integration' in scholarly debate, see Tariq Modood, *Multiculturalism: A Civic Idea* (Cambridge: Polity Press, 2007); Karen Schönwalder, 'Assigning the States Its Rightful Place? Migration, Integration, and the State in Germany', in *Paths of Integration: Migrants in Western Europe (1880–2004)*, ed. Leo Lucassen, David Feldman and Jochen Oltmer (Amsterdam: Amsterdam University Press, 2006) 78–97.
47 *Statistisches Jahrbuch für die Bundesrepublik Deutschland* (1953), Table 15. Available online: http://www.digizeitschriften.de/dms/img/?PID=PPN514402342_1952 %7Clog10 (accessed 13 January 2021).
48 B. Lewandowski (pseudonym) in Stachura, *Poles in Britain, 1940s–2000*, 8.

Map 14.1 Settlement of Danube Swabians in south-eastern Europe, 1930. © Bastiaan Willems.

14

Ethnopolitical humanitarianism

The post-war resettlement of 2,446 Danube Swabians to Brazil

Cristian Cercel

Introduction

Among the passengers aboard 7 ships that set sail between May 1951 and March 1952 from Europe (Genoa and Le Havre) to Santos in Brazil, there were 2,446 people – 500 families – whose final destination was in the state of Paraná, in the south of the country. There, about 250 kilometres from the state capital Curitiba, the migrants founded the settlement Entre Rios, near Guarapuava, and established the agricultural cooperative Agrária. The people in question were so-called *Volksdeutsche* (ethnic Germans from Eastern Europe), more precisely *Donauschwaben* (Danube Swabians). The starting point of their journey to Brazil via Italy and France had actually been Austria or, if seen in a slightly broader timeframe, Yugoslavia, Hungary and Romania, countries from which Danube Swabians fled westwards during and immediately after the final stages of the Second World War. The resettlement was organized by Schweizer Europahilfe (SEH), the predecessor of today's Swissaid. In Brazil, SEH's representatives negotiated with local and national authorities in order to get the necessary approvals for the resettlement and for the land acquisition that was indispensable for the project. In Austria, SEH selected the settlers and took care of the formalities implied by the migration. Moreover, in order to fund the action, SEH – with the support of the Swiss Political Department and of the Department of Economic Affairs – devised a complex financial scheme which involved convincing Brazilian authorities to grant supplementary import licences to Swiss companies.

Previous scholarship looked at the agricultural developments in Entre Rios after the migration, situated the action within the history of post-war Swiss developmental aid politics and considered issues of identity and memory.[1] By focusing on the multiple diasporic conditions in which Danube Swabian identifications have been embedded, and by reconstituting the development of this resettlement action as an instance of ethnopolitical humanitarianism, the chapter shows that notions of homeland and host society are fluid, contextual and plural, and that categories of forced and voluntary migration are interwoven. Moreover, by indicating that humanitarian organizations – and the states under whose banner they function – also engage in ethnic politics, the case study adds a potential fifth dimension to the model brought forth by Willems and Palacz in the introduction to this volume.[2] The case study shows that the relevant actors and stakeholders in diaspora politics can also be contextual and do not always easily fit within the typical pre-given categories and dimensions. In doing this, it indicates that analytical models should essentially focus on how to account for ethnicity and/or diaspora as action, not as bounded entities, but as legitimation mechanisms, as idioms, stances and claims.[3]

The chapter starts by discussing the complex web of allegiances, opportunities, pressures and constraints informing the construction of Danube Swabian (diasporic) identifications after the First World War up to the late 1940s. Then, the discussion of the resettlement to Brazil pays particular attention to the role played by issues of cultural and ethnopolitical belonging, identity discourses and diasporic frameworks. Thus, the text moots the implications of this case study for the study of histories of displacement and of refugeedom in general and for the analytical model proposed by Willems and Palacz in particular.

Danube Swabians in between diasporic conditions

At the onset of the Second World War, the so-called Danube Swabians numbered around 1.5 million.[4] Their identification discourses drew on them being the descendants of the settlers who had come to south-eastern Europe (more precisely to the regions of Banat, Bačka, Syrmia, Slavonia and Swabian Turkey) in several waves throughout the eighteenth century, at the behest of the Habsburgs. Mostly Germanophones, the eighteenth-century colonists had different origins and came in different phases, without sharing a proper group consciousness, other than, perhaps, a loose one as migrants/settlers. The denomination *Donauschwaben* as a reference to them and to their descendants was coined by geographers Robert Sieger and Hermann Rüdiger in the 1920s. Up until then, the slightly more indistinct designation *Schwaben* (Swabians) (Serbian *švaba*, Romanian *şvab*, Hungarian *sváb*) was used.[5]

Against the backdrop of the ethnicization and nationalization of social and political life that took place across Europe, especially since the second half of the nineteenth century onwards, the Germanophones in south-eastern Europe were caught between a series of identification pressures and opportunities. The imposition of the Austro-Hungarian Dualism and the related process of Hungarian nation-building, as well as German unification, played an important role in this context. The Catholic Church (most Danube Swabians were Catholic, with a minority being Protestant) was also a particularly relevant actor. Subsequently, following the disintegration of the Habsburg Empire, Danube Swabians became citizens of three different states – Yugoslavia, Romania and Hungary. In the first half of the twentieth century, there were also Danube Swabians who migrated to North and South America.[6]

That an umbrella-denomination and a group identification as Danube Swabians appear after the First World War is presumably linked to these political transformations, as well as to the growing scholarly and political interest in Germans abroad.[7] It was fundamentally a transnational identification inasmuch as it referred to people living in three different countries, united by the common origin/ancestry of (imperial) settlers. The Danubian reference established a direct connection with the eighteenth-century migration to south-eastern Europe, which took place by boat, down the Danube.[8] The Danube Swabian identification involved a potential triple diasporic condition: the diasporic condition of a people of settlers dispersed across state borders after the disintegration of the Habsburg Empire, the diasporic condition of 'Germans' abroad, imagined in relationship with Germany as a homeland/kin-state, as well as the diasporic condition of 'Austrians' abroad, imagined in relationship with Austria, the successor of the Habsburg Empire, which could also be seen as an external homeland/kin-state. The integration and assimilation pressures and offers that Yugoslavia, Romania and Hungary themselves had for their German minorities – of which Danube Swabians were just one part – were, in principle, in a tense relationship with these potential diasporic conditions, as well as with more local identifications.

Yet the ascent of Nazism largely succeeded in making the Danube Swabians into *Volksdeutsche*, a German diaspora with a special role in the European order-to-come. It also brought along Austria's unification with Germany, which radically changed or even eliminated the third aforementioned diasporic condition. Moreover, the envisaged – and subsequently very concrete – Nazi rule (directly or by proxy) in south-eastern Europe attenuated the diasporic condition implied by their dispersal in three different states. In Romania, allied with Nazi Germany until August 1944, and Hungary, first allied, then (March 1944) practically occupied, as well as in fragmented (and either occupied or allied) Yugoslavia, Danube Swabians generally enjoyed social and economic privileges. Against this background, Danube Swabians enrolled in significant numbers in the Wehrmacht and in the Waffen-SS. The opposition to Nazi rule came especially from left-wing ranks and to some extent from Catholic circles.[9]

However, the tables turned once the Nazis were defeated. From what was presumably a coveted identification, built both on privileges and social pressures, being a *Volksdeutscher* largely turned into a liability. In all three countries, Danube Swabians were subjected to persecutions and discriminatory measures: expropriations, deportations to the Soviet Union for forced labour, internment in work camps. The repressive measures against the Danube Swabians in Yugoslavia were particularly harsh, amounting to a process of ethnic cleansing. Of the more than 20 million Europeans who found themselves on the move in the final stages of the war and in its aftermath, between 10 and 12 million were those who fled or were expelled from Eastern Europe on account of their Germanness.[10] About 700,000 of them were Danube Swabians.[11]

The *Volksdeutsche* were specifically excluded from the mandate of the International Refugee Organization (IRO).[12] For the Allies and for the IRO, those who fled or were expelled as Germans constituted a 'German' problem. Having traditionally played the role of a kin-state for Germans in Eastern Europe and having played a key part in the political mobilization of the *Volksdeutsche*, Germany (both West and East) was indeed the main receiving country for these expellees. Nonetheless, Austria, which was in the process of re-becoming a nation state following the intermezzo of the unification with/annexation by the Third Reich, was also a country receiving expelled Germans, particularly from Yugoslavia, Czechoslovakia, Hungary and Romania. Austrian authorities were in principle keen to delimit themselves from the *Volksdeutsche*, not wanting Austria to be regarded as a successor state of the Third Reich.[13] Moreover, especially in the early aftermath of the war, both Allied occupation forces and Austrian authorities actually tended to favour the 'repatriation' of the *Volksdeutsche* to (West) Germany.[14] Nonetheless, in 1951–2 between 330,000 and 380,000 *Volksdeutsche* were living in Austria. The largest groups were the Sudeten Germans and the Danube Swabians, with the latter numbering between 140,000 and 170,000.[15]

In Austria, some of those speaking for the *Volksdeutsche* in general and for the Danube Swabians in particular were prone to point out their ties with the Austrian state, trying to legitimize their various claims – legal, moral or financial – by an emphasis on the common Habsburg past, as well as on lofty pan-German ideals (the two were not mutually exclusive). In this context, they could and often did resort to a self-identification as *Altösterreicher* (Old-Austrians), which implicated the existence of an Austrian historical duty on their behalf. Within such discourses, the victimhood of the *Volksdeutsche* was placed above that of the other refugees and DPs. However, at least up until the mid-1950s, when access to citizenship was eased, the stance of Austrian authorities with respect to the efforts of the *Volksdeutsche* to claim Austrian-ness was rather ambiguous, even while being fundamentally more open with respect to them as compared to other DPs and refugees. In this context, there were, for example, cases of Jewish refugees who tried to present themselves as German expellees, as this provided them with more chances to remain in Austria.[16]

At the end of the Second World War, Danube Swabians in Europe were thus essentially divided between five countries: Yugoslavia, Romania, Hungary, Germany and Austria. The population movements leading to this dispersal had an impact upon the diasporic allegiances and relationships in which Danube Swabian identifications could be embedded. At first glance, the migration from south-eastern Europe to Austria and Germany was the migration of a diaspora violently chased away from the host state(s) 'back' to the 'homeland'. Nonetheless, the fact that there were two states – and subsequently three, once the German Democratic Republic was officially established in 1949 – apt to be considered and potentially to act as homelands for the Danube Swabians complicates the picture. Furthermore, the forced diasporic return of Danube Swabians to the Austrian and German homelands led to a situation in which the relationship with the latter also had some features of a relationship with a host state, while the former host states in south-eastern Europe could turn (at least in part) into (imagined) homelands. Other expellee groups went through similar processes, as the example of the East Prussians in Germany indicates.[17]

A *Volk* in search of land or a diaspora in search of a host state

In October 1946, one of the participants at a Caritas conference in Salzburg, Father Josef Stefan, suggested that the resettlement of German 'refugees' could play an important part in solving Europe's displacement problem, indicating that the Vatican and the Swiss Bank could contribute to the implementation of such a solution.[18] Born in 1911 in Vukovar (present-day Croatia), Stefan was a Danube Swabian Franciscan cleric. After serving as a chaplain in the Wehrmacht towards the end of the war, in a German–Croatian division, he retreated together with the troops, ending up in Austria, where he took over the pastoral care for the *Volksdeutsche*, first for those in Salzburg, Upper Austria and Tirol and then for those in the entire country.[19]

His 1946 intervention was by no means a one-off position. Throughout the second half of the 1940s, Stefan actively lobbied for mass resettlement of Danube Swabians to Latin America, as documents kept in the Archives of the Archdiocese of Salzburg indicate. In migration-related contexts, even as he used the more general term *Volksdeutsche*, he tended to refer to Danube Swabians only. At the same time, Stefan also distinctly pushed for the recognition of a Danube Swabian identity, aiming to single out Danube Swabians within the broader group of expellees/*Volksdeutsche*.[20]

Stefan developed his idea of a mass migration to Latin America against the backdrop of an increased dissatisfaction with regard to Austria. He considered that *Volksdeutsche* had a special historical relationship with the Austrian motherland, a country that had been loved as no other while living 'in the hostile outland'. Nonetheless, this love was not reciprocated in the aftermath of the Second World War. The about-to-be-reborn Austrian state did not have the courage to accept the role of homeland for those ethnic Germans who had made their way onto its territory, nor that of kin-state for those still in south-eastern Europe.[21]

Contemplating emigration stemmed out of the difficulties in envisaging a future for the Danube Swabians in Austria. In a note addressed to the Salzburg archbishop Andreas Rohracher in April 1948, Stefan referred to two ways to solve the 'question' of the expelled Volksdeutsche, namely the procurement of land in Austria or overseas emigration. In his view, only land ownership could offer the *Volksdeutsche*/Danube Swabians the possibility of an independent existence as free peasants/farmers, as they used to be in south-eastern Europe. The fact that land in Austria was scarce called for emigration.[22] Thus, the emigration solution drew on the representation of *Volksdeutsche*/Danube Swabians as a people of settlers, a people needing (and deserving) land and space.[23] Interestingly, it does not seem he considered in any way the possibility of a return to south-eastern Europe.

Despite the disappointment with respect to Austria assuming neither homeland responsibilities (for those in Austria) nor kin-state responsibilities (for those still in south-eastern Europe) on their behalf, emigration ideas could still be legitimized by the discursive construction of *Volksdeutsche*/Danube Swabian identity as a fundamentally diasporic identity. Emigration was not meant to cut off the connections with the Austrian homeland. On the contrary, it could ideally be intermediated by Austrian diplomacy abroad, potentially laying the basis for a 'new era of Austrian cultural activity', undertaken by the *Volksdeutsche*, thus styled as an Austrian diaspora to be.[24] Germany as a potential homeland and kin-state as well as the Danube Swabians in Germany played only a marginal role in Stefan's considerations.[25]

Stefan's mass resettlement ideas focused first (1947 and 1948) on Argentina and Chile. In this context, he also referred to the mobilization of Danube Swabians in Argentina.[26]

His efforts might have contributed to the success of some small emigration actions, but they did not lead to any mass resettlement.²⁷ In March 1949, Brazil came up as a potential destination country, an option mediated by Monsignor Giuseppe Crivelli, the director of Caritas Switzerland.²⁸ Caritas was already contemplating emigration as a solution to the refugee problem in Europe. An exposé titled 'Auswanderung' (Emigration) – probably dated January/February 1947 – argued that around 30 million Europeans were willing to migrate. It made the case for initial small-group resettlement actions which would 'prepare the ground for a large migration'.²⁹ Such actions were mainly envisaged as agricultural colonization projects in Latin America.³⁰ Caritas's visions largely corresponded to the way Stefan imagined the relocation of Danube Swabians.

After the stricter caps of the 1930s, Brazil was in the early post-war again open to immigration.³¹ In the negotiations conducted in 1946 within the Special Committee on Refugees and Displaced Persons, which would lead to the establishment of the IRO, one of the Brazilian delegates emphasized that the country was ready to receive refugees and displaced people, underlining the preference for 'farmers, technicians, and qualified workers', who could reinforce the country's 'European origin'.³² In Brazil, the governor of the federal state of Goiás promoted 'the resettlement of Europe's homeless as a colonization project', offering 'cheap land which called for pioneer settlers and farmers'.³³ The First Brazilian Conference for Immigration and Colonization took place in Goiânia, between 30 April and 7 May 1949.³⁴

Against this background, Crivelli/Caritas mediated the organization of a research trip, which practically amounted to being a Danube Swabian exploratory mission. A so-called Danube Swabian study commission, consisting of Josef Stefan and engineer and agricultural expert Michael Moor travelled between December 1949 and March 1950 to Brazil, where they were joined by Georg Bormet, a priest from Bačka who was already living there. Hungarian-Swiss lawyer Janos Vayda acted as Caritas representative in Brazil, mediating meetings with relevant actors and stakeholders. Some of the incurred costs were covered by the Danube Swabian aid associations in Chicago and Brooklyn.³⁵

In its communication with the relevant Brazilian authorities, the commission regularly claimed to speak on behalf of large numbers of Danube Swabians. In a letter to the governor of Goiás, Stefan and Moor referred for example to 80,000 'families of Danube Swabians'. Nevertheless, for large-scale resettlement to happen, it was supposed to start with a first pioneer colonization action of a minimum of 500 families.³⁶

One of the outcomes of the research trip was a 33-page report on the possibilities of colonization in Goiás. It dealt at length with agricultural, technical and financial issues, making the case that Danube Swabians constituted a 'well structured ethnic body', having 'all premises for mounting an exemplary colonisation'. The desired resettlement was legitimized by depicting Danube Swabians as a people of 'agricultural colonists', known to be 'exceptionally efficient and proficient farmers', originating from 'West Germany', and who, called on by the Habsburg rulers, had settled '200 years ago in the lowlands of the Danube, Tisza, Sava and Drava', 'in order to reclaim the deserted land'. They succeeded in doing this, creating 'the most fruitful cultivated land, the most abundant granary of Central Europe'. Danube Swabians were neither economic migrants nor political refugees, the report underlined, but were evacuated 'in the course of the military events in the autumn of 1944 by the German military bodies'. The consequence thereof was their being 'scattered' 'across half Germany and Austria'.[37] The reference to the origin from 'West Germany' might have been meant to tap into the positive views of Germanness present in Brazilian society.

The recent migration to Germany and Austria was thus presented not so much as a return to the homeland – forced as it may have been – but as the source of a particular diasporic process. Danube Swabians were a diaspora par excellence, not a diaspora without a homeland, but a paradoxical diaspora within the homeland, aiming to become again – in toto – a diaspora outside the homeland. The report addressed questions related to educational, pastoral, and medical care, understood as quintessential for the production and reproduction of an in-group identity.[38] Strict boundaries had to be maintained, according to the authors of the report: it advised against mixed marriages with local girls, 'on social, but especially on medical grounds'.[39]

The collective action that Stefan contemplated was not only meant to offer individuals and families the opportunity to lead a better life but was also about ensuring the continued existence of the Danube Swabians as a *Volk*. Land ownership was thus a prerequisite of this continued existence.[40] Stefan's resettlement plans largely drew on arguments about the historical role of Danube Swabians as settlers in south-eastern Europe. According to him, Danube Swabians practically amounted to being a settler diaspora by choice. The (mass) migration to potential new host states was meant to reiterate this condition, by recreating a context similar to that of the initial settlement in south-eastern Europe, both at a larger and at a smaller level. The larger level referred to Danube Swabians significantly contributing to the agricultural and economic advancement of the new host states in Latin America, as they had done in south-eastern Europe. The smaller level referred to the possibility to 'realise . . . to a certain extent the village communities of the old Heimat'.[41] Even as they were not necessarily mainstream, Stefan was not an outsider in embracing such identity discourses. Other Danube Swabian intellectuals and ethnopolitical entrepreneurs were disseminating similar views.[42]

Schweizer Europahilfe as 'patron' of Danube Swabians

Caritas Switzerland, who mediated the Danube Swabian research trip to Brazil, was only one of several Swiss relief and aid organizations reunited under the banner of SEH. SEH was the continuator of Schweizer Spende an die Kriegsgeschädigten (*Swiss Donation for War-Affected*), a humanitarian umbrella institution founded immediately after the end of the war, which was also meant to contribute to the overcoming of the Swiss foreign policy isolation.[43] It was financed both by Swiss federal money and public donations and closely coordinated its activities with the Swiss Federal Political Department. A significant part of its early post-war activities focused on Austria and Germany.[44]

Caritas had been advancing resettlement ideas ever since the end of the war, building on a particular religious/Catholic understanding of and interest in migration and settlement politics. Drawing on this and also in response to the upcoming termination of the activities of the IRO, SEH started in the second half of 1949 to seriously contemplate resettlement schemes as a way of solving the 'refugee problem' in Europe.[45] Since they did not fall under IRO's mandate and with Germany and Austria appearing largely either incapable or unwilling to integrate them, it comes as little surprise that German expellees were particularly considered as candidates for such schemes.[46] But this also meant that SEH was compelled to engage with issues related to ethnicity in general, and to 'Germanness' in particular. In effect, as it tried to address the European displacement crisis, post-war humanitarianism in general had perforce to address ethnopolitical questions. Ethnic and ethnopolitical identifications and ascriptions underlay much of the forced migration processes which had led to the situation in the early post-war and continued to be a key perspective that those involved were using in order to make sense of what was happening.

With Brazilian authorities open towards such an action, in May 1950 the Danube Swabian resettlement project officially became an SEH project. Within SEH, the responsible institutions were Caritas and the Schweizerisches Arbeiterhilfswerk (SAH).[47] In Austria, the agricultural expert Michael Moor remained the Danube Swabian in charge, with Josef Stefan actually disappearing from the picture.[48]

Following SEH's lobbying, in August 1950, the Brazilian Presidency and the Council for Immigration and Colonisation (CIC) agreed to a 'trial project' consisting in the resettlement of 500 *Volksdeutsche* and Danube Swabian families (2,500 persons), to take place later that year. The approval letter also referred to subsequent migration of 97,500 people, which was nonetheless to constitute the object of further negotiations after the upcoming Brazilian elections, with a view towards implementation in 1951–2. The immigrants were supposed to be 'exclusively refugees of German origin, so-called "Volksdeutsche" and "Danube Swabians", who find themselves under the patronage of your organisation'. By amalgamating humanitarian and ethnic categories, the wording indicates the complex and fluid character of ethnic and political ascriptions, as well as the fact that SEH had in effect to manage an action of ethnopolitical humanitarianism. Signed by CIC's vice-president, the letter emphasized that the Swiss side was alone responsible for finding the necessary funds.[49] For Brazilian authorities, the resettlement was largely a 'Swiss' humanitarian and colonization action, and the immigrants stood under 'Swiss' patronage.

The Swiss resettlement-related efforts had at least four entangled dimensions: technical, financial, diplomatic and ethnopolitical. Potential institutional partners had to be found, funds had to be raised, an exact location had to be decided, land had to be bought, business and viability plans had to be drafted and, last but definitely not least, settlers – that is, Danube Swabian settlers – had to be selected. SEH set to ask for specialist opinions about the feasibility of the project, mainly as reviews of the Goiás report. Among those asked there were representatives of other Germanophone settlements in Brazil, Swiss technical experts, as well as experts affiliated with international organizations such as the Food and Agriculture Organization or the International Labour Office.[50] Eventually, on the basis of these reports and also following another research trip to Brazil which took place from March to May 1951, the choice was made to move the location of the initial settlement from Goiás to Paraná, in the proximity of the town of Guarapuava.[51]

SEH's takeover of the project brought along an involvement of the Swiss state. Largely since the beginning of the efforts towards resettlement, the Swiss Political Department (more precisely, its International Organizations division) and Swiss diplomatic representatives in Brazil closely followed and generally helped the efforts of SEH/Caritas.[52] The interest of the Political Department (and subsequently that of the Trade Division within the Department of Economic Affairs) had an important economic dimension. SEH's ideas about how to fund the 'colonisation plans in Brazil' involved the 'activation of Swiss industry ventures and banks'. Such ideas were positively received by Swiss federal authorities.[53] Thus, with Swiss state support, an intricate financing scheme was developed, centred around the granting of supplementary import licences by the Bank of Brazil for a series of products. The licences would then be used by Swiss firms in order to export those products on the Brazilian market. Parts of the profit pertained to SEH in order to finance the resettlement. The Swiss state also granted a so-called export risk guarantee to the companies involved. Moreover, since the action required funds in advance, it provided an advance cash float to SEH, that was to be recuperated from the aforementioned market transactions. Agricultural colonization, land reclamation and the opening up of new markets came together. The scheme involved some questionable currency transactions and eventually ended up at the centre of a political and financial scandal in Switzerland, criticism being also raised in Brazilian newspapers.[54]

The premise of the project was that out of the approximatively 110,000 Danube Swabians in Austria and the 'presumably more' in Germany, half were 'willing to emigrate'.[55] SEH accepted that the colonization – or at least the pioneer resettlement – had to have an exclusively Danube Swabian character.[56] Nevertheless, the sometimes interchangeable use of the terms 'Volksdeutsche' and 'Donauschwaben', and the fact that SEH's 'patronage' relied on a mediated relationship with those who were potentially part of the Danube Swabian group in Austria, was bound to create some difficulties. For example, at a meeting in March 1951, SEH's representatives addressed the officially sanctioned Danube Swabian character of the resettlement. The exchange took place in the context of some critical reactions in the Brazilian press concerning what was considered to be a Danube Swabian willingness to maintain rigid boundaries with respect to the local population (incidentally, a diasporic feature). Indicating that some Danube Swabians were already attending Portuguese classes in Linz, Berta Hohermuth, the head of SEH's emigration commission, argued that the issue was less about 'the readiness to become Brazilians, as it is about the stance of having to fulfil a "German cultural mission"'. In view of the envisaged subsequent migration of up to 100,000 people and the potential difficulties that its exclusively Danube Swabian character might have entailed, some voices at the meeting made the case for replacing the term 'Danube Swabians' in the internal official documents that were to be drafted. Monsignor Crivelli proposed to refer to 'refugees', so that 'refugees of other nationalities could also receive the permissions to enter Brazil'. To Berta Hohermuth, who emphasized that the official Brazilian agreement referred specifically to 'Donauschwaben', Janos Vayda, the Hungarian-Swiss representative of Caritas/SEH in Brazil, retorted that 'Volksdeutsch is no nationality, among them there are Germans, Yugoslavs, Romanians, Hungarians'.[57] This exchange indicates SEH's own difficulty in managing the presupposed ethnic character of the resettlement and its patronage over an ethnic group about whom it only had superficial knowledge and on whose identity politics it had no leverage. Yet despite such discussions, the project did not stop being a Danube Swabian one.

SEH's most matter-of-fact encounter with ethnicity-related issues stemmed out of the fact that 2,500 Danube Swabians willing to be settlers in Brazil had to be found among the presumed 100,000 Danube Swabian refugees in Austria. This was largely a shot in the dark, since there was no register of Danube Swabians. The initial thoughts in this respect suggested that the selection had to be made according to professional criteria as well as on the basis of the common origin of the settlers-to-be: 'It is planned to consider people who previously lived together and, in this context, to give preference to 3-5 particular villages.' Furthermore, in order to simplify the process, the 'village communities' that were to constitute the pool of selection were to be those 'where the majority of their people find themselves in Austria'. Yet even if SEH was looking for 'the best qualified elements for the settlement', the 'labour market-oriented criteria' had to be applied only to the 'head of the family'.[58] Unmarried adults were in principle to be excluded.[59] Thus, a logic mixing moral, humanitarian and market-related criteria and arguments was summoned in order to create a group of colonists who were supposed to create a settlement out of nothing and to establish an agricultural cooperative. Being a Danube Swabian did not suffice, one had to be a Danube Swabian who would fit in the settlement, both professionally and morally. The limitation to the selection pool that Austria could provide was no surprise, considering the fact that the resettlement as such had started as a plan concerning Danube Swabians in Austria and not least because in the context of the early post-war it would have been much more complicated, if not almost impossible, to organize a selection process across borders. This case study therefore demonstrates that very territorialized constraints can impact upon transnational migration.

The selection process started in early 1951, at a moment when it was in effect not yet certain where exactly in Brazil the new settlement would be located. In principle, SEH was fully in charge of the draft, opening to this purpose an office in Linz in February 1951. Brazilian representatives in Austria apparently expressed no interest in participating in the selection.[60] In turn, the process could not have taken place without some degree of mediation from the Danube Swabian organizations. The de facto leader of the still-unmade group of Danube Swabian settlers, Michael Moor, also wanted to have a say in this respect. Male liaison officers from the Donauschwäbische Arbeitsgemeinschaft (DAG), the Danube Swabian organization in Austria, had to act as intermediaries between SEH and the broader Danube Swabian group. They were supposed to represent eighteen or twenty-five communities from Yugoslavia, with one representing the entire Romanian Banat.[61] The apparent Yugoslav bias reflects both the fact that most Danube Swabians in Austria were actually originating from Yugoslavia, as well as Moor's preferences since he hailed from Inđija (India) in Vojvodina.

Eventually, the selection process was far from smooth, being marred by numerous difficulties and mishaps. By 31 March 1951, 1,668 applications had been officially submitted, for a total of 7,047 persons. The number was rather low considering the visions of subsequent mass resettlement and the estimates of around 140,000 non-naturalized Danube Swabians living in Austria.[62] Nevertheless, despite the selection difficulties overall, 2,446 settlers travelled to Brazil between May 1951 and March 1952. No subsequent mass rettlement followed.

SEH largely took for granted the representation of Danube Swabians as a people of colonists and peasants made into refugees by the Second World War, a representation which largely legitimized the purpose of the Brazilian resettlement action.[63] Its representatives assumed the existence of a rather unitary Danube Swabian community (in Austria), whose members were prone to emigrate, and set to carve out of it a small and concrete group of pioneer settlers. However, in attempting to do this, SEH was faced with the rifts and cracks within this imagined Danube Swabian community: 'We completely do not have to do with a unitary breed, but with people of extremely different behavioural, cultural and social shades.'[64] Moreover, according to the head of SEH's Linz office, W. Baumann, the 'existence as refugees' had left its mark on the Danube Swabians, demoralizing them and depriving them of some of the skills necessary to mount a colonization project.[65]

Baumann also saw significant differences between peasants and craftsmen, with the former supposedly more qualified for colonization work, while the latter were seen as more prone to leave the newly established settlement.[66] He singled out two particularly problematic aspects. On the one hand, he criticized the very individualistic outlook of Danube Swabians, which made it difficult to envisage the success of what was supposed to be, at least in SEH's view, a cooperativistic agricultural project. There were clear tensions between different visions of landownership. On the other hand, the internalized collectivistic aspects of the Danube Swabian self-identification, such as the so-called 'German cultural mission' and the feeling of superiority with respect to other people/ethnic groups, were also bound to cause difficulties.[67] In any case, the real migration-prone Danube Swabians were not the imagined Danube Swabians.

By taking over the patronage of the Danube Swabian resettlement action, SEH had to mix humanitarianism and ethnopolitics. SEH – and, by extension, the Swiss state, one could argue – purported to speak and to act on behalf of an ethnically defined group, while also being supposed to literally make that group, even if the selection pool was not as broad and inviting as SEH had hoped for. SEH had to operate within and engage with the complicated Danube Swabian web of identifications. The representation of Danube Swabians as refugees in Austria in need of aid was the key rationale for the resettlement. Nonetheless, this argument was potentiated by the presumed diasporic condition of the Danube Swabians as a people of settlers, with a colonization history in south-eastern Europe. The discourses and representations on which the latter was relying were however largely indebted to visions of a 'German cultural mission' that SEH was officially rejecting.

Conclusion

The post-war Danube Swabian resettlement to Brazil allows for a critical consideration of the quadratic relationship model proposed by Willems and Palacz. First of all, the case study attests that there is a lot to be gained by looking at refugee movements in (and out of) twentieth-century Europe beyond the typical approaches emphasizing victimhood/resilience and integration/assimilation. Second, it confirms that looking at refugees through an analytical lens indebted to a diaspora vocabulary is legitimate. After all, more often than not, forced migration tends to either create diasporas or to be directed against groups that then resort to a diaspora vocabulary in order to advance (some of) their claims. Refugeedom is thus often related one way or another to processes of diasporization. However, it is precisely this nexus, linking refugeedom and diaspora-ness almost perforce, that makes the role of humanitarian organizations – as well as of states engaging in humanitarian politics without being guided in this engagement by a duty framed as the responsibility of a kin-state/external homeland – particularly important. Such organizations engage in ethnopolitics, as SEH's involvement in the post-war Danube Swabian resettlement to Brazil duly shows.

The case study indicates that categories such as 'homeland' and 'host society' are themselves fuzzy and far from being in any way stable and clear-cut. Generally, scholarship on diasporas and ethnic groups emphasizes the fluid, constructed, contested and negotiated character of identity ascriptions and identifications. Diasporas are fundamentally categories of practice and action.[68] Yet closely related to this is the fact that categories such as host society for or homeland of a particular group are also far from being bounded, straightforward or unchanging. Analytical models ought to take this into account as well.

Notes

1 For example, Anton Hochgatterer, *Entre Rios. Donauschwäbische Siedlung in Südbrasilien*, Donauschwäbische Beiträge 84 (Salzburg: Haus der Donauschwaben, 1986); Gerd Kohlhepp, 'Espaço e Etnia', *Estudos Avançados* 11, no. 5 (1991): 109–42; Sama Bose, 'Neue Wege zur Lösung der Flüchtlingsproblematik. Das donauschwäbische Siedlungsprojekt der Schweizer Europahilfe in Brasilien, 1949–1952', *Studien und Quellen. Zeitschrift des Schweizerischen Bundesarchivs* 19 (1993): 157–74; Markus Schmitz, *Westdeutschland und die Schweiz nach dem Krieg. Die Neuformierung der bilateralen Beziehungen 1945–1952* (Zürich: Neue Zürcher Zeitung, 2003), 133–40; Marcus Nestor Stein, *O oitavo dia: produção de sentidos identitários na Colônia Entre Rios-PR* (Guarapuava: Unicentro, 2011); Méri Frotscher, 'A Lost Homeland, a Reinvented Homeland: Diaspora and the "Culture of Memory" in the Colony of Danube Swabians of Entre Rios', *German History* 33, no. 3 (2015): 439–61.
2 Bastiaan Willems and Michał Adam Palacz, 'Unwilling Nomads: A Four-Dimensional Model of Diaspora', in this volume.
3 Rogers Brubaker, 'The "Diaspora" Diaspora', *Ethnic and Racial Studies* 28, no. 1 (2005): 1–19.
4 G. C. Paikert, *The Danube Swabians: German Populations in Hungary, Rumania and Yugoslavia and Hitler's Impact on Their Patterns* (The Hague: Martinus Nijhoff, 1967), 3.
5 Mariana Hausleitner, *Die Donauschwaben 1868–1948. Ihre Rolle im rumänischen und serbischen Banat* (Stuttgart: Franz Steiner, 2014), 17–18.
6 See for example Benjamin Moore, *The Names of John Gergen: Immigrant Identities in Early Twentieth-Century Saint Louis* (Saint Louis: University of Missouri Press, 2021).

7 Consider for example that the appearance of the umbrella-term and group identification *Russlanddeutsche* (Russian Germans) takes place roughly in the same period. See Hans-Christian Petersen, 'The Making of Russlanddeutschtum. Karl Stumpp oder die Mobilisierung einer "Volksgruppe" in der Zwischenkriegszeit', in *Minderheiten in Europa der Zwischenkriegszeit. Wissenschaftliche Konzeptionen, mediale Vermittlung, politische Funktion*, ed. Silke Göttsch-Elten and Cornelia Eisler (Münster: Waxmann, 2017), 163–89.
8 Márta Fata, 'Migration im Gedächtnis. Auswanderung und Ansiedlung in der Identitätsbildung der Donauschwaben', in *Migration im Gedächtnis. Auswanderung und Ansiedlung im 18. Jahrhundert in der Identitätsbildung der Donauschwaben*, ed. Márta Fata (Stuttgart: Franz Steiner, 2013), 7–20.
9 Thomas Casagrande, *Die volksdeutsche SS-Division 'Prinz Eugen': die Banater Schwaben und die nationalsozialistischen Kriegsverbrechen* (Frankfurt am Main: Campus, 2003); Hausleitner, *Die Donauschwaben*; Mirna Zakić, *Ethnic Germans and National Socialism in Yugoslavia in World War II* (Cambridge: Cambridge University Press, 2017).
10 Mathias Beer, *Flucht und Vertreibung der Deutschen. Voraussetzungen, Verlauf, Folgen* (Munich: C.H. Beck, 2011), 12.
11 Ingomar Senz, *Die Donauschwaben* (Munich: Langen Müller, 2005), 126.
12 Tara Zahra, '"Prisoners of the Postwar": Expellees, Displaced Persons, and Jews in Austria after World War II', *Austrian History Yearbook* 41 (2010): 192; Gerard Daniel Cohen, *In War's Wake: Europe's Displaced Persons in the Postwar Order* (New York: Oxford University Press, 2017), 44–6.
13 Matthias Stickler, 'Vertriebenenintegration in Österreich und Deutschland – ein Vergleich', in *Verschiedene europäische Wege im Vergleich. Österreich und die Bundesrepublik Deutschland 1945/49 bis zur Gegenwart*, ed. Michael Gehler and Ingrid Böhler (Innsbruck: Studienverlag, 2007), 416–35.
14 Niklas Perzi, 'Flüchtlinge und Vertriebene in der Republik Österreich', in *Online-Lexikon zur Kultur und Geschichte der Deutschen im östlichen Europa* (16 April 2015). Available online: ome-lexikon.uni-oldenburg.de/p32875 (accessed 14 December 2021).
15 Ibid.; Zahra, 'Prisoners of the Postwar', 192.
16 Zahra, 'Prisoners of the Postwar'.
17 See the concluding essay by Willems and Palacz in this volume.
18 Archives of the Archdiocese of Salzburg, Salzburg (hereafter AES), 2.1. EB Rohracher Caritas Dez 44-1952, 'Protokoll über die am 10. Oktober in Salzburg, Dreifaltigkeitsgasse 12, stattgefundene Caritas-Konferenz', 1 October 1946.
19 Sabine Veits-Falk, 'Fürsorge und Seelsorge der katholischen Kirche für volksdeutsche Flüchtlinge in Salzburg', in *Erzbischof Andreas Rohracher: Krieg, Wiederaufbau, Konzil*, ed. Ernst Hintermaier, Alfred Rinnerthaler and Hans Spatzenegger (Salzburg: Anton Pustet, 2010), 165–86; Georg Wildmann, 'Beitrag der Kirchen zur Integration der Heimatvertriebenen in Österreich', *Donauschwaben in Oberösterreich*. Available online: https://www.donauschwaben-ooe.at/index.php?id=311 (accessed 6 December 2020). See also AES, 2.17, 18/55 Flüchtlingssachen Korrespondenz mit Nuntiatur Wien 1947–52, Josef Stefan, 'La question de l'émigration des réfugiés catholiques en Chile', n.d., 2. Also Josef Werni, 'Sein Werdegang in der Heimat', in *Salzburg und die Heimatvertriebenen: Pater Stefan und sein Werk*, ed. Ruth Medger-Hameria and Josef Werni (Salzburg: Donauschwäbische Verlagsgesellschaft, 1966), 49–63.

20 Ruth Medger-Hameria and Josef Werni (eds), *Salzburg und die Heimatvertriebenen: Pater Stefan und sein Werk* (Salzburg: Donauschwäbische Verlagsgesellschaft, 1966), 79.
21 Josef Stefan, *Um das Schicksal der Volksdeutschen. Nach einem Vortrag im Rahmen des Bildungswerkes und der Adalbert-Stifter-Gemeinde als Manuskript gedruckt* (Salzburg: Verlag der Flüchtlingsseelsorge, 1949), 27–9.
22 AES, 2.17, 18/55 Flüchtlingsangelegenheiten Korrespondenz Eb. Rohracher 1946–1953, Josef Stefan to Andreas Rohracher, 26 April 1948.
23 See also Márta Fata, '"Creatio ex nihilo" – Das sinnstiftende Narrativ der Donauschwaben im Wandel der Zeit', in *Das leere Land. Historische Narrative von Einwanderergesellschaften*, ed. Matthias Asche and Ulrich Niggemann (Stuttgart: Franz Steiner, 2015), 165–88.
24 Stefan, *Um das Schicksal*, 32.
25 Ibid., 27.
26 AES, 2.17, 18/55 Flüchtlingssachen Korrespondenz mit Nuntiatur Wien 1947–52, Josef Stefan, 'Bericht über die Auswanderungsbestrebungen des Flüchtlingsseelsorgeamtes Salzburg, Lehen, Ignac Harrerstrasse 2, Bar. 1', 6 February 1949.
27 Ibid.
28 AES, 2.17, 18/57 Flüchtlingsseelsorge Korrespondenz mit NCWC, Caritas Schweiz, YMKA 1947–53, Josef Stefan to Crivelli, 12 March 1949; Victor Conzemius, 'Crivelli, Giuseppe', in *Historisches Lexikon der Schweiz* (11 March 2004). Available online: https://hls-dhs-dss.ch/articles/009759/2004-03-11/ (accessed 14 December 2021).
29 AES, 2.1 EB Rohracher Caritas Dez 44–1952, Schweizer Caritasverband, 'Auswanderung', n.d.
30 Dieter Marc Schneider, *Johannes Schauff (1902–1990). Migration und 'Stabilitas' im Zeitalter der Totalitarismen*, R. Oldenbourg Verlag (Munich: De Gruyter, 2001), 102–3.
31 José H. Fischel de Andrade, 'Brazil and the International Refugee Organization (1946–1952)', *Refugee Survey Quarterly* 30, no. 1 (2011): 75; Sênia Regina Bastos and Maria do Rosário Rolfsen Salles, 'Polish Postwar Migration to Brazil, 1945–55', *Polish American Studies* 69, no. 1 (2012): 62.
32 Fischel de Andrade, 'Brazil and the International Refugee Organization', 76.
33 Henriette von Holleuffer, 'Seeking New Horizons in Latin America: The Resettlement of 100.000 European Displaced Persons between the Gulf of Mexico and Patagonia (1947–1951)', *Jahrbuch für Geschichte Lateinamerikas* 39 (2002): 143.
34 Antón Corbacho Quintela and Alexandre Ferreira da Costa, 'Uma conferência relativamente fracassada: I conferência brasileira de imigração e colonização', *Revista UFG* XIII, no. 10 (2011): 215–25.
35 Swiss Federal Archives, Bern (hereafter BAR), E2001E#1967/113#15481 Volksdeutsche 1950-1, Michael Moor, Josef Stefan and Dr Vayda, 'Bericht der donauschwäbischen Studienkommission über die Kolonisationsmöglichkeiten im brasilianischen Bundesstaat GOIAZ' (Rio de Janeiro (*sic*, C.C.), Brasil: Uniao Suiça de Caridade / Union Suisse de Charité / Schweizerischer Caritasverband. Delegaçao Geral para a America do sul, 1950), 2.
36 BAR, J2.211#1992/236#1121* Guarapuava, Paraná: Berichte über die donauschwäbische Siedlung, 1949–52, Michael Moor and Josef Stefan to Dr Jeronimo Coimbra Bueno, 1950.
37 BAR, Moor, Stefan, and Vayda, 'Bericht Goiaz', 5.
38 Ibid., 28–32.

39 Ibid., 32.
40 See for example AES, 2.17, 18/56 Kath. Flüchtingsseel- u. Fürsorge Flüchtlingsangelegenheiten U.S.A. Organisationen Hilfestellen 1947–51, Josef Stefan to American Aid Societies for the Needy and Displaced Persons of Central and South Eastern Europe, 23 October 1947.
41 BAR, J2.211#1992/236#1121*, Josef Stefan, 'Bericht über die Studienreise nach Süd- und Nordamerika', 15 November 1950, 26.
42 See for example A. K. Gauss, 'Volkstumsprobleme der Heimatvertriebenen im geschlossenen Binnenvolksraum', *Kulturspiegel. Blätter aus dem geistigen Schaffen der heimatlosen Donauschwaben* 2 (1949): 3–5.
43 Jean-Claude Favez, 'Le Don suisse et la politique étrangère. Quelques réflexions', in *Des archives à la mémoire. Mélanges d'histoire politique, religieuse et sociale offerts à Louis Binz*, ed. Barbara Roth-Lochner, Marc Neuenschwander and François Walter (Geneva: Société d'Histoire et d'Archéologie de Genève, 1995), 327–39; Peter Hug, 'Schweizer Spende an die Kriegsgeschädigten', in *Historisches Lexikon der Schweiz* (28 October 2011). Available online: https://hls-dhs-dss.ch/de/articles/043513/2011-10-28/ (accessed 14 December 2021); Schmitz, *Westdeutschland und die Schweiz nach dem Krieg*, 59–75 and 133–40.
44 Christian Koller, 'Vor 70 Jahren: Das Ende des Zweiten Weltkriegs in Europa und die Schweiz', *Schweizerisches Sozialarchiv* (8 May 2015). Available online: https://www.sozialarchiv.ch/2015/05/08/vor-70-jahren-das-ende-des-zweiten-weltkriegs-in-europa-und-die-schweiz/ (accessed 14 December 2021); Schmitz, *Westdeutschland und die Schweiz nach dem Krieg*.
45 BAR, J2.211#1992/236#1121*, 'Protokoll der Vorstandssitzung der Schweizer Europahilfe', 27 October 1949; BAR, J2.211#1992/236#1121*, J. Leupold, 'Protokoll der Sitzung der Kommission der Schweizer Europahilfe für Auswanderung und Siedlung (KEAS)', 12 November 1949; Bose, 'Neue Wege', 161–2.
46 BAR, Leupold, 'Protokoll', 12 November 1949.
47 BAR, J2.211#1992/236#1121*, J. Leupold, 'Aktennotiz über die Besprechung von Dienstag, den 16. Mai 1950 21.40-23.10 Uhr, im Bahnhofbuffet Bern, zwischen Fräulein Hohermuth, Herrn Dr. J. Vayda, Herrn Bertholet, Herrn Moor und Herrn Dr. Leupold' (Bern, 16 May 1950); BAR, J2.211#1992/236#1121*, 'Memorandum über die Besprechung von 15.5.1950 mit den Herren: Dr. Vayda, Bertolet, Ingenieur Moor und am 16.5. mit Herrn Dr. Cramer, in der Angelegenheit: Siedlung Goyaz / Brasilien' (Bern, 16 May 1950). On SAH see Antonia Schmidlin, 'Schweizerisches Arbeiterhilfswerk (SAH)', in *Historisches Lexikon der Schweiz* (31 October 2011). Available online: https://hls-dhs-dss.ch/de/articles/016634/2011-10-31/ (accessed 14 December 2021).
48 Stefan touches upon his removal from the resettlement action in his correspondence from late 1950. See for example AES, 2.17, 18/57 Flüchtlingsseelsorge Korrespondenz mit NCWC, Caritas Schweiz, YMKA 1947–53, Josef Stefan to Msgr. Crivelli, 22 November 1950.
49 BAR, J2.211#1992/236#1121*, Armando V.P. de Vasconcellos to Jean Vayda, 'N. 1514/223.2 Projekt der Schweiz. Caritas', 12 August 1950.
50 See BAR, J2.211#1992/236#1121*.
51 BAR, J2.211#1992/236#1121*, Jean Vayda and Michael Moor to Schweizer Europahilfe, 'Rapport Nr.', 31 March 1951; Hans Scavenius, 'Bericht ueber einem Besuch mit der Caritas-Kommission in Goiaz', April 1951; Hans Scavenius, 'Report of Trip to Parana with Caritas Mission', 17 May 1951.

52 See BAR, E2001E#1967/113#15481 and E2200.196-01#1968/206#106*, 'Donauschwaben', Guarapuava 1950-7.
53 BAR, J2.211#1992/236#1121*, Berta Hohermuth, 'Möglichkeiten der Einschaltung der Schweizer Industrieunternehmungen in die Finanzierung von Kolonisationsplänen in Brasilien (diktiert von Dr. Jean Vayda)', 16 May 1950.
54 BAR, E2001E#1970/1#134*, Documentation 1952, Franz Luterbacher and Alexander Sieben, 'Bericht über die Siedlungsaktion der Schweizer Europahilfe in Brasilien an die Direktion der Eidg. Finanzverwaltung', 26 June 1952.
55 BAR, 'Memorandum', 15-16 May 1950.
56 Ibid.
57 Swiss Social Archives, Zürich (hereafter SSA), Ar 20.950.34, Schweizer Europahilfe, 'Entwurf als Diskussionsbasis betr. Zusammenarbeit zwischen Schweizer Europahilfe, Finanzierungsgesellschaft "Emigrar", Genossenschaft "Agraria"' (Bern, 7 March 1951).
58 BAR, 'Memorandum', 15-16 May 1950.
59 BAR, J2.211#1992/236#1121*, 'Aktennotiz über die Besprechung von Fräulein Hohermuth mit den Herren Moor und Lobsiger vom 19. September 1950', 4 October 1950.
60 BAR, J2.211#1992/236#1121*, W. Baumann, 'Schlussbericht der Delegation Linz der Schweizer Europahilfe', 30 April 1952, Basel, 3.
61 Archives of the Province of Upper Austria, Linz, ZBST 2/6, Zentralberatungsstelle der Volksdeutschen, Donauschwäbische Landsmannschaft, Landesstelle Oberösterreich, Rundschreiben 6, Linz, 4 November 1950, 1; also Zentralberatungsstelle der Volksdeutschen, Donauschwäbische Landsmannschaft, Landesstelle Oberösterreich, Rundschreiben 7, Weihnachten 1950, 2.
62 BAR, J2.211#1992/236#1121*, W. Baumann, 'Schlussbericht der Delegation Linz der Schweizer Europahilfe über ihre Tätigkeit für die Auswanderungs-Aktion nach Brasilien (Februar 1951 bis März 1952)', 30 April 1952, 3.
63 BAR, J2.211#1992/236#1121*, W. Baumann, 'Donauschwaben als Kolonisten nach Brasilien', 25 March 1952.
64 Ibid., 2.
65 Ibid., 3-4.
66 Ibid., 6.
67 BAR, Baumann, 'Donauschwaben als Kolonisten'.
68 Brubaker, 'The "Diaspora" Diaspora'.

15

Anti-communists, communists and migrants in France, 1917–53

Aaron Clift

As it is now cliché to point out, France, unlike most other European states, has always been a country of immigration. While the rest of Europe witnessed massive out-migration in the nineteenth and early twentieth centuries, especially to the settler colonies of America and Australasia, France saw comparatively limited emigration (with the notable exception of that to its own settler colony of Algeria). Meanwhile, large numbers of migrants made their way to France. Traditional seasonal migrants along France's borders with Spain and Italy continued their pastoral movements despite the growth of the modern state with its new border controls. Political refugees fled Poland in the 1830s and 1860s, Germany in the 1840s and 1930s, Russia in the 1920s and Spain in the 1930s, to name only the most prominent. Jews escaping ethnic and religious discrimination in Central and Eastern Europe also came, especially from the 1880s to 1910s and in the 1930s. Large numbers of economic migrants sought work in the new industrial economy growing in France but especially in the North and around Paris, be they Belgians, Italians and Spaniards in the nineteenth century; Poles, Czechs and Yugoslavs in the interwar period; or migrants from France's African and Asian colonies after the Second World War.

In the post-war period, the French government encouraged immigration as part of its reconstruction and development strategy. Substantial immigration to fill labour shortages was envisioned by the Plan Monnet, the French government's plan for economic modernization and growth.[1] Between 1946 and 1952, France received 356,516 immigrants, officially.[2] There was also substantial illegal immigration, however, so the total number was probably closer to half a million.[3] These numbers did not include migration from Algeria, then officially considered as part of France, which began to expand rapidly in this period, with 100,000 crossing the Mediterranean in 1947 alone.[4] As a result, the non-citizen population expanded from 16.7 million in 1945 to 18.7 million in 1951, at the same time as 370,000 immigrants became naturalized French citizens.[5]

These diverse waves of migration were never uncontroversial. Contemporary anti-immigrant politicians can be placed in a long tradition of hostility to immigration in France, including Charles Maurras, ideologue of the Action Française, who saw what he called 'métiques' (metics, after the ancient Athenian term for foreigners) as a danger equal to his other boogeymen, Jews and Freemasons. Various governments, including the Vichy regime but also many republican administrations, restricted and discriminated against migrants: when the Nazis arrived in France in 1940, they found concentration camps already in existence, built by the Daladier government of the Third Republic to house Spanish Republicans. In a November 1947 poll, only 33 per cent of the French public expressed a positive opinion of immigration, compared to 57 per cent who rejected it.[6] Two years later, the numbers were even worse: 25 per cent positive, 63 per cent negative.[7]

Anxieties about immigration interacted with another great political movement of interwar and post-war France: anti-communism. Here is not the place to overview the long history of French anti-communism; it suffices to say that as soon as Bolshevism took power in Russia, lively anti-communist political movements began to develop in France. This movement reached its crescendo in the years immediately following the Second World War, when it responded to the widespread popularity and political success enjoyed by the Parti communiste français (PCF), which regularly enjoyed the support of about a quarter of the French voting population in the decades after 1945. This chapter will examine the complex interaction between anti-communism and migration in France, focusing on the interwar period as well as the years between the end of the Second World War and 1953, when the end of the Korean War and the death of Stalin combined with internal political changes in France to ease, slightly, Cold War tensions.

French anti-communists, like French society as a whole, displayed a variety of different reactions to migration, reflecting their preoccupations as well as differing social and political circumstances driving different migrant movements. Most often, they tended to divide migrants into two black and white categories of good, anti-communist refugees and bad, pro-communist infiltrators. The former included, above all, political refugees fleeing communist regimes in East-Central Europe; the latter encompassed politically suspect groups like Jews and Spanish Republicans. Not all migrant groups fell neatly into these two categories, however, giving rise to ambivalent attitudes. Most immigrants in France were economic migrants motivated by employment rather than politics, and these groups were the subject of intense contestation between communists and anti-communists for their allegiance. Poles and Czechs who filled the factories of the Nord and the Paris banlieues could be viewed as born anti-communists, given events in their home countries, but also as a potential reservoir of support for the PCF in light of their poor material conditions. The chapter will also discuss how communists themselves responded to these groups, arguing there was significant parallelism between communist and anti-communist reactions to migration.[8]

The four-dimensional model of diaspora presented by Willems and Palacz in the introduction to this volume helps illuminate the nature of the relationship between migrants, communists and anti-communists in post-war France. As this chapter is fundamentally a study of French reactions to migration, it focuses above all on the refugee–host society relationship. In this case, as in others presented in this volume, the existing political conflicts of the host society coloured the experiences of refugees as well as the reactions of the host society, as often crude assumptions were made about the political meaning of migration. Refugees then had to decide how they would locate themselves in relation to a divided host society. Both anti-communist and communist migrants practised a form of assimilation, though to different segments of French political society. In some cases, political conflict assisted the process of integration, as certain groups of migrants were celebrated for their (assumed) political beliefs and welcomed on that basis – a pattern observed in similar cases, such as Cuban and Vietnamese refugees in the United States.[9] Of course, it often had the opposite result, as xenophobia was strengthened by the perception of political threat attached to some migrant groups.

These differential experiences were closely related to diaspora relations with their respective homelands. Assumptions about political events in the homeland and diaspora reactions to them influenced the positive or negative appraisals of different migrant groups by French anti-communists. Relations between different diaspora communities were also crucial. French anti-communists were constantly comparing different migrant groups, fuelling their characterization of some as good and others as bad, generating rank orders which could have substantial effects on the communities in question. Didier Fassin has highlighted the importance of similar processes throughout the history of French debates over immigration, with some migrants placed above others (e.g. virtuous political refugees contrasted with criminal 'economic migrants').[10] A parallel process of comparison and evaluation was also practised by communists. Therefore each part of the four-dimensional nexus identified by Willems and Palacz, overlaid with the transnational and global context of the Cold War, inflected the relationship between migrant communities, communists and anti-communists in France.

'Bad' migrants: 'Communist' refugees

One prominent anti-communist concerned about immigration was Pierre Lhande, a Jesuit priest from the French Basque country, who in the 1920s travelled to the suburbs (banlieues) of Paris in order to assess the religious condition of the working-class communities there.[11] The result of his efforts was a three-volume work, *Le Christ dans la banlieue*, which presented a harrowing (from a Catholic perspective) and extremely influential (it was even adapted into a film in 1941) portrayal of a dechristianized, morally degenerate urban space where the Catholic faith had been replaced by the 'pseudo-religion communiste'.[12] Lhande linked his concerns about communism and immorality to immigration; these were areas, he wrote, where Paris dumped 'her undesirables, her Turks, her Serbs, her Czechoslovaks, her Arabs'.[13] Interestingly, Lhande does not seem to have distinguished between immigrants from the Middle East and North Africa and those from East-Central Europe: both groups were racialized, portrayed as products of 'the naked and dusty Orient' and viewed as a threat because of communist affiliations.[14] This may have had to do with the close residential proximity and socio-economic conditions of the two groups: they often lived side by side in the impoverished neighbourhoods on the outskirts of the city. To reach out to these areas, Lhande said Catholics would have to adopt the same missionary tactics they used in the 'pays barbares' (barbarous countries) of France's colonies.[15]

Anti-immigrant sentiments were also in evidence among anti-communists active in France's vibrant 'familialist' sector. Beginning in the late nineteenth century, concern with low birth rates had driven the development of the 'familialist' movement in France, a network of organizations which advocated for the rights and importance of the family and pushed the state to adopt natalist and family aid measures. This movement continued into the post-war period, even as birth rates finally started to rise as part of the 'baby boom'. It even gained semi-official status, as the state established bodies known as Union departmentales des associations familiales (UDAFs), under the umbrella of the Union nationale des associations familiales, which united familialist groups and gave a semi-public status, including responsibility for the allocation of family allowances. Many of these familialist groups were strongly anti-communist, especially those from a Catholic background. They developed a discourse which emphasized the threat of communism to the family, alleging that the PCF aimed to abolish the family and replace it with state tutelage of children. Some even believed that the communists wanted to eliminate fathers by replacing them with artificial insemination.[16]

Immigration was considered part of this communist plot against natality. Pierre-Marie Thibault, a familialist activist and member of the UDAF in the Catholic, Breton department of Morbihan, warned that 'the influx of foreigners in a nation which is "devitalising" and which is losing its capacity of assimilation constitutes, in effect, a veritable colonisation. In such a conjecture, France will lose her soul'.[17] While the French government, and some familialist organizations, tended to regard immigration as a 'solution' to the 'problem' of low birth rates, for Thibault and those who thought like him the confluence of a native French population who were not having enough babies with growing immigration was an existential threat to the French nation.

Fears that growing immigrant populations would 'replace' the native French had a long history. Anti-Semites in the era of the Dreyfus Affair, including Édouard Drumont and Maurice Barrès, argued Jews were seeking to replace the French, and after the Russian Revolution these fantasies became connected to communism.[18] Persecution, not only in Nazi Germany but also in other Central European states such as Poland, Hungary and Romania, combined with France's relatively open immigration policy (especially compared to other Western powers, which largely closed their doors to Jewish refugees in the period), led 50,000–60,000 Jews to migrate to France in the 1930s.[19] This influx inflamed an already-existing anti-Semitism, and was reflected in the policies of the Vichy government, which turned over Jewish refugees to the Nazis with alacrity, even while it was leery of handing over Jews with French citizenship (more for reasons of national sovereignty than humanitarian motives).[20]

As demonstrated by the case of Jewish refugees, anti-communist responses to migration often focused on groups seen to be particularly susceptible to communism. Jean Delcroix was a conservative and anti-communist agricultural activist, who edited a right-wing paper, *La Terre Nouvelle*, aimed at rural audiences. *La Terre Nouvelle* showed an obsessive concern with the supposed threat of communism to the French peasant and used anti-communism to support the campaigns of René Blondelle, secretary-general of the Fédération nationale des syndicats d'exploitants agricoles, to establish right-wing dominance in France's agricultural associations. A particular obsession of Delcroix's was the supposedly 'foreign' nature of the PCF. Besides common anti-communist tropes about the party's loyalty to the USSR rather than France, he frequently highlighted the presence of migrants in the party's leadership organs. For example, in an article entitled 'the "French" of the so-called French Communist Party', he drew attention to the fact that one member of the PCF central committee, Félix Garcia, was a Spanish republican refugee, while another, Maurice Kriegel-Valrimont, was a Jew from Polish Galicia.[21] For Delcroix, these individuals could not be truly 'French' and their presence in the PCF's leadership disproved the party's assertion to be a national party, making it a foreign body within the nation. There was just one problem with this 'analysis': Kriegel-Valrimont, who Delcroix termed 'Kriminel-Valrimont', may have been Jewish, but he was not an immigrant. He had been born to a French Jewish family in Alsace, not in Poland. This confusion demonstrates how hostile sentiments towards Jewish refugees often transitioned into a more generalized anti-Semitism which was suspicious of all Jews, even those born in France.

As highlighted by Delcroix, the two biggest groups in the category of 'bad' migrants for French anti-communists were Spanish Republicans and Jewish immigrants/refugees. The former constituted the largest group of refugees in France. After the outbreak of the Spanish Civil War in 1936, successive waves of anti-Franco Spaniards fled across the border into France, seeking refuge from war and right-wing authoritarianism in Spain. Each time Franco's Nationalist forces captured an area near the French border, there was a new influx, beginning with 15,000 Basques in September 1936; 120,000 following Franco's victory in the North in late 1937; and 25,000 after the Nationalist victory in Aragon in spring 1938.[22] These numbers were dwarfed by massive influx that followed the fall of Catalonia in February-March 1939, when half a million refugee Spaniards crossed into France in about two weeks.[23] This included soldiers from the Spanish Republican Army and the International Brigades (leftist volunteers who travelled to Spain to support the Republic), but also 170,000 civilians, including 70,000 children.[24]

They were not welcomed by the French right, who feared their leftist political affiliations. The fascist newspaper *Action française* described them as 'deserters, assassins, and burglars'.[25] This reaction was not restricted to the far-right, however. The moderate *La Dépêche de Toulouse* also described them as 'terrorist hordes'.[26] The refugees were interned in concentration camps like that at Argelès-sur-Mer, which held 100,000 people.[27] Many of these camps would later be repurposed by the Germans and the Vichy regime to hold Jews during the war. Within a year, two-thirds of the refugees returned to Spain, as for many of them the desire to return home and the harsh conditions of the internment camps outweighed the fears of Francoist repression.[28] This left 180,000, including many of the most politically 'compromised', in France.[29] Many joined the French Communist Party, and, in a parallel way to the anti-communist refugees from Eastern Europe who will be discussed below, sought to lobby the French government to support regime change in Spain.[30] Concerns about Spanish political refugees had an impact on French government policy, which tried to encourage them to move on from France to Latin America, signing several accords with countries in Central and South America with this end in mind, agreements which eventually led to the resettlement of 80,000 of them between 1946 and 1951.[31]

'Good' migrants: Anti-communist political refugees

French anti-communists were not invariably opposed to all immigration, however. Rather, they made comparisons between different migrant communities, accepting some while denigrating others. In a September 1950 article, Pierre Sérandour, the fiercely anti-communist editor of the agricultural journal *Le Moniteur du Progrès agricole et viticole*, enunciated the position of the paper and of most French anti-communists: France could not become 'le dépotoir' (landfill/rubbish dump) of the world, but had to be selective in who it admitted. In particular, anti-communist credentials must be closely considered when evaluating potential immigrants. 'Welcome unfortunate exiles who accept the laws of our country, YES! Admit those who come to prepare disorder and revolution among us, NO!', Sérandour wrote.[32] He was in little doubt about who belonged in each of these two groups: the first included refugees fleeing communist governments on the other side of the Iron Curtain; the second comprised Spanish republican refugees and East European Jews.

At least regarding the first group, Sérandour put his money where his mouth was. One of the anti-communist 'experts' he employed was an 'unfortunate exile': Lazar Kiciorgros, a refugee from Romania. Kiciorgros was a Romanian landowner who had his land expropriated by the communist government after the war and then emigrated to France. After coming to France, Kiciorgros worked for Sérandour spreading the word about the dangers communism presented to peasants. Using the experience of his native Romania as a guide, he argued French peasants should not be taken by communist deceptions which claimed they supported private property in agriculture or smallholding farmers.[33] Rather, he said this was a cover for their true objective of collectivization, with his own experience as evidence. He also regaled readers with horror stories of famine in his native land.[34]

Kiciorgros was just one example of the many political refugees from East-Central Europe who came to France fleeing communism in the 1940s and 1950s. In 1955, there were 73,000 Poles, 12,000 Hungarians and 8,000 Czechs registered as political refugees with the Office français pour les Réfugiés et Apatrides.[35] Of course, these represented only minorities of these migrant communities in France, though not negligible ones: 37 per cent of Czechs and 14 per cent of Poles in France were classed as political refugees.[36] Once in France, and especially in Paris, they organized into a variety of anti-communist intellectual and organizational networks. Many of these were set up under American auspices, including the National Committee for a Free Europe (1949), the Crusade for Freedom (1950), Radio Free Europe (1951), the Fund for Intellectual Freedom (1952) and the journal *News from Behind the Iron Curtain* (1952).[37] There were also French organizations, such as the Conseil de la Jeunesse libre de l'Europe centrale et orientale, created in 1953 and headquartered at 82 avenue Marceau, Paris.[38] These organizations attempted to inform the French and more generally West European publics on conditions behind the Iron Curtain and to turn them against communism.

The most famous incident involving a refugee from Central or Eastern Europe in post-war France was the so-called 'Kravchenko affair'. Victor Kravchenko was a Ukrainian member of the Soviet Communist Party who became a captain in Red Army before securing a diplomatic post in Washington. Previously an enthusiastic communist, he became disillusioned after witnessing the effects of collectivization in Ukraine and the Great Purges. Therefore, in 1944 he defected to the United States. In 1950, he published a best-selling memoir, *I Chose Freedom*, which purported to expose the ugly reality of Soviet communism. In no country was the impact of Kravchenko's revelations greater than in France. *Les Lettres Françaises*, a Communist-aligned literary journal, attacked Kravchenko as a liar, a coward and a corrupt American agent. Kravchenko responded by suing the publication for libel, leading to a court battle in which both sides brought in reams of witnesses and evidence to either prove or disprove Kravchenko's description of the USSR. Kravchenko eventually won his case, after sparking a notorious cause célèbre in France.[39]

In the generally pro-Soviet and philo-communist intellectual environment of 1940s and 1950s Paris, however, the response to this propaganda was often cold. Tony Judt has written of dismissiveness with which pro-communist French intellectuals often treated revelations of communist human rights violations.[40] This was reflected in the treatment of anti-communist political refugees, who were often stigmatized as fascist sympathizers by French pro-communists. The PCF described these migrants as 'those who betrayed their fatherland, served the Hitlerites, and do not offer a minimum of guarantees compatible with national security'.[41] Their rhetoric was a mirror image of anti-communist attacks on groups perceived as pro-communist. Anti-communists regarded communist migrants as a threat to France's national security; communists believed the exact same of anti-communist refugees. PCF supporters sometimes cried 'Down with the fascists of the île Saint-Louis!' in reference to the centre of Polish émigré life in Paris. A Czech refugee who arrived in May 1948 was told in the Prefecture of the Paris police that 'you are a fascist! Beneš, the democrat, stayed in Prague' – the PCF recruited quite successfully among police officers in this period.[42]

That would change in the coming years as PCF-aligned police (often former resistors) were removed and replaced with anti-communists (often former collaborators – Maurice Papon being the most infamous example). In the anti-communism of this period we find the roots of the behaviour that to this day troubles the relationship between the police and migrant communities in France. For example, in 1952, during police repression of communist demonstrations against NATO, two protestors were killed – both Algerian.[43] Thus the shift in the ranks of the police from communists to anti-communists did not fundamentally alter their attitude towards migrants – only the targets changed.

Forced migrants or not? The ambivalent position of economic migrants

Political refugees from East-Central Europe were only a minority among the migrants from these countries, however. The reality was that the vast majority of immigrants to France did not come for political reasons. Rather, they came looking for better economic conditions. These migrants technically fall outside the scope of this chapter, as officially they moved voluntarily rather than being 'forced'. In reality, the situation was more complex. Generally, one can object that emigrating due to poverty is as involuntary as doing so due to, say, political persecution. Specific to the post-war East-Central European-French migration corridor, the lines between political refugees and economic migrants were especially blurred. Economic migration from countries like Poland, Czechoslovakia and Yugoslavia was extensive before and after the war. During the interwar period, half a million Poles and 70,000 Czechs, among others, immigrated to France for economic reasons.[44] Indeed, in 1946, Poles constituted 24 per cent of all foreigners in France.[45] In the 1920s, immigration had accounted for 75 per cent of France's population growth.[46] This more than doubled the foreign-born share of the population, from 2.9 per cent in 1911 to 6.6 per cent in 1931.[47]

Many of these migrants claimed political refugee status, sometimes years after they had actually migrated, because of the protection from deportation it offered. This was especially true after the French government (for reasons elaborated below) signed treaties with Poland and Yugoslavia to encourage the return of economic migrants to those countries. Some did this because they had made lives in France and simply did not want to return to their home countries. Others genuinely straddled the traditional division between economic and political migrants: they may have immigrated for financial reasons before the communist takeovers in East-Central Europe, but then feared political persecution if they returned given the new political situation there.[48] This is an example of the way migrants used the political debates between communists and anti-communists for their own purposes. By identifying themselves as anti-communist political refugees, regardless of whether they actually were or not, they could seek greater acceptance by the French state and society.

Assumptions about the communist or anti-communist character of these economic migrants were not so easily made – which is not to say people did not try. While they could be seen, like the political refugees mentioned above, as born anti-communists, they were also a predominately poor or working-class group, making them a possible source of recruitment for the Communist Party. The latter view was a frequently expressed concern in the interwar period. As with farm labourers, the PCF and its affiliated unions had success organizing Polish miners. In 1931, while immigrants were 6.5 per cent of the total population and 7.4 per cent of the working population, they comprised 38 per cent of miners.[49] In a 1923 strike in mines of Pas-de-Calais, two-thirds of the 14,000 participants were immigrants, mainly Poles.[50] The local prefect wrote that the migrants were 'still uprooted, poorly adapted to our traditions' and 'prey to pernicious influences'.[51] A socialist leader claimed that Poles had a natural inclination towards 'autocracy' and this made them easy prey for the communists.[52] The French authorities worked with Polish clergy and Nationalist organizations to restrain communist influence.[53] For example, the Polish Workers Association (Związek Robotników Polskich – ZRP) was condemned by the communist unions as 'agents provocateurs of international fascism who wanted to deliver the Poles bound hand and foot to the French capitalists'.[54]

Similar concerns were in evidence in the agricultural sector. Before the war, in 1937, there had been major strikes by agricultural labourers, in part organized by the Communist Party.[55] During these strikes, French right-wingers had blamed immigrant labourers (predominantly Poles in the North and Spaniards in the South) for being the instigators of the disturbances; they implied that French farm workers had far too much good sense to engage in such foolish and subversive behaviour.[56] During the 1920s, 830,484 immigrants had filtered in and out of the French agricultural sector.[57] An annual average of 69,207 migrants on official farm worker contracts entered the country between 1919 and 1930, not including all those who entered unofficially.[58] Labour unrest was common: 25 per cent of the Poles broke their contracts over pay disputes, another 18 per cent because of excessive work and 11 per cent because of inadequate housing.[59] Sixty-one per cent were in precarious seasonal employment.[60] French farmers tended to blame this on communist influence. Interestingly, Polish elites tended to agree with them. The Polish government, concerned about Polish migrants coming into contact with dangerous ideas in France, had its consuls mediate labour disputes and funded Catholic missions which aimed to insulate Polish farm labourers from Marxist ideas.[61]

This stigma continued in the post-war period, when rights for agricultural labourers became a major topic of political debate. The PCF waged an active campaign to organize farm workers, including members of the aforementioned immigrant groups, into unions to push for measures such as the extension of the forty-hour workweek to agriculture. These proposals were fiercely contested by conservatives, who argued they would be the ruin of French farmers. *La Terre Nouvelle* accused the 'communist federation of agricultural workers' of regarding the farmers as enemies and stated that legislation proposed by the communists and Socialists to extend labour protections to agricultural workers would be disastrous for the industry.[62] They rejected the proposal to expand the forty-hour workweek to agricultural labour, and implored farm workers not to support this legislation, which, they claimed, would result in there being replaced by machinery, and thus to further rural depopulation.[63] The stance of *Le Moniteur* was little different. The paper described communist proposals as 'the ruin of social peace in the countryside'.[64] Similar to its policy towards Spanish republican refugees, the government responded to these concerns by encouraging the resettlement of East European migrants. It signed agreements with the new communist governments in Poland and Yugoslavia, which wanted more labour for their own reconstruction projects, to encourage the return of Poles and Yugoslavs from France to their home countries. Seventy thousand were repatriated through this process between 1946 and 1951.[65]

The PCF attitude towards them was as conflicted as that of its opponents. The communists generally rejected economic migration as liable to reduce pay for French workers, but they also actively courted immigrant communities; during the interwar period, its affiliated union the CGTU devoted 16 per cent of its budget to propaganda directed towards migrants.[66] They tried to square this circle by arguing they were anti-immigration but pro-immigrant, arguing that while employers used migrants as a 'reserve army of labour' this was not the fault of immigrants themselves.[67] They contended that by fighting for equal rights for immigrants in the workplace, they would actually reduce immigration since it would no longer be advantageous for employers if they could not pay migrants less.[68]

The anti-communist perception that the communists encouraged immigration to undermine France was therefore not reflected in the actual positions of the French Communist Party. Between 1944 and 1947, when the PCF was in government, controlling the Ministry of Labour, and through it the National Immigration Office (ONI), it favoured the planners' perspective that immigration was necessary for economic development.[69] After the PCF left (or rather, was expelled) from the cabinet in May 1947, it rapidly changed its stance, however. Between October 1948 and June 1961, all the official pronouncements of the Communist-aligned CGT trade union confederation on the topic were hostile to immigration.[70] This reflected the opinions of the party's working-class base, which predominantly regarded immigration as a way for employers to drive down wages. The aforementioned 1949 poll showed that the segments of the population most hostile to immigration were agricultural labourers (only 14 per cent positive towards immigration, 72 per cent negative), and industrial workers (19 per cent positive, 70 per cent negative): these were precisely the groups most likely to vote communist.[71] This was a change from the party's interwar position, which favoured open borders.[72] For example, when the French government signed an agreement with Italy to recruit Italian workers to come to France, the PCF and its Italian counterpart (the PCI) issued a joint declaration condemning the accord.[73] Both communist parties regarded the agreement as hostile to themselves: the PCF believed it was designed to undercut its members' wages while the PCI thought the Italian government hoped to use the emigration of 'surplus' Italian labour as a 'pressure release valve' for worker unrest in Italy.[74]

Anti-communists similarly attempted to organize migrants, despite their often-displayed hostility to them. For example, Jeanette Beaunez, an activist with the Catholic familial organization the Mouvement Populaire des familles (MPF), a social Catholic organization with an agenda of working-class liberation, spoke of her activities battling communist influence among immigrant communities in her municipality, the banlieue of Colombes.[75] 'PCF militants, who sensed betrayal in their fief and who described us as "populists" in their journal *La Voix Populaire*, did not make the task easy', Beaunez wrote.[76] Monsignor Alfred Ancel, one of the most prominent anti-communist pamphleteers in France, similarly worked to organize migrants in the Gerland neighbourhood of Lyon, a poor area populated first by Italians and later by Algerians.[77] More often than not, these approaches were met with failure as the PCF was well-entrenched in many migrant communities.[78]

Migrants twice over: The French diaspora in Russia

Besides refugees from communist East-Central Europe, another group fell into the category of 'good' migrants for French anti-communists: the returning French diaspora from Russia. This group had the supreme benefit, for French anti-communists, of both a direct experience of communism and being ethnically French. They thus had an influence out of proportion to their relatively small numbers. During the period of the Franco-Russian alliance (1894–1914), a significant number of French citizens moved to Russia for work, as part of the large-scale investment France made in its ally's economy. After the Revolution of 1917, most of them returned to France, but some did not, either by choice or because they were unable to escape the new communist state. The latter were only repatriated to France in 1946 after the good relations engendered by the Second World War enabled the Soviet and French governments to conclude a treaty governing their return.

One of these individuals was an industrial technician, Francisque Bornet. He was born in Lyon in 1887, but when he was five he moved to the Russian Empire with his father, who had obtained a post at Crédit Lyonnais' branch in Odessa. He went to school in Switzerland, but in 1909 he returned to Ukraine. He would end up remaining in the Russian Empire, and then the Soviet Union, until 3 November 1946.[79] He followed his father as a mining technician. After the Bolshevik seizure of power, he tried to flee back to the West but was arrested in the attempt. The Soviets compelled him to work as a manager and technician in various industrial enterprises along with other foreign experts who were unable to leave the USSR.[80] At first, foreign specialists like Bornet received privileged treatment from the Soviet state, but in the era of the great purges, in the later 1930s, these privileges were gradually withdrawn and his quality of life steadily deteriorated. He survived NKVD interrogation in 1938 but was imprisoned in various gulags in Siberia after 1941 as part of a general round-up of foreign experts that took place that year as a result of the German invasion.[81] There, like other inmates, he had to engage in forced labour before he was finally released in 1946 as part of the aforementioned treaty.[82]

He then returned to France and resolved to educate the French population on the horrors of communism. In his memoirs, he described the Soviet system of workers' participation as a façade: all decisions were actually made centrally, and marvellous feats of labour were the result of terror, not enthusiasm. He also analysed the totalitarian nature of the Soviet state, describing its restrictions on free expression and movement.[83]

In France, he linked up with the emerging political movement of the 'classes moyennes'. During this period, efforts were being made by activists to define a new 'middle-class' identity, distinct from the traditional notion of the bourgeoisie. This broad group was supposed to encompass artisans, small shopkeepers and the so-called 'new middle classes', middle managers and white-collar employees (called 'cadres' in French), especially in the emerging services economy. Activists like Roger Millot, a social Catholic engineer active in the Confédération générale des cadres, attempted to unite these disparate groups under the common umbrella of his own organization, the Comité national des classes moyennes (CNCM). Given that the members of this group had quite disparate economic positions and interests, the conception of the 'middle classes' that Millot and others (including Bornet) developed was a civilizational and cultural one, emphasizing their role as the defenders of Western civilisation against all enemies but especially Marxism. Bornet wrote for Millot and the CNCM's journal *Bon Sens* (common sense) about the dangers of communism. His personal experience of the Soviet system gave his descriptions of the way communism repressed the supposed innate independence and creativity of the middle classes a particular resonance for his middle-class French audience.[84]

The communists, however, had their own Bornet: Jules Cotte. Like Bornet, Cotte was an industrial technician who had moved to Russia before the First World War and lived in the USSR until 1946. Unlike Bornet, however, he enjoyed his participation in the construction of socialism, and when he returned to France he became an advocate for, rather than a critic of, the Soviet system.[85] The parallelism between communist and anti-communist reactions to migration is therefore further demonstrated by the fact that the communists transposed their own, pro-communist, 'expert' migrants against those of the anti-communists.

Conclusion

The nexus between anti-communism and migration in post-war France demonstrates the multiple relationships highlighted by the four-dimensional model proposed by Willems and Palacz. Diasporas and host societies impacted one another. The political conflict around communism both helped and hindered the integration of different migrant communities, as some were stigmatized as dangerous communist sympathizers, while others were welcomed as vanguards of anti-communism. Moreover, migrants themselves intervened in these debates, on both sides. Anti-communist refugees lent their support and 'expertise' to French anti-communist movements, while communist migrants backed the PCF. These activities were often driven by relations with the homeland. In particular, anti-communist refugees from communist countries sought to gain French support for political change in their lands of origin – while Spanish republican refugees sought the same from the opposite end of the political spectrum. Conversely, homeland governments worked with French authorities to influence the political perspectives of migrants. Finally, different diaspora communities interacted with one another. The very contrast between 'good' and 'bad' migrants so frequently drawn by French anti-communists probably assisted the acceptance of the former. Most migrants did not fall easily into either category, but these comparisons had a substantial impact on their lives as the French government adopted policies that favoured the groups that came out ahead in this comparison – for instance, by granting refugee status to East European political migrants – and disfavoured those who did not – for example, encouraging Spanish republican refugees to leave the country for Latin America.

Notes

1. Xavier Lannes, *L'immigration En France Depuis 1945* (La Haye: Martinus Nijhoff, 1953), 15–17.
2. Ibid., 60.
3. Ibid., 66.
4. Ibid., 42.
5. Ibid., 61.
6. Georges Photios Tapinos, *L'immigration Étrangère En France, 1946–1973* (Paris: Presses Universitaires de France, 1975), 40.
7. Ibid.
8. In line with Bloomsbury's stylistic guidelines, this chapter will use the lower-case 'communist' to refer to the ideology and its adherents, but the upper-case 'Communist' to refer to the institutional political party and its members.
9. Katherine O'Flaherty, 'Seeking the "Mother of Exiles": A Cultural and Political History of American Refugee Policy in the Twentieth Century' (PhD diss., University of Maine, 2010), 5 and 25–6.
10. Didier Fassin, 'Compassion and Repression: The Moral Economy of Immigration Policies in France', *Cultural Anthropology* 20, no. 3 (2005): 362–87.
11. Jeanne Moret, *Le père Lhande, pionnier du Christ dans la banlieue et à la radio* (Paris: Beauchesne, 1964).
12. Pierre Lhande, *Le Christ dans la banlieue* (Paris: Plon, 1927); Pierre Lhande, *Le Dieu qui bouge* (Paris: Plon, 1930); Pierre Lhande, *La croix sur les fortifs* (Paris: Plon, 1931).
13. Lhande, *Le Christ dans la banlieue*, 34.
14. Ibid., 21.
15. Ibid., 34.
16. S. de Lestapis, *Au dela du marxisme et l'organisation des familles* (Paris: Éditions Spes, 1946), 25.
17. Pierre-Marie Thibault, 'Peut-on rejeuner la population française?', *Familles Morbihannaises* no. 10, May 1946, 2.
18. Laurent Joly, *Naissance de l'Action Française* (Paris: Grasset, 2015); Patrick Weil and Nicolas Truong, *Le sens de la République* (Paris: Grasset, 2015); Gérard Noirel, *Le venin dans la plume: Édouard Drumont, Éric Zemmour et la part sombre de la République* (Paris: La Découverte, 2019). Similar demographic fears concerning Jewish migrants were present in other European countries in the same time period, for example in Germany – see Jack Wertheimer, *Unwelcome Strangers: East European Jews in Imperial Germany* (New York and Oxford: Oxford University Press, 1987) – or in the Vienna of Karl Lueger – see Peter G. J. Pulzer, *The Rise of Political Anti-Semitism in Germany and Austria* (New York: John Wiley & Sons, 1964); John W. Boyer, 'Karl Lueger and the Viennese Jews', *The Leo Baeck Institute Year Book* 26, no. 1 (1981):

125-41; Robert Wistrich, 'Karl Lueger and the Ambiguities of Viennese Antisemitism', *Jewish Social Studies* 45, no. 3/4 (1983): 251-62.
19 Vicki Caron, 'Prelude to Vichy: France and the Jewish Refugees in the Era of Appeasement', *Journal of Contemporary History* 20, no. 1 (1985): 157.
20 Michael Marrus and Robert O. Paxton, *Vichy France and the Jews* (New York: Basic Books, 1981), 363-5.
21 Jean Delcroix, 'Les Français du Parti communiste dit français', *La Terre Nouvelle* 37 (22 February 1950), 1.
22 Scott Soo, *The Routes to Exile: France and the Spanish Civil War Refugees, 1939-2009* (Manchester: Manchester University Press), 33. See also David Messenger's contribution in this volume.
23 Soo, *The Routes to Exile*, 38.
24 Ibid., 39.
25 Quoted in Ralph Schor, *L'opinion française et les étrangers en France, 1919-1939* (Paris: Publication de la Sorbonne, 1985), 676.
26 Quoted in Marie-Claude Rafaneau-Boj, *Odyssée pour la liberté: Les camps de prisonniers espagnols, 1939-1945* (Paris: Denoël, 1993), 40.
27 Soo, *The Routes to Exile*, 58.
28 Ibid., 83.
29 Ibid.
30 Louis Stein, *Beyond Death and Exile: The Spanish Republicans in France, 1939-1955* (Cambrdige, MA: Harvard University Press, 2013), 182-6.
31 Lannes, *L'immigration En France Depuis 1945*, 63-4.
32 Pierre Sérandour, 'Dire toute la verité', *Le Moniteur du Progrès agricole et viticole* 128 (24 September 1950): 1.
33 L. Kiciorgros, 'En Roumanie, le communisme a commencé par défendre la propriété', *Le Moniteur du Progrès agricole et viticole* 117 (28 May 1950): 2.
34 L. Kiciorgos, 'L'Exploitation agricole communiste: Premiers résultats en roumanie', *Le Moniteur du Progrès agricole et viticole* 118 (4 June 1950): 2.
35 Antoine Marès, 'Exilés d'Europe Centrale de 1945 à 1967', in *Le Paris des étrangers depuis 1945*, ed. Antoine Marès and Pierre Milza (Paris: Éditions de la Sorbonne, 1995), 132.
36 Ibid., 133.
37 Ibid., 137.
38 Ibid., 138.
39 Guillaume Malaurie, *L'affaire Kravchenko* (Paris: R. Laffont, 1982).
40 Tony Judt, *Past Imperfect: French Intellectuals, 1944-1956* (Berkeley and Oxford: University of California Press, 1992).
41 Tapinos, *L'immigration Étrangère En France*, 42-3.
42 Quoted in Marès, 'Exilés d'Europe Centrale de 1945 à 1967', 134.
43 Michel Pigenet, *Au Coeur de l'Activisme Communiste des Années de Guerre Froide: 'La manifestation Ridgway'* (Paris: Éditions L'Harmattan, 1992).
44 Marès, 'Exilés d'Europe Centrale de 1945 à 1967', 129.
45 Ibid., 130.
46 Gary S. Cross, *Immigrant Workers in Industrial France: The Making of a New Laboring Class* (Philadelphia: Temple University Press, 1983), 3.
47 Ibid., 18.
48 Marès, 'Exilés d'Europe Centrale de 1945 à 1967'.
49 Tapinos, *L'immigration Étrangère En France*, 8.

50 Cross, *Immigrant Workers in Industrial France*, 88.
51 Quoted in ibid., 88.
52 Ibid., 171.
53 Ibid., 90–1.
54 Quoted in ibid., 93–4.
55 John Bulaitis, *Communism in Rural France: French Agricultural Workers and the Popular Front* (London: I.B. Tauris, 2008), 148.
56 Ibid.
57 Cross, *Immigrant Workers in Industrial France*, 73.
58 Ibid., 74.
59 Ibid., 80.
60 Ibid.
61 Ibid., 80–1.
62 L. Prault, 'La fédération communiste des travailleurs agricoles considère les exploitants comme des "ennemis"', *La Terre Nouvelle* 45 (15 April 1950): 1–2.
63 'Sur 848.000 salariés agricoles 285.000 seulement seraient assujettis à la loi de 40 heures proposée par les communistes', *La Terre Nouvelle* 77 (2 December 1950): 1.
64 'Veut-on faire le jeu des communistes ?', *Le Moniteur du Progrès agricole et viticole* 149 (24 February 1951): 1 and 3.
65 Lannes, *L'immigration En France Depuis 1945*, 62.
66 Cross, *Immigrant Workers in Industrial France*, 171.
67 Freeman, *Immigrant Labor and Racial Conflict in Industrial Societies*, 231.
68 Ibid., 234.
69 Gary P. Freeman, *Immigrant Labor and Racial Conflict in Industrial Societies: The French and British Experience, 1945–1975* (Princeton: Princeton University Press, 1979), 228.
70 Ibid., 229.
71 Tapinos, *L'immigration Étrangère En France*, 42.
72 Leah Haus, 'Labor Unions and Immigration Policy in France', *The International Migration Review* 33, no. 3 (1999): 693.
73 Lannes, *L'immigration En France Depuis 1945*, 49–51.
74 Freeman, *Immigrant Labor and Racial Conflict in Industrial Societies*, 246–7.
75 Geneviève Dermenjian, *Femmes, famille et action ouvrière: pratiques et responsabilités féminines dans les mouvements familiaux populaires, 1935–1958* (Villeneuve-d'Ascq: GRMF, 1991), 71.
76 Ibid., 73.
77 Olivier de Berranger, *Alfred Ancel: 1898–1984: un homme pour l'Évangile* (Paris: Le Centurion, 1988), 183.
78 Joseph Jacquet and Alfred Ancel, *Un Militant ouvrier dialogue avec un évêque* (Paris: Éditions ouvrières Éditions sociales [diffusion] Messidor, 1982), 16.
79 Francisque Bornet, *Je reviens de Russie* (Paris: Plon, 1947), 1–3.
80 Ibid., 14–15.
81 Ibid., 43, 51 and 96–8.
82 Ibid., 178–80.
83 Ibid., 57–65.
84 Francisque Bornet, 'Une critique et un témoignage sur la bureaucratie Soviétique', *Informations industrielles et commerciales* 112 (13 June 1947): 1.
85 Jules Cotte, *Un ingénieur français en U.R.S.S.* (Paris: Calmann-Lévy, 1946).

Conclusion

Polish refugees and East Prussian expellees: Applying the four-dimensional model

Bastiaan Willems and Michał Adam Palacz

Introduction

The wars and political upheavals of the first half of the twentieth century triggered multiple intertwined refugee movements that displaced millions of people across and beyond Europe. These movements are often examined and discussed in isolation from each other, reflecting the national narratives of historical uniqueness which centre on the familiar themes of victimhood and integration. The final chapter of this volume elucidates how a transnational framework can be used to tie the lived experience of individual refugee groups into a broader narrative of forced migration as a phenomenon independent of national histories. The preceding chapters presented new empirical findings on understudied aspects of forced migration in the era of the two world wars and have engaged with one or more dimensions of the conceptual model of diaspora that was proposed in the introduction to this volume. The concluding chapter uses the model itself as a point of departure and demonstrates how to engage with all four dimensions of the diasporic relationship, based on the case studies of Polish wartime refugees in Britain and East Prussian expellees in post-war Germany. As such, it proposes a new way of looking at two diasporic communities whose experiences are well known in the literature but have mostly been analysed from either 'host society' or 'homeland' perspective. This chapter shows how to reinterpret such cases using our model and thus integrates them within a common transnational framework. The historiographies of both these 'neighbouring' Eastern European diasporas have largely been shaped by collective memories of victimhood and resilience on the part of forced migrants and their descendants, and politically charged narratives of 'assimilation' espoused by host societies. Looking at Polish refugees and East Prussian expellees through the lens of a four-dimensional relationship with the host society, homeland, own diaspora and other migrant communities demonstrates that there is a significant added value to be found in approaching refugee movements in twentieth-century Europe not as individual cases of national victimhood and integration, but as de-homogenized experiences which taken together offer new perspectives on the developments that spurred European history.[1] What follows is therefore a schematic overview of these two case studies. They are not meant to be exhaustive analyses of themes, such as flight, expulsion, discrimination and integration, but rather show how the four-dimensional model of diaspora can be applied by historians of forced migration in the first half of the twentieth century.

Polish refugees in Great Britain

Background

Around 300,000 Polish soldiers and civilian refugees arrived in Britain during or immediately after the Second World War. The Polish wartime diaspora in Britain was a heterogenous community (with Jews and Ukrainians being the largest minorities), formed by several associative cohorts with a common geographical route, form of displacement, time of departure from Poland, time of arrival in Britain and shared wartime experiences.

The first large group of Polish refugees arrived in Britain after the fall of France in the summer of 1940. This cohort contained both soldiers and civilians, including many prominent politicians, academics and other members of the pre-war elite who escaped from Poland to continue in exile their struggle against Nazi Germany. There was also a sizeable group of Polish Jews who already before the war emigrated to Western Europe, largely due to anti-Semitic discrimination and violence in interwar Poland. Smaller groups of Polish citizens arrived in Britain from France via the prolonged and more dangerous route across the Iberian Peninsula or managed to escape from occupied Poland via the Baltic countries and Scandinavia.[2] The largest number of Polish refugees, however, arrived in Britain with the so-called Anders' Army. Following the German invasion of the USSR, Stalin allowed General Władysław Anders to recruit an army from Polish prisoners of war (POWs) as well as civilians who had been deported from pre-war Poland's eastern borderlands into forced labour camps and penal settlements in Arctic Russia, Siberia and Soviet Central Asia. More than 100,000 Polish soldiers, including several thousand Polish Jews, were evacuated to the Middle East in 1942. The Anders' Army took part in fighting on the Italian front and was transferred to Britain in 1946.[3]

Unlike other cohorts which were dominated by adult males, a characteristic feature of the refugees from the Soviet Union was the relatively large number of women and children. This was a consequence of General Anders' attempt to improve the living conditions of Polish deportees in the USSR by drafting women into the military and sending children to military orphanages and schools.[4] After the war, civilian dependants of the Anders' Army were transferred to Britain from temporary camps in India, East Africa and the Middle East.[5]

The Polish Armed Forces in the West also recruited Polish deserters from the *Wehrmacht* and the Organisation Todt. They were mostly ethnic Poles from pre-war Poland's western borderlands, who were administratively classified by the Nazis as German nationals eligible for conscription and who were either captured or willfully surrendered to the Allies, and were subsequently transferred to Britain.[6] Another group of displaced persons from pre-war Poland arrived from occupied Germany after 1945. This cohort included Polish POWs and concentration camp inmates who were liberated by British and American troops as well as former forced labourers, including both ethnic Poles and Polish Ukrainians, who were brought to Britain within the framework of the European Volunteer Workers scheme.[7]

Only a third of the refugees returned to communist-dominated Poland after the end of the war, while the rest permanently settled in Britain or re-emigrated to other countries. Around 160,000 Polish nationals lived in Britain in 1950, mostly in London, in the industrial North of England, in Flintshire and Glamorgan in Wales, and in Edinburgh and Glasgow in Scotland. The Poles became the first large immigrant community in post-war Britain.[8]

Host society

There was relatively little contact between Polish and British people in the interwar period. France was Poland's major political and military ally, and educated Poles were usually fluent in French but could rarely speak English.[9] One of the Polish refugees, a medical student, admitted in his diary that before the war Great Britain seemed to him as exotic as Ivory Coast![10] An average Briton's attitude towards Poland was likely similar when thousands of Polish soldiers arrived in the summer of 1940.[11] However, unlike refugees from Nazi Germany and fascist Italy who were interned in Britain as 'enemy aliens', the Poles were generally met with sympathy as wartime allies. The Polish government-in-exile relocated from Paris to London and reorganized its troops under British operational command. Despite wartime restrictions of civil liberties, numerous Polish political, social and cultural organizations were allowed to flourish in Britain.

The magnanimous reception of Polish refugees was largely predicated on the expectation that these brothers-in-arms would return home after Allied victory over Nazi Germany. Post-war reality made this impossible or undesirable for thousands of Poles, especially those who came from territories annexed by the Soviet Union as well as Polish Jews who often lost their entire families in the Holocaust. The Labour government responded to this situation with a long-term plan to resettle 150,000 Polish ex-servicemen and their families who remained in Britain. This scheme was the first large-scale official plan to integrate an ethnic minority in British history. The collective arrangement of employment and housing, orchestrated through the Polish Resettlement Act of 1947, prevented economic conflicts between Polish refugees and British workers.[12]

Regardless of government policies, many Britons remained sympathetic to the Poles because of the remarkable contributions made by Polish soldiers to the Allied cause. What is more, due to the predominance of men among the wartime diaspora (males made up 75 per cent of the refugees),[13] marriages between Polish men and British women became commonplace in post-war Britain and facilitated the integration of the newcomers. The Poles nevertheless encountered widespread hostility until the 1960s. Anti-Polish sentiments were strongest in Scotland, where the majority of Polish soldiers had been stationed during and immediately after the war.[14] Many refugees experienced difficulties in finding suitable employment and housing in post-war Britain, and were therefore forced to develop their own strategies to avoid discrimination and prejudice. Most of them applied for British citizenship and some even Anglicized or completely changed their distinctively foreign names. One Polish doctor's job applications were rejected forty times before he changed his surname from the unpronounceable Chrząszcz to a more familiar Chauncey.[15] Another strategy adopted by Polish refugees in order to escape fierce competition and xenophobic sentiments in post-war Britain was to join the colonial service in Africa, Asia or the Caribbean. Many disenchanted refugees eventually left Britain for good and re-emigrated to more promising destinations, such as the United States, Canada, Australia or New Zealand. In the long run, however, the integration of Polish refugees was hindered not only by instances of discrimination and prejudice but also by the desire of many Poles to preserve their national identity, as they believed that Polish culture was threatened in the homeland by Soviet domination.[16]

Homeland

A self-imposed mission to preserve national culture abroad was characteristic for the Polish wartime diaspora in Britain. Apart from collective efforts to restore Polish independence through military service in the Polish Armed Forces in the West, individual refugees contributed to the national cause in a variety of ways. Professional and personal contacts with the host society were used as an opportunity to disseminate news from occupied Poland, including information about German and Soviet atrocities. Poles who found a safe haven in Britain supported their less fortunate compatriots with material and financial means. These donations were distributed via the Polish Red Cross in London, for example, to Polish POWs in Germany and the Soviet Union.[17] Difficult decisions on whether to remain in Britain after the war were determined by multiple factors, but many refugees motivated the refusal to return home with opposition to the Soviet domination of Poland. Although the Polish government in London was diplomatically de-recognized by Britain in 1945, it continued to operate until the fall of communism in 1990. A number of Polish political parties remained active in post-war Britain and elections to a parliament-in-exile were held in 1954. Many Poles who remained loyal to the government-in-exile became stateless. They avoided any contacts with communist Poland and some of them would even go as far as to regard applying for British citizenship as a form of national treason.[18]

While exile politics largely lost relevance in the mid-1950s, it was the network of autonomous Roman Catholic parishes and Saturday schools that played an especially important role in preserving Polish identity in post-war Britain. Polish Catholic refugees used religious narratives, rituals and artefacts to fulfil their spiritual needs and to symbolically connect with their lost homeland.[19] At the same time, however, the amalgamation of Polish national identity with Roman Catholicism, together with instances of anti-Semitism among Polish refugees, led to the further alienation of Jews from the Polish diaspora in Britain.[20] While the Yiddish-speaking, working-class refugees were rather quickly integrated into local Jewish communities of East European origins, for example, in the East End of London, the Polish-speaking, middle-class Jews maintained a separate identity and generally distanced themselves both from Catholic Poles and British Jews.[21]

Diaspora

The origins of the global Polish diaspora can be traced back to the late eighteenth and early nineteenth centuries, when, following the failure of national uprisings against foreign domination, Polish exiles sought refuge in Western Europe and North America. The Poles who settled in Britain between the 1830s and the 1860s were numerically small (around 1,000 men) but constituted the most radical section of the so-called 'Great Emigration' – the political, military and intellectual elite who in the nineteenth century consciously chose exile in order to preserve in independence the political and cultural values of the Polish nation.[22] Following this historical model, the Polish wartime diaspora was imagined as a continuation of the Second Polish Republic (1918–39). In fact, the Polish government-in-exile set up a global network of educational and welfare institutions for the benefit of its displaced citizens. This remarkable network was partially preserved in Britain after 1945 in order to facilitate the resettlement of Polish refugees. The spatial distribution of Polish communities and the emergence of residential 'ghettoes' in many British towns were, in turn, determined by the Labour government's policy of allocating demobilized Polish soldiers and displaced persons to specific sectors of the post-war economy, for example, mining and agriculture, and by its decision to initially house them in special camps and hostels, some of which survived until the 1960s.[23]

Notwithstanding their gradual integration with the host society, many Poles in Britain continued to live in a parallel universe of Polish parishes, ex-servicemen's clubs, political parties, social and cultural centres as well as schools and hospitals. Diasporic ties with friends and relatives in the Middle East or North America were, moreover, as important to them as day-to-day contacts with British neighbours and long-distance relationships with families back in Poland. Although generally invisible to the British public, formal and informal Polish networks facilitated the settling down of refugees who struggled to resume personal lives and professional careers in a culturally alien environment. For instance, the Polish Medical Association, established in 1944 in London and still existing today, successfully lobbied the British government for the right of Polish refugee physicians to permanently register as medical practitioners in Britain.[24]

On the one hand, many refugees, especially those who came from ethnic minority backgrounds or who married non-Polish spouses, were rarely involved with Polish diasporic institutions and often maintained only sporadic contacts with fellow Poles. On the other hand, a sense of belonging to the global Polish diaspora motivated many parents to pass down to their children the knowledge of Polish language and a hybrid Polish-British cultural identity. British Poles achieved a high degree of upward social mobility in the second and third generations. In the 1980s they supported the Solidarity movement and raised funds, food, clothing and medicines for their economically depressed 'homeland'.²⁵ The Polish community in Britain has been rejuvenated by the arrival of at least 800,000 Polish immigrants since Poland's accession to the European Union in 2004. Despite reported conflicts with the wartime diaspora, the newcomers inherited a well-preserved network of Polish organizations and numerous historical role models of how to successfully combine cultural pluralism with socio-economic integration.

Other diasporas

Polish refugees arrived in Britain as part of a larger movement of European people displaced by fascism and communism. During the Second World War, Poles in Britain established especially close contacts with refugees from other Slavic countries, such as Czechoslovakia and Yugoslavia.²⁶ After 1945 Poles became the largest group of East European political exiles in Britain. Cooperation between refugees emerged in the context of the Cold War. Polish émigré scholars founded in 1950 the Central European Society of Professors and Lecturers which grouped academic refugees from different communist countries, mostly Poles and Hungarians. The Society established a Central European School in London, where courses on the history, economy and contemporary politics of the region were taught in the English language.²⁷

In the early post-war years many demobilized Polish soldiers found employment as unskilled workers in agriculture and industry. The Poles often worked alongside other displaced persons from continental Europe, mostly Ukrainians, Latvians, Yugoslavs and Germans, who were recruited by the British government as part of the European Volunteer Workers scheme to cover labour shortages in key sectors of the economy.²⁸ Polish refugees might have shared with their co-workers the opposition towards communist domination of their respective homelands, but conflicts occasionally arose, as the Poles were biased against displaced persons from those nations that were collectively accused of collaborating with the Nazis.

The improvement in the socio-economic status of Polish refugees coincided with the arrival of the so-called Commonwealth immigrants in post-war Britain. In the North of England, for example, textile factory jobs left in the 1960s by upwardly mobile Poles were filled in by new arrivals from Pakistan.²⁹ The relationship between the Polish community and the South Asian, African and Caribbean diasporas has not been adequately studied from a historical perspective, but it has been suggested that the acceptance of Polish refugees by the host society was inadvertently hastened by the growing preoccupation with race.³⁰ Xenophobic prejudice towards 'white' Poles might have been overshadowed in the 1960s and 1970s by racist attitudes towards Commonwealth immigrants.

East Prussian expellees in post-war Germany

Background

In the summer of 1944 the Red Army reached the borders of East Prussia, Germany's easternmost province. In the months that followed the majority of its inhabitants would flee westwards, hoping to stay ahead of the Soviet troops. By the time most of these people left their homes, the Allied powers had already made far-reaching plans to divide East Prussia between Poland, Russia and Lithuania, which, as Winston Churchill stated in a speech to the British House of Commons on 15 December 1944, included the mass transfer of its German population – a measure which served 'to prevent war-breeding problems' in the future.[31] Behind political statements such as these lay the grim realities of flight and forced expulsion, which caused the deaths of tens of thousands of East Prussians.

Host society

To those refugees who commenced their flight prior to May 1945, their destination was the heartlands of the Greater German *Reich*, but this would not be the society that would come to host them. After its defeat, 'Germany' underwent a complete transformation: the areas east of the rivers Oder and Neisse were handed to Poland, Austria regained its independence and what remained of Germany was divided into two parts, East and West, which in 1949 would become the Federal Republic of Germany (FRG) and the German Democratic Republic (GDR), respectively.[32] In West Germany, they found themselves labelled as 'Easterners' or even as 'Polacks' – language which until very recently they had employed themselves to discriminate their neighbours.[33] The use of this language towards them was not a new phenomenon: between the unification of Germany in 1871 and the beginning of the Second World War close to a million East Prussians had left their province for the mines of the Ruhr and had been subject to similar prejudices.[34] After the war the discrimination these refugees faced was more concrete and became openly antagonistic. Those westerners whose houses had survived the Allied bombing campaigns were forced to share their homes with them, which often led to outright hostility. At the same time, the large presence of women among this group meant that they were also blamed for the spread of STDs and the increase of divorces. Many refugees suffered a loss of status: some former self-employed landowners had to accept jobs as farmhands, while educated East Prussians were often simply placed in the countryside. These people had few friends or acquaintances to turn to: since authorities feared that keeping intact the old community structures would hamper their integration, refugees hailing from the same area were often deliberately separated and spread out over different towns and villages.[35]

In East Germany, meanwhile, East Prussians' experiences were not only shaped by structural hardships, but also by the identity politics of the new communist regime. Since devoting attention to their flight and expulsion would negatively impact the relation between East Germany and other communist states (primarily Poland and the Soviet Union), their plight was silenced. They were to consider themselves part of a group of over 4 million 'new citizens' (*Neubürgern*) – the euphemistic term used for German refugees hailing from the areas east of the rivers Oder and Neisse. Adding insult to injury, from July 1950 onwards (following the Treaty of Görlitz) these rivers were officially inaugurated as the 'border of peace' between the GDR and Poland.[36]

Despite their 'invisibility', the refugees' circumstances would nevertheless leave their mark on domestic policy and put tremendous pressure on the new state. 'New citizens' made up about a quarter of the population of East Germany, but since this group mainly consisted of women and children, they initially required 43 per cent of the country's total welfare support. Meanwhile, the regime implemented land reform measures, which were to serve as a double-edged sword: not only would these measures dismantle the estates of the former landed nobility (the *Junkers*), but in an effort to integrate the 'new citizens', who traditionally came from a rural background, many of the resulting smaller plots were allocated to them. This inevitably created friction as the country's traditional inhabitants felt that the 'new citizens' disproportionately profited from the new GDR dictatorship at the expense of long-established community structures. Similarly, since the communist authorities had been fairly thorough in the denazification of local administrations, positions opened up that were filled by expellees, prompting a fear that these new officials would challenge the existing social make-up.[37] In the shadow of a lost war, the two host societies were unable and often unwilling to accommodate their 'fellow Germans'. To many refugees, the new Germany was an alien and unforgiving place, and in some cases the challenges to integrate appeared so insurmountable that they made the decision to abandon their homeland altogether and travel further. Revealingly, United States migration statistics from 1956 show that refugees and expellees from the former eastern German provinces comprised 37 per cent of the migrants arriving from the FRG, even though they only made up 17.5 per cent of its population.[38] The vast majority of East Prussians (and other expellee groups) would nevertheless permanently settle down in the FRG and the GDR, although many of them would continue to cherish the hope that they would one day be able to return to their homeland.

Homeland

East Prussian expellee groups, when discussing their province, adhere to a strict victim narrative. This story devotes sustained attention to their own lived experience of 'flight and expulsion' (a common set phrase: 'Flucht und Vertreibung'), which started in 1944, as the Red Army approached their province.[39] The members of the East Prussian diaspora draw attention to historic parallels and tend to promote the idea that their province has always been an embattled vanguard of Germany that had to stand up to the westward encroachment of the 'Slavs'.[40] This 'struggle' is widely seen as being as old as the German colonization of the province itself: a narrative that had been pushed with fervour from the late nineteenth century onwards, and which reached its peak in the interwar period, during which the members of the diaspora grew up.[41] East Prussia's Nazi *Gauleiter*, Erich Koch, summarized this stance in 1937 by writing in a guide about the province that 'The history of East Prussia is one of struggle. Struggle shaped the East Prussian people, it created their spiritual attitude.'[42] When a decade earlier, in the early 1920s, a monument was put up to commemorate the 1914 victory at Tannenberg (in the east of the province), its shape was deliberately reminiscent of a Medieval castle.[43] In the 1950s and 1960s, the first decades after their flight and expulsion, East Prussians stuck to this narrative and framed their homeland as an embattled vanguard for western values, as such seeking to dissuade policy makers from considering their province as 'a colonial area on the edge of the European cultural landscape' but rather the easternmost part of the western occident, the *Abendland*, which could not be abandoned to Slavdom.[44] In line with this, East Prussian expellees directed attention to the more 'timeless' characteristics of their province, such as its agriculture, its tradition of cattle breeding, and its 'dark forests and crystal lakes'.[45] The emphasis on these 'banal nationalist'[46] symbols served a dual purpose: not only did they convey a sense of guardianship but they also served as a 'way in' to criticize the area's new inhabitants – Russian and Polish settlers – who supposedly did not know how to appreciate and cultivate what their lands had to offer. Members of the East Prussian diaspora successfully perpetuated these sentimental notions of their province, ensuring that the idea of the area as traditionally German is still one that resonates well, both domestically and abroad.[47]

Diaspora

Central in the representation of their province (and by extension that of themselves) is the diaspora itself. Rather than explaining their departure from East Prussia – be it flight, evacuation or expulsion – as a result of their role in the previous years of National Socialist rule, they instead highlighted their traumatic plight as a way to move conversations away from questions of complicity during the Third Reich. East Prussia's former inhabitants 'close ranks', as it were, and do not wish to discuss the Nazi era, which means that, as the author Alison Owings observed when she interviewed an East Prussian woman, she 'simply was not forthcoming about the first eleven and a half years of the Third Reich. Then the chronology got to the point when Soviet troops were moving forward to [her former hometown] Tolnicken. And [she] became a different witness.'[48] By consistently referring to their province as a 'peaceful island' where during the war the 'plight of the times' could be forgotten,[49] they present their victimhood as unprovoked and disproportionate.

East Prussian expellees carefully guard the narrative of their flight. Sustained attention is paid to their flight over the *Frische Haff* (Vistula Lagoon) and *Frische Nehrung* (Vistula Spit), and the sinking of the liners *Steuben*, *Goya* and *Wilhelm Gustloff* and other ships during the maritime evacuation of their province. *Grossadmiral* Karl Dönitz, who after the war claimed that his *Kriegsmarine* (Navy) organized mass evacuation efforts, has been put on a pedestal – even though little evidence suggests that during these final months of the war the evacuation of refugees was of any priority to the Navy High Command.[50] The Nobel laureate Günter Grass noticed in preparation to the novel *Im Krebsgang*, which tells the story of the sinking of the liner *Wilhelm Gustloff* (with a death toll placed at between 6,000 and 9,000 deaths – the largest naval disaster in history), that diverting from the official line invites heavy criticism from expellees. He saw how even Heinz Schön, who almost single-handedly brought the topic of the sinking of the liner *Wilhelm Gustloff* to the public attention, was met with considerable hostility when he showed understanding for the Soviet perspective which, since the *Wilhelm Gustloff* served as a troop transport, did not consider its sinking a war crime.[51] Rather than critically examining the era, its actors or its broader context, East Prussian expellees lay the blame almost exclusively on a select number of Nazis, most noteworthy Erich Koch, who they feel prevented evacuation.[52] This also means that little attention is drawn to the acts of genocide that happened during 1944-45. Even though tens of thousands of refugees passed (the fully operational) Stutthof concentration camp on their way from Königsberg to Danzig – many were even accommodated in former inmate barracks – the camp remains absent in refugees' memoirs.[53] Similarly, when in 1994 Martin Bergau published his memoirs, in which he described how as a Hitler Youth he had been ordered to assist in the execution of 3,000 Jews in January 1945 near the coastal town of Palmnicken, he was promptly deemed a *Nestbeschmutzer* (nest polluter), with the expellee newspaper *Das Ostpreußenblatt* printing a review that considered '[h]is efforts to fit his little life into the great historical processes [to be] disturbing'.[54]

Other diasporas

In the early post-war years, the members of the East Prussian diaspora pursued one main goal: the re-establishment of Germany's 1937 borders, which would allow most of them to return home. It was a desire that they shared with every other expellee group in Germany, and both in East and West Germany these groups hoped to get the issue on the political agenda. In East Germany proponents of the idea (among them even Wilhelm Pieck, the first President of the GDR) were quickly forced to abandon this position, since raising the issue was deemed to be perpetuating ideas of the previous German regimes. In May 1946, for example, Polish deputy prime minister Stanisław Mikołajczyk 'warned' his compatriots that 'we know the Germans and know that they're always the same. . . . One day it may turn out that the German communists also use their influence to try to revive German imperialism, which threatens Poland'.[55] Meanwhile, in West Germany, the Allied military authorities feared that when the expellees' ideas would gain traction it could lead to social and political unrest, which in 1946 led to a ban of refugee and expellee organizations, known as the '*Koalitionsverbot*'.[56] Refugee groups nevertheless kept pushing for what they considered their *Heimatrecht* ('right to one's homeland'), which they connected to the Wilsonian 'right of self-determination' – effectively arguing that they not only wanted to return to their homes, but that these homes ought to be German land where they would not be subject to foreign rule.[57] The geopolitical situation offered no real room for these ideas, but when in 1949 the first free elections were held in the FRG these demands could not be ignored. Counting 12 million in number, the expellees represented a massive voting bloc, which all major political parties courted by promising to guarantee Germany's old borders – even though most politicians were aware that there was little room to act on these promises.[58]

How limited the international leeway was became clear in the debates surrounding the post-war refugee crisis. The 1951 United Nations Convention Relating to the Status of Refugees restricted the definition of the refugee to those who were unable or unwilling to return to their country of nationality.[59] The Convention deliberately used 'country of nationality' rather than 'home country' to exclude German expellees who were thus considered to still be in the country of their nationality, that is, Germany.[60] On the other hand, the predicament of the expellees was acknowledged in West Germany through the 1949 establishment of the Federal Ministry for Displaced Persons, Refugees and War Victims (*Bundesministerium für Vertriebene, Flüchtlinge und Kriegsgeschädigte*), and followed by legislation that sought to recompense refugees for their lost properties, and which regulated the refugees' legal situation.[61] Facing competition from other German victim groups, such as bombed-out urban populations, the expellee groups understood that in order to have their plight acknowledged they would have to form a united front, leading to the 1957 establishment of the League of the Expellees (*Bund der Vertriebenen*).[62] Although the rural Protestant inhabitants of East Prussia had little in common with the predominantly industrial 'red' Silesians, and even less with Germans hailing from the Romanian Banat or from the Sudetenland, combined they formed a powerful lobby that actively opposed rapprochement with those (communist) states that controlled former German territory. This hard-line stance impacted Germany's foreign policy until the late 1960s but eventually ensured that after the first thaws of the Cold War had set in under Chancellor Willy Brandt the League of the Expellees, and smaller expellee organizations like it, lost in importance.[63]

After the fall of communism, and especially after 1992, many former inhabitants of East Prussia took the opportunity to visit their places of birth, such as the Kaliningrad *Oblast*, which from 1945 onwards had been under Russian rule. However, this seldom translated into an understanding of the 'new' inhabitants, most of whom had themselves been forced to leave their homes in Russia and resettle the area in the decade following the war.[64] More recently, the different German expellee groups co-opted World Refugee Day (20 June), which the United Nations established in 2001, convincing the German Federal Government in 2015 – at the time of the largest refugee crisis since the war – to rebrand it a 'Remembrance day for the victims of flight and expulsion' (*Gedenktag für die Opfer von Flucht und Vertreibung*), which 'commemorates victims of flight and expulsion and in particular the German expellees'.[65] In the last decade, a vocal section of the East Prussian diaspora, including its older generation, has found its way to social networks, such as Facebook, where they created somewhat of a 'digital *Heimat*' for themselves. Part and parcel of these platforms, unfortunately, is the use of polarizing and often aggressive language, which in the case of East Prussians is directed at current-day refugee groups that in their opinion do not deserve the sympathy and welcome they feel they were denied.

Conclusion

Both the Polish and the East Prussian examples introduce us to the depth of tragedy that was experienced by these two diasporic groups, but, more importantly, by briefly outlining these two cases we can identify common themes within forced migration in Europe in the period of the two world wars. The two case studies are open-ended and do not follow a spatial-temporal structure, that is, 'from homeland to host society', as this seemingly logical order would perpetuate an incorrect narrative suggesting that, with time and exposure to the host society, the refugees' symbolic and material ties to the homeland diminish. The added value of considering these two forced migrations through the lens of the four-dimensional model of diaspora is that it helps to flesh out how the collective experiences of displacement shaped later behavioural patterns of the two groups and the ways in which these are related to each other. How close the two neighbouring diasporas are entwined, and the virtue of not treating them as separate cases but as part of a single larger history of forced migration out of Eastern Europe, is well illustrated by a diary entry of the Nazi propaganda minister Joseph Goebbels, dated 25 January 1945:

> The English authoritative newspapers are constantly trying to present our situation in the East more favourably than it is in reality. . . . One can easily imagine the fear that prevails in London today, especially since Stalin has just broadcasted that in the case of Königsberg's fall Field Marshal Paulus and General Seydlitz intend to set up a Free German government in the city, which would plead for a separate peace. If that were the case, it would be a repetition of the Polish example [the Lublin Government] for London and Washington, which of course would be sensational. With his broadcast, Stalin announces his intention to completely ignore the British and the Americans, at least regarding those parts of the *Reich* which he intends to conquer.[66]

The East Prussians and the Poles had had a troubled relationship for centuries, as they both laid claim to some of the same contested territories in their border regions, but after 1945 the westward advance of the Soviet Union and the fear of living under a communist regime made their displacement a common fate. Despite a shared hope of returning to their Eastern European homelands, for the majority of Polish refugees and East Prussian expellees this displacement became permanent. Many of them have nevertheless passed on a deeply felt attachment to the East Prussian *Heimat* or the Polish *ojczyzna* (fatherland) to the second or even third generations of the diaspora.

The comparative case study of Polish wartime refugees in Britain and East Prussian expellees in post-war Germany demonstrates the full potential of using the four-dimensional model of diaspora as an analytical tool. Looking at the experience of forced migration and the subsequent formation of diasporic communities from the vantage points of 'host society', 'homeland', 'diaspora' and 'other diasporas' allows historians to transcend national narratives of victimization that became entrenched not only in the collective memory of refugees but also in much of the historiography. This model also enables one to approach forced migration from a genuinely transnational perspective, as it situates individual and collective experiences within the broader context of Europe's moving peoples and shifting borders. Even though the volume focuses on the 'Old Continent' in the first half of the twentieth century, the model can be applied to other periods and regions of the world.

Finally, while the transnational character of cross-border refugee movements is more obvious, also the experience of internally displaced people cannot fully be understood without breaking out of the confines of national history. East Prussian expellees settling in West Germany in theory never left their country but, especially in the first post-war decade, they felt as out of place in the 'host society' as Polish refugees in Britain. By focusing on the four aspects of diasporic relationship rather than on international legal definitions and national typologies, the proposed model therefore allows one to include all groups of forced migrants who were displaced both internally and across state borders in Europe during the era of the two world wars. These 'unwilling nomads' profoundly shaped the course of European history and continue to do so.

Notes

1. For a Europe-wide view of the issues relating to refugees in the post-1945 era, see particularly David Nasaw, *The Last Million: Europe's Displaced Persons from World War to Cold War* (New York: Penguin Press, 2020).
2. Jerzy Zubrzycki, *Polish Immigrants in Britain: Study of Adjustment* (The Hague: Martinus Nijhoff, 1956), 54–5; Keith Sword, with Norman Davies and Jan Ciechanowski, *The Formation of the Polish Community in Great Britain, 1939–1950* (London: School of Slavonic and East European Studies, University of London, 1989), 21–45; Halik Kochanski, *The Eagle Unbowed: Poland and the Poles in the Second World War* (London: Allen Lane, 2012), 204–44.
3. Zubrzycki, *Polish Immigrants in Britain*, 55–6; Sword et al., *Formation of the Polish Community*, 61–4.
4. Helena Bauer et al. (eds), *Książka Pamiątkowa Szkół Młodszych Ochotniczek* (London: Związek Szkół Młodszych Ochotniczek, 1976), 19–41; Maria Maćkowska, *Pomocnicza Służba Kobiet w Polskich Siłach Zbrojnych w okresie 2 wojny światowej* (London: Veritas Foundation Publication Centre, 1990), 8–16 and 80–8.
5. Zubrzycki, *Polish Immigrants in Britain*, 58.
6. Sword et al., *Formation of the Polish Community*, 51–2.
7. Zubrzycki, *Polish Immigrants in Britain*, 56–61; Sword et al., *Formation of the Polish Community*, 338–9.
8. Zubrzycki, *Polish Immigrants in Britain*, 62–71, Sheila Patterson, 'Immigrants and Minority Groups in British Society', in *The Prevention of Racial Discrimination in Britain*, ed. Simon Abott (London: Oxford University Press, 1971), 21–53; Sheila Patterson, 'The Poles: An Exile Community In Britain', in *Between Two Cultures: Migrants and Minorities in Britain*, ed. James L. Watson (Oxford: Basil Blackwell, 1977), 214–41.
9. Tadeusz Radzik, *Szkolnictwo polskie w Wielkiej Brytanii w latach drugiej wojny światowej* (Lublin: Wydawnictwo Polonia, 1986), 58.
10. Edinburgh University Archives, Edinbugrh (hereafter EUA), GD46/Box 5. Diary of Zdzisław Golarz (Teleszyński), 25 December 1942.
11. Zubrzycki, *Polish Immigrants in Britain*, 80; Józef Gula, *The Roman Catholic Church in the History of the Polish Exiled Community in Great Britain* (London: School of Slavonic and East European Studies University of London, 1993), 64; Tomasz Ziarski-Kernberg, *The Polish Community in Scotland* (Hove: Cladra House, 2000), 14–24.
12. Patterson, 'Immigrants and Minority Groups', 51–3; Colin Holmes, 'Immigration into Britain', *History Today* 35, no. 6 (1985): 16–17; Colin Holmes, *John Bull's Island: Immigration and British Society, 1871–1971* (Houndmills, Basingstoke and London:

Macmillan, 1988), 247–50. Cf. Mieczysław Nurek, *Gorycz zwycięstwa: Los Polskich Sił Zbrojnych na Zachodzie po II wojnie światowej, 1945–1949* (Gdańsk: Wydawnictwo Uniwersytetu Gdańskiego, 2009) and Jerzy Adam Radomski, *Demobilizacja Polskich Sił Zbrojnych na Zachodzie w latach 1945–1951* (Cracow: Fundacja Centrum Dokumentacji Czynu Niepodległościowego, 2009).

13 Zubrzycki, *Polish Immigrants in Britain*, 63.
14 Peter D. Stachura, 'The Emergence of the Polish Community in Early Postwar Scotland', *Slavonica* 4, no. 2 (1997): 27–40.
15 Wiktor Tomaszewski, *Na szkockiej ziemi. Wspomnienia wojenne ze służby zdrowia i z Polskiego Wydziału Lekarskiego w Edynburgu*, 2nd edn (London: White Eagle Press, 1976), 242–3.
16 Zubrzycki, *Polish Immigrants in Britain*, 153–89; Laura Hilton, 'Cultural Nationalism in Exile: The Case of Polish and Latvian Displaced Persons', *The Historian* 71, no. 2 (2009): 280–317.
17 EUA, IN14/3: Records of the Polish School of Medicine, Minutes of Faculty Meetings, 24 March 1942.
18 Sword et al., *Formation of the Polish Community*, 317.
19 Michał Adam Palacz, 'Polish diasporic Catholicism in Scotland', in *The Bloomsbury Handbook of Religion and Migration*, ed. Rubina Ramji and Alison Marshall (London: Bloomsbury Academic, 2022), 55–72.
20 Aaron Goldman, 'The Resurgence of Antisemitism in Britain during World War II', *Jewish Social Studies* 46, no. 1 (1984): 42–3; David Engel, *Facing a Holocaust: The Polish Government-in-Exile and the Jews, 1943–1945* (Chapel Hill and London: The University of North Carolina Press, 1993), 108–37; Michał Adam Palacz, 'Christian-Jewish Relations in the Polish School of Medicine at the University of Edinburgh, 1941–1949', *Gal-Ed: On the History and Culture of Polish Jewry* 25 (2017): 55–81.
21 Zubrzycki, *Polish Immigrants in Britain*, 214–15.
22 Jerzy Zubrzycki, 'Emigration from Poland in the Nineteenth and Twentieth Centuries', *Population Studies* 6, no. 3 (1953): 248–72; Peter Brock, 'Polish Democrats and English Radicals 1832–1862: A Chapter in the History of Anglo-Polish Relations', *The Journal of Modern History* 25, no. 2 (1953): 139–56; Jerzy Zdrada, *Wielka Emigracja po Powstaniu Listopadowym* (Warsaw: Krajowa Agencja Wydawnicza, 1987).
23 Zubrzycki, *Polish Immigrants in Britain*, 68–71; Patterson, 'Immigrants and Minority Groups', 51–3.
24 The National Archives, Kew, MH 76/338: Letter from the Polish Medical Association to Aneurin Bevan, 19 July 1946.
25 James Walvin, *Passage to Britain. Immigration In British History and Politics* (Harmondsworth: Penguin Books, 1984), 164.
26 Piotr S. Wandycz, *Czechoslovak-Polish Confederation and the Great Powers, 1940–1943* (Bloomington: Indiana University Publications, 1956); Vojtech Mastny, 'The Czechoslovak Government-in-Exile During World War II', *Jahrbücher für Geschichte Osteuropas* 27, no. 4 (1979): 548–63; Sword et al., *Formation of the Polish Community*, 163–4.
27 Stanisław Mauersberg, 'Nauka i szkolnictwo wyższe w latach 1939–1951', in *Historia Nauki Polskiej. Tom V: 1918–1951, Część I*, ed. Bogdan Suchodolski (Wrocław: Zakład Narodowy im. Ossolińskich, 1992), 396–411.
28 Zubrzycki, *Polish Immigrants in Britain*, 58–61; Sword et al., *Formation of the Polish Community*, 338–9.

29 Muhammad Anwar, *The Myth of Return: Pakistanis in Britain* (London: Heinemann Educational Books, 1979). For a similar development in Croydon, see Sheila Patterson, *Immigrants in Industry* (London and New York: Oxford University Press, 1968).
30 V.G. Kiernan, 'Britons Old and New', in *Immigrants and Minorities in British Society*, ed. Colin Holmes (London: George Allen & Unwin, 1978), 54.
31 'Reds' Polish Demands Backed by Churchill', *The Atlanta Constitution* (16 December 1944): 1. See also: Richard Krickus, *The Kaliningrad Question* (Lanham: Rowman & Littlefield, 2002), 30-1.
32 Mary Fulbrook, *A History of Germany 1918-2014: The Divided Nation* (Chichester: Wiley Blackwell, 4th edn, 2015), 113-41.
33 Andreas Kossert, *Kalte Heimat: Der Geschichte der deutsche Vertriebenen nach 1945* (Bonn: Bundeszentrale für politische Bildung, 2008), 43.
34 Wilhelm Schivelbusch, *Three New Deals, Reflections on Roosevelt's America, Mussolini's Italy and Hitler's Germany, 1933-1939* (New York: Picador, 2007), 224-5.
35 Kossert, *Kalte Heimat*, 50-9.
36 Katarzyna Stokłosa, *Polen und die deutsche Ostpolitik 1945-1990* (Göttingen: Vandenhoeck und Ruprecht, 2011), 76-9.
37 Michael Schwarz, 'Staatsfeind "Umsiedler"', in *Die Flucht: Über die Vertreibung der Deutschen aus dem Osten*, ed. Stefan Aust and Stephan Burgdorf (Bonn: Bundeszentrale für politische Bildung, 2005), 225-30.
38 Klaus J. Bade, 'From Emigration to Immigration: The German Experience in the Nineteenth and Twentieth Centuries', *Central European History* 28 (1995): 511 and 515.
39 See particularly: Theodor Schieder (ed.), *Dokumentation der Vertreibung der Deutschen aus Ost-Mitteleuropa, Die Vertreibung der deutschen Bevölkerung aus den Gebieten östlich der Oder-Neisse*, Vol. 1 (Munich: Deutschen Taschenbuch Verlag, 1984).
40 Gregor Thum, 'Megalomania and Angst: The Nineteenth-Century Mythization of Germany's Eastern Borderlands', in *Shatterzones of Empire: Coexistence and Violence in the German, Habsburg, Russian and Ottoman Borderlands*, ed. Omer Bartov and Eric Weitz (Bloomington: Indiana University Press, 2013), 23-41.
41 See for example the widely read 'Battlefields in East Prussia': Wehrkreiskommando I, *Schlachtfelder in Ostpreußen* (Königsberg: Königsberger Allgemeine Zeitung Volz & Co., 1932), 3.
42 Andreas Kossert, *Damals in Ostpreußen, Der Untergang einer deutschen Provinz* (Munich: Pantheon, 2008), 104.
43 Stefan Goebel, *The Great War and Medieval Memory: War, Remembrance and Medievalism in Britain and Germany, 1914-1940* (Cambridge: Cambridge University Press, 2007), 36-8 and 127-34.
44 Bastiaan Willems and Joe Schuldt, 'The "European Boundaries" of the East Prussian expellees in West-Germany, 1948-1955', *Novoe Proshloe/The New Past* 2 (2018): 36.
45 The clearest examples of this practice are the front pages of the different expellee pages (such as the *Ostpreussen-Warte*, the *Wir Ostpreußen*, and the *Das Ostpreußenblatt*), which, rather than featuring news items, were mainly filled with generic pictures of East Prussian cities and landscapes.
46 Michael Billig, *Banal Nationalism* (London: Sage, 1995), 6-7.
47 For example: Max Egremont, *Forgotten Land, Journeys among the Ghosts of East Prussia* (New York: Farrar, Straus and Giroux, 2011).
48 Alison Owings, *Frauen: German Women in the Third Reich* (New Brunswick: Rutgers University Press, 2011), 143.

49 Karl Springenschmid, *Raus aus Königsberg! Wie 420 ostpreußische Jungen 1945 aus Kampf und Einsatz gerettet wurden* (Kiel: Arndt, 1993), 20.
50 Bastiaan Willems, *Violence in Defeat: The Wehrmacht on German Soil, 1944–1945* (Cambridge: Cambridge University Press, 2021), 209–13.
51 Günter Grass, *Im Krebsgang* (Göttingen, Steindl, 2002), 96–7 and 103.
52 Kurt Dieckert and Horst Großman, *Der Kampf um Ostpreussen. Der umfassende Dokumentarbericht* (Stuttgart: Motorbuch Verlag, 1998), 119–32.
53 On Stutthof concentration camp in 1945, see Danuta Drywa, *The Extermination of Jews in Stutthof Concentration Camp* (Gdańsk: Stutthof Museum in Sztutowo, 2004), Ch. IV.
54 Martin Bergau, *Todesmarsch zur Bernsteinküste: Das Massaker an Juden im ostpreußischen Palmnicken im Januar 1945, Zeitzeugen erinnern sich* (Heidelberg: Universitätsverlag Winter, 2007), 217 and 221; Kurt Gerdau, 'Nicht ohne Ungereimheiten', *Das Ostpreußenblatt* 9 (2 March 1996): 11 ['Störend wirken seine Bemühungen, sein kleines Leben in die großen geschichtlichen Abläufe einzuordnen'].
55 Fritjof Meyer, 'Das Trojanische Pferd', in *Die Flucht*, ed. Aust and Burgdorf, 235–8.
56 Heinrich Süssner, 'Still Yearning for the Lost Heimat: Ethnic German Expellees and the Politics of Belonging', *German Politics and Society* 22 (2004): 4.
57 Pertti Ahonen, 'Domestic Constraints on West German Ostpolitik: The Role of the Expellee Organizations in the Adenauer Era', *Central European History* 31 (1998): 37.
58 Ibid., 41–2.
59 United Nations High Commissioner for Refugees, 'Convention and Protocol Relating to the Status of Refugees', 2010. Available online: https://www.unhcr.org/3b66c2aa10?fbclid=IwAR3HsZzL8UOgHsmlGQrAKWNYTghqHOdRB387-PF4LgjWxw6xacfkaRmlmYE (accessed 17 August 2021).
60 Rune Johansson, 'The Refugee Experience in Europe after World War II: Some Theoretical and Empirical Considerations', in *The Uprooted. Forced Migration as an International Problem in the Post-War Era*, ed. Göran Rystad (Lund: Lund University Press, 1990), 230–4.
61 Willems and Schuldt, 'The "European Boundaries" of the East Prussian Expellees', 33–4.
62 Michael Schwarz, *Funktionäre mit Vergangenheit: Das Gründungspräsidium des Bundesverbandes der Vertriebenen und das 'Dritte Reich'* (Munich: Oldenbourg, 2013), 7–19.
63 Pertti Ahonen, *After the Expulsion: West Germany and Eastern Europe 1945–1990* (Oxford: Oxford University Press, 2003).
64 See Eckhard Matthes (ed.), *Als Russe in Ostpreußen: Sowjetische Umsiedler über ihren Neubeginn in Königsberg / Kaliningrad nach 1945* (Stuttgart: Edition Tertium, 2000).
65 Bundesministerium des Innern, für Bau und Heimat, '20. Juni wird Gedenktag für Opfer von Flucht und Vertreibung'. Available online: https://www.bmi.bund.de/SharedDocs/kurzmeldungen/DE/2014/08/gedenktag-fuer-die-opfer-von-flucht-und-vertreibung.html (accessed 30 August 2021).
66 Elke Fröhlinch, *Die Tagebücher von Joseph Goebbels 1945, Teil II, Band 15: Januar – April 1945* (Munich: K.G. Saur, 1995), 214.

Concluding remarks

Pertti Ahonen

At the end of this ambitious and far-ranging volume, it seems appropriate to reflect on the book as a whole and to ask what it adds to the considerable amount of high-quality literature that already exists on the history of forced migrations in twentieth-century Europe. Why, in other words, should historians of forced migrations pay attention to this study? And what new impulses could it offer for the future development of this thriving field of scholarship?

I would like to highlight five areas in which *A Transnational History of Forced Migrants in Europe* enhances the existing historiography in significant ways. First, the editors' emphatic focus on the transnational is important in itself. Few phenomena are as inherently transnational as cross-border migrations and their manifold consequences. However, as Willems and Palacz point out, forced migrations have often been harnessed to serve nationally defined narrative frameworks, typically as stories of either singular victimhood or exceptional integrative success – or indeed both, with the latter following the former once the forcibly uprooted victims have settled into the nation state to which they purportedly belong, due to their ethno-national characteristics. In keeping with this paradigm, much of the scholarship on forced migrations in twentieth-century Europe has also been nationally focused. However, as a welcome corrective to that long-term trend, important studies that view these migrations and their consequences through a transnational lens have started to appear in recent years.[1] This book makes a major contribution to that emerging corpus of literature, a contribution that is made all the more notable by the volume's additional, distinctive merits.

A significant one of these derives from the book's contextualization of forced migrations within what the editors label a 'longer arc of European history', stretching from the First World War and its antecedents to the Second World War and its aftermath. Most previous studies have adopted a considerably narrower timeframe. The Second World War and its temporal hinterland, a period which Peter Gatrell and Nick Baron have aptly called 'violent peacetime', has caught the lion's share of scholarly attention, as could be expected, given the unprecedented scale of the brutal uprooting of European populations that took place during this era.[2] To a lesser but still considerable extent, the forced migrations that unfolded around the First World War have also been analysed insightfully, not least from the perspective of the precedents and models that they helped to set for later cases of expulsion.[3] However, studies that incorporate the two world wars and their consequences into a single framework that also includes the interwar years have remained very few, and one of this volume's notable contributions is to have provided a model for this kind of integrated analysis.⁴ In theory, the 'longer arc of European history' could be extended further in both directions: into the forced removals and demographic re-engineering projects that began on Europe's southern and eastern periphery in the 1870s – launching what Donald Bloxham has labelled 'the great unweaving' of populations – and also into the different kinds of forced migrations that took place during and after the Cold War, both within Europe and between Europe and other parts of the world.⁵ However, an overly wide chronological scope would have undermined the coherence and analytical depth of this volume, and the editors' decision to frame the book around the era of the two world wars is sensible and convincing. It is to be hoped that their work will provide impetus for further comprehensive, long-term histories of European forced migrations.

The volume's third significant contribution to the historiography is closely linked to the previous point; the editors have aimed for a broad scope, not only in the time periods covered but also in the types of forced migrations and personal experiences addressed. This is quite atypical of the field as a whole. For instance, in the area in which I have done most of my own empirical work – post-Second World War Central Europe in general and Germany in particular – different types of forced migrants have usually been studied separately. The sizeable literature on ethnic German expellees has remained largely distinct from that on displaced persons (DPs) of other nationalities, for example, and more generally, too, works that 'look at the many different kinds of refugees and dislocated people in the same context' have been lacking, as Jessica Reinisch has observed.⁶ At the same time, the rare studies that have focused specifically on the post-war interaction of distinct population groups, such as Adam Seipp's local-level study of the relations among DPs, ethnic German expellees, American occupation forces and local German residents in the small Bavarian garrison town of Wildflecken, have been particularly valuable in highlighting complex societal and transnational dynamics.⁷

Similar observations about discrete categories and literatures for particular kinds of uprooted people also apply more broadly across the period covered in this volume. There are strong and vibrant historiographies on many of the specific population groups addressed in the individual chapters: the First World War evacuees and internees, political émigrés of the interwar years, refugees from fascist rule, populations targeted by Nazi resettlement schemes, and so on, but little in the way of integrative studies that seek to examine these categories together, or at least to draw explicit connections between them. Against this background, the editors' decision to adopt a very broad definition of forced migrants, a definition that makes it possible to bring a wide range of unwilling nomads under one analytical umbrella, is laudable. On this point, Willems and Palacz deserve to be quoted at some length:

> It is generally accepted now that the boundary between 'forced' and 'voluntary' migration is often blurry and that the experiences of people on the move can be better represented as a spectrum rather than as a dichotomy. We have therefore adopted a broad category of involuntary migrants that includes all people in Europe whose movement across and within state borders in the first half of the twentieth century was primarily caused by war, persecution, and political upheaval. The case

studies presented in this volume range from deportees and refugees with limited agency whose displacement was caused by forces beyond their control to political émigrés who consciously chose exile in order to continue their struggle against a repressive regime. (p. 2)

This expansive, yet clearly delineated, definition of the term 'forced migrant', in turn, underpins the book's fourth major source of strength: its exceptionally wide scope in general and the inclusion of enlightening cases and approaches that do not necessarily jump to mind when thinking of twentieth-century forced migrations in particular. Here it will suffice to single out two examples of the fresh perspectives on offer, starting with Katrin Sippel's chapter on the cultural impact of female refugees from National Socialism who passed through Portugal between the late 1930s and the mid-1940s. Although the vast majority of these women stayed in Portugal only briefly, in transit between their original abodes and more permanent places of exile, and therefore typically did not even try to adjust to the host society and its very conservative gender roles and other behavioural norms, they nevertheless became highly significant agents of long-term cultural change in Portugal. However, contrary to what the reader might expect, it was not their 'political activism' but rather their 'day-to-day behaviours' that proved to have a much greater long-term effect on Portuguese habits and national mentalities' (p. 145). Refugee women defied and altered prevailing local norms in public behaviour, dress, culinary habits and other areas of daily life, thereby opening up new possibilities for local women and initiating major transformation processes in Portuguese society. All of this is highly enlightening as a case study in the gendered, transnational interaction between refugees and local populations in mid-twentieth-century Portugal, but, on a more general level, it also exemplifies how complex – and ultimately unpredictable – the dynamics between forced migrants and host societies can be.

Another chapter worthy of a special mention is Jill Meißner-Wolfbeisser's close reading of the role of one particular Austrian émigré, Stefi Kiesler, as a largely forgotten but highly influential cultural and linguistic mediator within the German-speaking literati community in the United States in the 1930s and 1940s. In a study that accentuates the potential of microhistorical approaches to illuminate broad historical processes, Meißner-Wolfbeisser shows how Kiesler, a long-term public librarian in the German-language section of the New York Public Library, became a pivotal bridge-builder among German-speaking émigré intellectuals in New York. On one level, therefore, the chapter provides a study of personal networks among forced migrants struggling to find their footing in a host society. At the same time, it also underscores the multidimensional sociocultural importance of the physical space of the library, at least for certain types of forced migrants: as an entrance point to a new culture and language, as a bridge to the mother tongue, 'as a place of encounter both with members of the host society and with old acquaintances from the homeland' (p. 113), and even as a 'multicultural gathering place' that can bring together local residents and émigrés of many different backgrounds and nationalities (p. 114).

Meißner-Wolfbeisser's multi-level analysis of the German émigré intellectuals' interactions with each other, with the surrounding society, with the old homeland

and with other exile groups also links directly to this volume's fifth and probably most notable contribution to the historiography of forced migrations and their consequences: the four dimensional model of diasporic relationships (p. 4) laid out in the introduction and applied, with varying levels of explicitness, in the individual chapters. As Willems and Palacz explain, the model draws on a long tradition of historical and social science research on diasporic communities, an approach that is highly suitable to a volume like this, with its transnational focus on 'the experiences of different types of forced migrants' (p. 3), especially the processes through which the migrants adjust to their new, post-migration circumstances. However, whereas scholars have generally analysed diasporic relationships through a three-fold model comprising the lost homeland, the new host society and the diasporic community forcibly transported from the former to the latter, Willems and Palacz develop this model further. They propose to apply it with heightened flexibility, 'as a spectrum that varies from one individual to another, changes over time and is mediated by age, gender, psychosexual identity, ethnic background, religious beliefs and socio-economic class' (p. 5). More innovatively, they also 'suggest adding a fourth dimension to the triad of "host society", "homeland" and "diaspora": interaction with other diasporas' (p. 5). With this extra dimension, the editors accentuate the often complicated relationships among different national and ethnic groups that find themselves in exile, relationships that can fluctuate between 'coexistence, cooperation or conflict' (p. 5).

This revised, four-dimensional model of diasporic relationships is a very useful analytical device that has a good deal of potential for explorations of the experiences of forced migrants, on both the individual and collective levels. Willems and Palacz themselves describe its value as follows: 'The proposed conceptual model of diaspora can be used by transnational historians as an analytical tool that offers the possibility of looking at the formation of migrant communities as a phenomenon in itself, and not only in relation to the national histories of the respective countries of origin and settlement, as implied by the traditional paradigm of linear assimilation' (p. 5). That evaluation seems apt, and the chapters of this book go a long way towards validating the editors' expectations.

In taking stock of this volume and its contributions, it seems appropriate to finish by asking how it could help to develop and renew the field in the future. Which issues addressed on the preceding pages could perhaps be examined further by other scholars of forced migrations, and how? One intriguing possibility, raised explicitly by Cristian Cercel in his contribution on the transnational arrangements through which around 2,500 'ethnic Swabians' came to be resettled in Brazil in the early 1950s and echoed implicitly in Chelsea Sambells's chapter on European cross-border child evacuation schemes before and during the Second World War, is the addition of a fifth dimension to the proposed model of diasporic relationships. As highlighted by Cercel and Sambells in their respective chapters and acknowledged by the editors in the introduction, international humanitarian organizations have frequently played a key role in the resettlement of modern-day forced migrants, providing aid and relief, developing employment opportunities, facilitating cross-border relocation schemes and engaging in a panoply of other activities. In the context of twentieth-century Europe, the relevant actors have been many and varied, ranging from such international juggernauts as the American Relief Administration of the post-First World War era or the United Nations Relief and Rehabilitation Administration and its successor, the International Refugee Organization of the 1940s and early 1950s, to many smaller entities, including the Schweizer Europahilfe examined by Cercel or the Second World War era Swedish voluntary refugee committees explored, in part, by Sambells.

The case studies by Cercel and Sambells provide concrete examples of how the activities of international organizations have frequently had a major impact on the life trajectories of forced migrants and their communities. They also accentuate some of the ways in which humanitarian organizations have tended to 'engage in ethnic politics', to borrow Cercel's expression (p. 216), helping to draw and re-draw boundaries between perceived ethno-national groups and to valorize particular groups over others. Furthermore, these two chapters cast light on the complicated dynamics between humanitarian organizations, the states to whose interests they are linked – politically, economically or administratively – and the wider national and international contexts in which they operate. The systematic inclusion of relevant international organizations into the diasporic nexus outlined in this volume, potentially as its fifth dimension, alongside those of the homeland, the host society, the primary diaspora and other diasporas, would therefore seem well worth considering, given the additional analytical breadth that such a move promises to deliver.

Another area in which the new avenues for investigation opened up in this book could still be developed further by other scholars has to do with questioning and partly deconstructing concepts and analytical categories that are sometimes taken too much at face value in the relevant literature. To be sure, to a considerable extent the volume does precisely that. The transnational emphasis throughout is an important achievement in itself, as already discussed, given the prevalence of nationally focused approaches in much of the previous historiography. The model of diasporic relationships applied in the volume, with its four or potentially even five dimensions, offers enhanced analytical purchase in several directions. At the same time, the constituent elements of that model come under perceptive scrutiny in a number of contributions. In his penetrating analysis of population movement, evacuation and internment in Habsburg Galicia during the First World War, for instance, Serhiy Choliy stresses that the resulting diasporas 'proved to be a short-lived phenomenon' that 'rapidly disappeared after the collapse of imperial regimes' (p. 23). Cristian Cercel echoes the same point about the contingent character of diasporic categorizations on a more general level, emphasizing 'the fluid, constructed, contested and negotiated character of identity ascriptions and identifications' that apply to the concept of 'diaspora' (p. 226). Cercel also helps to disaggregate the other two dimensions of the diasporic model introduced by Willems and Palacz. Through his examination of the complicated journeys of some 2,500 'Danube Swabians' from multiple points of origin in south-eastern Europe to Austria and subsequently on to Brazil, with the assistance of the Schweizer Europahilfe organization, he concludes that 'far from being bounded, straightforward or unchanging', categories such as 'host society for or a homeland of a particular group' can themselves be 'fluid, contextual and plural' (pp. 215, 226). These kinds of probing insights about the diasporic model and its constituent parts offer plentiful opportunities for future investigation, both empirically, in particular case studies, and more generally, on the level of the model itself and its potential transnational and comparative applications.

One key issue in need of additional exploration and disaggregation in future studies is the tension between collective ethno-national and political categorizations of forced migrants, imposed by national and other authorities, and subjective perceptions of belonging and group identity among the migrants themselves. In much of the historical literature, particularly the more general literature, in which forced migrations typically feature only in passing, there is a tendency to employ seemingly precise ethno-national categories when discussing their victims: so many million Poles uprooted here, that many 'ethnic Germans' expelled there, and so on. However, upon closer examination, such apparently neat classifications frequently break down, revealing much more fluid and ambiguous realities, especially at the grassroots level.

Several contributions in this volume highlight these kinds of complexities. Serhiy Choliy, for example, argues that '[t]he most important factor that influenced the fate of those persons who moved or were removed from Galicia during the First World War was their categorization by the host societies, either Austro-Hungarian or Russian', categorizations that were often quite arbitrary and failed to 'correlate with a person's behaviour or political views' (p. 21). Bradley Nichols, in turn, reminds us of how porous the boundaries separating ethno-national in- and out-groups could be, even – or perhaps especially – in Nazi Germany, where pseudo-racial classification schemes were supposed to create strict dividing lines between desirable and undesirable elements. In his insightful analysis of the Third Reich's so-called Re-Germanization Procedure (*Wiedereindeutschungsverfahren*), a wartime policy aimed at 'reclaiming' select foreign nationals from across Europe on the basis of their alleged Germanic heritage, Nichols stresses the ambiguity and fluidity of ethno-national classification criteria. As he points out, 'the long history of cultural syncretism' in many of the regions targeted by the Nazis, along with 'the frequency with which they had changed hands, made it incredibly difficult to figure out who was who' (p. 167). The editors of this volume, then, are undoubtedly right in concluding that 'migrant identities in the first half of the twentieth century were hybrid, individualized and constantly reconstructed in response to socio-economic forces and political pressures' (p. 9).

Examinations of forced migrants' hybrid identities and the external pressures under which they were (re-)formed and (re-)drawn can be developed further in the future, building on what has been accomplished in this volume and elsewhere. The interaction of the twin processes of attempted categorizations from above and reactions and responses from below can be explored in any number of forced migration contexts. After all, the division of target populations into discrete groups, defined by degrees of perceived belonging and exclusion, and the drawing of boundaries between them are key elements in the planning and implementation of any involuntary migration, and the practical consequences of these policies have almost invariably been very complicated. There already exists some excellent literature on the tensions between official categorizations and subjective experiences in particular cases of forced migration. Highly perceptive recent studies have explored ethno-national ambiguities in the borderlands between Germany and Poland during and after the Second World War, for example.[8] However, much more work of a similar kind is still needed, both regional case studies and, even more acutely, broader transnational and comparative analyses.[9]

To close these brief remarks, I would like to widen the perspective beyond the specific remit followed by this volume's editors and contributors by suggesting that the book's most far-reaching potential contribution to migration history may lie in encouraging the further dismantling of walls and fences that still tend to separate different branches of the relevant historiography. As shown previously, this study does transcend many conventional dividing lines in the literature: the time period and the types of involuntary migrations covered are both commendably broad, and the proposed model of diasporic relationship promises to bring together disparate strands of scholarship. However, there is still room for additional integrative efforts in the future. This seems particularly pertinent at the interface between migrations defined as 'voluntary' or 'involuntary'. While acknowledging that 'the boundary between "forced" and "voluntary" migration is often blurry' and casting their net quite wide, the editors of this volume have nevertheless chosen to exclude 'migrants whose displacement was mainly induced by economic and environmental factors' (p. 2). That is a perfectly justifiable decision – all successful studies need clear parameters, after all – but in the broader field of migration history one of the main ways forward would seem to consist of increasingly comprehensive works in which all kinds of migratory movements – wherever on the voluntary-involuntary continuum they happen to fall – are addressed within a single analytical and narrative framework. Excellent examples of such integrative approaches have recently begun to appear, on both the national and transnational planes.[10] Hopefully many others will soon see the light of day, as migration historians continue to grapple with what Peter Gatrell has described as their 'greatest challenge': the writing of 'displacement into the larger processes of historical change'.[11] In those endeavours, *A Transnational History of Forced Migrants in Europe* can provide significant inspiration and stimulus, as a concrete example of the kinds of studies that the field needs in order to develop further: broad, transnational and far-ranging books that ask big, ambitious questions and present probing challenges to the received wisdom.

Notes

1 For some key studies that offer transnational perspectives, often in close connection with comparative ones, see Jessica Reinisch and Matthew Frank (eds), 'Refugees and the Nation State in Europe, 1919-1959', special issue of the *Journal of Contemporary History* 49, no. 3 (2014); Jessica Reinisch and Matthew Frank (eds), *Refugees in Europe, 1919-1959: A Forty Years' Crisis?* (London: Bloomsbury Academic, 2017); Jan C. Jansen and Simone Lässig (eds), *Refugee Crises 1945-2000: Political and Societal Responses in International Comparison* (Cambridge: Cambridge University Press, 2020); Peter Gatrell, *The Making of the Modern Refugee* (Oxford: Oxford University Press, 2013).

2 Peter Gatrell and Nick Baron, 'Violent Peacetime: Reconceptualising Displacement and Resettlement in the Soviet East European Borderlands after the Second World War', in *Warlands: Population Resettlement and State Reconstruction in the Soviet East*

European Borderlands, 1945–1950, ed. Peter Gatrell and Nick Baron (Basingstoke: Palgrave Macmillan, 2009), 255–68.

3   As just one excellent example, see Peter Gattrell and Liubov Zhvanko (eds), *Europe on the Move: Refugees in the Era of the Great War* (Manchester: Manchester University Press, 2017).

4   An insightful attempt to provide this kind of a longer framework is Reinisch and Frank, *Refugees in Europe, 1919–1959*.

5   Donald Bloxham, 'The Great Unweaving: Forced Population Movement in Europe, 1875–1949', in *Removing Peoples: Forced Removal in the Modern World*, ed. Richard Bessel and Claudia Haake (Oxford: Oxford University Press, 2009), 167–208.

6   Jessica Reinisch, 'Introduction', in *The Disentanglement of Populations: Migration, Expulsion and Displacement in Post-War Europe*, ed. Jessica Reinisch and Elizabeth White (London: Palgrave Macmillan, 2011), xv.

7   Adam R. Seipp, *Strangers in the Wild Place: Refugees, Americans and a German Town, 1945–1952* (Bloomington: Indiana University Press, 2013). On these points, see also Pertti Ahonen, 'Germany and the Aftermath of the Second World War', *Journal of Modern History* 89, no. 2 (2017): 355–87.

8   See, for example, John J. Kulczycki, *Belonging to the Nation: Inclusion and Exclusion in the German-Polish Borderlands, 1939–1951* (Cambridge, MA: Harvard University Press, 2016); Hugo Service, *Germans to Poles: Communism, Nationalism and Ethnic Cleansing after the Second World War* (Cambridge: Cambridge University Press, 2013).

9   One such effort is the project 'Expellees and Ethno-National Categorizations in Europe, 1943–1948', which was launched in September 2021 under my direction, with four years of funding from the Academy of Finland. The four-person research team explores the complex ways in the ethnicity and national belonging of select groups of forced migrants uprooted from historically multi-ethnic border regions was defined, perceived and negotiated as a key component of wider projects of nation (re-)building in four European polities – Germany, Hungary, Italy and Finland – during the transitional 'postwar moment' between approximately late 1943 and 1948.

10 For strong examples of such integrative literature, see Jan Plamper, *Das neue Wir: Warum Migration dazugehört. Eine andere Geschichte der Deutschen* (Frankfurt am Main: S. Fischer 2019) and Peter Gatrell, *The Unsettling of Europe: How Migration Reshaped a Continent* (New York: Basic Books, 2019).

11 For the quotation, see Peter Gatrell, 'Refugees – What's Wrong with History', *Journal of Refugee Studies* 30, no. 2 (2017): 184.

Further reading

Ahonen, Pertti, Gustavo Corni, Jerzy Kochanowski, Rainer Schulze, Tamás Stark, and Barbara Stelzl-Marx. *People on the Move: Forced Population Movements in Europe in the Second World War and its Aftermath*. Oxford and New York: Berg, 2008.
Bartov, Omer, and Eric Weitz (Eds). *Shatterzones of Empire: Coexistence and Violence in the German, Habsburg, Russian, and Ottoman Borderlands*. Bloomington: Indiana University Press, 2013.
Bessel, Richard, and Claudia B. Haake (Eds). *Removing Peoples: Forced Removal in the Modern World*. New York: Oxford University Press, 2009.
Bloxham, Donald. *Genocide, the World Wars, and the Unweaving of Europe*. Portland, OR: Valentine-Mitchell, 2008.
Bloxham, Donald. 'The Great Unweaving: Forced Population Movement in Europe, 1875–1949'. In *Removing Peoples: Forced Removal in the Modern World*, edited by Richard Bessel and Claudia Haake, 167–208. Oxford: Oxford University Press, 2009.
Gatrell, Peter. *A Whole Empire Walking: Refugees in Russia during the World War I*. Bloomington: Indiana University Press, 1999.
Gatrell, Peter. *The Making of the Modern Refugee*. Oxford: Oxford University Press, 2013.
Gatrell, Peter. *The Unsettling of Europe: How Migration Reshaped a Continent*. New York: Basic Books, 2019.
Gatrell, Peter, and Liubov Zhvanko (Eds). *Europe on the Move: Refugees in the Era of the Great War*. Manchester: Manchester University Press, 2017.
Manz, Stefan, Panikos Panayi, and Matthew Stibbe (Eds). *Internment during the First World War: A Mass Global Phenomenon*. London and New York: Routledge, 2019.
Marrus, Michael R. *The Unwanted: European Refugees in the Twentieth Century*. Oxford: Oxford University Press, 1985.
Nasaw, David. *The Last Million: Europe's Displaced Persons from World War to Cold War*. New York: Penguin Press, 2020.
Reinisch, Jessica, and Elizabeth White (Eds). *The Disentanglement of Populations: Migration, Expulsion and Displacement in Post-War Europe*. London: Palgrave Macmillan, 2011.
Reinisch, Jessica, and Matthew Frank (Eds). 'Refugees and the Nation State in Europe, 1919–1959', special issue of the *Journal of Contemporary History*, 49, no. 3 (2014).
Reinisch, Jessica, and Elizabeth White (Eds). *Refugees in Europe, 1919–1959: A Forty Years' Crisis?* London: Bloomsbury Academic, 2017.
Stibbe, Matthew. *Civilian Internment during the First World War: A European and Global History, 1914–1920*. London: Palgrave Macmillan, 2019.

Index

Adriatic Sea   60, 62, 68
AJDC, see American Jewish Joint Distribution Committee
AK, see Armia Krajowa
Aleksandar I of Yugoslavia   60, 64–7, 69
Allies
   and DPs   184, 199–200, 203–5
   and expellees   208, 217–18, 251, 254
   and Poles   209, 246–7, 251, 254
Alsace-Lorraine   62, 167–8, 170, 173–4, 235
Altenberg, Peter   109, 114
American Jewish Joint Distribution Committee   188, 192
anarchists   156, 159
Anders, Władysław   199, 246
anti-communism   86, 204, 231–42
anti-communist refugees   232, 235, 237, 241
anti-fascism   59–61, 64–7, 69–70, 157–8
anti-immigrant hostility   231, 233, 239–40, 247, 251, see also xenophobia
anti-Semitism, see also pogroms
   in DP camps   186
   in France   234–5
   in Poland   234, 246
   of Polish refugees in Britain   248
   in Russian Empire   15, 17
   in Sweden and Switzerland   120, 127
Arabs   185, 233
Argentina   59–60, 69, 174, 219
Armenian genocide   153
   refugees from   3, 159–60
Armia Krajowa   203–4
Arons, Ruth   140–1
assimilation, see also integration
   forced in Nazi Germany   165–6, 170–2, 174
   of migrants in France   232, 234
   narratives of   1, 9, 245
   paradigm of   5, 146, 226
   of Poles in Germany   202, 208–9
   of Russian refugee children   99
Aufbau (newspaper)   105, 108, 113
Australia   173, 184, 248
Austria   108, 110, 251, see also Austria-Hungary
   Anschluss of   119, 121, 123, 131, 136
   Danube Swabians in   215, 217–19, 221–5, 265
   diaspora   108–9, 217, 219
   Lower Austria   17, 29, 45–6
   refugees from   137, 142
   Upper Austria   17, 29, 45, 219
Austria-Hungary
   Austrian Littoral   48–9, 59, 62 (*see also* Julian March)
   collapse of   62–4, 75, 216–17
   in First World War   13–24, 29–40, 51–3, 77, 108
   Jewish middle class in   113
   Ukrainians in   78

Bačka   216, 220
Balkans   31, 60
Balts   185, 206–7
Banat   216, 224, 254
banlieues   232–3, 240
Barcelona   152
Basque Country   152, 233
   nationalists   160
   refugees in France   235
Belarussians   85, 97, 99
Belgium   64, 94, 98, 129, 188, 208
Belgrade   63, 66–7, 95
Berlin   4, 78–86, 106, 140
   Ukrainian Scientific Institute in   79, 82, 86
Bevin, Ernest   193–4
Bidault, Georges   159–61
Bilbao   152
Bohemia   17, 32, 46
Bolsheviks   76–7, 80, 82, 232, 240

Index

borderlands
  of Austria-Hungary 13, 35
  Czechoslovak 81
  ethnic minorities in 59
  of Germany and Poland 256, 266
  of Nazi Germany 167–8
  Polish 80–1, 246
  of Russian Empire 77
Bornet, Francisque 240–1
Brazil 215–16, 220–1, 223–6, 264–5
Britain
  Commonwealth immigrants in 250
  House of Commons 206, 251
  Hungarian refugees in 250
  immigration policy in 120–2
  Kindertransport to 120, 123–6, 131
  Labour government (1945-1951) 247, 249
  occupation of Germany 183–95, 199–209
  Pakistani immigrants in 250
  Polish refugees in 4, 200–1, 207, 245–50, 256–7
  Russian emigrants in 89–90, 94
  and Spanish Republicans 156–7, 160–1
  support for *White* Russians 85
British Guiana 123–4, 126
Bruck an der Leitha refugee camp, *see under* refugee camps
Buenos Aires 175
Bug (river) 199, 203
Bukovina 14, 16, 18–19, 47–8
Bulgaria 19, 31, 89, 94, 98–9

Caldas da Rainha 144–5
Canada 78, 173, 184, 248
Caritas (Catholic charity) 218, 220–3
Catalonia 152–3, 235
  Catalan Nationalists 160
Catholicism, *see also* Greek Catholics
  in Austria-Hungary 34
  of Danube Swabians 216–17
  and Jewish refugees 124
  and migrants in France 233–4, 238, 240–1
  of Polish refugees 248–9
Central Committee of Liberated Jews in the British Zone 184, 186–7, 189, 191–4

Central Europe 75, 77–8, 81, 105, 131, 138
Central Jewish Committee, *see* Central Committee of Liberated Jews in the British Zone
Central Powers 20, 48, 76–7
Chamberlain, Neville 122–4
Chicago 220
Chile 219
Churchill, Winston 204, 251
Church of England 124
citizenship
  American 108, 110, 112
  Austrian 4, 17–19, 29–31, 34, 51, 218
  British 207, 248
  French 152, 231, 234, 240
  German 19, 166, 169, 173–4, 202
  Yugoslav 65, 70, 216
civil rights 17, 30–1, 166
CNT, *see Confederación Nacional del Trabajo*
Čok, Ivan Marija 66–9
Cold War 208, 232–3, 250, 255, 262
colonies
  agricultural projects in Brazil 220, 222–5
  British 248
  ethnic German settlements in Eastern Europe 216, 225, 252–3
  French 231, 233
  Portuguese 138–9
  postcolonial theory 166
  resettlement of Jewish refugees in 124
communism
  Communist Party of France 232, 234–41
  in East-Central Europe 232, 236, 238, 240, 250–1, 254–6
  in East Germany 251–2, 254
  German communists 154
  Italian communists 154, 240
  in Poland 173, 239, 247–8
  Spanish communists 156, 158
  in Yugoslavia 67, 173, 239
concentration camps
  Bergen-Belsen 183, 189–90, 193
  Dachau 174
  in First World War 17, 23, 32

Mauthausen   155–6
  in Nazi Germany   123, 155–6, 171,
    183–90, 247
  for Spanish Republicans in
    France   232, 235
  Stutthof   254
Confederación Nacional del Trabajo   158,
  160
conscription   15, 246
Continuation War   128, *see also* Winter
  War
Craener, Vera   113–15
Crivelli, Giuseppe   220, 223
Croatia   43, 60, 66, 219
Croats   49, 59–60, 63–6, 68, 70
Cuban refugees   233
Curitiba   215
Cyprus   194
Czechoslovakia
  German expellees from   204, 218
  interwar   2, 21, 65, 77
  Kindertransport from   124
  migrants in France   231–3, 236–8
  refugees in Britain   250
  Russian refugees in   89, 94, 96, 98–9
  Ukrainians in   78–9, 81, 84
Czernowitz   18

Dalmatia   62
Danube Swabians   215–26, 264–5
Delcroix, Jean   234–5
Dembitzer, Salomon   142, 144
demobilized soldiers   24, 78, 249–50
Denmark   126–7
deportations
  from Alsace-Lorraine   167–8, 174
  in First World War   17–20, 33–4
  to Soviet Union   217, 246
  of Spanish Republicans   155–6
diaspora, *see also* homeland; host society
  concept of   4, 113, 165, 173, 175, 218,
    221, 256
  four-dimensional model of   4–5, 8–9,
    13, 21, 43, 61, 185, 201, 215,
    225–6, 232, 241, 245–57,
    264–7
  interaction with other   22–3, 39, 53,
    114, 154–5, 200–2, 207, 209,
    233, 241

Displaced Persons   173–4, 183–5, 199,
  208, 218, 250, 262, *see also*
  European Volunteer Workers;
  Westward Ho!
  DP camps   173, 184–6, 194–5, 199,
    203–6
  Jewish DP camp Bergen-
    Belsen   183–95
  Latvian DPs   250
  Polish DPs   186, 199–209, 247, 249
  Soviet DPs   199, 203
  Ukrainian DPs   87, 185, 206, 208,
    247, 250
  Western DPs   199, 203
Döblin, Alfred   106–7, 115
Dominican Republic   122
Donauschwaben, see Danube Swabians
DPs, *see* Displaced Persons

East Africa   246
East-Central Europe, *see* Eastern Europe
Eastern Europe   59, 75, 79–81, 83, 85–6,
  96
  diasporas   245, 256
  ethnic Germans in   215, 217
  refugees from   75, 232–3, 235–8,
    250
East Germany, *see* Germany, Democratic
  Republic of
East Prussia   201, 250–2, 255–6
  diaspora   252–5
  expellees from   202, 245, 250–7
Edinburgh   247
Ehrenstein, Albert   106, 108, 115
enemy aliens   16–17, 22–3, 31, 115,
  247
England   130, 247, 250, *see also* Britain
Entente Powers   62, 77
epidemic diseases   18, 34, 36–7, 40,
  49–50, 52
Ernst, Max   107, 143
Estonia   89, 92–4, 97–9
Estoril   138, 143
Esztergom internment camp, *see under*
  internment camps
Ethiopia   68
ethnic cleansing   171, 217
ethnic Germans, *see* Volksdeutsche
European Union   250

European Volunteer Workers 247, 250,
    see also Westward Ho!
evacuations
    of children 119–31, 264
    of concentration camp inmates 183, 186
    from East Prussia 253–4
    from Galicia 13–23
    from Istria 43–53
Evian Conference 119, 121–2, 124–6, 131
expulsions
    in Austria-Hungary 31
    of East Prussians 202, 245, 250–7
    of ethnic Germans 3, 204, 208, 217–19, 222, 262
    of WED candidates 165–6, 174–5

fascism 113–14, 153, 193, 235, 237–8, 250
FFI, see French Resistance
Figueira da Foz 141–2
Finland 89, 92–4, 96–9, 127–8
Fiume, see Rijeka
Food and Agriculture Organization 222
forced labour 155–6, 184, 199–202, 204, 217, 240, 246–7
France
    Algerian immigrants in 231, 237, 240
    anti-communism and migrants in 231–42
    anti-fascist organizations in 69
    Belgian immigrants in 231
    diaspora in Russia 240
    economic migrants in 231–3, 237–9
    familialist movement in 233–4, 240
    German occupation of 127–8, 136–7, 155–6
    Hungarian refugees in 236
    Italian immigrants in 231, 240
    and Poland 247
    Poles in 231–2, 236–9
    Russian emigrants in 89–90, 94, 98
    Spanish immigrants in 238
    Spanish Republican refugees in 152–61
    and Ukraine 86
    Vichy regime 128–30, 155–6, 167–8, 232, 234–5

    and Yugoslavia 64, 68
Franco, Francisco 152–3, 155–6, 158, 160–1, 235
Frankfurt am Main 170
Franz Joseph I of Austria 44
freedom of movement 30–1, 48, 155–6
French Forces of the Interior, see French Resistance
French Resistance 153, 156–9, 161, 199

Galicia 13–24, 29–40, 47–8, 82, 97, 167
    diasporas from 21–4
    Jews in 14–15, 17, 19, 21, 35
    Poles in 14–15, 19, 34, 39
    Ukrainians in 14–16, 18–19, 21, 29–35, 38–9
Gatrell, Peter 261, 267
GDR, see Germany, Democratic Republic of
gender roles 141–2, 263
General Government 167
Geneva 128
    Convention of 1951, see United Nations, Conventions Relating to the Status of Refugees
genocide 123, 131, 166, 175, 183, 254,
    see also Armenian genocide; Holocaust
George, Manfred 105, 108
German People's List, see Volksliste
Germany, see also Nazi Germany
    American occupation of 185, 192, 199, 203, 262
    British occupation of 183–95, 199–209
    Democratic Republic of 217–18, 251–2, 254
    diaspora 108–9, 217
    Federal Republic of 174, 208–9, 217–18, 251–2, 254–5, 257
    German Empire 20, 22, 62, 77, 86, 108
    and Poland 80, 84, 86
    Poles in 201–3, 208–9
    Russian emigrants in 89–90, 94–5, 98
    Weimar Republic 75, 79–83, 85–6
Gestapo 122, 167
Glasgow 247

Gmünd refugee camp, *see under* refugee camps
Goiás, State of 220, 222
Göllersdorf internment camp, *see under* internment camps
Graz 29, 35-7
Great Britain, *see* Britain
Greece 67, 175
Greek Catholics 14, 16, 33-5
Grzelka, Feliks 174-5
Guarapuava 215, 222
Guggenheim, Peggy 140, 143
Gurs internment camp, *see under* internment camps

Habsburg Empire, *see* Austria-Hungary
Hamburg 194-5
Heimat 221, 255-6, *see also* homeland
Helsinki 96-7
Himmler, Heinrich 165, 169-73, 202
Hitler, Adolf 109, 120, 122, 129, 156
Holocaust 131, 189, 194-5, 247
  survivors of 184, 186, 188-91
homeland 4-5, 23, 39, 53, 61, 87, 111, 168, 174-5, 195, 200-1, 215, 217-19, 221, 226, 233, 241, 245, 248, 250, 252-6, 263, *see also* diaspora; host society
host society 1-2, 4-5, 21, 23, 39, 53, 61, 99-100, 110, 137-8, 145-6, 153-5, 158-9, 161, 185, 195, 201-2, 215, 218, 226, 232, 241, 245, 247-50, 255-7, 263, 266, *see also* diaspora; homeland
Hull, Cordell 121
humanitarianism 127, 215, 222, 225
  humanitarian organizations 120-31, 216, 221, 226, 264-5
human rights 121, 237
Hungary 17-18, 45-6, 70, 130, 185, 215-18, 234
hybrid identity 5, 170, 249, 266

IGC, *see* Intergovernmental Committee on Refugees
illegal immigrants 136, 193-4, 231
integration
  of migrants in France 232, 241

narratives of 110, 115, 125, 146, 226, 245, 261
  of Polish refugees in Britain 247-50
  of refugees in Germany 208, 251-2
  of refugees in Yugoslavia 61, 63
Intergovernmental Committee on Refugees 121-2, 160-1
International Brigades 235
international community 120-1, 131, 191
International Labour Office 222
international law 3, 31, 119-21, 126-7
International Refugee Organization 206-9, 217, 220-2, 265
internment
  of civilians in Austria-Hungary 13-24, 29-40, 48, 53
  of refugees in Britain 247
  of Spanish Republicans in France 152-3, 155, 161, 235
  of Ukrainian soldiers 78, 84
internment camps
  Esztergom 32
  Göllersdorf 35-6
  Gurs 154
  Katzenau 29, 32, 35-6
  Kufstein 32, 38
  Miskolc 32
  Satmar-Nemeti 32
  Schwaz 32, 38
  Spielberg 17
  Thalerhof 17, 21-2, 29, 32-9
IRO, *see* International Refugee Organization
Iron Curtain 173, 236
irredentism 18, 30, 60
  Italian 29, 33, 39, 46, 62
Israel, State of 4, 184, 190, 192-4
Istria 43-53, 62
Italians 19, 29-33, 35, 38, 49, 64
Italy
  Fascist 59, 66-8, 152, 247
  Italian front (1915-18) 22, 51
  Italian front (1943-5) 246
  Kingdom of 33, 43-6, 52, 62-3

Jackson, Alvin 111
Jehovah's Witnesses 126

Jewish DP camp Bergen-Belsen, *see under*
    Displaced Persons
Jews
  Austrian   119, 185
  in Britain   125, 248–9
  Czechoslovak   122
  Eastern European   191, 231, 236,
    248
  in France   231–2, 234–6
  in Galicia   14–15, 17, 19, 21, 35
  German   119–20, 122–3, 185
  Nazi persecution of   126, 130
  Polish   184, 246–8
  refugees   122–3, 126, 136, 156, 161,
    218, 234–5
  in Russia   19
  in Switzerland   130
Joint, *see* American Jewish Joint
    Distribution Committee
Julian March   59–70
  diaspora   65–6, 70
  Union of the Yugoslav Emigrants
    from   63, 66–9

Kaliningrad (Königsberg)   254–6
Karl I of Austria   17, 51
Katzenau internment camp, *see under*
    internment camps
Kiesler, Frederick (Friedrich)   105–6, 113
Kiesler, Stefi   105–15, 263
Kindertransport   120, 123–6
Kingdom of Serbs, Croats and Slovenes,
    see Yugoslavia
Koch, Erich   252, 254
Königsberg, *see* Kaliningrad
Konovalets, Jevhen   82, 84
Korean War   232
Korostovets, Vladimir   85–6
Kraus, Karl   108, 114
Kravchenko, Victor   236–7
Kriegel-Valrimont, Maurice   234–5
Kristallnacht   119, 122–4, 131, 136, 195
Kryha, Oleksandr (Alexander von)   81–2
Kufstein internment camp, *see under*
    internment camps
Kyiv   20, 76

LaGuardia, Fiorello   205
La Terre Nouvelle (newspaper)   234, 239

Latin America   64, 154, 216, 219–21,
    235, 242
Latvia   89, 92–4, 96, 99
League of Nations   3, 67, 121, 159–61
Lemberg (Lwów, L'viv)   18, 20, 22, 91,
    95, 97
Le Moniteur du Progrès agricole et viticole
    (agricultural journal)   235, 239
Linz   29, 223–5
Lisbon   136–8, 140–5
Lithuania   89, 92, 94, 97–9, 251
Ljubljana   62–4, 66
London   86, 121, 188, 204, 247–9
Losa, Ilse   138–41, 144
L'viv, *see* Lemberg
Lwów, *see* Lemberg
Lyon   128, 240
Lypynskyi, Viacheslav   81, 85

Makovsky, Vasyl'   19, 22–3
Maribor   68
von Mattanovich, Erwin   35–6
Mediterranean Sea   44, 62, 231
Mexico   122
Middle East   68, 233, 246, 249
Miskolc internment camp, *see under*
    internment camps
mobilization of soldiers   15–16, 22–3
Mocidade Portuguesa Feminina   136,
    139, 143
Moor, Michael   220, 222, 224
Moravia   17, 45–6
Moscow   95
MPF, *see Mocidade Portuguesa Feminina*
Mundo Gráfico (magazine)   136, 142, 145
Munich   82, 84
  Agreement   119, 122–3, 131
Muslims   175
Mussolini, Benito   66, 68

Nansen, Fridtjof   3, 160
  International Office for Refugees   93
  passports   84 (*see also* stateless
    persons)
  refugees (*see* stateless persons)
national homogenization   21, 59, 70, 120,
    165, *see also* nation-building
nationalism
  Italian   29, 60, 62

Polish 29
Russian 29
Serbian 29
Slovene 60, 66
Ukrainian 29, 78, 82, 84, 86
Yugoslav 60, 63, 65–7, 69–70
national minorities 39, 59, 61–5, 67–70
    protection of 89
National Socialism 136, 161, 189, 217, 263
nation-building 2, 59, 69–70, 79, 166, 216, *see also* national homogenization
Natonek, Hans 111–12, 115
naturalization 129, 166, 169, 173, 225, 231, *see also* citizenship
Nazi Germany
    forced migration to 167–75, 199, 203, 209
    Nazi Party 172
    negotiations with 160–1, 165
    refugees from 105, 120–30, 136, 247
    and Spain 152
    and Ukraine 85–7
Nazism, *see* National Socialism
neutrality 126–7, 129–30, 137
New York 98, 106–7, 109–12, 114–15, 188, 263
    New School for Social Research in 111
    Public Library 107–8, 110–14, 263
New Zealand 248
Nicholas II of Russia 33, 75
North Africa 233
North America 216, 249
Norway 127
    refugees from 4
November pogrom, *see* Kristallnacht
NSDAP, *see* Nazi Party

Organization for Rehabilitation through Training 187
ORT, *see* Organization for Rehabilitation through Training
Orthodox Church 16, 19, 33–5, 84–5, 90, 175
Ostarbeiter 169, 171, *see also* forced labour

Ottoman Empire 2, 19–20, *see also* Turkey

Palestine 120, 123–4, 126, 184–8, 193–4
Pan-Slavism 15, 18, 21, 64
Paraná, State of 215, 222
Paris 78, 106, 188, 231–3, 237, 247
    Peace Conference 62, 66, 69 (*see also* Versailles, Treaty of)
Pas-de-Calais 129, 238
PCF, *see under* communism
Perpignan 154, 157
Petliura, Symon 78
Petrushevych, Jevhen 82, 84
Pinthus, Kurt 110–11, 113, 115
pogroms 122, 136, 184, *see also* Kristallnacht
Poland
    Armed Forces in the West 246, 248
    communist regime in 239, 247–8
    diaspora 246–50
    evacuation from 48, 124, 130
    forced migration from 167, 173–4
    government-in-exile 199–200, 206–7, 247–9
    interwar 21, 24, 77, 79, 249
    occupation of 203, 246–8
    partition of 91
    Provisional Government of National Unity 199
    repatriation to 199–200, 202–7, 238
    Russian emigrants in 89, 92–9
    Ukrainians in 78, 81, 84, 86–7
Polish-Bolshevik War 77, 80
political refugees 109, 121–2, 126, 160, 231–8, 242, 250
Poltavets-Ostrianytsia, Ivan 81–2
popular front 67, 156
Porto 138, 140–1, 144
Portugal 136–46, 263
    Estado Novo regime 137–8, 145
Potsdam Conference 199
Pottendorf refugee camp, *see under* refugee camps
POWs, *see* prisoners of war
Prague 78–9, 82, 91, 94, 98, 122
    Ukrainian Free University in 79
prisoners of war
    Austro-Hungarian 16, 19, 21–2, 24

Polish   203–4, 246–8
  Russian   49, 92
Przemyśl   18
Pula   43–7, 51–2
Pushkin, Alexander   94–6
Pyrenees   152–4, 156–7, 161

quota-based immigration   122–3, 184, 193

racism   167–70, 174–5, 233, 250
Rapallo, Treaty of   59, 62–3, 80
RCM, *see* Refugee Children's Movement
Red Army   200, 236, 250, 252
Red Cross movement   127–8
  German Red Cross   168
  International Red Cross   175
  Polish Red Cross in London   248
  Swiss Red Cross   130
refugee camps
  Bruck an der Leitha   49
  Gmünd   21, 39, 48–50, 53
  Pottendorf   48–50
  Steinklamm-Rabenstein   48–9
  Wagna   46, 48–50, 53
Refugee Children's Movement   124–5, *see also* Kindertransport
refugee crisis   23, 121–2, 124, 126, 254–5
refugee status   3, 157, 238, 242, *see also* United Nations, Conventions Relating to the Status of Refugees
Re-Germanization Procedure   165–75, 266
repatriation   206–7, 209, 240
resettlement
  of Danube Swabians   215–26
  of DPs   206–9
  of Jewish refugees   119–24
  in Nazi Germany   165–75
  of Polish refugees   247, 249
revisionism   60, 62, 67, 69–70
Riga   96
  Treaty of   77
Rijeka (Fiume)   44, 62
Robertson, Brian   190–1
Roma and Sinti   126
Roman Catholics, *see* Catholicism

Romania   77–9, 89, 185, 215–18, 234, 236
Roosevelt, Franklin Delano   121, 123, 204
Rosensaft, Josef   186, 191–4
Rostov-on-Don   20, 22
Rothmund, Heinrich   122, 127, 129–30
Rovinj   45, 51
Ruhr area   200–2, 209, 251
Russia, *see also* Soviet Union
  Day of the Russian Child   90, 98–9
  diaspora   84–5, 95
  Far East   21, 78
  refugees from   3, 89–99, 153, 159–60, 231
  Russian Charitable Society   92, 96–7
  Russian Culture Day   90, 94–8
  Russian Empire   13–24, 30–3, 83, 175, 240–1
  Russian Civil War   21–2, 79, 84–5
    Whites in   76–7, 80, 83, 85, 159–60
  Russian Revolution (1917)   20, 24, 64, 75–6, 89, 153, 234, 240
Russophiles   14, 16–17, 21–2, 29–35, 39

Saar refugees   160
Saint Petersburg   76
Salazar, Antonio de Oliveira   137–8
Salazarism   138, 141
Salzburg   39, 109, 218–19
Satmar-Nemeti internment camp, *see under* internment camps
Schutzstaffel   122, 165, 167–74
  Waffen-SS   217
Schwaz internment camp, *see under* internment camps
Schweizer Europahilfe   215, 221–6, 265
Scotland   247
SEH, *see Schweizer Europahilfe*
self-determination   2, 62, 185, 191–4, 254
Sérandour, Pierre   235–6
Serbia   31, 33
Serbophiles   29, 31, 33, 39
Serbs   19, 30–1, 33, 60, 65–6, 70, 168
SHAEF, *see* Supreme Headquarters, Allied Expeditionary Forces
She'erit Hapletah   184, 188–9, 194–5
Sheptytsky, Andrzej   20
Shoah, *see* Holocaust
Siberia   20–1, 204, 240, 246

Skoropadski, Pavlo   76–8, 80–3, 85–6
Slavonia   29, 31–2, 35, 39, 216
Slavs   15, 18, 62, 252, *see also* Pan-Slavism
Slovaks   15, 19
Slovenes   49, 59–60, 63–6, 68, 70, 170, 172
Slovenia   167–8, 173
Sobkowiak, Roman   174–5
Social Democrats, *see* socialists
socialists   122, 156, 158, 239
South America, *see* Latin America
South-eastern Europe   33, 216–19, 221, 225, 265
South Tyrol   29, 31–2, 35, 39, 47, 62
Soviet Union
   deportations in   175, 217, 246
   and East Prussian expellees   251, 253, 255–6
   emergence of   21, 92
   and Finland   127–8
   and France   234, 236–7, 240–1
   and Poland   200–1, 203, 209, 246–8
   Polish Jews in   184
   and Russian refugees   160
   and Ukraine   79–80, 86–7
   and Weimar Republic   81, 83
Spain   152–61, 231, 235, *see also* Spanish Republic
Spanish Civil War   67, 128, 152–3, 155, 159, 235
Spanish Republic   152–3, 156–7, 235
   army   152, 235
   diaspora   153, 155–6, 158, 161
   refugees   152–61, 232, 234–6, 239, 241–2
Spielberg internment camp, *see under* internment camps
SS, *see* Schutzstaffel
Stalin, Joseph   83, 199, 204, 208, 232, 246, 256
stateless persons   84, 119, 160, 184, 192, 194–5, 248
Stefan, Josef   218–22
Steinklamm-Rabenstein refugee camp, *see under* refugee camps
Styria   17, 29, 46
Sudeten Germans   122, 218, *see also* Volksdeutsche

Sudetenland   119, 122, 131, 255
Supreme Headquarters, Allied Expeditionary Forces   183, 203
Sweden   119–20, 122, 126–8, 130–1
Switzerland
   and Danube Swabians   220–1, 223 (*see also Schweizer Europahilfe*)
   evacuation of children to   126–31
   refugee policy in   119–20, 122
   Russian refugees in   94, 98
   Skoropadskyi in   81, 85

Tarnopol (Ternopil)   18, 20
Terezín, *see* Theresienstadt
Thalerhof internment camp, *see under* internment camps
Theresienstadt (Terezín)   17, 22, 32, 38, 187
Third Reich, *see* Nazi Germany
Tillinger, Eugen   142, 144
Todt Organization   156
Torberg, Friedrich   108, 112, 115
Transcarpathia   14
transnational history   3–5
Trieste   44–5, 62–4, 66
Turkey   94, 98, 160, 175, *see also* Ottoman Empire
Tyrol   32, 38–9, 48, 219

UGT, *see Unión General de Trabajadores*
UK, *see* Britain
Ukraine
   diaspora   75, 79, 81, 83–7
   Hetman of   77, 81–2
   identity   14, 78, 85, 87
   refugees from   4, 85
   Soviet Ukraine   79–80, 236
   Ukrainian National Republic   76, 78, 80, 82
   Ukrainian state   75–7, 83
   Weimar Germany and   79–80
   Western Ukrainian National Republic   76, 78, 82, 84
Ukrainophiles   14–15, 21–2, 34
UN, *see* United Nations
UNE, *see Unión Nacional Española*
Unión General de Trabajadores   158, 160

Unión Nacional Española   156, 158–60
United Kingdom, *see* Britain
United Nations   160, 194, 255
    Conventions Relating to the Status of Refugees   3, 121, 254–5 (*see also* refugee status)
    Relief and Rehabilitation Administration   173–4, 191, 199, 202–7, 265
United States of America
    and Britain   201, 209
    German expellees in   252
    and Jewish refugees   119–24, 126–7, 184
    Polish refugees in   236
    Russian refugees in   93–4, 98
    Ukrainian immigrants in   78
    Yugoslav emigrants in   60, 69
UNRRA, *see* United Nations Relief and Rehabilitation Administration
Unser Sztyme (newspaper)   186–90
USA, *see* United States of America
USSR, *see* Soviet Union

Val d'Aran invasion   158–9
Vatican   34, 219
Vavryk', Vasyl'   22–3
Venezia Giulia, *see* Julian March
Versailles, Treaty of   2, 75, 79, 89, *see also* Paris, Peace Conference
Vienna
    Jews in   112–14, 122, 140
    Nunciature in   34
    refugees in   17, 35, 38
    Stefi Kiesler in   105–6, 111
    Ukrainian émigrés in   78–9, 81–2
Vietnamese refugees   233
Volksdeutsche   208–9, 215, 217–18, 222–5, 262, *see also* Danube Swabians; Sudeten Germans
Volksliste   202, 209

Wagna refugee camp, *see under* refugee camps
Wales   247
Warsaw   4, 78–9, 91, 93, 95, 97
    Russian House in   91–2, 96
    Ukrainian Scientific Institute in   79
    Uprising (1944)   203
Washington, DC   111, 236
WED, *see* Re-Germanization Procedure
Wehrmacht   217, 219, 246
Western Europe   75, 126, 128, 184, 246, 249
Westward Ho! (resettlement scheme)   206–7, *see also* European Volunteer Workers
Wiedereindeutschungsverfahren, see Re-Germanization Procedure
Wilhelm Gustloff   253–4
Wilson, Thomas Woodrow   2
Winter War   127–8, *see also* Continuation War
Wollheim, Norbert   189–91, 194–5
Wrangel, Pyotr   85

xenophobia   153, 170, 248, 250, *see also* anti-immigrant hostility

Yalta Conference   204
Yugoslavia
    Danube Swabians in   215–18, 224
    and emigrants from Italy   59–70
    forced migration from   168, 173–4
    and France   231, 237–9
    government-in-exile   68
    refugees from   62, 250
    Russian refugees in   89, 94, 98–9

Zagreb   63, 66
Zelenevskyi, Hnat   81–2
Zionism   195
Zweig, Stefan   108, 138
Zweig-Winternitz, Friderike   115, 138–9

www.ingramcontent.com/pod-product-compliance
Lightning Source LLC
Chambersburg PA
CBHW052214300426
44115CB00011B/1683